9.95

Roman Rosdolsky

THE MAKING OF MARX'S 'CAPITAL'

IN TWO VOLUMES

Translated by Pete Burgess

VOLUME 1

Pluto Press

viii · *Contents*

> PART FOUR. The Section on the Circulation Process   315
> Introductory Remark   315

21. The Transition from the Production Process of Capital to the Circulation Process of Capital. Excursus on the Realisation Problem and the First Scheme of Reproduction   317

22. Circulation Time and Its Influence on the Determination of Value   334

23. The Turnover of Capital and Turnover Time. The Continuity of Capitalist Production and the Division of Capital into Portions   345

24. The Characteristic Forms of Fixed and Circulating (Fluid) Capital   351

> PART FIVE. Capital as Fructiferous. Profit and Interest   367

25. The Transformation of Surplus-Value into Profit. The General Rate of Profit   367

26. The Law of the Falling Rate of Profit and the Tendency of Capitalism Towards Breakdown   376

27. Fragments on Interest and Credit   383
    1. The extent to which the original outline envisaged the treatment of these themes   383
    2. The *Rough Draft* on interest-bearing capital   386
    3. The category of 'capital as money'   389
    4. Critique of Proudhonism   391
    5. The *Rough Draft* on the role of credit in the capitalist economy   392
    6. The barriers of the credit system   395
 Appendix. On Recent Criticisms of Marx's Law of the Falling Rate of Profit   398

> PART SIX. Conclusion   413

28. The Historical Limits of the Law of Value. Marx on the Subject of Socialist Society   413
    1. Marx on the development of human individuality under capitalism   413

Contents · ix

    2. The role of machinery as the material precondition of socialist society   425
    3. The withering away of the law of value under socialism   428

29. The Reification of the Economic Categories and the 'True Conception of the Process of Social Production'   437

PART SEVEN. Critical Excursus   445

30. The Dispute Surrounding Marx's Schemes of Reproduction   445
    I. Introduction   445
        1. A note on the formal aspect of the schemes of reproduction in Volume II   445
        2. The 'approximation to reality' of Marx's schemes of reproduction   450
        3. The basic presupposition of Marx's schemes of reproduction   454
        4. The schemes of reproduction and the realisation problem   457
    II. The discussion between the 'Narodniks' and the 'Legal' Marxists in Russia   460
        1. Engels's debate with Danielson   460
        2. Bulgakov's and Tugan-Baranovsky's interpretation of Marx's analysis of extended reproduction   464
    III. Lenin's theory of realisation   472
    IV. Hilferding's interpretation of Marx's schemes of reproduction   483
    V. Rosa Luxemburg's critique of Marx's theory of accumulation   490
        1. The historical and methodological background   490
        2. The schemes of reproduction and technical progress   494
        3. The neo-Harmonist applications of the schemes   497

31. The Problem of Skilled Labour   506
    I. Böhm-Bawerk's critique   506
    II. Marx's probable solution   505

32. A Note on the Question of 'False Rationalisation'   521

33. Joan Robinson's Critique of Marx   530
    I. Marx's theory of value   530

1. Marx as a 'value fetishist' — 530
2. Marx's 'rigmarole' — 538
3. Marx's search for a social elixir. The problem of value in a socialist society — 541
II. Marx's theory of the essence of capitalist exploitation and his concept of capital — 544
III. Concluding remarks — 549

34. Neo-Marxist Economics — 552
I. A seemingly dogmatic controversy — 552
II. On the method of Marx's economics — 561
III. Concluding remark — 570

Bibliography — 573
Index — 579

Author's Preface

In 1948, when I first had the good fortune to see one of the then very rare copies of Marx's *Rough Draft*,[1] it was clear from the outset that this was a work which was of fundamental importance for marxist theory. However, its unusual form and to some extent obscure manner of expression made it far from suitable for reaching a wide circle of readers. I therefore decided, first, to provide a 'commentary' on the work and, second, to make a scientific evalution of some of the new findings which it contained. The first exercise (mainly covered by Parts II-VI) necessitated an exposition of the *Rough Draft*'s most important arguments, as far as possible in Marx's own words. The second required detailed discussions of particular aspects, which are to be found in the first, introductory, and seventh, concluding, parts of this work.

Completion of the work presented a number of difficulties. Inhabiting a city whose libraries contained only very few German, Russian or French socialist works (let alone such indispensable periodicals as Kautsky's *Neue Zeit*) I was restricted to the few books in my own possession, and often doubted the practicability of the venture. But this was not the only problem. The more the work advanced, the clearer it became that I would only be able to touch upon the most important and theoretically interesting problem presented by the *Rough Draft* – that of the relation of Marx's work to Hegel, in particular to the *Logic* – and would not be able to deal with it in any greater depth.

Of all the problems in Marx's economic theory the most neglected has been that of his method, both in general and, specifically, in

---

[1] The *Rough Draft* was printed in Berlin in 1953, by the Dietz Verlag, under the title *Grundrisse der Kritik der politischen Ökonomie (Rohentwurf), 1857-1858*. Until that time there were only three or four copies of the original Moscow edition in the West. [The *Grundrisse* has been published in an English edition, translated with an Introduction by Martin Nicolaus, Harmondsworth: Penguin 1973.]

its relation to Hegel. Recent works contain for the most part platitudes which, to echo Marx's own words, betray the authors' own 'crude obsession with the material' and total indifference to Marx's method.

What would one make of a psychologist who was interested only in Freud's results, but rejected the question of the *manner* in which Freud obtained those results as being irrelevant or even 'metaphysical'? One could only shrug one's shoulders. But this is precisely how most present-day critics of, and 'experts' on, Marx judge his economic system. Either they totally refuse to discuss his dialectical method because they are opposed to 'metaphysics' (such as the adherents of 'modern theory') – this has the advantage of avoiding a real study of this method – or the critique is restricted to a few platitudes, better left unsaid. This even applies to such a prominent critic as Joseph Schumpeter.

Schumpeter writes in one of his last works that, although the author of *Capital* was a neo-Hegelian, it would be a 'mistake and an injustice to Marx's scientific powers . . . to make this element the master key to the system'. Of course, 'Marx retained his early love during the whole of his lifetime. He enjoyed certain formal analogies which may be found between his and Hegel's argument. He liked to testify to his Hegelianism and to use Hegelian terminology. But this is all. Nowhere did he betray positive science to metaphysics.'[2]

What Schumpeter says here is, of course, nothing new. As early as 1922 Lukacs already complained about the bad habit of 'regarding the dialectic as a superficial stylistic ornament . . . Even otherwise conscientious scholars like Professor Vorländer, for example, believed that they could prove that Marx had "flirted" with Hegelian concepts "in only two places" and then again in a "third" place. Yet they failed to notice that a whole series of *categories of central importance and in constant use* stem *directly* from Hegel's *Logic*. We need only recall the Hegelian origin and the substantive and methodological importance of what is for Marx as fundamental a distinction as the one between *immediacy* and *mediation*. If this could go *unnoticed* then it must be just as true even today that Hegel is still treated as a "dead dog", and this despite the fact that he has once again become *persona grata* and even fashionable in the universities. What would Professor Vorländer say if a historian of philosophy contrived *not to notice* in the works of a successor of Kant, however critical and original, that

[2] J.A.Schumpeter, *Capitalism, Socialism and Democracy*, London: Unwin 1966, pp. 9-10.

the "synthetic unity of apperception", to take but one instance, was derived from the *Critique of Pure Reason*.'[3]

It is clear that the four decades which have passed since the publication of Lukacs's pioneering study have brought no change. Admittedly, Schumpeter was not a professor of philosophy, as Vorländer was, and as an economic specialist was not, perhaps, obliged to read Lukacs's book (or, let us say, Lenin's *Philosophical Testament* which contains more or less the same). However he should not have simply passed over Marx himself. For example, the following well-known passage comes from Marx's own correspondence.

'I am getting some nice developments, e.g. I have overthrown the entire doctrine of profit as previously conceived. In the method of working it was of great service to me that by mere accident I leafed through Hegel's *Logic* again.'[4]

Does this really sound like mere 'formal analogies' or the simple use of Hegelian 'phraseology'? Shouldn't we rather conclude that even the most serious and professorial critics of Marx are guilty of a somewhat superficial approach?[5]

Marx's *Rough Draft* will put an end to this superficiality. If Hegel's influence on Marx's *Capital* can be seen explicitly only in a few footnotes, the *Rough Draft* must be designated as a massive reference to Hegel, in particular to his *Logic* – irrespective of how radically and materialistically Hegel was inverted! The publication of the *Grundrisse* means that academic critics of Marx will no longer be able to write without first having studied his method and its relation to Hegel. And whilst the *Rough Draft* does present a formidable task for both the opponents and supporters of marxism, its publication will

---

[3] G.Lukacs, *History and Class Consciousness*, London: Merlin 1971, xliv. What Lukacs says also applies to marxist theory in the period of the Second International. For example, O.Bauer answers the question 'What connects the mature Marx with Hegel?' in 1911 in the following way. It is 'the epistemological reflection on the essence of science, which is not a mere reflection of events, but rather "a product of the thinking head which appropriates the world in the only way it can" [a quote from Marx's Introduction to the *Grundrisse*], that is a piece of Kant, implanted in Hegel – developed by Marx, without Kant's knowledge, in Hegel's language, but free from the ontological re-interpretation of Kant by Hegel.' (*Der Kampf* VI, pp.189-190).

[4] *Marx-Engels Werke (MEW)* Vol.29, p.260.

[5] This fact was perfectly clear to Marx's philosophically educated contemporaries. Thus, Lassalle compared Marx's *A Contribution to the Critique of Political Economy* with Hegel's *Phenomenology* and praised Marx as a 'Ricardo become socialist, and a Hegel become economist'. However, Engels regarded the 'German dialectical method', which underlay Marx's economic system, 'as a result which was of less significance than the materialist interpretation'.

in the final analysis raise the general level of economic writing on Marx.[6]

In conclusion, a few words about the author. I am, by profession, neither an economist nor a philosopher. I would not have dared to write a commentary on the *Rough Draft* if a school of marxist theoreticians still existed today – as it did in the first thirty years of this century – which would have been better equipped to carry out this task. However, the last generation of notable marxist theoreticians for the most part fell victim to Hitler's and Stalin's terror, which interrupted the further development of the body of marxist ideas for several decades. Given these circumstances I feel obliged to offer this work to the reading public – as defective and incomplete as it might be – in the hope that a new generation will follow for whom, once more, Marx's theory will be a living source both of knowledge and the political practice which this knowledge directs.

March 1967

[6] Unfortunately the author was far too optimistic in this respect (this Foreword was completed in 1955) . . . For, although Marx's *Grundrisse* has been in print for fourteen years it has passed almost unnoticed. The single, pleasing, exception is the work devoted to the *Grundrisse* by the Japanese scholar Kojiro Takagi. We should also cite *Der Begriff der Natur in der Lehre von Marx*, by Alfred Schmidt 1962. [An English translation by Ben Fowkes was published under the title *The Concept of Nature in Marx*, London: New Left Books 1971.] This work attaches great importance to the *Grundrisse* as a means of understanding the 'mature Marx'.

Translator's Note

The Making of Marx's 'Capital' was not an easy work to translate. Not only was the translator confronted with the usual problems of giving a correct rendering of German philosophical and economic terms into English, but also with Rosdolsky's own somewhat inaccessible style. In general, a uniform translation of key concepts is provided, with some notable exceptions. The word *aufheben* for example, is rendered as suspend, transcend, annul and abolish – depending on the needs of the overall context. This seemed a superior method to that of offering one rigid 'correct' translation, which, as can be seen in the current English edition of the *Grundrisse*, gives rise to some awkward and obscure meanings. The same applies to the concept *Bestimmung*, which is normally translated as 'character' or 'determination', except in the chapter on money, where it is given as 'function'.

Where possible references have been given to an English edition, although in some cases the translation may not accord one hundred per cent with the English reference cited: this applies in the case of *Capital* Volumes II and III, and the *Grundrisse*, where certain concepts have been retranslated, or originally awkward or archaic formulations eliminated. For example, the German *Verwertung* has been generally changed from the original 'self-expansion of value' (*Capital* Vols. II and III) and 'realisation' (*Grundrisse*) to 'valorisation'. Because of the superiority of the recently published Penguin edition of *Capital* Volume I, translated by Ben Fowkes, references for Volume I of *Capital* are given to this edition. For those readers who still use the Lawrence and Wishart edition references are given in brackets after the Penguin reference. Thus, *Capital* I p.781 (629). In addition a number of references to the MEGA were translated independently, before the appearance of any of the volumes of the Marx-Engels *Collected Works*. Page references to the latter were added later. Certain abbreviations are also employed, derived in part from Rosdolsky's own. For example, *Theories of Surplus-Value* is shortened to *Theories, Contribution to*

xvi · *Translator's Note*

the Critique of Political Economy to *Contribution* etc. Such abbreviations are clarified in the relevant first reference or footnote to the works in question, and on the following page.

The English *Grundrisse* is not a complete translation of the entire contents of the Dietz Verlag *Grundrisse* : one notable text, the *Urtext: 'Zur Kritik'*, the original draft of the *Contribution to the Critique of Political Economy*, is left, as yet untranslated : references to this text are therefore references to the original German version, contained in the Dietz Verlag edition. This is made clear at the appropriate points.

Italicisation in the text follows Rosdolsky's emphasis, not any italicisation which may be present in the original works cited.

I would like to thank Ben Fowkes for his help in checking the translation and elucidating a number of textual and conceptual points. And to PT for much support during a long job.

Pete Burgess

Abbreviations

Contribution	*A Contribution to the Critique of Political Economy*
Grundrisse	Nicolaus translation of the *Grundrisse*
Grundrisse, German edn.	1953 Dietz edition of the *Grundrisse*
MEW	Marx-Engels *Werke*
Rough Draft	Nicolaus translation of the *Grundrisse*
Selected Correspondence	Moscow 1975 edition unless otherwise indicated
Theories	*Theories of Surplus-Value*

Acknowledgements

Material quoted from Karl Marx, *Capital*, Volume I, translated by Ben Fowkes, Harmondsworth, Penguin 1976, pp.40, 76, 89-90, 103, 127-9, 132-3, 135, 138, 143, 149-50, 152-4, 162, 164-7, 170-5, 181-3, 187-8, 190-2, 196-200, 208-9, 227-9, 230, 232-3, 240, 242-3, 268-9, 271, 274-5, 280, 289-90, 296, 300, 305, 308-9, 312, 316-7, 329, 344-5, 365, 419-22, 425, 432-3, 437, 439, 445, 451, 453, 468, 515, 548-9, 578, 618, 655, 659, 661, 664, 667, 705, 712-4, 719, 724, 728-30, 732-4, 753, 763, 768-72, 781-2, 785, 788-90, 793, 798-9, 869, 911. Copyright © Ben Fowkes 1976.

And from Karl Marx, *Grundrisse*, translated by Martin Nicolaus, Harmondsworth, Penguin 1973, pp.85, 87, 95-6, 101-7, 122-3, 126, 134-49, 151, 153-69, 172-4, 188-91, 194-5, 197-204, 206-13, 218, 221-6, 228, 231-5, 238-49, 251-2, 254-9, 263-5, 267, 270-2, 274-9, 282-9, 293-308, 310-1, 313-9, 322, 324-7, 331, 334-41, 346, 354-64, 367, 375-6, 385-6, 389, 395, 399-411, 413-6, 420-3, 426, 435-6, 439-44, 446-7, 449-66, 469-70, 486-9, 497-8, 503, 505-17, 519, 523-4, 529, 533-49, 551-2, 554, 556, 558, 567-8, 585-90, 595, 599, 603, 605-8, 611, 620-30, 632-5, 639-40, 645-7, 649-52, 659-61, 663, 666, 669-76, 679, 682, 684-5, 692-4, 699-703, 705-7, 709-12, 715, 718-21, 723, 732, 745-51, 753-4, 759-63, 767, 769, 774-7, 787, 791, 814, 817, 830-2, 839, 843-4, 846, 851-3, 871, 881. Copyright © Martin Nicolaus 1973.

Reprinted by permission of Penguin Books Ltd and Random House Inc.

PART ONE
Introduction

1.
The Origins of the Rough Draft

The manuscript which this book deals with has a long prehistory. As Marx pointed out in a letter to Lassalle,[1] it was the fruit of fifteen years of study, during the course of which he set about the problems of political economy from constantly renewed perspectives, and in doing so created the basis of his own system of political economy. We should therefore begin by clarifying the stages by which Marx's work grew to maturity.

Marx's wide-ranging critique of politics and political economy, which dates from the years between 1844 and 1846, was the first of these stages.[2] Unfortunately, only fragments of this work remain. They were published in the *Marx-Engels Gesamtausgabe* as the *Economic and Philosophical Manuscripts*.[3] Marx appears here primarily as a philosopher, seeking to apply his recently acquired 'humanist' — or more correctly 'materialist' — interpretation of history in the crucially important field of 'social economy'. He therefore often simply takes over the traditional economic categories in order to demonstrate

---

[1] *Selected Correspondence*, Moscow: Progress Publishers 1975, pp.96-97.
[2] See *K.Marx, Chronik seines Lebens*, henceforth referred to as *Chronik*, pp.22-23, 25-26, 30, 32, 35, 37 and also *MEW* Vol.27, pp.16, 23, 25, 78, 79.
[3] London: Lawrence and Wishart 1970. First published in the *Marx-Engels Gesamtausgabe (MEGA) Abteilung* I Vol.3, Berlin 1932.

4 · *The Making of Marx's 'Capital'*

There Marx writes to Engels: 'By the way, you must let me know what your views on Proudhon are. They interest me all the more now, as I'm occupied with the composition of the "Economics" '.[16] Accordingly, Engels advised Marx to inform Löwenthal, the Frankfurt publisher who had objected to Marx's way of arranging the work, that 'it would be impossible to throw aside your entire plan; that you've already begun to draft the *Kritik*,[17] etc.'[18] Finally Marx wrote to Engels, on 13 February 1855, immediately after the collapse of all the publication plans, saying 'I've contracted an eye-complaint as a result of reading through my own note-books on economics, if not to draft the thing, at least to master the material and have it ready for working through.'[19] From all this one could conclude that a final preparation of a draft of the planned 'Economics' was at least begun. What actually happened to this manuscript, however, and why it failed to survive are questions which will probably never be answered.

As far as the content and construction of the proposed work are concerned, we are thrown back on the meagre information in Engels's letter of 27 February, which we have already cited, and the preceding letter from Marx of 24 November 1851. Both letters show that Marx abandoned his earlier intention to include a Critique of Politics in the work,[20] as he wanted to confine himself more to a 'final settling of accounts' with previous political economy and the systems constructed by the socialists. Accordingly, the entire work was planned to consist of three volumes. The first was to have contained the critique of traditional economic categories,[21] the second, the critique of the socialists, and the third the history of economics itself.[22] Had Marx begun the work with the section on the history of economic doctrines, as Löwenthal wanted, he would have had to 'throw aside' this very plan.[23] Naturally, Marx could not approve such a change in the outline; on the other hand his financial situation was so desperate that he

[16] *ibid*. p.359.
[17] See next paragraph.
[18] *MEW* Vol.27, p.373.
[19] *MEW* Vol.28, p.434.
[20] See the beginning of this chapter. This already constitutes a modification of Marx's earliest outlines which, besides political economy and politics, also included a critique of law, morals and above all, philosophy (see Marx's own Preface to the *Economic and Philosophical Manuscripts*).
[21] The 'Critique of Economics' should be understood here as Marx outlined it to Lassalle eight years later: 'It is a presentation of the system and simultaneously through this presentation of it, a criticism of it.' (*Selected Correspondence*, p.96.)
[22] Cf. *Chronik*, p.114.
[23] Ryazanov's misleading remarks should be corrected in this light.

could not break off negotiations for this reason alone. Engels therefore advised him to agree to Löwenthal's suggestion, if it became absolutely necessary, with the proviso that Löwenthal would have to commit himself to two volumes of the history of economic doctrines, instead of one, since in such a situation numerous 'anticipations of the criticism' would be inevitable. 'After this would come the socialists as the third volume and, as the fourth – (the *Critique*), that is what would remain from the whole – the renowned "positive", what you "really" want. The matter does have its problems in this form, but it has the advantage that the much sought after secret is not revealed until the end, only after the curiosity of the citizen has been pent up for three volumes, thus revealing to him that one is not dealing in patent medicines.' In addition, 'it would be best', in the then prevailing political situation, 'to begin with the most harmless section – the History'.[24]

Some light is thrown on the studies which Marx pursued in 1850-51, and the progress he had made as an economist since 1847, by letters in which he and Engels discuss questions of political economy – above all, the extremely interesting exchange of opinions in January 1851 on Ricardo's theory of rent.[25] Here Marx already presents his basic objections to Ricardo's explanation of rent, which we later encounter in the *Theories of Surplus-Value* and in Volume III of *Capital*. Engels found these objections so devastating that he jokingly replied, 'There is no doubt that your solution is the right one, and that you have acquired a new claim to the title of the economist of ground-rent. If there were any right and justice left in the world the earth's total ground-rent should now be yours for at least a year, and even that would be the least to which you are entitled.' He added, 'If an article by you on ground-rent could be published in a translation in an English review it would attract enormous attention ... This is one more reason why you should hasten to complete and publish the "Economics".'[26]

Of equal importance in this context is Marx's letter on 3 February 1851, in which he communicates his critique of 'Currency theory' to Engels, and where we can see how he also differs from Ricardo on the theory of money.[27]

Of particular interest is the detailed discussion in the correspondence over Proudhon's book (*The General Idea of the Revolution*

---

[24] *MEW* Vol.27, p.373.
[25] *Selected Correspondence* ed. Dona Torr, London: Martin Lawrence 1934, pp.27, 132.
[26] *ibid*. p.32.
[27] *MEW* Vol.27, pp.173-77 and (Engels's reply) 200-201.

6 · *The Making of Marx's 'Capital'*

in the Nineteenth Century), published in 1851, as Marx produced a large pamphlet on it, which he offered to several publishers, again without success.[28] Like several of his early works, the manuscript of this pamphlet has been lost. We know only that this text was, for some time, in the hands of a close acquaintance of Marx, Wilhelm Pieper, who promised to offer it to German publishers during his tour there in 1851,[29] and further, that Marx wanted to publish the same text in the form of a series of articles under the title *Newest Revelations of Socialism or the General Idea of Revolution in the Nineteenth Century by P.J. Proudhon. A Critique by Karl Marx*, in *Revolution*, published by Weydemeyer in New York.[30] However, a previously unpublished manuscript was found among Marx's papers, which is mentioned in the editorial comments to the *Grundrisse*,[31] and bears the title *The Completed Money System (Das vollendete Geldsystem)*. This may well be a fragment of the pamphlet against Proudhon. However, whether this is so or not, the detailed discussion in the *Correspondence*[32] is certainly a substitute for the lost pamphlet. In addition, we see from the *Chronik* that Marx submitted a treatise, *Modern Literature on Political Economy in England from 1830 to 1852*, to the publisher Brockhaus in August 1852, in which he proposed to discuss the following subjects,[33] 1) 'the general works' and 2) the 'special writings' on 'population, colonies, the bank question, protective tariffs and freedom of trade etc.' Since Brockhaus turned it down it almost certainly remained as a mere outline.

From the summer of 1852 until the autumn of 1856 Marx's work on the *Critique of Political Economy* was interrupted by his professional work as a journalist. This did not of course mean that the research which he engaged in for this purpose had no significance for his work in political economy. On the contrary; Marx had to make himself familiar with practical details, since many of his reports dealt with 'noteworthy economic events in England and on the Continent'. Although these lay 'strictly speaking outside the sphere of political economy',[34] they did prove useful to him later. We need only refer to his numerous articles on economic conditions, on questions of trade policy, on the English working-class movement and

[28] *Chronik*, pp.110-11 and *MEW* Vol.28, pp.312, 358-59.
[29] *MEW* Vol.28, pp.369, 383.
[30] *Chronik*, p.116.
[31] *Grundrisse*, German edn. p.987.
[32] *MEW* Vol.28, pp.296-304, 306, 308-11, 312-15, 317-18.
[33] *Chronik*, p.126.
[34] *A Contribution to the Critique of Political Economy*, London: Lawrence & Wishart 1971, p.23. (Hereafter referred to as *Contribution*.)

strikes. Moreover, his reporting on Irish and Scottish agrarian conditions, and on English policy in India, proved to be extremely useful in this respect, as they provided the stimulus for a very thorough study of the 'Asiatic forms of production' and the remnants of agrarian communism in Europe and Asia. As a consequence, the sections on economic history in his work on political economy underwent a significant deepening and enrichment.[35]

So much, then, on the actual prehistory of the *Rough Draft* of 1857-58. How the *Rough Draft* itself arose, and how the first part of it came to be published, after a thorough re-working, under the title *A Contribution to the Critique of Political Economy* at the beginning of 1859, is dealt with in such detail in the article by Ryazanov and in the Editor's Foreword to the *Grundrisse*[36] that we shall confine ourselves to the most essential points here.

Characteristically, it was the outbreak of the economic crisis of 1857 which was responsible both for the immediate decision to write the *Rough Draft*, and the feverish hurry with which this was done. (The entire work, almost 50 proof-sheets, was completed in nine months, between July 1857 and March 1858.)[37] The economic crisis filled the 'Two-man Party' – as Engels's biographer, Mayer, named the two friends – with high hopes,[38] and it was therefore only natural that Marx wanted to commit at least the fundamentals of his economic theory to paper 'before the deluge',[39] that is, before the beginning of the expected European revolution. Of course, his revolutionary prognosis was based on an illusion; but such illusions have often

---

[35] It would certainly be rewarding to make a closer comparison of the topics in economic history which Marx dealt with on the one hand in the *New York Tribune*, and on the other in *Capital*.

[36] *Grundrisse*, German edn. pp.VII-XIV.

[37] See the editorial notes on pp.VII-VIII, 4, 150 and 842 of the German edition of the *Grundrisse*. The inaccurate information on pp.162-78 of the *Chronik* should be corrected in this light.

[38] It suffices here to cite a few characteristic passages from the Marx-Engels correspondence. 'Despite being deep in financial distress myself,' wrote Marx, 'I haven't felt so cosy since 1849, owing to this outbreak.' And Engels replied on 15 November 1857. 'The general aspect of the Stock Market' (which Engels visited through his work) 'has been highly amusing in the last few weeks. The fellows are absolutely furious over my attack of peculiarly good spirits. Indeed the stock exchange is the only place where my present dullness turns into elasticity and bouncing. Naturally, I prophesy the worst at the same time; that makes the asses twice as enraged.' (*MEW* Vol.29, pp. 207, 210.)

[39] *ibid.* p.225: 'I'm working like a madman right through the night, gathering my economic studies together so that I'll at least have the outlines (*Grundrisse*)' – hence the title given to the *Rough Draft* – 'clear before the deluge'.

proved themselves to be fruitful! So too in this case. Marx wrote to Engels on 18 December 1857, 'I'm working colossally – usually until 4 a.m. My task is twofold; 1) to work out the fundamentals of the economics . . . 2) the *present crisis*. On that, apart from the articles in the *Tribune* I'm simply keeping a record, which, however, takes up a lot of time. I think that we'll do a pamphlet together in the spring on history, by way of reintroducing ourselves to the German public – to say that we're still there and haven't changed, "always the same". I've sketched out three big books – England, Germany, France . . . all the material on America is in the *Tribune*. It can be put together later.'[40] This project too remained a mere outline, if we disregard the detailed notes for the chapter on France (in Marx's letter to Engels of 25 December 1857)[41] and the numerous articles devoted to the financial and commercial crises published in the *New York Tribune*.[42] The extent to which Marx's intensive concern with the symptoms of the 1857-58 crisis had sharpened his theoretical gaze can be seen from the brilliant excursus in the *Rough Draft* on the realisation problem and on crisis.[43] To this extent we are richly compensated for the fact that the intended pamphlet never appeared.

Just as apparent as his hope for a 'year if disruption in 1858',[44] is the other motive which impelled Marx to work on the *Rough Draft*; namely, his desire to deal with the 'false brothers' of the socialist workers' movement, the Proudhonists. It was certainly no accident that the *Rough Draft* began with a devastating polemic against the Proudhonist, Darimon, and the so-called Labour-Money system, and that also the refutation of Proudhonism occupies considerable space in the remainder of the text. As we know from his correspondence, Marx himself regarded this as one of the most crucial scientific results of the first part of his work (i.e. the book entitled *A Contribution to the Critique of Political Economy*.)[45] As the specifically Proudhonist variety of socialism is of very little importance today Marx appears

[40] *ibid.* p.232.
[41] *ibid.* pp.236-40.
[42] See *Chronik*, pp.164-65.
[43] See Chapter 21 of this work.
[44] *MEW* Vol.29, p.245.
[45] Thus he wrote to Weydemeyer on 1 February 1859: 'These two Chapters will also destroy the foundation of the Proudhonist socialism, now fashionable in France, which wants to leave private property in existence but to organise the exchange of private products; which wants commodities but not money. Communism must first of all get rid of this "false brother" '. (*Selected Correspondence*, p.106.) And similarly in Marx's letter, 22 July 1859, to Engels: 'In case you write anything about it [i.e. about the *Contribution*], 'you must not forget, 1) that Proudhonism is destroyed in it, at the roots, and

to have placed a 'disproportionate' emphasis on this particular aspect.

In our opinion the theoretical destruction of Proudhonism fades far into the background in the face of the second result stressed by Marx; namely, that his analysis of the commodity and of money exposed 'the specifically social and in no way absolute character of bourgeois production'. However, we should not overlook the fact that, in this case too, theory was fertilised by practice, and that the confrontation with Proudhonism contributed very substantially to the development of Marx's theory of money. But this is a perspective which we shall have to reserve for the section devoted to this theory.

2) that the specifically social and by no means absolute character of bourgeois production is analysed there as already present in the very simplest form, that of the commodity.' (*MEW* Vol.29, p.463.)

2.
The Structure of Marx's Work

1. THE ORIGINAL OUTLINE AND ITS CHANGES

It is known that Marx had two outlines which he wanted to use as the basis for his principal work; the first dates from 1857, and the second from 1866 (or 1865).[1] Between the two lay a a nine-year period of experimentation and continual searching for a form of presentation which would be adequate to the material. At the same time a progressive narrowing down of the original outline occurred, which corresponded, however, with an expansion of the part which remained.

In the 1857 outline the complete work was divided into six 'Books' (called also 'Sections'[2] and 'Chapters'.[3]) The first of these was to have dealt with capital, the second with landed property, the third with wage-labour, the fourth with the state, the fifth with foreign trade and the sixth with the world market and crises. Marx wanted to preface the whole work with an 'Introduction', in which the 'universal, abstract characteristics, which obtain in more or less all societies' would be discussed.[4] However, by the turn of 1858 he had already decided to dispense with this Introduction as it seemed to him that 'any anticipation of yet-to-be proved results would be a distraction'.[5]

[1] We move the date of the production of the second outline to 1865 because the structure of the work in Marx's letter to Engels of 31 July 1865 corresponds exactly to the structure in his letter to Kugelmann of 13 October 1866.

[2] See *Grundrisse* pp.287-88 ('section on wages'), p.530 ('section on international intercourse') and p.227, where all six divisions of the work are referred to as 'sections'.

[3] 'Chapter on Capital' (*Contribution*, p.19); 'Chapter on Wage-Labour' *Grundrisse*, p.399, 817 (latter in the German edition); *MEW* Vol.29, p.337. 'Chapter on Wages', *Grundrisse*, p.336; *Theories* I, p.404 and *Theories* III p.312.

[4] See the 'torso' of this Introduction in *Grundrisse*, pp.81-111. It should be noted here that in the text of the *Rough Draft* itself several references can be found to the quoted Introduction and the themes dealt with there. *ibid.* pp.298, 320, 362.

[5] *Contribution*, p.19. In fact such an Introduction is mentioned again in Marx's proposal of 1863.

The structure of Marx's work · 11

According to the original outline the last three of the six books of the work (on the state, foreign trade and the world market) were only to have been sketched out, confined – as Marx said – to 'the broad outlines'.[6] Nevertheless, one of these books is the subject of a letter to Kugelmann, written on 28 December 1862, proof that at that time they had not yet been finally excluded from the plan of the complete work.[7] However, this must have taken place soon afterwards, as Marx's 1864-65 manuscript (which Engels used as the basis for Volume III of *Capital*) makes no mention of these books and merely allots them – or at least one of them, on the world market – to an 'eventual continuation' of the work.[8] And so one restriction of the original plan had already been decided by then.

The second restriction concerns Books II and III, which were to have dealt with landed property and wage-labour. It is impossible to say precisely when Marx finally dispensed with these books. Even Marx's proposals for the first and third sections of the book on capital, which date from January 1863 and were published by Kautsky, provide no conclusive answer. However, the basic themes of the books on landed property and wage-labour were incorporated in the manuscripts of Volumes I and III of the final work, which took shape between 1864 and 1866. In this way the six books which were originally planned were reduced to one – the *Book on Capital*.

Let us now turn to the expansion of the book which remained. It is clear that a great deal of material from the deleted books, especially II and III, must have been transferred to the first, insofar as they contained 'the basic and properly economic, development'.[9] But not only that. According to the original outline the book on capital was also divided into four sections, which were supposed to deal with, a) 'capital in general', b) competition, c) credit and finally d) share-capital. Accordingly, the first two versions of the work, that is, the *Rough Draft* and the second manuscript of 1861-63, were also confined in essence to the analysis of 'capital in general'.[10] In writing

[6] Marx to Lassalle, 11 March 1858 (*MEW* Vol.29, p.554).
[7] Marx says in this letter on the subject of his second large manuscript, which he was working on at that time, and which he had thought of publishing under the changed title, *Capital, a Contribution to the Critique of Political Economy*: 'It is the quintessence . . . and the development of the following (with the exception of the relation of the different forms of the state to the different economic structures of society) could be easily carried out by others on the basis of what has been provided.' (*MEW* Vol.30, p.639.)
[8] *Capital* III, p.110.
[9] See the letter to Lassalle of 11 March 1858.
[10] The extraordinary importance of this concept in Marx's methodology is shown later in Section IV/B. of this Chapter.

sufficient to show that at the time of their drafting Marx had already established the outline of *Capital* [by which Kautsky means the final version] in its fundamentals. . . . Five years before the publication of the first volume, *Capital* as a whole was not only thought out in general terms, but actually already finalised in the same organised form in which it eventually appeared in public. This follows directly from a comparison of the outline with the List of Contents of Volume I. They coincide almost completely. The line of reasoning which Marx developed in the first volume as "Historical tendencies of capitalist accumulation", and which leads to the expropriation of the expropriators, is clearly to be understood under "change in the appearance of the law of appropriation". There are only two significant differences between the preliminary plan and the final edition of the first volume. In the plan Marx adheres strictly to his intention of providing the history of the theories on particular points of political economy at the end of the exposition of each of them in the form of a summary, as was done in the *Critique*[18] [i.e. the *Contribution*] . . . It will surely be seen as appropriate that the presentation of the history of the theory was partly reserved for an overall description in a specific fourth volume, and partly given in individual footnotes, depending on the circumstances.'

'But why,' Kautsky continues, 'didn't Marx deal with productive labour in the first volume, as he originally intended? One cannot suppose that he wanted to exclude it completely from the scope of his researches in *Capital*, because it is too important to it. Where did he think he could bring it in if he excluded it from the first volume? Unfortunately we are not in a position to say anything about that, we haven't the slightest clue to a definite answer.'

We read, in the same preface by Kautsky that : 'The final form of the book fits even more closely to the preliminary outline in the third volume than in the first. If we disregard the digressions on the history of the theory of rent and profit, mentioned above, which were planned and then dropped, the only difference between the third volume (insofar as it was finished) and his first plan lies in the order of the material. In the preliminary outline the exposition of the laws of ground-rent precedes the discussions of trade profit and money interest. The order is reversed in the third volume. The one seems to me to be just as good as the other, and does not constitute a substantial difference.'[19] This, then, is Kautsky's view. As with his com-

---

[18] The *Rough Draft* also contains sections specifically on 'Theories of Surplus-Value and Profit'.
[19] *Theories* (Kautsky's edition) III, VIII-X.

ments on productive labour, his entire commentary is likewise based on a misunderstanding. He simply notes the fact that Point 5 of the outline for the first section corresponds fairly precisely to the contents of Chapters 16 and 17 of Volume I of *Capital*, and that Chapter 16, dealing with 'Absolute and Relative Surplus-Value', begins with an examination of the definition of the concept of productive labour, which was intended to extend and complete the earlier analysis of this concept 'from the standpoint of the simple labour process'. In fact, in Chapter 16 Marx restricts himself to a short resumé of his research on this subject and, apart from that, refers the reader to the 'Fourth Book' of his work (according to the 1866 outline); that is, to the *Theories*, published by Kautsky himself, where a more extensive examination of this question can be found [on pages 152-300 of Part I of the English edition].

Nor can one agree with Kautsky that 'the line of reasoning which Marx developed in the first volume as "Historical Tendencies of Capitalist Accumulation" is to be understood under "Change in the Appearance of the Law of Appropriation" '. It is nothing of the sort. What it has much more to do with, is the fact that the law of appropriation in a simple commodity economy must change into the capitalist law of appropriation when the transition to bourgeois production has taken place. Marx devoted an entire sub-chapter of Volume I of *Capital*[20] to this idea and in fact it represents the crux of his criticism of the classical school.

However, these are only details. Kautsky's assertion as to the alleged 'almost total' correspondence between the January 1863 outline and the contents of Volume I and III of *Capital* is a much more serious error. It must be obvious that, in contrast to the *Rough Draft*, the outline for Section I includes such topics as the 'Struggle for the Normal Working-Day', 'Simple Co-operation', 'Division of Labour', 'Ratio of Wage-Labour to Surplus-Value', 'Primitive Accumulation', 'Theory of Colonisation' – that is, the topics which correspond to Chapters 10, 13, 14, 17, 26 and 33 of Volume I. However what is totally absent is an analysis of the category of the wage and its forms – the material which Marx deals with in Part VI of Volume I. From this we can conclude that Marx reserved this topic for a separate *Book on Wage-Labour*. Thus, the proposal for Section I

[20] See the first sub-chapter of Chapter 24: 'Capitalist Production on a Progressively Increasing Scale. Transition of the Laws of Property that Characterise Production of Commodities into Laws of Capitalist Appropriation.' (See also *Grundrisse*, pp.238, 295, 457-58, 469-70, 501, 673-74 and in the German edition pp.903-904; and *Theories* I, p.86, III, pp.377-78, 483.)

seems to correspond more to the original outline of 1857, than to that of 1866.

The matter is more complicated as far as Section III is concerned. In the first place, with regard to ground-rent, one can hardly agree with Kautsky that the question is simply one of a 'difference in the ordering of the material'. In fact Marx says in the proposal itself that he simply wants to deal with the problem of ground-rent as a digression in order to 'illustrate the difference between value and the price of production',[21] which should connect directly with the analysis of the 'transformation of the values of commodities into prices of production'. On the other hand we regard it as important that the proposed outline departs from the former method of subdividing the *Book on Capital*, insofar as it dispenses with a separate treatment of competition. However, the proposed outline still lacks an analysis of credit and share-capital. (Kautsky's reference to Point 8 of the proposed outline in no way suffices, as Marx deals with the category of interest in the *Rough Draft*[22] and in the *Theories of Surplus-Value*,[23] although he expressly excludes the credit system from consideration.[24])

We therefore conclude that the proposed outline of January 1863 remained for the most part within the framework of the original plan, although one can already detect a departure from it. This hypothesis is substantiated by a reading of the *Theories* themselves (that is the published sections of the 1861-63 manuscripts). There are numerous points in the *Theories* where the reader is referred sometimes to the separate *Book on Wage-Labour* and landed property, and sometimes to the further sections of the *Book on Capital* (as referred to in the original outline).

Let us begin with the latter. We should first mention that the outlines published by Kautsky were drafted by Marx when the manuscript of the *Theories* was almost finished. This explains why references can be found in the *Theories* to both the particular section

---

[21] Hence, this only concerns Marx's theory of absolute rents. (Cf. *Theories* (Kautsky's edition), II, p.329, 'Absolute rent is the surplus of value over the price of production of products of the soil. Differential rent is the surplus of the market price of the product of better soils over the value of its own product.') (Cf. *MEW* Vol.26, 2, p.137.) Cf. also Marx's letter to Engels of 2 August 1862: 'I now intend after all to bring the theory of rent already into this volume as a supplementary chapter, i.e. as an "Illustration" of a principle laid down earlier.' (*Selected Correspondence*, p.120.)
[22] See Chapter 27 below.
[23] *Theories* III, pp.453-96.
[24] See, for example, *Grundrisse*, pp.790, 805, 854; *Theories* II, pp.212, 482, 492, 513, 533; *Theories* III, pp.53, 466.

on credit[25] and also to that on competition.[26] One thing is clear from the outset. In the *Rough Draft* it is repeatedly stressed that a thorough treatment of the problem of the average rate of profit and prices of production is not possible until the analysis of 'many capitals',[27] i.e. competition.[28] However, in the *Theories* Marx was compelled to deal with Smith's and Ricardo's theories of value and surplus-value; but he could not have done this had he not dealt in detail with the question of the establishment of the general rate of profit and the transformation of values into prices of production. So it became necessary, in the course of the work itself, to go far beyond the limits of the original section on 'capital in general'. It is true that several questions (which we later find dealt with in Volume III of *Capital*) are assigned to the 'Chapter' or 'Section' on competition.[29] However, the fact that so much of the material originally destined for the special section on competition was already anticipated in the Manuscript of 1861-63 finally led, as we have already seen in Marx's proposed outline, to the complete elimination of this section, and consequently to the substitution of the new outline for the old.

A different result emerges if we consider the references to the *Book on Landed Property* and the *Book on Wage-Labour* which can be found in the *Theories*. Marx emphasises once more, in the section of Part II of the *Theories* dealing with Ricardo's theory of rent, that all he wants to do is 'set forth the general law of rent as an illustration of my theory of value and cost prices' since, he adds, 'I do not intend to give a detailed exposition of rent till dealing with landed property *ex professo*'.[30] The references to the *Book on Wage-Labour* are equally clear. This was the book in which Marx wanted to examine, among other things, the important question of skilled labour,[31] and remuneration for the so-called 'unproductive services'.[32]

[25] Cf. the previous note.
[26] See *Theories* II, pp.202, 238, 454, 468, 483, 492, 504, 513; III, pp.53, 311, 356.
[27] See Section IV/B. of this chapter on the category of 'many capitals'.
[28] *Grundrisse*, pp.435-36, 567, 760.
[29] Most informative in this respect is surely the example of 'counteracting tendencies to the tendency of the rate of profit to fall'. In Part III of the *Theories* (pp.311-12) the study of these 'tendencies' is still referred to the specific chapter on the 'competition of capitals'. However in Volume III of *Capital* there is an entire chapter dealing with 'Counteracting Influences' to the decline in the rate of profit.
[30] *Theories* II, p.269. Cf. ibid. pp.30, 37, 103-104.
[31] *Theories* III, pp.165.
[32] *Theories* I, pp.404.

In this respect he still adhered to his original outline.

As a final piece of evidence we want to draw upon the manuscript for Volume III of *Capital*, published and partially re-edited by Engels, as this manuscript was first produced in the years 1864-65, that is, at the time when, in our opinion, the transition from the old to the new outline took place.

As far as the originally envisaged section specifically on competition is concerned, several topics (appearing in more detail) were allotted to a 'Special Analysis of Competition' in the manuscript of 1864-65.[33] However, the key thing here is the perspective which Marx had already set out on Page 1 of the manuscript.

'In their real movement, capitals face each other in concrete forms of this kind, for which the form of capital in the direct production process, as also its form in the process of circulation, appears merely as specific moments. The forms of capital, as we develop them in this book, progressively approach the form in which they appear on the surface of society, in the action of the different capitals upon one another, in competition, and in the everyday consciousness of the agents of production.'[34] Hence the previous fundamental separation of the analysis of 'capital in general' and that of competition is dropped here, which naturally did not rule out the necessity of assigning certain specific problems to a separate section on competition.[35]

The question of the Section on Credit (and share-capital) cannot be resolved so definitively. Marx's own statements indicate that Volume III was supposed to contain a thorough analysis of the credit system.[36] Marx therefore also broke with the old outline on this point. However, in the first section of the manuscript of 1864-65 we find the comment that the presentation of the credit system 'should remain outside the scope of my work'.[37]

Furthermore, at the beginning of Chapter 25 of *Capital*, Volume III, Marx says, 'An exhaustive analysis of the credit system and of the instruments which it creates for its own use (credit-money etc.) lies beyond our plan.'[38] These are statements which seem to indicate

---

[33] See *Capital* III, pp.83, 118, 196, 235, 831.
[34] *ibid.* p.25. Cf. *ibid.* p.828.
[35] It should be mentioned here that, according to Marx's intention, the 'special analysis of competition' was mainly to have dealt with the 'real movement of market price', i.e. with the problem which constitutes the main object of analysis of so-called contemporary academic theory.
[36] See *MEW* Vol.31, p.296 and *MEW* Vol.32, pp.74, 204.
[37] *Capital* III, p.110.
[38] *ibid.* p.400. (Cf. Chapter 27 below.)

a certain indecision, which would certainly have been overcome had Marx had the chance to draft the manuscript in a form ready for printing – in particular Part V, which existed mainly in the form of notes.[39]

So much on competition and credit. But how does this relate to the material which should have been dealt with in Books II-VI of the work, according to the original outline?

As far as the *Book on Landed Property* is concerned, the work on the *Theories* led Marx to go beyond Point 4 of the proposed outline for Section III of January 1863. He by no means confined himself to an 'Illustration of the difference between values and prices of production' in the *Theories*, i.e. to an exposition of the theory of absolute rent, but in addition provided a detailed critique of Ricardo's theory of differential rent. Both problems – absolute and differential rent – were then dealt with in the 1864-65 manuscript, although the examination of differential rent now came first.[40]

In the manuscript of Volume III, published by Engels, there is not only a separate chapter on the rents for building land and mines and on the price of land, but also an exhaustive inquiry into the 'Genesis of capitalist rent' – thus fulfilling an intention which had already been stated in Volume II of *Theories*.[41] Part VI of Volume III, which was produced as a result, ought to have covered the crucial themes of the *Book on Landed Property*, as it was originally envisaged; although Marx emphasises that 'a systematic treatment of landownership, which is beyond the scope of our plan' not only involved a consideration of the different historical forms of

[39] Cf. Engels's Foreword to Volume III of *Capital*, pp.2-21.
[40] In fact the change in the order can be traced back to Engels, who, however, simply followed Marx's outline note on pp.726-27 of Volume III.
[41] The following passage is meant here: 'The following problems should now be set forth: 1. The transition from feudal landownership to a different form, commercial land rent, regulated by capitalist production, or, on the other hand, the conversion of this feudal landed property into free peasant property. 2. How rent comes into existence in countries such as the United States, where originally land has not been appropriated and where, at any rate in a formal sense, the bourgeois mode of production prevails from the beginning. 3. The Asiatic forms of landownership still in existence.' (*Theories* II, p.42) Marx returns to all but the last of these points in the manuscript of Volume III. We should perhaps still mention in this connection that Marx also intended (as we can infer from the footnote on p.869 (711) of Volume I of *Capital*) 'to demonstrate in detail how the famine and its consequences have been deliberately exploited both by the individual landlords and by the English Parliament through legislation so as to accomplish the agricultural revolution by force and to thin down the population of Ireland to the proportion satisfactory to the landlords'. Marx did not return to this point either.

landed property, but also several of the specific questions which relate to modern landed property itself.[42] On the other hand we know from Engels's Preface to Volume III of *Capital* that in the seventies 'Marx engaged in entirely new special studies for the part on ground-rent. For years he had studied the Russian originals of statistical reports inevitable after the "Reform" of 1861 in Russia and other publications on landownership and had taken extracts from them . . . Owing to the variety of forms both of landownership and of the exploitation of agricultural producers in Russia, this country was to play the same role in the part dealing with ground-rent that England played in Book I in connection with industrial wage-labour.'[43] We cannot say what effect this would have had in changing the manuscript on ground-rent.

Why the manuscript of 1864-65 contains no references of any kind to a separate *Book on Wage-Labour* can be easily explained. The manuscript was already drafted according to Marx's new outline and consequently all the themes of the earlier book on wage-labour came into the scope of Volume I of the work, which dealt with the production process.

Finally, as far as the original Books IV-VI (state, foreign trade, world market) are concerned we should like to refer here to the section from Volume III of *Capital*[44] which has already been cited, where Marx excludes the question of 'Competition in the World Market' from the scope of his research for *Capital*. The same applies to the problem which relates very closely to this, namely that of the business cycle – 'the alternation of prosperity and crisis' – 'whose further analysis', as Marx repeatedly stressed 'falls outside our field of study'[45] and was perhaps intended for an 'eventual continuation' of the work. This does show, however, that Marx's theory of crises had 'gaps', in the sense that he never again had the opportunity of dealing with the problem at its most concrete level. To this extent Rosa Luxemburg's criticism[46] contains an element of truth.

So much for the changes in the outline which can be established by looking at the manuscripts for *Capital* itself. What conclusions can we draw from our inquiry? First, that the transition from the old outline to the new did not take place before 1864-65; second, that on the subject of the changes in the outline we must draw a

[42] *Capital* III, pp.614, 615, 618.
[43] *ibid*. p.7 of Engels's Preface.
[44] *ibid*. p.110.
[45] *ibid*. pp.360, 362, 831.
[46] Rosa Luxemburg, *The Accumulation of Capital*, London: Routledge and Kegan Paul 1963, pp.165-70.

sharp distinction between the original Books I-III and Books IV-VI. As far as these last books are concerned our inquiry suggests the conclusion that they were never really 'abandoned'. That is to say, their subject matter was never fully assimilated within the second structure of the work, but rather held back for the 'eventual continuation' itself. And since the subjects under consideration are only dealt with intermittently in *Capital*, the so-called 'gaps theory' does seem to have some justification. (This is, in fact, Grossmann's term. Of course he himself denies that there are any 'gaps' in Marx's *Capital*.[47])

The position is quite different in the case of Books II and III. These had to be incorporated into the new structure because *Capital* would have been inconceivable without a treatment of the questions which they deal with. (The same of course applies to Sections b) – d) of the *Book on Capital* as in the original plan.) So our present problem, that of the change in the outline, only arises in connection with these latter parts of the former structure – namely Books II and III and Sections b) – c) of the first book.[48]

III. PREVIOUS EXPLANATIONS OF THE CHANGE IN THE OUTLINE

(The attempted explanations of Grossmann and Behrens)

This is sufficient on the outward history of the change in the outline. But what about the reasons for the change, and how do they relate to the methodology of Marx's work? It is indicative (and at the same time quite appalling) that this question, which is so fundamental to an understanding of Marx's system, was not brought up until Grossmann, the author of the *Akkumulationsgesetz*, did so in 1929.[49] However, like several other post-war authors who dealt with this subject, he did not succeed in answering the question.

Grossmann is of course right when he says that: 'A change in the outline of *Capital* could not have been an accidental matter, nor a technical question of the presentation, a question of clarity, for

---

[47] H.Grossmann, *Das Akkumulations- und Zusammenbruchsgesetz des kapitalistischen Systems*, p.417.

[48] Accordingly we shall limit ourselves in this chapter to Books I-III and only refer occasionally to Books IV-VI in the course of the work.

[49] See Grossmann, *Die Änderung des Aufbauplans des Marxschen 'Kapital' und ihre Ursachen* in *Archiv für die Geschichte des Sozialismus und der Arbeiterbewegung*, 1929, pp.305-38.

example.' Rather, as he says, it must be traced back to something 'internal'; that is, methodological reasons must be found. However, the reasons Grossmann himself gives are so inadequate that we have to regard his attempted explanation as a complete failure.[50] According to Grossmann the question can be solved quite simply. Whereas Marx's work in its final form is structured according to the individual functions of industrial capital from a scientific viewpoint, the original outline merely represents an empirical division of the material to be dealt with.[51] It was not until later, in 1863, that Marx – in connection with his study of the problem of reproduction – 'necessarily arrived at the point where he could no longer take the given world of appearance as the object of his analysis'. It was not until then that he succeeded in advancing 'from the visible surface manifestations of profit and the different forms of capital to a comprehensive vision of the totality, aggregrate surplus-value and aggregate capital. This made it impossible to adhere to the original outline.'[52] So, in fact, the abandonment of this outline amounted to breaking out of what was essentially a Vulgar-Economic shell, which had imprisoned Marx until 1863!

Grossmann's study was sharply criticised by Behrens.[53] In contrast to Grossmann, Behrens seeks to derive the change in the outline from the 'essence of the materialist dialect'. What he actually comes up with is this: 'If Marx originally set out from an external point of view, with the division into six books, and followed the traditional classification of economics up to that time, he now constructed his work [i.e. according to the amended outline] along strictly scientific lines.'[54]

Despite his criticism of Grossmann's 'external-mechanistic' method, it is evident that Behrens's own explanation resembles it

[50] Cf. the penetrating criticism of Grossmann's study in O.Morf's book: *Das Verhältnis von Wirtschaftstheorie und Wirtschaftsgeschichte bei Karl Marx*, 1951, pp.75-78.
[51] Here in Grossmann's own words: 'Whereas the articulation of the 1859 outline into six sections is from the standpoint of the material to be dealt with: Capital, Landed Property, Wage-Labour, Foreign Trade etc. the structure of the work in the final outline is from the standpoint of knowledge ... methodological considerations [lead] to the abstraction and separate representation of the individual functions of industrial capital from their diverse reality, without regard to the material. The material as a whole is only dealt with within the representation of each of the functions from the respective functional standpoints.' (*op. cit.* p.311.)
[52] *ibid.* pp.319-20.
[53] Fr. Behrens, *Zur Methode der politischen Ökonomie*, 1952, pp.31-48.
[54] *ibid.* pp.32-33.

exactly. Both of them (equally externally) want to derive the change in the outline from Marx's preoccupation with a particular area of investigation.[55]

Both 'localise' the time of the change to 1863[56] on the basis of an arbitrarily interpreted passage of the *Correspondence* and, finally, they both interpret Marx's original outline as being in accordance with the methodology of Vulgar Economics. The 'dialectical' accessories which Behrens uses to decorate his argument make no difference at all.

It would be a pure waste of time to look at these superficial attempts at an explanation any more closely. The intention of the original outline must be derived from an analysis of the *Rough Draft*, and the later *Capital* manuscripts themselves, if we are to find a solution to the problem of the change in the outline.

IV. THE METHODOLOGICAL IMPORT OF THE ORIGINAL OUTLINE

A. The first three 'Books'

1. Marx on the method and object of political economy

Does not the articulation of the work, which is to be found in the first outline, coincide at least outwardly with the conventional divisions of bourgeois economics? It does, but only outwardly: and the task of marxist research consists in proceeding to the essence of the

---

[55] The difference is simply that, according to Grossmann, Marx first came upon the idea in the course of his work on problems of reproduction, which he allegedly began in 1863, that 'instead of an analysis of the given empirical material, the function of the creation of surplus-value has to stand in the foreground' (Grossmann, *op. cit.* p.320); whereas according to Behrens Marx owes this sudden inspiration to his 'renewed critical confrontation with classical bourgeois economics', with its theories of surplus-value (Behrens, *op. cit.* p.44). It is sufficient here to mention that Marx first became occupied with the problem of reproduction in 1858 (*Rough Draft*), and that, on the other hand, all the essential points which Marx used against Smith's and Ricardo's methodology can be found in the *Rough Draft*.

[56] The relevant passage here is this. Marx wrote to Engels on 15 August 1863: 'My work is proceeding well in one respect. It seems to me that with the final working out the points are taking on a tolerable popular form – with the exception of a few unavoidable M-Cs and C-Ms... At any rate it will be 100 per cent easier to understand than No. 1 [i.e. the *Contribution*]. Moreover, when I look at the concoction and see how I've had to overturn everything and compose the historical part to some extent out of quite unknown

matter, to the basic methodological assumptions, which distinguish Marx's classification from the conventional one, and not in allowing itself to be deceived by superficial similarities.

The outline we are discussing here was first drafted by Marx in September 1857, at the end of the chapter dealing with the 'Method of Political Economy', which forms the Introduction preceding the *Rough Draft*.[57] It follows that any initial clarification of the real intention behind Marx's original outline should be looked for in this chapter.

Marx shows here that the method of 'ascending from the abstract to the concrete' is the only scientific way of 'appropriating the concrete and reproducing it as the concrete in thought'. 'The concrete is concrete', so runs the now famous sentence of the Introduction, 'because it is the synthesis of many determinations, hence the unity of the diverse'.[58] Therefore it can only be fully understood by means of thought as a 'process of synthesis'; that is, by means of the progressive reconstruction of the concrete from the most simple, abstract definitions of the concrete itself. On the other hand if scientific (in this case economic) analysis begins directly with the 'real and concrete', with the 'actual preconditions' themselves, for example population or the world market, then it has an indistinct and completely undefined picture of reality to deal with. Because : 'Population is an abstraction if I leave out, for example, the classes of which it is composed. These classes in turn are an empty phrase if I am not familiar with the elements on which they rest. E.g. wage-labour, capital etc. These in turn presuppose exchange, division of labour, prices etc. . . . Thus, if I were to begin with population, this would be a chaotic conception of the whole, and I would then, by means of further definition, move analytically towards ever more simple concepts : from the imagined concrete towards ever thinner abstractions until I had arrived at the simplest definitions. From there the journey would have to be retraced until I finally arrived back at population, but this time not as a chaotic conception of the whole, but as a rich

material, I find it really amusing that Lassalle has "his" Economics well in hand . . .' Behrens and Grossmann want to conclude from this that the words 'how I've had to overturn everything' relate directly to the change in the outline. However, what is more likely is that the 'overturning' does not mean the original outline, but rather all previous economics, in which case Grossmann's and Behrens's fixation on 1863 as the time of the change lacks any foundation.

[57] *Grundrisse*, pp.100ff.

[58] Cf. Hegel, *Encyclopädie der philosophischen Wissenschaften im Grundrisse* (1870) p.60. 'The concept as concrete, and in fact any particular is essentially in itself a unity of diverse determinations.'

totality of many definitions and relations.' And it is precisely for this reason that a correct and scientific method of political economy must ascend 'from the simple, such as labour, division of labour, need, exchange-value . . . to the state, exchange between countries and the world market',[59] in order that the development of the capitalist mode of production can be followed through until it is grasped in its totality.

We refer to this section, which has been quoted so often, because it provides us with some explanation of Marx's outline of 1857 and because it demonstrates that this outline (as did *Capital* later) 'follows the path from abstract definitions to the concrete', and was in no way arranged in a form corresponding 'to the point of view of the raw material'.[60] This is not all, however. The original outline was clearly drawn up so that the process of synthesis, the 'ascent from the abstract to the concrete' occurs there several times. This can be seen particularly clearly in the changes to the outline on page 108 of the *Grundrisse*. In this version the inquiry proceeds from general categories (exchange-value, money, price), through an analysis of the 'inner structure of production' – the categories of capital, landed property and wage-labour – in order to arrive at the synthesis of bourgeois society in the form of the state. Here bourgeois society is studied 'in its relation to itself', which naturally offers quite new perspectives. However, this is still not the final stage of concretisation! For the domestic economy must be understood in its external relations to other capitalist (and non-capitalist) countries, and ultimately as one element in a totality which embraces all countries. Only then do we arrive at the category 'world market' and the 'world economy' as a 'rich totality of many definitions and relations'. Finally, the same procedure of the ascent from 'the abstract to the concrete' is repeated in the *Book on Capital*, where Marx begins with 'capital in general' in order to reach, via an examination of competition and the credit system, capital in its most developed form, share-capital.[61]

So we see that what distinguishes the original outline is primarily the view of the bourgeois economy as an 'organic whole', the perspective of a totality – of the 'all-pervasive, determining supremacy of the whole over the parts' (G.Lukacs).[62] A view far removed from the method of bourgeois economics, which brings outward appearances into a purely external relation with one another. Accord-

[59] *Grundrisse*, pp.100-101.
[60] Morf, *op. cit.* p.35.
[61] Cf. Marx's letter of 2 April 1858 to Engels. *Selected Correspondence*, pp.97-101.
[62] *History and Class Consciousness*, p.27.

ingly Marx stresses in the same chapter of the Introduction that 'it would be wrong and impractical' to deal 'with the economic categories in the same sequence as that in which they were the determining factors in history. Their sequence is determined, rather, by the relation which they bear to each other in modern bourgeois society, which is precisely the opposite of what seems to be their natural order or the order of their succession in history.' Marx states further, 'This must be kept in mind because it has an immediate and decisive bearing on the arrangement of the categories. For example, nothing seems more natural than to start with rent, with landed property, because it is bound up with land, the source of all production and all existence, and with the first form of production in all reasonably settled societies – namely agriculture. But nothing could be more erroneous.' For 'in all forms of society there is a certain form of production which predominates over all the rest, and whose relations determine the rank and influence of all others.' For example, under capitalist production agriculture becomes more and more a branch of industry, and as such, subordinate to capital. And it is precisely for this reason that in the theoretical analysis of the bourgeois social order, capital 'as the all-prevailing economic power of bourgeois society', 'must form the starting-point as well as the end and be developed before landownership'. (And their 'mutual relation should not not be studied until after they have been looked at separately'.)[63]

2. The 'trinity formula' of bourgeois economics

However, if the category of capital constitutes 'the starting point as well as the end', why did Marx intend to follow the *Book on Capital* with separate books on landed property and wage-labour? Doesn't this indicate a certain inconsistency or methodological immaturity in the original outline?

Not at all. We first have to remember that the threefold division of the material in bourgeois economics did not always serve apologetic ends, and that we should distinguish between classical and Vulgar Economics in this respect at least. We know that Marx was unmerciful in his demolition of the 'trinity formula' of Vulgar Economics, with its theory of three 'factors of production' – capital, land and labour – understood not simply as three different sources of income, but at the same time as independent sources of value creation, working harmoniously together. ('As for example, the peasant,

[63] *Grundrisse*, pp. 106-107.

the ox and plough, and the land in agriculture, which despite their dissimilarities work harmoniously together in the real labour process'.[64]) He shows that 'the mystification of the capitalist mode of production, the reification of social relations is accomplished' in this formula, because it unthinkingly compounds the historically determined social forms of production with the material aspects of the real labour process : 'the enchanted, perverted, topsy-turvy world in which Monsieur le Capital and Madame la Terre do their ghost-walking as social characters and at the same time directly as mere things.'[65] However, this characterisation only applies to Vulgar Economics proper, or the elements[66] of it which were undoubtedly to be found in the classical school.[67] Secondly, the 'trinity formula' does contain a certain germ of truth, because owing to the separation of the real producers from the means of production, the value created by the annual addition of new labour divides into three parts, which take on the shape of three different kinds of revenue, and form the annual income of the three social classes – the capitalists, landowners, and the workers. 'These, then, are relations or forms of distribution for they express the relations under which the newly-produced total value is distributed among the owners of the various productive agencies.'[68]

Indeed : 'If labour were not defined as wage-labour the form in which it takes its share of products would not appear as wages.'[69]

[64] *Theories* III, p.503.
[65] *Capital* III, p.830. Accordingly, it is stressed in the Introduction that it would be a 'complete illusion' to derive ground-rent 'simply from the earth' or wages 'as simply from labour'; these forms of distribution presuppose the modern form of landed property modified by capitalism, and modern wage labour.
[66] *Theories* III, p.500.
[67] However as far as classical political economy is concerned, 'it seeks to grasp the inner connection in contrast to the multiplicity of outward forms. It therefore reduces rent to surplus profit, so that it ceases to be a specific, separate form and is divorced from its apparent source, the land. It likewise divests interest of its independent form and shows that it is a part of profit. In this way it reduces all types of revenue and all independent forms and titles under cover of which the non-workers receive a portion of the value of commodities, to the single form of profit. Profit, however, is reduced to surplus-value since the value of the whole commodity is reduced to labour; the amount of paid labour embodied in the commodity constitutes wages, consequently the surplus over and above it constitutes unpaid labour, surplus labour called forth by capital and appropriated gratis under various titles.' (*ibid*. p.500.) To this extent the threefold division of the material in Classical Economics has no connection with the 'trinity formula' of Vulgar Economics.
[68] *Capital* III, p.877.
[69] *Grundrisse*, p.95.

On the other hand, if the ruling class did not possess a monopoly of the means of production they could not compel the worker to perform surplus labour, and would therefore not be in a position to appropriate the different parts of the surplus-value produced by the worker in the form of manufacturers' profits, interest and rent. So the distribution of products is preceded by a 'distribution of the elements of production', the 'separation of the ability to work, as the worker's commodity, from the means of production, the property of non-workers'.[70] 'The distribution of products is evidently only a result of this distribution, which is comprised within the process of production itself and determines its structure.'[71] From this perspective 'the so-called relations of distribution are themselves relations of production', only under a different form.[72] It therefore follows from this that it is foolish 'to view the bourgeois forms of production as absolute, but the bourgeois forms of distribution as historically relative, and hence transitory'.[73] However, it does *not* follow that the forms of distribution should only be given secondary importance in economics. On the contrary; these forms continually react upon the relations of production. 'The specific features and therefore also the specific limitation ... enters production itself as a determining factor which overlaps and dominates production.'[74] 'Ricardo, whose concern was to grasp the specific social structure of modern production and who is the economist of production *par excellence* declares for precisely that reason that distribution, and not production, is the proper study of modern economics.'[75]

However, in the last analysis, Marx's main concern was also to consider the forms of appearance of distribution 'which serve as the starting-point for the Vulgar Economists', as the necessary obverse of the relations of production: to establish 'the three major classes of developed capitalist society – the landowners, capitalists and wage-labourers – corresponding to three great forms of revenue – ground-rent, profit and wages – and the class struggle, an inevitable concomitant of their existence, as the actual consequence of the capitalist

[70] *Capital* II, p.389.
[71] *Grundrisse*, p.96.
[72] *ibid*. p.832.
[73] *Theories* III, p.84.
[74] *ibid*. In this sense profit and interest are denoted as 'determining determinates' in the Introduction to the *Grundrisse*.
[75] *Grundrisse*, pp.96-97. (Cf. p.95-96) 'Thus economists such as Ricardo, who are the most frequently accused of focusing on production alone, have defined distribution as the exclusive object of economics, because they instinctively conceived the forms of distribution as the most specific expression into which the agents of production of a given society are cast.')

The structure of Marx's work · 31

period'.⁷⁶ Accordingly Volume III of *Capital* ends with an analysis of the revenues of the social classes. In addition, however, according to the outline of 1857, the analysis of capital, landed property and wage-labour was to have opened out into a study of the 'three great social classes', and the 'exchange between them'. In other words, Marx expected the analysis of the relations of production to lead on to that of the relations of distribution.⁷⁷ And so a considerable correspondence between the original outline and the final one can also be established on this issue.

3. *The three fundamental social classes*

From what has been said it is now clear how we should interpret the projected threefold division of the inquiry in the first outline into the three separate books on capital, landed property and wage-labour; it was necessary 'to investigate the economic conditions of existence of the three main classes into which modern bourgeois society is divided'.⁷⁸ What determines this class division? (Or, as it states in the fragment of Chapter 52 of Volume III of *Capital* – 'What makes wage-labourers, capitalists and landlords constitute the three great social classes?')⁷⁹

As far as workers and capitalists are concerned there is clearly only one answer; their functions in the production process.⁸⁰ This is quite evident in relation to wage-labour. The capitalist social order would be inconceivable without the category of wage-labour. In order to expand its value, capital must constantly have available a class of people who entirely lack the means of production and who therefore have to purchase a portion of the value-product created by them through the performance of surplus labour. The role and existence of the capitalist class is also given by their function in the production process (this naturally only applies to industrial capital).⁸¹ Marx writes in his *Marginal Notes on Adolph Wagner*: 'I

⁷⁶ *Capital* III, p.7. Cf. *MEW* Vol.32, pp.74-75.
⁷⁷ See *Grundrisse*, pp.108, 264.
⁷⁸ *Contribution*, p.19.
⁷⁹ *Capital* III, p.886.
⁸⁰ In this sense Marx speaks at one point of 'functionally determined social classes'.
⁸¹ 'Industrial capital is the only mode of existence of capital in which not only the appropriation of surplus-value, or surplus-product, but simultaneously its creation, is a function of capital. Therefore with it the capitalist character of production is a necessity. Its existence implies the class antagonism between capitalists and wage-labourers ... the other kinds of capital, which

represent the capitalist as a necessary functionary of capitalist production, and indicate at length that he does not only "deduct" or "rob", but enforces the production of surplus-value and thus first helps to create what is to be deducted; I further show in detail that even though in the exchange of commodities only equivalents are exchanged, the capitalist begins to obtain surplus-value as soon as he has paid the worker the real value of his labour-power – and he is fully entitled to do this by the law which corresponds to this mode of production.'[82] Or as we read in the *Theories* : 'The capitalist is the direct exploiter of the worker, not only the direct appropriator, but the direct creator of surplus labour. But since this can only take place for the industrial capitalist in and through the process of production, he is himself a functionary of this process, its director.'[83] From this viewpoint, since 'materialised labour and living labour represent the two factors which have to be brought into contact with each other before capitalist production can take place . . . capitalists and wage-labourers are the sole functionaries and factors of production, whose

appeared before industrial capital amid conditions of social production that have receded into the past or are now succumbing, are not only subordinated to it, and the mechanism of their functions altered in conformity with it, but move solely with it as their basis, hence live and die, stand and fall with this basis.' (*Capital* II, p.57.)

[82] Marx adds, 'however all this does not make the "profit of capital" a "constitutive" element of value, but rather only proves that in the value which is not "constituted" by the labour of the capitalist, there is a part which he can "rightfully" appropriate, i.e. without violating the laws corresponding to the exchange of commodities.' (*MEW* Vol.19, pp.359-60: see English translation in *Theoretical Practice*, Issue 5, spring 1972, p.44.)

[83] 'Indeed', Marx wrote in 1863, 'capitalist production itself has brought it about that the labour of superintendence walks the streets, separated completely from the ownership of capital, whether one's own or other people's. It has become quite unnecessary for capitalists to perform this labour of superintendence. It is actually available separate from capital, not in the sham separation which exists between the industrial capitalist and the moneyed capitalist, but that between industrial managers, etc. and capitalists of every sort.' But this proves 'that the capitalist as functionary of production has become just as superfluous to the workers as the landlord appears to the capitalist with regard to bourgeois production.' (*Theories* III, p.497.) And then two years later Marx points out that the development of joint-stock companies would lead 'to the transformation of the actually functioning capitalist into a mere manager, an administrator of other people's capital, and of the owner of capital into a mere owner, a mere money capitalist'. 'In stock companies the function is divorced from capital ownership, hence also labour is entirely divorced from ownership of the means of production and surplus labour. This result of the ultimate development of capitalist production is a necessary transitional phase towards the reconversion of capital into the property of producers, although no longer as the private property of the individual

relation and confrontation arise from the essence of the capitalist mode of production.'[84]

For this very reason we must make a sharp distinction between the industrial capitalist and the large landowner. If we assume the capitalist mode of production, 'the capitalist is not only a necessary functionary, but the dominating functionary in production', whereas the landowner 'is quite superfluous in this mode of production'. Although he was 'an important functionary in the ancient world and the Middle Ages', he has 'become a useless excrescence in the industrial world'.[85] Therefore Marx considers that it is only consistent for economists, especially Ricardo, to 'start from a division into two, between capitalist and wage-labourer, and only bring in the landowner who draws rent at a later stage, as a special outgrowth ... Far from being an error on the part of Ricardo[86] ... this reduction of the classes participating directly in production, hence also in the value produced and then in the products in which this value is embodied, to capitalists and wage-labourers, and the exclusion of the landowners (who only enter *post festum*, as a result of conditions of ownership of natural forces that have not grown out of the capitalist mode of production but have been handed down to it from the past) ... is an adequate theoretical expression of the capitalist mode of production, grounded in its essence, and it expresses its *differentia specifica*.'[87] It does not however follow that the landowner 'is not a necessary agent for capitalist production',[88] that he is unnecessary for the maintenance of this form of production, or that the capitalist economy could have arisen and developed without landownership.

---

producers, but rather as the property of associated producers as outright social property.' (*Capital* III, pp.436-37.) When 'sociologists' such as J.Burnham present the replacement of the functioning capitalist by the industrial manager as some major novelty, one really doesn't know whether this is a question of plagiarism or simple ignorance. More likely the second, as one cannot really attribute a knowledge of marxism to Burnham ('The Witchdoctor', as Trotsky called him).

[84] *Theories* II, p.152. Cf. *Capital* III, pp.879-80: 'In view of what has already been said, it is superfluous to demonstrate anew that the relation between capital and wage-labour determines the entire character of the mode of production. The principal agents of this mode of production itself, the capitalist and the wage-labourer, are as such, mere embodiments, personifications of capital and wage-labour; definite social characteristics stamped upon individuals by the process of social production; the production of these definite social relations.'
[85] *Theories* II, p.44.
[86] The quote is directed against Rodbertus.
[87] *ibid*. pp.152-53.
[88] *ibid*. p.152.

On the contrary; if land were 'at everybody's free disposal, then a principal element for the formation of capital would be missing. A most important condition of production and – apart from man himself and his labour – the only original condition of production could not be disposed of, could not be appropriated. It could not thus confront the worker as someone else's property and make him into a wage-labourer. The productivity of labour ... in the capitalist sense, the "producing" of someone else's unpaid labour would thus become impossible. And this would put an end to capitalist production altogether.'[89] Looked at in this way, 'private ownership of land, private ownership by one person which presupposes non-ownership on the part of other persons – is the basis of the capitalist mode of production.'[90] For this reason capital simply cannot exist without landed property ('which it includes as its antithesis'), and therefore the change in the conditions of labour within capital presupposes not only 'the expropriation of the direct producers from the land', but also at the same time 'a definite form of landownership'.[91]

In fact, 'the form of landed property with which the incipient capitalist mode of production is confronted does not suit it. It first creates the form appropriate to it by subordinating agriculture to capital . . . landownership thus receives its purely economic form through the removal of all its former political and social embellishments and associations',[92] and is reduced to the category of capitalist ground-rent. And so it should not be forgotten that 'capitalist production starts its career on the presupposition of landed property, which is not its own creation, but which was already there before it'. As a consequence the influence capital can exert on landownership is limited. 'All that capital can do is to subject agriculture to the conditions of capitalist production.'[93] However, it cannot prevent a separate class of monopolistic owners of the means of production

---

[89] ibid. p.44.
[90] Capital III, p.812. In fact, the sole concern of capital is that 'the land and soil are not under common ownership, that they confront the working class as means of production which do not belong to it, and this aim would be completely attained if it became state property, i.e. if the state drew the rents'. 'The radical bourgeois proceeds then theoretically to the denial of private landownership which he would like to make into the common property of the bourgeois class, of capital, in the form of state ownership. However, courage is lacking in practice, since an attack on one form of property – a form of the private ownership of the conditions of work – would be very risky for the other forms.' (Theories II, p.44.)
[91] Capital III, p.870.
[92] ibid. p.617.
[93] Theories II, p.243.

from continuing to exist apart from and alongside the real capitalists in the shape of the large landowners. This class, 'confronts capital as alien power and a barrier . . . in its endeavour to invest in land',[94] and can squeeze from it a portion of the surplus-value produced by the workers. The 'private ownership of natural objects' is certainly 'not a source from which flows value, since value is only materialised labour. Neither is it the source from which surplus-value flows . . . This ownership is however a source of revenue . . . a claim to unpaid labour, gratis labour.'[95] In fact the landowner 'has a claim – through landed property (to absolute rent) and because of the physical differences of the various types of land (differential rent) – which enables him to pocket a part of this surplus labour or surplus-value, to whose direction and creation he contributes nothing'. (Marx adds here: 'Where there is a conflict, therefore, the capitalist regards him as a mere superfetation, a Sybaritic excrescence, a parasite on capitalist production, the louse that sits upon him.')[96]

4. *The 'transition from capital to landed property' and from 'landed property to wage-labour'*

We have spent some time on the question of landed property and the role which it plays in the capitalist mode of production. We shall see why this discussion was necessary when we come to the study of one particular line of thought which is crucial for the understanding of the original outline, and which can be found in both the *Rough Draft* and the *Correspondence*,[97] where Marx discusses the transition from capital to landed property, on the one hand, and, on the other, that from landed property to wage-labour.

The *Rough Draft* says on the subject of the first transition: 'In

---

[94] *Capital* III, p.764.
[95] *Theories* II, p.42.
[96] *ibid.* p.328.
[97] We can quote the second here, as it only consists of two sentences. Marx wrote to Engels on the subjects of Books II and III of his work, 'The transition of capital to landed property is at the same time historical, as the modern form of landed property is a product of the effect of capital upon feudal and other landed property. Similarly the transition of landed property to wage-labour is not only dialectical but historical, since the final product of modern landownership is the general positing of wage-labour, which in turn appears as the basis of the entire thing.' (*Selected Correspondence*, p.97.) Cf. Engel's reply of 9 April 1858: 'This arrangement of the whole into six books could not be better and pleases me a great deal, although I still don't see the dialectical transition from landed property to wage-labour clearly.' (*MEW* Vol.29, p.319.)

the money market [with which the *Book on Capital* was to have been concluded] capital is posited in its totality . . . but capital, not only as something which produces itself . . . but at the same time as a creator of values, must posit a value or form of wealth specifically different from capital. This is ground-rent. This is the only value created by capital which is distinct from itself, from its own production. By its nature as well as historically, capital is the creator of modern landed property, of ground-rent; just as its action therefore appears also as the dissolution of the old form of property in land. The new arises through the action of capital upon the old . . .'[98]

Consequently, as Marx himself stresses, the 'transition from capital to landed property' is to be understood in a double sense – both dialectically and historically. The second sense requires no further elucidation after the foregoing discussion. However, the dialectical transition should be understood as follows : The special form of wealth which capital itself creates is value based on labour. But apart from this there is also the 'value of natural agents' (agricultural land, waterfalls, mines etc.), which as such are not products of labour but which 'are appropriated, hence possess exchange-value and enter as values into the calculation of the cost of production'.[99] This value can only be explained by the Theory of Rent – and modern ground-rent represents a particular creation of capital, the only creation of capital 'as value distinct from itself, from its own production'. So the question is answered : 'How does it come about that commodities which contain no labour possess exchange-value, or in other words, how does the exchange-value of purely natural forces arise?'[100] Naturally 'value' here only has a figurative meaning, i.e. it cannot be directly explained by the theory of value as such, but rather, presupposes 'further developments'.[101] However, this is one reason why Marx did not intend to deal with landownership i.e. the theory of

[98] *Grundrisse*, pp.275-76.
[99] *ibid.* p.715.
[100] *Contribution*, p.62-63.
[101] 'It is also quite correct that the "value or price of land", which is not produced by labour, appears directly to contradict the concept of value and cannot be derived directly from it. This proposition is all the more insignificant when used against Ricardo, since its author does not attack Ricardo's theory of rent in which precisely Ricardo sets forth how the nominal value of land is evolved on the basis of capitalist production and does not contradict the definition of value. The value of land is nothing but the price which is paid for capitalised ground-rent. Much more far-reaching developments have therefore to be presumed here than can be deduced *prima facie* from the simple consideration of the commodity and its value, just as from the simple concept of productive capital one cannot evolve fictitious

ground-rent, until after the analysis of the category of capital – apart from the historical considerations which suggested this.

So much for the conceptual and historical interaction between landed property and capital. Marx continues: 'Now the question arises as to how the transition from landownership to wage-labour came about? Historically the transition is beyond dispute. It is already given in the fact that landed property is the product of capital.[102] We therefore always find that wherever landed property is transformed into money-rent through the reaction of capital on the older forms of landed property (the same thing takes place in another way where the modern farmer is created) and where, therefore, at the same time agriculture, driven by capital, transforms itself into industrial agronomy, there the ... serfs, bondsmen, tenants for life, cottagers, etc. become day labourers, wage-labourers,' i.e. we find that 'wage-labour in its totality is initially created by the action of capital on landed property, and then, as soon as the latter has been produced as a form, by the landowner himself. The latter then "clears", as Steuart says, the land of its excess mouths, tears the children of the earth from the breast at which they were raised, and thus transforms labour on the land, which appears by its nature as the direct source of subsistence, into a mediated source of subsistence, a source purely dependent on social relations ... There can therefore be no doubt that wage-labour in its classic form, as something permeating the entire expanse of society, which has replaced the very earth as the ground on which society stands, is initially created only by modern property[103] ... This is why landed property leads back capital, the object of gambling on the stock exchange, which is actually nothing but the selling and buying of entitlement to a certain part of the annual tax revenue.' (Marx on the text *Observations on Certain Verbal Disputes*, *Theories* III, pp.110-11.) Cf. *Capital* I, p. 677 (537): 'In the expression "value of labour" the concept of value is not only completely extinguished, but inverted, so that it becomes its contrary. It is an expression as imaginary as the value of the earth. These imaginary expressions arise, nevertheless, from the relations of production themselves. They are categories for the forms of appearance of essential relations.'

[102] Of course, only modern landed property is meant here.

[103] Marx says before this that 'The inner construction of modern society or capital in the totality of its relations, is therefore posited in the modern relations of modern landed property.' (*Grundrisse*, p.276.) And in another passage: 'It is therefore precisely in the development of landed property that the gradual victory and formation of capital can be studied, which is why Ricardo, the economist of the modern age, with great historical insight, examined the relations of capital, wage-labour and ground-rent within the sphere of landed property, so as to establish their specific form.' (*Grundrisse*, p.252.)

to wage-labour. It is nothing more than the extension of wage-labour from the cities to the countryside i.e. wage-labour distributed over the entire surface of society.'[104] In this respect, 'England has been the model country for the other continental countries'. On the other hand the same necessity for (modern) capitalist landownership is shown, 'if within one society the modern relations of production are fully developed, i.e. if capital is developed to its totality, and this society then seizes a new territory, as, for example, in the colonies'; then 'it finds, or rather its representative the capitalist finds, that his capital ceases to be capital without wage-labour, and that one of the presuppositions of the latter is not only landed property in general, but modern landed property; landed property which, as capitalised rent, is expensive, and which, as such, excludes the direct use of the soil by individuals. Hence Wakefield's theory of colonies,[105] followed in practice by the English government in Australia. Here landed property is artificially made more expensive in order to transform the ['indigenous'] workers into wage-labourers, to make capital act as capital . . .' And Marx stresses that it is precisely for this reason that 'Wakefield's theory is infinitely important for a correct understanding of modern landed property'.[106]

At the same time the transition from landed property to wage-labour is not only historical, but also dialectical: 'Capital, when it creates landed property, therefore goes back to the production of wage-labour as its general creative basis.[107] Capital arises out of circulation and posits labour as wage-labour; takes form in this way; and developed as a whole, posits landed property as its precondition as well as its opposite.[108] It turns out however that it has thereby only created wage-labour as its general presupposition. The latter must then be examined by itself.'[109]

[104] Cf. *Capital* II, pp.119-20: 'To the extent that labour becomes wage-labour, the producer becomes an industrial capitalist; for this reason capitalist production first appears in its full extent when the direct rural producer is a wage-labourer.'
[105] Cf. *Capital* I, Chapter 33 'The Modern Theory of Colonisation'.
[106] *Grundrisse*, pp.276-78.
[107] The expression which Marx uses here shows a close relation to Hegel's *Logic*, in particular to the theory of foundation, developed in Volume II. Cf. Hegel *Science of Logic*, Vol.I p.82. 'If it is considered that progress is a return to the foundation, to that origin and truth, then it must be admitted that this consideration is of essential importance ... Thus consciousness is led back on its road from immediacy with which it begins, to absolute knowledge as its inmost truth.'
[108] Cf. the sentence from *Capital* III, p.879, according to which capital includes landed property as its 'antithesis'.
[109] *Grundrisse*, pp.278-79.

5. The real function of the threefold division

It is clear that what Marx is basically discussing here is the construction of his work, the question of the order in which the categories which express the class structure of bourgeois society, namely capital, landed property and wage-labour, should be presented. The answer which emerges from the analysis of the mutual relation of these categories is as follows : the category of capital, as the decisive, all-prevailing and ruling relation of bourgeois society must be elaborated before everything else. This means capital in its pure form, leaving out of consideration all the forms to be derived from the relation of capital itself. Only then can modern landed property be developed insofar as it is a creation of capital, a product of its effect on pre-capitalist economic forms. However wage-labour, although it represents both conceptually and historically the fundamental condition for capital and the capitalist mode of production, requires for its full development the precondition that this mode of production has taken hold of the totality of social relations and transformed even the rural producers into wage-labourers. Consequently, we can only study this category exhaustively after we have studied capital and landed property.

It can be seen, then, that the reasons which Marx had for the threefold division of his inquiry, and for the sequence which was to be observed, do not have the slightest relation to 'external considerations', or the conventional 'factors of production' theory of bourgeois economics. Rather, they are the product of the inner nature of the capitalist mode of production itself, of the historical and logical succession of the categories which constitute it, and which in fact required – at least temporarily – the dismemberment of the object of the analysis, especially at the outset, where 'the essential issue was to grasp the pure, specific economic forms and hence with not joining together things that do not belong together'.[110] Thus Marx then felt obliged not only to disregard the category of landed property in the *Rough Draft* of 1857-58, but also to omit a more detailed examination of the forms of wages in order to work out the concept of capital in its purity.[111] (And so the analysis of ground-rent could follow the analysis

---

[110] *ibid.* p.732.
[111] Cf. Marx's letter to Engels of 2 April 1858, *Selected Correspondence*, pp.97-98. 'Throughout this section [i.e. the section on "Capital in general"] it is assumed that wages always remain at minimum ... further, landed property is taken as = 0, that is, landed property as a particular economic relation does not yet concern us. This is the only possible way to avoid dealing with all relations when discussing each particular relation.'

40 · *The Making of Marx's 'Capital'*

of capital as it does in the final version of Marx's work, being placed at the end of Volume III.) It is in this sense, that is as a provisional, but unavoidable 'blueprint' that the original threefold division of the work into separate books on capital, landed property and wage-labour should be interpreted. Nevertheless, the question remains as to what particular reasons necessitated the later abandonment of this blueprint; but before we tackle this we should clarify the changes which occurred in the original outline of Part I of the work, namely the *Book on Capital*.

B. The *Book on Capital*

1. The original subdivision of the 'Book on Capital'

According to the outline of 1857-58 the book should have been divided into the following sections:[112]

    a) Section on 'capital in general'.
        1. Production process of capital
        2. Circulation process of capital
        3. Profit and interest.
    b) Section on competition.
    c) Section on the credit system.
    d) Section on share-capital.

Of this, only the first section was carried out in the shape of the *Rough Draft* (1857-58), which was confined, as we have already said, to the analysis of 'capital in general', in contrast to his later work. As far as the remaining sections were concerned i.e. b), c) and d), a similar process occurred to the one we were able to establish in the case of Books II and II. That is, they were indeed dropped as independent sections, but at the same time their contents were incorporated into the new structure of the work. Here, too, a narrowing down of the original scheme took place, but this corresponded to a broadening of the first part, i.e. the section on 'capital in general'. Since, whereas

---

[112] In the changes to the outline on pages 264 and 275 of the *Grundrisse* there is another breakdown of the *Book on Capital* into six sections, which – besides the earlier four sections – contains 'Capital as money market' as the fifth, and 'Capital as the source of wealth' as the sixth. However, these last two subjects could have been equally well dealt with in sections c) and d), which probably explains why they are not mentioned in later changes.

Moreover, it is precisely these two variations which reveal how 'Hegelian' the structure of the *Rough Draft* is!

The structure of Marx's work · 41

the first two volumes of *Capital* do not fundamentally go beyond the analysis of 'capital in general', the third volume is the place where competition, credit and share-capital are introduced, in the originally envisaged order, even if not quite as extensively as Marx had intended at the outset. This also shows that the original strict separation of the categories was simply a means of methodological abstraction, and could therefore be discarded as soon as the main task – the analysis of 'capital in general' – had been carried out. This is, therefore, the category which is most important to understand, and upon which we now concentrate our attention.

2. *'Capital in general' and 'many capitals'*

As we already know, the *Rough Draft* not only excludes, in principle, all the themes which came under the scope of the original Books II-VI, but also those which were to have been looked at in Sections b) – d) of the first Book.[113] From the outset Marx wishes to deal with 'capital in general'. But what does this concept mean? What level of abstraction does it represent?

To begin with we shall content ourselves with the answer to be found in Marx's letter to Kugelmann of 28 December 1862. It says there that the restriction to 'capital in general' excludes a study of the competition of capitals and the credit system.[114] Competition involves the 'action of capital upon capital', which presupposes a multiplicity of capitals; whereas with credit, 'capital appears in relation to the individual capitals as a general element'.[115] In both cases the issue is one of the real movement of real capitals – capital in concrete reality, and not in some 'ideal average'.[116] We read in the

---

[113] We say in principle because the *Rough Draft* contains many digressions which go beyond the framework of 'capital in general', and which fit into other parts of Marx's work, according to their content. Cf. Marx's letter to Engels of 31 May 1858: 'The devil is namely that everything is completely higgledy-piggledy in the manuscript (which would be a thick volume when printed), and there is a great deal which is actually intended for parts which come much later.' (*MEW* Vol.29, p.330.)

[114] 'The second part is finally completed . . . it is the continuation of Notebook I [i.e. the *Contribution*] but is published independently under the title *Capital* . . . In fact it only embraces what was to have made up the third chapter of the first section, namely capital in general. Hence competition and credit are not included.' (*MEW* Vol.30, p.639.)

[115] Marx's letter to Engels of 2 April 1858, *Selected Correspondence*, p.97.

[116] Likewise, in the *Theories*, competition and credit are often contrasted with 'capital in general' or the 'general nature of capital' as the 'real move-

42 · The Making of Marx's 'Capital'

Rough Draft that 'Capital exists and can only exist as many capitals and its self-determination therefore appears as the mutual interaction of these upon one another', it is (note the repeated echoes of Hegel's terminology) by its essence, 'that which repels itself from itself', and must therefore necessarily 'repel itself from itself'.[117] Therefore, production based on capital, 'posits itself only in its adequate forms, insofar as and to the extent that free competition develops'.[118] Of course, 'as long as capital is weak it still relies on the crutches of past modes of production, or those that pass away with its appearance'. However, 'as soon as it begins to sense itself and become conscious of itself as a barrier to development it seeks refuge in forms which, by restricting competition, seem to make the rule of capital more complete, but which are at the same time, the heralds of its dissolution and that of the mode of production resting on it.'[119] In its heyday, however, the rule of capital can only be made real in and through competition.

Marx says that bourgeois economics has 'never understood' this positive aspect of competition. In fact, free competition has only been understood, 'in a negative way; i.e. as the negation of monopolies, corporations, legal regulations'. But competition 'is very far from having only this historical significance, or being merely a negative force'. It is simultaneously 'the relation of capital to itself as another capital, i.e. the real behaviour of capital as capital' and, through it, 'what corresponds to the concept of capital is posited as an external necessity for the individual capital'. Hence, conceptually, competition is, 'none other than the inner nature of capital appearing and realised as the interaction of many capitals', which 'force the inherent determinants of capital upon one another, and upon themselves'.[120] As such, competition is the 'essential locomotive force of the bourge-

---

ment of capital' and as 'concrete relations'. (cf. *Theories* II, pp.492, 510-11, 529: III, pp.53, 311, 465.)

[117] *Grundrisse*, pp.414, 421: 'Since value forms the foundation of capital, and since it therefore necessarily exists only through exchange for countervalue, it thus necessarily repels itself from itself. A universal capital, one without alien capitals confronting it, with which it exchanges – is therefore a nonthing. The reciprocal repulsion between capitals is already contained in capital as realised exchange-value.' Hence 'state capitalism' would only be possible with several capitals, organised by the state, confronting each other.

[118] *ibid.* p.650.

[119] *ibid.* p.651. Here, as early as 1857 Marx predicts the form of monopoly capitalism. (This could be called a 'vision'; we prefer the less mystical 'dialectic'.)

[120] *ibid.* pp.650-51, 414. 'Generally competition is the means by which capital carries through its mode of production.' (*ibid.* p.730.)

ois economy', even though it does not produce its laws, but only realises them, even if it cannot explain them, but merely renders them visible.[121] So nothing could be more incorrect than to confuse the analysis of these laws with the analysis of competition, or of the relations of credit which presuppose competition. To understand the forms of appearance we first have to examine what appears in these forms. This is particularly important because everything in competition is presented, and must be presented,[122] in an inverted form (not price determined by labour, but labour by price etc.), so that in it capital appears to 'determine price, give work, regulate production', in a word, to be the 'source of production'.[123] Thus in order to be able to inquire directly into the inherent laws of capital we must abstract from competition and its accompanying characteristics, and begin with 'capital as such', or 'capital in general'. 'The introduction of many capitals must not interfere with the investigation here. The relation of the many is better explained after we have studied what they all have in common, the quality of being capital.'[124]

However, what are the characteristics which all capitals have in common? Quite clearly, they are those which apply to capital, and not to any other forms of wealth, and in which the particular historical character of the capitalist mode of production is expressed.

The Classical Economists (here Marx has Smith in mind) often saw capital as 'accumulated (objectified) labour' which 'serves as a means to new labour'. However, 'it is just as impossible to make the transition directly from labour to capital as it is to go from the different human races to the banker, or from nature to the steam-engine – to develop the concept[125] it is necessary to begin not with labour, but with value, and precisely, with exchange-value already developed in the movement of circulation.'[126] One such exchange-value is money, to the extent that it neither functions simply as a means of

[121] *ibid.* p.552. (Cf. the excellent explanation in Grossmann's *Das Akkumulations- und Zusammenbruchsgesetz*, pp.96-99.)
[122] 'So as to impose the inherent laws of capital upon it as an external necessity, competition seemingly turns all of them over. Inverts them.' (*Grundrisse*, p.761.) Cf. *Capital* III, pp.45, 209, 225 etc.
[123] *Grundrisse*, p.275.
[124] *ibid.* p.517.
[125] 'For the whole of capitalist production is based on the fact that labour is bought directly so that a part of it can be appropriated without purchase in the prices of production; which part is sold however in the product – since this is the basis of existence of capital, its very essence . . .' (*Theories* I, p.293.)
[126] *Grundrisse*, p.259. Cf. Chapter II of Section III of this work, where this argument is dealt with in more detail.

exchange nor petrifies into a hoard, but rather maintains and multiplies itself in circulation through the mediation of alien labour. Thus, the first distinguishing feature of capital, as distinct from mere value or money, is that it is a value 'which breeds surplus-value', and that it rests on a particular historically determined relation – the relation of wage-labour. Admittedly, 'many things are subsumed under capital which do not seem to belong with it conceptually. Capital is lent, for example. It is stockpiled etc. In all these designations it seems to be a mere thing, and to coincide entirely with the material in which it is present.'[127] However, we are dealing here 'neither with a particular form of capital, nor with one individual capital as distinct from other individual capitals etc. We are witness to the process of its becoming.[128] This dialectical process of its becoming is only the ideal expression of the real movement through which capital comes into being.[129] The later relations are to be regarded as a development from this germ.'[130]

What all capitals have in common is their capacity for expanding their value (*Verwertungseigenschaft*) – the fact that they appropriate (directly or indirectly) the surplus-value created in the capitalist production process. The analysis of 'capital in general' must, therefore, begin with the investigation of the production process. This must show how money, 'goes beyond its simple quality of being money' and becomes capital, how it then produces surplus-value through the consumption of human labour and finally how the production of surplus-value for its part, leads to the reproduction of both capital and the relation of capital itself. All this can be developed without our having to pay attention to the presence of several capitals and the differences between them, for regardless of how the different individual capitals divide the surplus-value created in the production process, they cannot 'distribute more than the total

---

[127] *Grundrisse*, p.513.

[128] Accordingly the real object of analysis of the *Rough Draft* is referred to in many places as the 'general history of the rise of capital', its 'self-determination' or 'self-formation'. (*ibid.* pp.403, 414, 529.)

[129] 'Since we speak here of capital as such, capital in the process of becoming, we are not yet concerned with anything else in addition – in that many capitals are not yet present for us – nothing but it itself and simple circulation . . .' (*ibid.* p.729.) In the *Rough Draft* (and also in *Capital* and the *Theories*) capital in its becoming is contrasted to capital which has become, which is complete, in the sense that it is capital 'as it appears as a whole, as the unity of the circulation and production process' (*Theories* III, p.483; *Theories* II, p.513), or the 'finished form of capital'. (*Capital* III, p.209.)

[130] *Grundrisse*, p.310.

surplus-product among themselves'.[131] This cannot explain, but only obscure, the emergence of surplus-value; because in the form of profit surplus-value appears to be produced in equal amounts by all sections of capital, and capital itself appears 'as the source of wealth, independent of labour'.[132] So if the basic presupposition of the capital relation is to be understood, i.e. the relation of capital to labour and the role of surplus-value as the driving force of capitalist production, we must begin not with 'many capitals', but with capital or 'capital in the whole society'[133] i.e. with 'capital in general'. Only then is the real development of the concept of capital possible.

However, the life-cycle of capital is not confined to the direct production process. In order for capital to renew itself the product of capital, including surplus-value, must 'be transformed into money, not as in earlier stages of production where exchange is in no way concerned with production in its totality, but only with superfluous production and superfluous products'.[134] The phase of the production process must be complemented by that of the circulation process. And so the movement of capital becomes a circuit in which forms grow (fixed and circulating), which harden into specific forms of the existence of capital from being temporary determinations of it. In addition these forms are to be understood as distinctions within the abstraction 'capital in general' ('particularisation of capital'[135]), because they 'characterise every kind of capital',[136] and must therefore be understood without regard to the reciprocal action of 'many capitals'. On the other hand, capital's passage through the different phases of circulation appears 'as a restriction on production through the specific nature of the barriers posited by capital itself'. Circulation takes time, and during this time capital is unable to create any surplus-value. The expansion of its value (*Verwertung*) does not depend only on the length of time (labour-time) in which capital (sic!) creates values, but equally on the period of circulation in which these values are realised.[137]

[131] Cf. *ibid*. p.684. 'The profit of the capitalists as a class or the profit of capital as such must exist before it can be distributed . . .'
[132] *ibid*. p.759.
[133] 'We are concerned here with capital as such, say the capital of the whole society. The differentiation of capital does not concern us yet.' (*ibid*. p.346.)
[134] *ibid*. p.406.
[135] *ibid*. p.275. Similarly the concept of 'particularisation' is a specifically Hegelian one (in the same way that Marx's use of such terms as 'universality', 'particularity' and 'individuality' are based on Hegel's *Logic*).
[136] *Grundrisse*, p.449.
[137] *ibid*. p.627.

Accordingly, the surplus-value of capital 'no longer appears to be simply determined by the surplus labour appropriated by it in the production process'. It is no longer measured by its real standard, 'the ratio of surplus to necessary labour', but by the size of the capital itself. 'One capital of a certain value produces in a certain period of time a certain surplus-value.'[138]

Thus, surplus-value now assumes the transformed and derived form of profit, and the rate of surplus-value takes on the form of the rate of profit. (With this we come to the final, third section of the *Rough Draft*.) The only requirement is that the aggregate profit of the capitalist class has to coincide with the aggregate surplus-value appropriated by that class.[139] On the other hand, individual capitalists can pocket either more or less than the surplus-value which would correspond to what has been created in their own production process. Marx does not refer to this question in the *Rough Draft* until the 'study of many capitals', as the establishment of a general rate of profit and the transformation of values into prices of production which corresponds to it, presuppose competition and hence occur at a level which is excluded from the study of 'capital in general', according to Marx's original outline.[140]

It must be evident here that in the sentences we have just quoted Marx is already speaking about the capital of the entire capitalist class, the 'aggregate social capital' – in contrast to particular individual capitals.

However, what is the significance of this concept in Marx's methodology? This can be discovered in a very important marginal comment in the *Rough Draft*. We read there: '*Capital in general*, as distinct from particular capitals, does indeed appear 1) *only as an abstraction*; not an arbitrary abstraction, but one which grasps the specific differences which distinguish capital from other forms of wealth . . . These are the features common to each capital as such or which make every specific sum of values into capital. And the distinctions within this abstraction are likewise abstract particularities which characterise every kind of capital, in that it is either their position or negation (e.g. fixed or circulating capital); 2) however, capital in general, as distinct from particular real capitals, is itself a real existence. This is recognised by ordinary economics, even if it is not understood, and constitutes a very important moment in its theory of equilibrations. For example, capital in this general form,

[138] *ibid.* p.746.
[139] *ibid.* pp.787-88.
[140] *ibid.* pp.759-60.

The structure of Marx's work · 47

although belonging to individual capitalists . . . forms the capital which accumulates in the banks or is distributed through them, and as Ricardo says, [141] distributes itself so admirably in accordance with the needs of production. Similarly, through loans etc. it forms one level between different countries[142] . . . therefore while the general is on the one hand only a conceived mark of distinction it is at the same time a particular real form alongside the form of the particular and individual.' (Marx adds, 'We will return later to this point, which, while having more of a logical than an economic character, will nonetheless have great importance in our inquiry. The same also in algebra. For example, a,b,c are numbers as such, in general; but then again they are whole numbers as opposed to a/b, b/c, c/b, c/a, b/a etc., the latter however presupposing the former as their general elements.'[143])

And, in another part of the *Rough Draft*, Marx says, 'To examine capital in general is no mere abstraction. If I regard the total capital of, for example, a nation, as distinct from total wage-labour (or landed property), or if I regard capital as the general economic basis of a class as distinct from another class, then I regard it in general. Just as when I look at man physiologically, for example, as distinct from the animals.'[144]

The extraordinary importance of these marginal notes by Marx is immediately obvious. As an example we can take his treatment of the 'Reproduction and Circulation of the Aggregate Social Capital' in Volume II of *Capital*. It states here on the 'Circuit of commodity-capital' : 'But just because the circuit C' . . . C' presupposes within its sphere the existence of other industrial capital in the form of C(equal to $L+MP$) . . . it clamours not only to be considered the general form of the circuit i.e. not only as a social form in which every single industrial capital . . . can be studied, hence not merely as a form of movement common to all individual industrial capitals, but simultaneously also as a form of movement of the sum of the individual capitals, consequently of the aggregate capital of the capitalist class –

---

[141] See e.g. D. Ricardo, *Principles of Political Economy*, 1971, p.152.
[142] Marx continues here: 'If it is therefore e.g. a law of capital in general that, in order to realise itself it must posit itself doubly, and must realise itself in this double form, then, e.g. capital of a particular country which represents capital par excellence in antithesis to another, will have to lend itself out to a third country in order to be able to realise itself.' And Marx adds, 'this double positing, this relating to self as an alien, becomes damned real in this case' (*Grundrisse* pp.449-50.)
[143] *ibid.* p.450.
[144] *ibid.* p.852.

C

a movement in which that of each individual industrial capital appears as only a partial movement which intermingles with the other movements and is necessitated by them. For instance, if we look at the aggregate of commodities annually produced in a certain country and analyse the movement by which a part of it replaces the productive capital in all individual businesses, while another part enters into the individual consumption of the various classes, then we consider C′ . . . C′ as a form of movement of the social capital as well as of the surplus-value or surplus-product generated by it. The fact that the social capital is equal to the sum of the individual capitals . . . and that the aggregate movement of the social capital is equal to the algebraic sum of the movements of the individual capitals, does not in any way exclude the possibility that this movement as the movement of a single individual capital may present other phenomena than the same movement does when considered from the point of view of a part of the aggregate movement of social capital, hence in its interconnection with the movements of its other parts, and that the movement simultaneously solves problems the solution of which must be assumed when studying the circuit of a separate individual capital instead of being the result of such a study.'[145]

From this perspective the individual capitals are to be regarded simply as 'fragments' (*Bruchstücke*) of social capital, 'whose movement, as well the movement of individual capitals, is at the same time an integrating link in the movement of aggregate capital', which – although only the sum of individual capitals – exhibits a character different from that of the capital of each individual capitalist.[146] The 'aggregate capital of society' is therefore to be understood as a whole, as a real 'existence distinct from particular real capitals'. The same applies (as the marginal note shows) in Marx's study of credit : 'Here [in the money-market], in its supply and demand, capital steps forth in reality and emphatically *as being in itself, the common capital of a class*, something which, in the case of industrial capital, only occurs in the course of movement and competition between the individual spheres.'[147] Credit is therefore seen by Marx as a 'form in which capital tries to posit itself as distinct from individual capitals, or the individual capital as distinct from its quantitative barrier'.[148] However, the real character of aggregate social capital is demonstrated most

[145] *Capital* II, pp.99-100.
[146] *ibid.* pp.397ff.
[147] *ibid.* III, p.368.
[148] *Grundrisse*, p.659.

clearly in share-capital: 'In [this] form capital has worked itself up to its final form, in which it is posited, not only *in itself*, in its substance, but is posited also in its form as social power and product.'[149]

So much on the 'general concept of capital' – as distinct from the study of the 'concrete relations'[150] i.e. 'capital in its reality'.[151] As we have already said, this concept, for Marx, is simply an abstract and dialectical *image* 'of the real movement, by which capital *becomes*'. It follows from this that 'what comes later is already contained' in the general concept of capital, in embryonic form. That is, not only the 'civilising' and progressive tendencies, but also the contradictions which lead out beyond its limits.[152] (There are numerous examples to be found in the *Rough Draft*; we refer here only to the development of machinery,[153] the credit system and the realisation problem[154]). However, on the other hand, 'all moments of capital, which appear involved in it when it is considered from the point of view of its general concept, obtain an independent reality and further, only show themselves, when it appears as real, as many capitals. The inner living organisation, which takes place in this way within

[149] *ibid*. p.530. We should note here that the contrast of 'in itself' and 'posited existence' is also taken from Hegel's *Logic*.
[150] Cf. *Capital* II, p.461; III, pp.25, 110, 113.
[151] The distinction between the two methods of study is illustrated in the following example. 'Capitals have different sizes. But the size of each individual capital is equal to itself, hence, insofar as only its quality as capital is concerned, any size. But if we examine two capitals in comparison to each other, then the difference in their sizes introduces a relation of a qualitative character. Size itself becomes a distinguishing quality. This is an essential aspect, of which size is only one single instance, of how the study of capital as such differs from the study of one capital in relation to another capital, or the study of capital in its reality.' (*Grundrisse*, pp.684-85.)
[152] 'The simple concept of capital has to contain its civilising tendencies etc. in themselves; they must not as in the economics books up to now, appear merely as external consequences. Likewise the contradictions which are later released, demonstrated as latent within it.' (*ibid*. p.414.) Cf *ibid*. p.331. 'The exact development of the concept of capital is necessary since it is the fundamental concept of modern economics, just as capital itself, whose abstract reflected image is its concept, is the foundation of bourgeois society. The sharp formulation of the basic presuppositions of the relation must bring out all the contradictions of bourgeois production, as well as the boundary where it drives beyond itself.'
[153] 'It is easy to develop the introduction of machinery out of competition and out of the law of the reduction of production costs which is triggered by competition. We are concerned here with developing it out of the relation of capital to living labour, without reference to other capitals.' (*ibid*. pp.776-77.)
[154] 'The antithesis of labour-time and circulation time contains the entire doctrine of credit...' (*ibid*. p.660.)

and through competition, thus develops all the more extensively.'[155] In particular, 'the simultaneity of the different orbits of capital, like that of its different aspects, becomes clear only after many capitals are presupposed. Similarly the course of human life consists of passing through different ages. But at the same time all ages exist side by side, distributed among different individuals.'[156]

3. The structural relation of 'the Rough Draft' to 'Capital'

Those readers who are acquainted with the contents of Marx's *Capital* will of course appreciate the importance of these extracts from the *Rough Draft*, for what Marx wrote here in 1857-58 in fact also turns out to be the programme for the later work. Like the *Rough Draft*, Volumes I and II of *Capital* are restricted to the 'abstract study of the phenomenon of the formation of capital',[157] or the analysis of the process of circulation and reproduction 'in its fundamental form', where it is 'reduced to its most abstract expression',[158] that is, to 'capital in general'. (Hence the assumption made throughout that commodities are sold at their values.[159]) The real methodological difference first emerges in Volume III of *Capital*. When the *Rough Draft* speaks of profit, the general rate of profit, and its tendency to fall, this is still a question of 'profit in general', the 'profit of the capitalist class', but not the profit of 'one individual capital at the expense of another'.[160] The study of the latter (i.e. primarily the transformation of values into prices of production, and the

On the subject of realisation; *ibid.* p.447. Cf. *Theories* II, p.493 : 'As we have already found in the study of money . . . namely that it includes the possibility of crises, this emerges even more in the study of the general nature of capital, without having to develop the further real relations, which constitute all the presuppositions of the real production process.'
[155] *Grundrisse*, p.520.
[156] *ibid.* p.639. Cf. *ibid.* p.661 : 'The simultaneity of the process of capital in different phases of the process is possible only through its division and break up into parts each of which is capital, but capital in a different aspect. This change of form and matter is like that in the organic body. For example, if one says the body reproduces itself in 24 hours, this does not mean it does it all at once, but rather the shedding in one form and the removal in another is distributed, and takes places simultaneously . . . (Here then the transition to many capitals).'
[157] Cf. *Capital* I, p.269 (166).
[158] *Capital* II, pp.461, 510.
[159] 'Study of capital in general in which the prices of commodities are assumed to be identical with the values of commodities ' (*Theories* II, p.515.)
[160] *Grundrisse*, p.767.

division of surplus-value into business profit, interest etc.) goes beyond the context of 'capital in general'. However, Volume III of *Capital* 'progressively approaches the form' in which 'the forms of capital appear on the surface of society, in the action of the different capitals upon one another, in competition, and in the everyday consciousness of the agents of production'.[161] At this point the limits of 'capital in general' – as the concept had been elaborated by Marx in the *Rough Draft* – are far exceeded. Problems can now be dealt with, which could only be hinted at in the earlier stages of the inquiry[162] – problems whose solution only becomes possible if we proceed from the 'final pattern of economic relations, as it appears on the surface . . . to its inner, basic but hidden essential structure, and the conception corresponding to it'.[163]

We therefore consider that the categories of 'capital in general' and 'many capitals' provide the key to the understanding of not only the *Rough Draft*, but also the later work, i.e. *Capital*. One should not of course exaggerate the structural similarity of the two works. It should not be overlooked that the later reorganisation of the original *Book on Capital* led, and had to lead, to a certain change in the use of the concepts which underlay this book, and that therefore the meaning which these concepts have in *Capital* does not always coincide with the one we have encountered in the *Rough Draft*.

It is of course true that in *Capital*, as in the *Rough Draft*, the 'real inner movement' of capitalist production is constantly contrasted with its 'apparent' movement displayed in competition. And similarly the Hegelian distinction between 'essence' and 'appearance' is consistently employed.[164] We read in Volume I : 'The general and necessary tendencies of capital are to be distinguished from the forms of their appearance . . . the way in which the immanent laws of capitalist production manifest themselves in the external movement of the individual capitals, assert themselves as the coercive laws of competition . . . does not have to be considered here . . . but this much is clear : a scientific analysis of competition is possible only if

---

[161] *Capital* III, p.25.

[162] One example of this is the definition of the concept of 'socially necessary labour', which – as with the definition of accumulation – was only looked at 'abstractly, as one aspect of the immediate process of production', (*Capital* I, p.710 (565), and which could only be developed further from the standpoint of the 'concrete conditions' in Volume III (see the next chapter for a more detailed discussion).

[163] *Capital* III, p.209. (The concept is only an image of the 'hidden essential structure' i.e. the actual prevailing social relations.)

[164] Cf. Lukacs, *History and Class Consciousness*, p.7, n.9.

52 · *The Making of Marx's 'Capital'*

we can grasp the inner nature of capital, just as the apparent motions of the heavenly bodies are intelligible only to someone who is acquainted with the real motions, which are not perceptible to the senses.'[165] Similarly in Chapter VI of Volume III : 'The phenomena analysed in this chapter require for their full development the credit system and competition on the world market . . . these more concrete forms of capitalist production can only be comprehensively presented, however, after the general nature of capital is understood.'[166] In fact, all these efforts would not be necessary, 'if the appearance and the essence of things directly coincided';[167] but then 'all science would be . . . superfluous'. Since this is not the case, scientific investigation must proceed from the 'surface appearances' to the 'inner essence', the 'essential structure' of the economic process in order to be able to discover the 'law of appearances',[168] and to understand that this appearance itself is necessary.[169] As far as this aspect is concerned the methodological orientation of *Capital* is no different from that of the *Rough Draft*. The difference lies elsewhere : namely, that in *Capital* Marx regards that part of his inquiry which 'progressively approaches the surface forms in competition' (i.e. Volume III) as also belonging to the 'general analysis of capital'. Hence the scope of the latter analysis expands, and the framework of the analysis of competition is narrowed down.[170] This is proof that the distinction between 'capital in general' and 'many capitals', which forms the basis of the *Rough Draft*, also represents, first and foremost, a 'blue-

[165] *Capital* I, p.433 (316).
[166] *Capital* III, p.110. 'In a general analysis of this kind it is usually always assumed that the actual conditions correspond to their conception, or, what is the same, that actual conditions are represented only to the extent that they are typical of their general case.' (cf. in addition p.831.) 'We leave this outside our scope, and we need present only the inner organisation of the capitalist mode of production, in its ideal average as it were.'
[167] *ibid.* p.817. (Cf. Marx's letter to Engels of 27 June 1867, *Selected Correspondence*, pp.178-79, and to Kugelmann of 11 July 1868, *ibid.* pp.195-97.)
[168] *Capital* I, p.421 (307).
[169] Marx says in one of his notebooks from 1851, on the subject of Ricardo's view of competition that Ricardo 'abstracts from what he considers to be accidental. Another is to present the real process, in which both what he regards as accidental movement, but which is constant and real, and its law, the average relation, appear as equally fundamental'. (*Grundrisse*, German edn. p.803. Cf. *MEGA* III, pp.530-31.)
[170] In contrast to the *Rough Draft*, in *Capital* the field of the 'theory of competition' is confined to the analysis of the 'real movement of market prices' (in antithesis to prices of production), and the study of competitive struggles on the world market. See *Capital* III, pp.110, 235, 764, 831.

print', without which Marx's economic system could never have developed, but which – like any working hypothesis – can only lay claim to full validity within specified limits.

V. THE SCOPE OF AND PROBABLE EXPLANATION FOR THE CHANGE IN THE OUTLINE

What, then, are the results of our inquiry? In other words: what does the change consist in, and how can it be explained?

The first question is not difficult to answer (see the schema at the end of this chapter). We believe that we can conclude from our examination of the *Capital* manuscripts that the last three books of the six originally planned were never definitely 'abandoned' by Marx, but rather destined for the 'eventual continuation' of the work. So the real change in the outline only relates to Books I-III; it consists in the fact that the second book (on landed property) was embodied in Volume III of the final work, while the material for the third book (on wage-labour) was incorporated in the last section but one of Volume I. However, in the case of the *Book on Capital*, i.e. Part I of the original outline, a regrouping took place in the sense that Sections b)–d) of this book were absorbed into Volume III of *Capital* in the same order, while the first two volumes of the work correspond almost completely to Section a) of the original *Book on Capital*. That is, they are confined to the analysis of 'capital in general'.

It is true of course that what has been said here only relates to the outward regrouping of the material dealt with in Marx's system. What motives lay behind it?

One thing is certain. They are not the reasons suggested by Grossmann and Behrens! Rather, the change in the outline can be explained by reasons already touched upon in the course of this analysis; namely, that once Marx had accomplished the most fundamental part of his task – the analysis of industrial capital – the former structure of the work, which had served as a means of self-clarification, became superfluous. The *Rough Draft* itself provides an important pointer here because, although this manuscript was drafted entirely in accordance with the intentions of the original outline, none of the basic lines of thought which Marx later developed in Volumes I and II of *Capital* are missing – with the exception of the chapter on the wage and its forms. (We refer here to the sections of the outline dealing with the production and circulation process.) This shows that the entire analysis of the production and circulation process of capital could have been carried out without going into any of the topics envisaged for the proposed book on wage-labour and landed property. All that this analysis presupposed was the existence of the relation of wage-labour – but this coincides, conceptually, with that of capital itself. Everything else could, and had to be disregarded in the first instance so that the category of capital could be elaborated in its pure form.[171] In this respect the strict separation of the areas of the inquiry, which formed the basis of the original outline, was maintained throughout. However, what was initially useful and necessary eventually had to turn out to be a superfluous and obstructive limitation. (All the more so as adhering to this separation would have had to lead to the constant repetition of what had already been presented.) The blueprint had served its purpose and could therefore be dropped in the further stages of the analysis, without leading to any fundamental changes in the results which had already been obtained. This meant that the separate books on landed property, and wage-labour could be given up, with their essential parts incorporated into the new work which only dealt with 'capital'. Both are to be found there, where they properly belong; the *Book on Landed Property* in Volume III, because the real theoretical problem of ground-rent could only be solved at this stage of the analysis, as a continuation of the already completed analysis of industrial capital, and its 'secondary' and 'derived'[172] forms.[173] In contrast, the *Book on Wage-Labour* goes directly into the analysis of the production process of capital, i.e. into Volume I – in order to create one of the necessary 'links' between the value-theory in Volume I and the theory of prices of production developed in Volume III, by means of an

---

[171] Cf. *Grundrisse*, p.817. 'The fixed definitions become themselves fluid in the further course of development. But only by holding them fast at the beginning is their development possible without confounding everything.'

[172] 'Industrial capital, which is the basic form of the relation of capital, as it rules bourgeois society and from which all other forms only appears as secondary or derived – derived, like interest-bearing capital; secondary, i.e. as capital in a particular function (which belongs to its circulation process) such as commercial . . .' (*Theories* III, p.468.)

[173] We read in Chapter XLIV of Volume III of *Capital*: 'We must clarify in our minds wherein lies the real difficulty in analysing ground-rent from the viewpoint of modern economics . . . the difficulty is not to explain the surplus-product produced by agricultural capital and its corresponding surplus-value in general. This question is solved in the analysis of the surplus-value produced by all productive capital in whatever sphere it may be invested. The difficulty consists rather in showing the source of the excess of surplus-value paid the landlord by capital invested in land in the form of rent, after equalisation of the surplus-value to the average profit among the various capitals, after the various capitals have shared in the total surplus-value produced by the social capital in all spheres of production . . .' (*Capital* III, p.782.)

analysis of the category of the wage and its forms. (This last point will be dealt with in more detail in the appendix to this chapter, devoted to the *Book on Wage-Labour*.)

List of draft outlines and outline notes considered by the author, which relate to the structure of Marx's work.

1) September   1857   *Grundrisse*, p.108
2) October   1857   *Grundrisse*, pp.227-228
3) November   1857   *Grundrisse*, p.264
4) November   1857   *Grundrisse*, p.275
5) February   1858   Letter to Lassalle 22 February 1858, *Selected Correspondence*, p.96.
6) April   1858   Letter to Engels 2 April 1858, *ibid.* pp.97-98
7) June   1858   *Grundrisse*, German edn., pp.855-859
8) January   1859   *Contribution*, p.19
9) February-March 1859 *Grundrisse*, German edn., pp.969-978
10) December   1862   Letter to Kugelmann 28 December 1862, *MEW* Vol. 30
11) January   1863   *Theories* I, p.414-416
12) July   1865   Letter to Engels 31 July 1865, *MEW* Vol. 31
13) October   1866   Letter to Kugelmann 13 October 1866, *ibid.*
14) April   1868   Letter to Engels 30 April 1868, *Selected Correspondence*, p.191-195

THE ORIGINAL PLAN (6 Books)	THE CHANGED PLAN
I. ON CAPITAL	'CAPITAL' (3 Volumes):
a) Capital in general	
1) Production process	I. Production process of capital (Sections):
	1) Commodity and money
	2) Transformation of money into capital
	3-5) Absolute and relative surplus-value
	6) Wage
	7) Accumulation process
2) Circulation process	II. Circulation process of capital
3) Profit and interest	III. Process of capitalist production as a whole.
	1-3) Profit and profit rate
b) Competition	4) Merchant capital
c) Credit system	5) Interest and credit
d) Share-Capital	
II. ON LANDED PROPERTY	6) Ground-Rent
	7) Revenues.
III. ON WAGE LABOUR	

IV. STATE

V. FOREIGN TRADE

VI. WORLD MARKET

Unbroken lines: changes within the first three books
Dotted line: changes within the *Book on Capital.*

Appendix I.

The Book on Wage-Labour

1. Themes which were to have been included in the book

One thing which should be noted from the outset is that we cannot say exactly which themes were to have come under the scope of the *Book on Wage-Labour*, as we have no precise information on this subject. We are dependent chiefly on a comparison of the *Rough Draft* with the later work. Thus, as already mentioned, there is no analysis of the wage in the *Rough Draft*; in addition it also lacks any material dealing with the length of the working day, the exploitative practices of capital, and factory legislation, which Marx treated in such detail in Volume I of *Capital*. According to the original outline all this was to have been analysed in the *Book on Wage-labour*. We can find numerous remarks throughout the *Rough Draft* and Marx's later manuscripts which prove that this assumption is not an arbitrary one.

The task of the 'Theory of Wage-Labour' is defined in the *Contribution* in the following way: 'Given labour-time as the intrinsic measure of value, how are wages to be determined on this basis.'[1] In other words: in general the amount of value, which the worker receives in exchange with capital, is measured by the objectified labour which is necessary to reproduce the worker's capacity to work, that is to physically maintain himself and his offspring. However, how the 'more or less' which the worker actually receives as wages is determined 'is of such little relevance to the general relation that it cannot be developed from the latter as such'.[2] The 'real movement of wages' depends rather on laws which rule in the labour market (as distinct from the market for commodities[3]), whose analysis has to be reserved for a separate theory of wage-labour.[4]

[1] *Contribution*, p.62.
[2] *Grundrisse*, p.282.
[3] 'IV. The exchange of a part of the capital for living labour-capacity can be regarded as a particular moment, and must be so regarded, since the labour market is ruled by other laws than the product market etc ... Moment IV belongs in the section on wages etc.' (*ibid*. p.521.)
[4] Cf. *Theories*. 'A rise or fall in wages can be the consequence of a change in the supply and demand for labour-power or a consequence of a temporary

But let us proceed further: 'The basis for the development of capitalist production is in general that labour-power, as the commodity belonging to the worker, confronts the conditions of labour as commodities maintained in the form of capital, existing independently of the workers . . . The determination of the value of labour-power, as a commodity, is of vital importance . . . It is only on this basis that the difference arises between the value of labour-power and the value which that labour-power creates – a difference which exists with no other commodity, since there is no other commodity whose use-value, and therefore also the use of it, can increase its exchange-value or the exchange-values resulting from it. Therefore the foundation of modern political economy, whose business is the analysis of capitalist production, is the conception of the value of labour-power as something fixed, as a given magnitude, as indeed it is in practice in each particular case.'[5] Marx also uses this premise as a matter of course when he approaches the analysis of capital and the formation of capital; that is, he initially assumes that the 'worker is paid the economically just wage i.e. the wage as determined by the general laws of economics'.[6]

This was the only way in which the laws of the formation of

rise or fall in the price of necessary consumption goods (in comparison to luxuries), changes in which can re-enter through changes in the supply and demand for labour-power, and the increase or fall in wages which this occasions. The extent to which such rises or falls of wages bring about a rise or fall in the rate of profit has as little to do with the general law of the rise or fall of the rate of profit, as the market price of commodities has to do with the determination of their values. This is to be looked at in the Chapter on the real movement of wages.' (This is taken from Kautsky's edition of the *Theories*, where Marx's original text was somewhat re-edited on the grounds of its difficulty.) This question is dealt with in *Capital* Volume III, Chapter XI, 'Effects of General Wage Fluctuations on Prices of Production'.

[5] *Theories* I, p.44. Cf. *Grundrisse*, p.817: 'Besides it is practically sure, that . . . however the standard of necessary labour may differ at various epochs and in various countries . . . at any given time the standard is to be considered and acted upon as a fixed one by capital. To consider those charges themselves belongs together to the chapter treating of wage-labour.'

[6] *Theories* I, p.426. We must, however, remark here that in the *Rough Draft* (and to a certain extent in the *Theories*) Marx tended to regard the 'economically just wage' as being identical with the physically minimum wage. This incorrect view was not corrected until later. (See Engels's note in Marx's *Poverty of Philosophy*, pp.51-52.)

In addition: as a comparison with the original text of the *Theories* shows, Kautsky felt it necessary to erase all the places where Marx refers to the 'minimum wage' and replace them with his own corrections in order not to expose any of Marx's 'weak points'. (The two sections from Kautsky's edition which we have cited must have been left intact due to an oversight.)

surplus-value could be set out in their pure form, without 'bringing in accompanying circumstances which were distracting and foreign to the actual course of development'. Naturally, these 'fixed presuppositions' had to be dropped as soon as the analysis was transferred from general relations to more concrete ones; likewise the assumption of the 'economically just wage', i.e. the sale of labour-power at its value. In concrete reality capital strives to increase its valorisation (*Verwertung*), on the one hand by pushing down wages below the value of labour-power, and on the other by extending the duration of work beyond its normal limits (which amounts to the devaluation of labour-power). Both of these methods[7] were to have first been studied in the *Book on Wage-Labour*. 'It is beside the point here,' it says in the *Rough Draft*, 'that capital, in practice as well as in general tendency, directly employs price as e.g. in the truck system, to defraud necessary labour [i.e. the worker] and reduce it below its measure ... the contradictions must follow from the general relations themselves and not from the fraud of individual capitalists. The further forms which this assumes in reality belong to the doctrine of wages.'[8] For the same reason, the 'forcible extension of the working day beyond its natural limits' – which belongs together, among other practices, with night-work and the inclusion of women and children in the work-force – is assigned in the *Rough Draft* to the Chapter on Wage-Labour (alternatively referred to as the 'wage of labour').[9]

In contrast to the slave or serf relation the capacity to work of the free wage-labourer 'appears in its totality as his property, one of his moments, over which he, as subject, exercises domination, and which he maintains by alienating it'.[10] Consequently the share of the worker in his own product assumes the form of the wage. ('If labour did not possess the characteristic of wage-labour, then the manner in which it shares in the products would not appear as wages ... an individual who participates in production in the form

[7] Such methods are still employed, in all their brutality, in the 'underdeveloped' parts of the capitalist world (for example in Central and South America, Asia and Africa).
[8] *Grundrisse*, p.426.
[9] See the following passages in the *Rough Draft*: 'The working day itself does not recognise daylight as a limit; it can be extended deep into the night; this belongs to the chapter on wages.' (*ibid.* p.336.) And: 'Surplus labour can also be created by means of forcible prolongation of the working day beyond its natural limits; by the addition of women and children to the labouring population ... but this is mentioned here only in passing, belongs in the chapter on wage-labour.' (*ibid.* p.399.)
[10] Marx adds, 'This to be developed later in wage-labour.' (*ibid.* p.465.)

of wage-labour shares in the products, in the results of production, in the form of wages.'[11] Although it is important to go into the transformed shape which the value of labour-power must already assume in the general analysis of capital, a study of the different forms which the wage itself exhibits appears to be superfluous at the outset. And as we cannot find such an analysis in the *Rough Draft* we can conclude that it was reserved for the *Book on Wage-Labour*. Consequently this would have been the place where Marx first considered the different forms of the wage; in fact not only the two basic forms – time and piece wages[12] – but also such forms of payment as profit-sharing,[13] 'natural wages' etc. In addition, according to the original outline, the determination of the value of so-called personal services was also to have been first examined in the *Book on Wage-Labour*, inasmuch as these services are paid according to the laws of wages proper.[14]

We should also mention in this context that Marx (as already noted)[15] considered examining the laws of the reduction of so-called qualified labour to simple average labour in the *Book on Wage-Labour*. This appears surprising at first sight, especially if one supposes there to be a 'gap' here in Marx's theory of value (as most authors who have written on this question have done). However, Marx had already solved the main problem, namely that of the reduction of different human labours, in their individual and concrete character, to undifferentiated simple average labour. Looked at in this way, the question of the relationship of skilled to unskilled labour simply represents a special case, which is reducible in the final analysis to the question of the 'different value of labour-powers', the study of which, as Marx stressed,[16] could proceed in the section on wage-labour. (We shall see in Chapter 31 of this book how Marx thought this problem could be solved).

---

[11] *ibid.* p.95.
[12] We read in the *Rough Draft*: 'The piece-work system of payment . . . is only another form of measuring time . . .; it is here, in the examination of the general relations, altogether beside the point.' (*ibid.* p.282.)
[13] 'The recently and complacently advanced demand that the workers should be given a certain share in profits is to be dealt with in the section on wage-labour.' (*ibid.* p.288.)
[14] 'The question of how the value of these services is regulated and how this value itself is determined by the laws governing wages has nothing to do with the examination of the relation we are considering, and belongs to the Chapter on Wages.' (*Theories* I, p.404.)
[15] See p.19.
[16] *Theories* III, p.165.

2. Why did Marx abandon the separate 'Book on Wage-Labour'?

So much then for the themes which Marx initially wanted to include within the scope of a book specifically on wage-labour. Most of them were later taken up in Volume I of *Capital*.[17] As can be seen, they are all questions which were irrelevant for the general development of the capital relation in its 'pure' form, and they could therefore be disregarded in the first instance. However, our concern here is not so much to become acquainted with the outlines of Marx's original plan, but rather to discover the reasons which later prompted him to give it up. The further history of the *Book on Wage-Labour* seems to provide some valuable pointers in this respect.

We saw that the proposed outline of 1863 for Section I, published by Kautsky, signified a change in the outline of 1857-58 inasmuch as it contains a separate item on the 'Working Day' which was originally to have been dealt with in the *Book on Wage-Labour*. However, everything seems to indicate that in 1863 Marx was still keeping to his old outline, and consequently to a separate *Book on Wage-Labour*.

The first time that we can confirm that this book was finally abandoned is in Volume I of *Capital*. This is shown by the extensive empirical and historical analyses, which underpin the sections on absolute and relative surplus-value and on the process of accumulation, and which include for the most part themes which, according to the old outline, were not to have been taken up until the *Book on Wage-Labour*. We do not have to stress how much liveliness and persuasiveness these detailed analyses contributed to the presentation of Volume I. However, the essential results of the analysis for this section (as the example of the *Rough Draft* shows) could have been presented without this evidence, as Marx had originally intended.[18] On the other hand what seems much more important is the fact that Marx assimilated the main part of the proposed *Book on Wage-Labour* into Volume I - namely the analysis of the wage and its forms, which was still absent from the 1863 plan. We cannot say when he decided to do this, although it was not before 1864. How-

---

[17] The question of skilled labour and the examination of the 'real movement of wages' were not taken up, the latter for the same reason that Marx had for disregarding the 'real movement of market prices'. (*Capital* III, p.765.)

[18] Cf. Marx's letter to Engels of 10 February 1866. 'I was unable to proceed with the theoretical section proper' [of Volume I. Marx is referring here to his illness]. 'My brain was too weak. Consequently I expanded the section on the "Working Day" in a historical sense, which lay outside the scope of my original plan.' (*MEW* Vol.31, p.174.)

ever, the reasons can be clearly seen in a letter from Marx to Engels of 27 June 1867.

The letter reads, 'How is the value of a commodity transformed into its price of production, in which (1) the whole labour seems to be paid in the form of wages; (2) but surplus labour, or surplus-value, assumes the form of an increase in price, called interest, profit etc., over and above the cost price (equals price of the constant part of capital plus wages)?

The answer to this question presupposes:

1. That the transformation of e.g. the value of a day's labour-power into wages, or the price of a day's labour has been explained. This is done in Chapter 5[19] of this volume...' (i.e. Volume I.[20])

Thus, Marx himself states here why he chose to incorporate the analysis of wages and their forms into Volume I (i.e. into the *Book on Capital*, according to the earlier schema), although this was not in line with his original intentions. It was to construct a necessary link to the theory of the prices of production, which was to be presented later in Volume III. And if this does not seem to offer a direct answer to the question of the causes of the change in the outline, then the sudden alterations in the *Book on Wage-Labour* do appear to prove one thing; that the strict separation of the categories of capital and wage-labour, which the old outline envisaged, could only be taken up to a certain point, and then had to be abandoned. This is one more proof that our hypothesis on the change in the outline is the correct one.

---

[19] This must have been an error on Marx's part (or his handwriting must have been incorrectly deciphered), as the subject mentioned here was in fact dealt with in Chapter 19 of Volume I and not in Chapter 5. We read there: 'The wage form thus extinguishes every trace of the division of the working day into necessary and surplus labour, into paid labour and unpaid labour. All labour appears as paid labour . . . In slave labour, even the part of the working day in which the slave is only replacing the value of his own means of subsistence, in which he therefore actually works for himself alone, appears as labour for his master . . . In wage-labour, on the contrary, even surplus labour or unpaid labour, appears as paid. In one case, the property relation conceals the slave's labour for himself; in the other case the money relation conceals the uncompensated labour of the wage-labourer.' (*Capital* I, p.680 (539-40).) Cf. *Capital* III, p.30 'The capitalist mode of production differs from the mode of production based on slavery, among other things, by the fact that in it the value, and accordingly the price of labour-power, appear as the value or price of labour itself, or as wages.' (Marx thus refers the reader to Chapter XIX.)

[20] *Selected Correspondence*, p.179.

Appendix II.

Methodological Comments on Rosa Luxemburg's Critique of Marx's Schemes of Reproduction

Marxist literature provides numerous references to the incorrectness of Luxemburg's criticism of the schemes of reproduction in Volume II of *Capital*. What is strange, however, is the neglect of the methodological premises which she adopted as the starting-point of her criticism, although this seems to be the most interesting aspect, and the point at which one really should begin.

Luxemburg herself saw two methodological questions as being at the heart of her critique. One : should the processes of the economy be reviewed from the standpoint of individual capital, or from that of aggregate social capital? Two : is this latter method consistent with the abstraction of a society composed solely of capitalists and workers?

Rosa Luxemburg had no doubts about the answer to the first question. We read in her *Anti-Critique*[1] : 'The self-sufficient existence of the individual capital is indeed only an external form, the surface of economic life, which only the Vulgar Economists regard as the essence of things and their sole source of knowledge. Beneath that surface and through all the contradictions of competition there remains the fact that all individual capitals in society form a whole. Their existence and movement are governed by common social laws, which, with the unplanned nature and anarchy of the present system, only assert themselves behind the backs of individual capitalists and in opposition to their consciousness in a roundabout way, and purely through deviations from the norm.'

For this reason Luxemburg considers that any serious theory in the field of political economy must study economic processes 'not from the superficial standpoint of the market, i.e. the individual capitalist, the favourite platform of the Vulgar Economist', but rather

---

[1] Published in *Imperialism and the Accumulation of Capital*, Luxemburg and Bukharin, London: Allen Lane 1972. Henceforth referred to as the *Anti-Critique*.

from that of 'aggregate capital, i.e. in the final analysis the only correct and appropriate standpoint'.

'This is precisely the standpoint which Marx systematically developed for the first time in Volume II of *Capital*, but on which his entire theory is based.' For only then did Marx succeed in 'extracting from the chaos of contradictions and fumbling attempts of Quesnay, Adam Smith and their poor imitators, for the first time, and with classical clarity, the fundamental distinction between the two categories, individual capital and aggregate capital'. 'Marx's economic theory stands and falls with the concept of aggregate social capital as a real economic magnitude, which finds its tangible expression in aggregate capitalist profit and its distribution, and whose invisible movement initiates all visible movements of individual sums of capital.'[2]

Nevertheless, continues Luxemburg, Marx adhered to the theoretical abstraction of a purely capitalist society not only in Volume I of *Capital*, but also in Volumes II and III. He therefore approached the problem of the 'reproduction and circulation of aggregate social capital' with an assumption which made any genuine solution of this problem impossible. She writes, 'It was at this point that I believed I had to start my critique. The theoretical assumption of a society of capitalists and workers only – which is legitimate for certain aims of the investigation (as in the first Volume of *Capital*, the analysis of individual capital and its practice of exploitation in the factory) – no longer seems adequate when we deal with the accumulation of aggregate social capital. As this represents the real historical process of capitalist development, it seems impossible to me to understand it if one abstracts it from all conditions of historical reality. Capital accumulation as the historical process develops in an environment of various pre-capitalist formations, in a constant political struggle and in reciprocal economic relations.[3] How can one capture this process in a bloodless theoretical fiction which declares the struggle and the relations to be non-existent? Here it seems necessary, in the spirit of marxist theory, to abandon the premise of the first volume, and to carry out the inquiry into accumulation as a total process, involving the material exchange of capital and its historical environment. If

[2] *Anti-Critique*, pp.73, 86, 103.
[3] We should add to this not only capital accumulation, but also the circulation of capital in general. Since, 'Within its process of circulation, in which industrial capital functions either as money or as commodities, the circuit of industrial capital, whether as money-capital or as commodity-capital, crosses the commodity circulation of the most diverse modes of social production, so far as they produce commodities.' (*Capital* II, p.113.)

one does this, then the explanation of the process follows freely from Marx's basic theories, and is consistent with the other portions of his major works on economics.'[4] It must be admitted that the categories of 'individual capital' and 'aggregate social capital' represent a fundamental difference of methodology which divides Marx's economic theory from bourgeois, and especially Vulgar Economic, theory.[5] But in saying this have we in fact grasped what is most essential in Marx's method? Does this distinction really provide us with the key to the understanding of Marx's work and its structure? Surely not. Luxemburg thinks that the individual volumes of *Capital* are differentiated by the fact that Marx confines himself to the analysis of individual capital in the first, and only proceeds to the analysis of capital in its social connections in the second and third. This is not in fact the case. The category of aggregate capital is counterposed to that of individual capital in many places in Volume I. This procedure is used to establish some very significant theoretical results, such as for example, in the study of the factors which influence the rate and mass of surplus-value;[6] and in Part 7, in the inquiry into the process of the accumulation of capital etc.[7] The main difference is rather that the first two volumes do not go beyond the analysis of 'capital in general' whereas the third volume does and therefore represents the transition to the analysis of 'many capitals'

[4] *Anti-Critique*, p.61. Cf. the more detailed proof of this line of argument in *Accumulation of Capital*, Chapter 25 and 26.

[5] Cf. Chapter 2 of this work.

[6] 'The labour which is set in motion by the total capital of the society, day in, day out, may be regarded as a single working day. If, for example, the number of workers is a million, and the average working day is 10 hours, the social working day will consist of 10 million hours. With a given length of this working day, whether the limits are fixed physically or socially, the mass of surplus-value can be increased only by increasing the number of workers, i.e. the size of the working population. The growth of population here forms the mathematical limit to the production of surplus-value by the total social capital. And, inversely, with a given population this limit is formed by the possible lengthening of the working day.' (*Capital* I, p.422 (307).)

[7] Cf. *ibid.* p.713 (568): 'The illusion created by the money-form vanishes immediately if, instead of taking a single capitalist and a single worker, we take the whole capitalist class and the whole working class. The capitalist class is constantly giving to the working class drafts, in the form of money, on a portion of the product produced by the latter and appropriated by the former. The workers give these drafts back just as constantly to the capitalist class, and in this way, obtain their allotted share of their product. The transaction is veiled by the commodity-form of the product, and the money-form of the commodity.' Cf. *ibid.* p.719 (573): 'From the standpoint of society then, the working class even when it stands outside the direct labour process is just as much an appendage of capital as the lifeless instruments of labour are.'

and their interaction with one another, i.e. capital 'in its reality'.

In other words: the concepts of 'individual capital' and 'capital in general' are by no means identical. The second is much broader than the first, with the result that, according to Marx, 'the aggregate capital of society' can be studied most successfully in the context of 'capital in general' – and in fact, must be. The best example of this is provided by Part III of Volume II, precisely the one criticised by Rosa Luxemburg. And thus we come to her second methodological question; whether the study of economic processes from the standpoint of aggregate capital can be made consistent with the abstraction of a society composed solely of capitalists and workers?

It is clear that the criticisms which Luxemburg makes against the schemes of reproduction in Volume II would only have been justified if Marx had wanted to portray the process of the reproduction of social capital by means of these schemes, not simply in its 'abstract expression', in its 'fundamental form',[8] but also in the course of its actual historical development. We know that he did not. Luxemburg has to assume this because she considers that when we analyse aggregate social capital – in contrast to individual capital – we not only have to deal with economic processes in their entirety, but at the same time, with the direct, concrete reality of capitalism. Only then is it possible to understand why she saw the analysis in Part III as a 'bloodless fiction' and why she accused Marx of abstracting 'from all the conditions of historical reality', in this respect. From all the conditions? If we look closer, it turns out that although Luxemburg speaks of all conditions, she actually only means one – namely the existence of a non-capitalist environment, the so-called third person. And this is no accident, for if one wanted to take Luxemburg at her word, and make the validity of the economic laws discovered by Marx dependent on the strict consideration 'of all the conditions of historical reality', not only would the schemes of reproduction prove to be 'fictions', but so too would the entire results of the analysis in *Capital*. It is well known that any theoretical abstraction will always come off second best in the court of naked empiricism.

It certainly is true that the accumulation of capital 'as a historical process' presupposes 'from the first to the last' a milieu of pre-capitalist economic formations, with which it ceaselessly interacts.[9] However, it presupposes many other things 'from the first to

---

[8] See p.50 above.

[9] This is dealt with very nicely by Trotsky in his *Permanent Revolution*. 'Capitalist development – not in the abstract formulae of the second volume

the last' such as competition within and between countries, the failure of values to coincide with prices, the existence of an average rate of profit, external trade, the exploitation of countries where the productivity of labour is lower by their more fortunate competitors etc. These are all things which Marx rightly disregards in his abstract schemes of reproduction, but which, like the 'historical environment of capitalism', cannot be passed over when one adopts the standpoint of 'reality', as conceived empirically.

In other words: the confrontation of the schemes with historical reality either proves too much, or nothing at all. Luxemburg's inconsistency emerges clearly at this point. But not only at this point! She refers with satisfaction to the alleged gaping contradictions which emerge between the reproduction schemes in Volume II and the 'conception of the entire capitalist process and its development, as set out by Marx in Volume III of *Capital*'.[10] However, she herself repeatedly (and correctly) maintained that Marx not only proceeded under the assumption of a society composed solely of capitalists and workers in Volumes I and II, but also in Volume III[11] – i.e. he proceeded from an assumption which supposedly excluded a correct conception of the accumulation process from the outset! How can one reconcile the statements? How could Marx, using the same assumptions which led him astray in Volume II, arrive at diametrically opposed conclusions in Volume III – conclusions which Luxemburg regarded as correct. Again too much is proved here – more than is compatible with the starting-point of Luxemburg's critique. It is not difficult to discover the source of all these errors, once one has read the *Rough Draft*. It lies in the complete neglect of Marx's category of 'capital in general', and further in the failure to appreciate the role which is allotted to the abstraction 'a pure capitalist society' in marxist methodology. Marx himself says on this: 'In considering the essential relations of capitalist production it can therefore be assumed that the entire world of commodities, all spheres of material production ... are (formally or really) subordinated to the capitalist

of *Capital*, which retain all their significance as a stage in analysis, but in historical reality – took place and could only take place by a systematic expansion of its base. In the process of its development, and consequently in the struggle with its internal contradictions, every national capital turns in an ever-increasing degree to the reserves of the "external market", that is, the reserves of the world-economy. The uncontrollable expansion growing out of the permanent internal crises of capitalism constitutes a progressive force up to the time when it turns into a force fatal for capitalism.' (p.153.)

[10] *Accumulation of Capital*, p.345.
[11] ibid. p.331.

mode of production (for this is what is happening more and more completely; this is the objective in principle, and only if this is attained will the productive powers of labour be developed to their highest point). On this premise, which expresses the limit [of the process] and which is therefore constantly coming closer to an exact presentation of reality, all labourers engaged in the production of commodities are wage-labourers, and the means of production in all these spheres confront them as capital.'[12]

Naturally this does not mean that Marx for one moment confused this methodological assumption with the reality of capitalism. His main concern was to understand the capitalist mode of production in concrete reality. However he regarded the method of the 'ascent from the abstract to the concrete' as being the only adequate scientific means of achieving this – he had already outlined this method in his Introduction and he later employed it in the *Rough Draft* and *Capital*. That is: according to Marx, in order to examine the inherent laws which form the basis of the capitalist mode of production, the 'development' of capital, in both its production process, and the processes of reproduction and circulation, had to be studied initially in 'ideal average', as a 'general type', in which all the 'concrete forms' of capital (e.g. the existence of non-capitalist strata) were to be disregarded.

And this analysis was in no way confined to the analysis of individual capital (which would be in accordance with Luxemburg's conception) since the 'capital of society as a whole' can and must also be conceived of as 'capital as such' or 'capital in general' in line with the particular aims of the analysis.[13] Let us remind the reader of the section from the *Rough Draft* quoted in the previous chapter: 'If I contemplate the aggregate capital of a country, e.g. as distinct from aggregate wage-labour, or if I look at capital as the general economic basis of a class, then I look at it in general.' One cannot agree at all that this represented a 'bloodless fiction' – in contrast to the study of individual capital.

Admittedly we could ask here whether the reproduction process of aggregate social capital presupposes a multiplicity of capitals? And whether therefore the study of this process should be excluded from the analysis of 'capital in general' and be assigned to that of 'many

[12] *Theories* I, pp.409-10. Cf. *Capital* III, p.175: 'But in theory it is assumed that the laws of capitalist production operate in their pure form. In reality there exists only approximation; but this approximation is the greater the more developed the capitalist mode of production and the less it is amalgamated with the survivals of former economic conditions.'

[13] *Grundrisse*, p.346.

capitals' i.e. competition? (Marx himself may have had similar thoughts for a while, as one could conclude from one passage in the *Rough Draft*.)[14] However, what the reproduction process of social capital requires conceptually is simply the existence of exchange relations between the two departments of social production – the industry producing the means of production, and that producing the means of consumption (which one can imagine as being represented simply by two separate capitals), but not competition in its real sense. Of course 'multiplicity is given once one has duality', and hence 'a transition from capital' in general to 'particular capitals, real capitals' would follow.[15] However, this in no way excludes an abstract inquiry within the framework of 'capital in general'. And this is also the reason why such an inquiry can already be found in Volume II of *Capital* – before Marx proceeded to the study of the 'action of many capitals upon each other', the average rate of profit etc. However, we do not have to go back to the *Rough Draft* to convince ourselves of the soundness of this interpretation, since Marx advocates this same standpoint with unmistakeable clarity in the *Theories of Surplus-Value* (well known to Luxemburg, and held in high regard by her).

We read in the Introductory Remarks to the chapter on 'Crises' in Part II of the *Theories*: 'Here we need only consider the forms which capital passes through in the various stages of its development. The real conditions within which the actual process of production takes place are therefore not analysed. It is assumed throughout, that the commodity is sold at its value. We do not examine the competition of capitals, nor the credit system, nor the actual composition of society, which by no means consists only of two classes, workers and industrial capitalists, and where therefore consumers and producers are not identical categories. The first category, that of the consumers (whose revenues are in part not primary, but secondary, derived from profits and wages), is much broader than the second category (producers), and therefore the way in which they spend their revenue, and the very size of the revenue, give rise to very considerable modifications in the economy and particularly in the circulation and reproduction process of capital. Nevertheless, just as the examination of money – both insofar as it represents a form altogether different from the natural form of commodities,

---

[14] *ibid.* p.521.
[15] *ibid.* p.449. (This passage does in fact refer to credit, as does a similar passage in *Theories* II, p.211; however, the point which is made can be applied to the process of reproduction.)

70 · *The Making of Marx's 'Capital'*

and also in its form as means of payment – has shown that it contained the possibility of crises; the examination of the general nature of capital, even without going further into the actual relations which all constitute prerequisites for the real process of production, reveals this still more clearly.'[16]

In contrast, in another part of the same volume we read, 'But now the further development of the potential crisis has to be traced – the real crisis can only be deduced from the real movement of capitalist production, competition and credit – insofar as the crisis arises out of the special aspects which are peculiar to capital as capital, and not merely comprised in its existence as commodity and money.'[17]

And as if in a foreboding of the fact that he would be criticised if he ever disregarded the 'actual relations' at this level of the analysis, Marx wrote, a few lines later : 'Furthermore it is necessary to describe the circulation or reproduction process before dealing with the already existing capital[18] – capital and profit[19] – since we have to explain, not only how capital produces, but also how capital is produced. But the actual movement starts from the existing capital – i.e. the actual movement denotes developed capitalist production, which starts from and presupposes its own basis. The process of reproduction and the predisposition to crisis which is further developed in it are therefore only partially described under this heading and require further elaboration in the chapter[20] on Capital and Profit.'[21]

For : 'The crises in the world market must be regarded as the real concentration and forcible adjustment of all the contradictions of bourgeois economy. The individual factors, which are condensed in these crises, must therefore emerge and must be described in each sphere of the bourgeois economy and the further we advance in our examination of the latter, the more aspects of this conflict must be

[16] *Theories* II, pp.492-93. Luxemburg quotes the same passage in her book without giving the slightest attention to the most important thing there – Marx's distinction between the 'general nature of capital' and the 'real relations'.
[17] *Theories* II, pp.512-13.
[18] See Note 129 on p.44.
[19] We know that in the draft outline on p.978 of the German edition of the *Grundrisse* this denotes a part of the work which corresponds to Volume III of *Capital* as far as its subject matter is concerned.
[20] This should read 'Section' or 'Book'.
[21] *Theories* II, p.513. Marx himself refers here to the relation between the section on Crises in Volume III of *Capital* and that on the reproduction schemes in Volume II (which deals with the supposed contradiction which Luxemburg saw between Volumes II and III).

Methodological comments on Rosa Luxemburg · 71

traced on the one hand, and on the other hand it must be shown that its more abstract forms are recurring and are contained in the more concrete forms.'[22] There are therefore 'a multitude of moments, conditions, possibilities of crisis, which can only be investigated by observing the concrete relations, namely the competition of capitals and credit.'[23] Marx therefore dispensed with their presentation at this stage. According to his outline the detailed analyses of the social process of reproduction and crises as concrete phenomena were, in the main, to have been reserved for a later part of his work[24] as at this stage of the analysis Marx had two other principal concerns. 1. why does the 'general possibility of crisis become reality'[25] for the first time in the capitalist mode of production, and 2. how, despite this, a 'moving equilibrium in an expanding capitalism is possible' (although this is very relative and subject to periodic disturbances).[26] This does not of course exclude the concretisation of the analysis at a subsequent stage: in fact, it demands it.[27] (One example of a successfully concrete analysis is provided by Chapter XV of Volume III of *Capital*. One should also note Marx's methodological remarks on p.878 of that volume where he expressly refers to the necessity for further concretisation.)

So one can see that the 'bloodless fiction' for which Luxemburg rebukes Marx is none other than the study of the social reproduction process in the context of 'capital in general'. This demonstrates the extent to which she misinterpreted the method of *Capital*, and consequently what little trust we can place in her critique of Marx's reproduction schemes. (It shows too how right Lenin was when he described the failure to understand the methodology of *Capital* as the weakest aspect of marxist economic theory at the time of the Second International.)[28] It is true that Luxemburg energetically points out the basic distinction between the study of economic processes from the perspective of individual capital, and from that of aggregate social capital; these pages are among the best in her book. However,

---

[22] *ibid.* p.510.
[23] *ibid.* p.512.
[24] 'I exclude Sismondi from my historical survey here because a critique of his views belongs to a part of my work dealing with the real movement of capital (competition and credit).' *Theories* III, p.53.
[25] *Theories* II, p.514.
[26] Bukharin, *Imperialism and the Accumulation of Capital*, p.154.
[27] It must be significant in some sense that the methodological remarks made in Volume II of the *Theories* did not come to the attention of either Luxemburg or her critics.
[28] See Lenin, *Collected Works*, Vol.38, p.180.

at the same time she confuses the equally fundamental distinction between 'capital in general' and capital 'in reality', 'many capitals'. In her view only individual capital permits an abstract method of study, whereas the category of aggregrate social capital should be used as a category to represent direct reality.

Hence her constant references to 'historical reality' versus 'theoretical fiction', her mistaken critique of Marx's reproduction schemes, and finally her inability to undertake a concrete marxist theoretical development of the valid kernel of her book, namely, her insistence on the conflict between capital's limitless drive for valorisation, and the restricted purchasing power of capitalist society, as one of the principal sources of capitalism's political and economic expansion.

And regardless of how unsatisfactory her own solution to this question might have been, she retains the merit of having placed this perspective back in the centre of discussion; a perspective which follows directly from Marx's theory itself, but one which posed intractable problems for the reformist epigones of the Second International.

3.
Karl Marx and the Problem of Use-Value in Political Economy[1]

Before proceeding to a presentation of the contents of the *Rough Draft* we want to raise a methodological question which has been very neglected in previous marxist literature,[2] the answer to which, however, contributes fundamentally to our knowledge of the *Rough Draft*. The issue is that of the role of use-value in Marx's economics.

I.
Among Marx's numerous critical comments on Ricardo's system the most striking can be found only in the *Rough Draft*, namely that Ricardo abstracts from use-value in his economics,[3] that he is only 'exoterically concerned'[4] with this important category, and that consequently for him it 'remains lying dead as a simple presupposition'.[5]

We should now examine this criticism more closely. Strangely enough, it concerns not only Ricardo, but also many of Marx's pupils, as it has been a tradition among marxist economists to disregard use-value, and place it under the scope of the 'knowledge of merchandise' (*Warenkunde*). For example, Hilferding in his reply to Böhm-Bawerk: 'The commodity is the unity of use-value and value, but we can regard that unity from two different aspects. As a natural thing it is the object of a natural science – as a social thing, it is an object of a social science, political economy.

The object of economics is the social aspect of the commodity, of the good, insofar as it is a symbol of social inter-connection. On

---

[1] Originally published in the Swiss journal *Kyklos*, 1959.
[2] We can name two works which constitute an exception: first, the work of the Russian economist I.I.Rubin on *Marx's Theory of Production and Consumption* of 1930, which was unfortunately unavailable to the author; second (at least in part) Grossmann's last work *Marx, die klassische Nationalökonomie und das Problem der Dynamik*, (mimeographed) New York.
[3] *Grundrisse*, p.267.
[4] *ibid.* p.647.
[5] *ibid.* p.320.

the other hand the natural aspect of the commodity, its use-value, lies outside the domain of political economy.'[6]

At first glance this appears to be simply a paraphrase of the well-known section from Marx's *Contribution*. However, how does this passage actually read in Marx?

'To be a use-value is evidently a necessary prerequisite of the commodity, but it is immaterial to the use-value whether it is a commodity. Use-value as such, since it is independent of the determinate economic form, lies outside the sphere of investigation of political economy. It belongs in this sphere only when it is itself a determinate form.'[7]

It must be conceded that the original differs considerably from the copy,[8] and that Hilferding's arbitrary reproduction of these sentences is tantamount to clumsy distortion of Marx's real view.

Or, we can take a more recent marxist author, P.M.Sweezy. In his work the *Theory of Capitalist Development*, which is intended to popularise Marx's economics, we read: 'Marx excluded use-value (or as it would now be called, 'utility') from the field of investigation of political economy on the ground that it does not directly embody a social relation. He enforces a strict requirement that the categories of economics must be social categories, i.e. categories which represent relations between people. It is important to realise that this is

---

[6] R.Hilferding, *Böhm-Bawerk's Criticism of Marx*, Clifton NJ: Kelley, 1949, p.130.

[7] *Contribution*, p.28.

[8] Bernstein noticed this immediately and chafes Hilferding in his discussion of the latter's text (in *Dokumenten des Sozialismus* 1904 Heft 4, pp.154-57) on the subject of the discrepancy between his formulation of the question and Marx's own. He writes, 'Marx is not so daring as to throw use-value completely out of political economy', and if Hilferding does this, 'then he stumbles from his lofty position as an interpreter of Marx into depths far below those of the university professors whom he holds in such low regard'. However, these sarcastic remarks do not obscure the fact that Bernstein himself had no idea how to deal with the discrepancy, and was only able to solve it through a convergence of Marx's theory with the economists of the 'psychological school'.

Hilferding's reply turned out to be very weak. 'Use-value can only be designated a social category when it is a conscious aim of society, when it has become an object of its conscious social action. It becomes this in a socialist society, whose conscious management sets as its aim the production of use-values; however, this is in no way the case in capitalist society . . . However, although use-value can be designated as a social category in a socialist society it is not an economic category, not an object of theoretical economic analysis, since a consciously directed relation of production does require this analysis.' (*Neue Zeit* No.4, 1904, pp.110-11.)

in sharp contrast to the attitude of modern economic theory ...'[9]

Sweezy's presentation does not differ substantially from that normally found in popularisations of marxist economics.[10] However, in his case the mistake is even less forgivable, as not only did he have access to the *Theories of Surplus-Value*, but also the *Marginal Notes on A.Wagner*,[11] where Marx discusses the role of use-value in his economic theory in great detail.

He says there on Wagner, 'Only a *vir obscurus*, who has not understood a word of *Capital* could conclude: Because Marx dismisses all the German professional twaddle on "use-value" in general in a footnote on "use-value" in the first edition of *Capital* and refers the reader who would like to know something about real use-value to "manuals dealing with merchandise"[12] therefore use-value plays no role for him ... If one is concerned with analysing the "Commodity", the simplest concrete economic entity, all relations which have nothing to do with the object of analysis must be kept at a distance. However, what there is to say about the commodity, as far as use-value is concerned, I have said in a few lines; but, on the other hand, I have called attention to the characteristic form in which use-value – the product of labour[13] – appears in this respect; namely, "A thing can be useful and the product of human labour, without being a commodity. Whoever directly satisfies his own needs with the

[9] *op. cit.* p.26.
[10] The philosopher Marcuse goes to the other extreme when he writes, 'when Marx declares that use-value lies outside the scope of economic theory, he is at first describing the actual state of affairs in classical political economy. His own analysis begins by accepting and explaining the fact, that, in capitalisms, use-values appear only as the "material bearers of exchange-value" (*Capital* I, p.126(36)). His critique then refutes the capitalist treatment of use-values and sets its goals on an economy in which this relation is entirely abolished.' (*Reason and Revolution*, p.304.)

The arbitrariness of this interpretation is immediately obvious. In the first place the passage quoted from the *Contribution* is not concerned exclusively with classical political economy, but with political economy in general. Secondly, Marx nowhere states that use-values are only 'material depositories of exchange-value', but rather that they are so 'at the same time', which is quite another question. Finally, Marx never set himself the task of combatting the capitalist treatment of use-values, but rather of scientifically explaining the fact, peculiar to capitalism (and to commodity production in general), that for use-values to be able to satisfy human needs, they must first prove themselves as exchange-values.

[11] Marx's last economic work, printed in *MEW* Vol.19, pp.355-89. An English translation was published in *Theoretical Practice*, Issue 5, spring 1972.
[12] See *Contribution*, p.28.
[13] This should read, 'insofar as it is the product of labour'.

product of his own labour creates, indeed, use-values, but not commodities. In order to produce the latter, he must not only produce use-values, but use-values for others, social use-values . . .".[14] Hence use-value itself – as the use-value of a "commodity" – possesses a historically specific character . . . It would therefore be sheer word-spinning to use the opportunity provided by the analysis of the commodity – because it presents itself as, on the one hand a use-value or good, and on the other a "value" – to add on all kinds of banal reflections about use-values or goods which do not form part of the world of commodities [in the way that standard university economics does] . . . On the other hand the *vir obscurus* has overlooked the fact that I do not stop short in my analysis of the commodity at the double manner in which it presents itself, but immediately go on to say that in the double being of the commodity there is represented the twofold character of labour, whose product the commodity is: useful labour, i.e. the concrete modes of labour which create use-values, and abstract labour, labour as the expenditure of labour-power, irrespective of whatever "useful" way it is expended (on which my later representation of the production process is based); that in the development of the value-form of the commodity, in the last instance of its money-form and hence of money, the value of commodity is represented in the use-value of the other, i.e. in the natural form of the other commodity; that surplus-value itself is derived from a "specific" and exclusive use-value of labour-power, etc. etc. That is, use-value plays a far more important part in my economics, than in economics hitherto,[15] but N.B. that it is only ever taken into account when this arises from the analysis of given economic forms, and not out of arguing backwards and forwards about the concepts of words "use-value" and "value".'[16]

This then is Marx's view. It is clear from this that the traditional marxist interpretation of Hilferding, Sweezy *et al.* cannot possibly be correct, and that in this instance the authors mentioned above – without knowing it – do not follow their teacher, Marx, but rather Ricardo, the man he criticises.

II.

However, what is the basis of Marx's critique, and how should we actually interpret the objections to Ricardo which are mentioned at the beginning?

---

[14] Quoted from *Capital* I, p.131 (40).
[15] Marx refers here, of course, to the economics of Smith and Ricardo.
[16] *MEW* Vol.19, p.371.

The problem of use-value · 77

To answer this we have to go back to the basic methodological assumptions of the marxist system. We know that, in contrast to the Classical school, Marx's entire theoretical effort was directed at uncovering the 'particular laws which govern the emergence, existence, development and death of a given social order, and its replacement by another higher one'.[17] He thus regarded the capitalist mode of production as 'merely a historical mode of production, corresponding to a certain limited epoch in the development of the material conditions of production',[18] and the categories of bourgeois economics as 'forms of thought expressing with social validity the conditions and relations of a definite, historically determined mode of production'.[19]

But how can theory arrive at a knowledge of such particular laws, which have only a historical claim to validity? And how can these laws be brought into consonance with the general economic determinants which apply to all social epochs since 'all epochs of production have certain features in common', a fact which 'arises already from the identity of the subject, humanity, with the object, nature'.[20] Consequently, nothing is easier than 'to confound or extinguish all historical differences under general human laws', by picking out these common characteristics.[21] For example, 'even though the most developed languages have laws and charac-

[17] J.J. Kaufmann's description of Marx's method of investigation – quoted by Marx in the Afterword to the Second Edition of Volume I of *Capital*, p.102 (19).
[18] *Capital* III, p.259.
[19] *Capital* I, p.169 (76).
[20] *Grundrisse*, p.85. Hence, 'no society can go on producing, in other words, no society can reproduce, unless it constantly reconverts a part of its products into means of production, or elements of fresh products'. (*Capital* I, p.711 (566). For this purpose, therefore, it must maintain a certain production between the growth of the industries producing the means of production, and those producing the means of consumption (Departments I and II in Marx's schemes of reproduction), accumulate reserves etc. On the other hand, in any society, a certain quantity of surplus labour has to be carried out by the members of that society in order that it may have 'at its disposal, so to speak, a fund for development, which the very increase in population makes necessary' (*Theories* I, p.107). 'If we strip both wages and surplus-value, both necessary and surplus labour of their specifically capitalist character, then certainly there remain not these forms, but merely their rudiments, which are common to all social modes of production.' (*Capital* III, p.876.) And finally, 'No society can prevent the disposable labour-time of society one way or another from regulating production.' (*MEW* Vol.32, p.12.) And consequently this material basis of the determination of value will also have considerable significance under socialism. (Cf. *Capital* III, p.851.)
[21] *Grundrisse*, p.87.

teristics in common with the least developed, nevertheless, those things which determine their development' must express 'the distinction between what they have in general and what they have in common'. Similarly the task of political economy is, above all, the investigation of the laws of development of the capitalist period, which it studies 'so that in their unity' (the unity between this period with earlier ones through the features which they have in common), 'the essential difference is not forgotten'.[22]

But what constitutes development in the sphere of the economy? It is precisely that process in which it expresses its specific social character! 'To the extent that the labour-process is solely a process between man and nature, its simple elements remain common to all forms of social development. However, each definite historical form of this process marks a further development in its material basis and social forms.'[23] Here it is the social forms which are the decisive factor – as distinct from their naturally given 'content'. They alone represent the active, forward-moving element,[24] for 'natural laws cannot be abolished at all. What can change in historically different circumstances is only the form in which these laws assert themselves.'[25]

We cannot go any more closely here into the fundamental marxist distinction between 'Form' and 'Content' in economics. (The influence of Hegel's *Logic* is easily discernible here.[26]) One fact though is certain: for Marx it is the *economic* forms which serve to distinguish the particular modes of production, and in which the social relations of economic individuals are expressed. For example, as he says when

---

[22] *ibid.* p.85.
[23] *Capital* III, p.883.
[24] Cf. Hegel's *Science of Logic*, Volume II, p.79. 'Matter is determined as indifferent: it is the *passive* as against the active . . . Matter must be formed and Form must materialise itself – must in Matter give itself self-identity and persistence.'
[25] Marx's letter to Kugelmann, 11 July 1868. *Selected Correspondence*, p.196.
[26] The Russian political economist I.I.Rubin wrote in another context: 'One cannot forget that, on the question of the relation between content and form, Marx took the standpoint of Hegel and not of Kant. Kant treated form as something external in relation to the content, and as something which adheres to the content from the outside. From the standpoint of Hegel's philosophy, the content is not in itself something to which form adheres from the outside. Rather, through its development, the content itself gives birth to the form which was already latent in the content. Form necessarily grows from the content itself.' (*Essays on Marx's Theory of Value*, Detroit: Black and Red 1972, p.117.)

criticising Rossi : 'the "forms of exchange" seem [to Rossi] to be a matter of complete indifference. This is just as if a physiologist were to say that the different forms of life are a matter of complete indifference, since they are all only forms of organic matter. It is precisely those forms that are alone of importance when the question is the specific character of a mode of social production. A coat is a coat. But have it made in the first form of exchange, [a] and you have capitalist production and modern bourgeois society; in the second, [b] and you have a form of handicraft which is even compatible with Asiatic relations or those of the Middle Ages etc.'[27] For, 'in the first case the jobbing tailor produces not only a coat, he produces capital; therefore also profit; he produces his master as a capitalist and himself as a wage-labourer. When I have a coat made for me at home by a jobbing tailor, for me to wear, that no more makes me my own entrepreneur (in the sense of an economic category) than it makes the entrepreneur tailor an entrepreneur when he himself wears and consumes a coat made by his workmen.'[28]

And in another passage : 'The agricultural labourers in England and Holland who receive wages which are "advanced" by capital "produce their wages themselves" just like the French peasant or the self-sustaining Russian serf. If the production process is considered in its continuity, then the capitalist advances the worker as "wages" today only a part of the product which he produced yesterday. Thus the difference does not lie in the fact that, in one case, the worker produces his own wage, and does not produce them in the other ... The whole difference lies in the *change of form*, which the labour fund produced by the worker undergoes, before it returns to him in the form of wages ...'[29]

Hence it is the specific social forms of production and distribution which, in Marx's view, constitute the real object of economic analysis; and it is just this 'lack of the theoretical understanding needed to distinguish the different form of economic relations' combined 'with a crude obsession with the material' which characterises

   a) The form in which the tailor produces the coat for sale ready-made.
   b) The form in which the tailor is provided with the material and a wage by the person who wants the coat.

   [27] Marx's comments here refer to the following sentence from Rossi: 'Whether one buys ready-made clothes from a tailor, or whether one gets them from a jobbing-tailor who has been given the material and a wage, as far as the results are concerned the two actions are perfectly similar.' (*Theories* I, p.295.)
   [28] *Theories* I, pp.295-96.
   [29] *Theories* III, p.424. (Cf. *Grundrisse*, p.87.)
D

previous economics, even in its best representatives.[30] Only R. Jones and Sismondi are exempt from this criticism.[31])

With this we come to the end of our methodological excursus. Meanwhile the reader will have noticed that we have simultaneously answered – in very general terms – the question of the role of use-value in Marx's economics. How did that passage run which we quoted at the beginning, from Marx's *Contribution*? In its 'independence from the determinate economic form' use-value 'lies outside the sphere of investigation of political economy. It belongs in this sphere only when it is a *determinate form itself*.' In other words, whether use-value should be granted economic significance or not can only be decided in accordance with its relation to the social relations of production. It is certainly an economic category to the extent that it influences these relations, or is itself influenced by them. However, apart from that – in its raw 'natural' characteristics – it falls outside the scope of political economy. Or, as it says in the *Grundrisse*: 'Political economy has to do with the specific social forms of wealth or rather the production of wealth. The material of wealth, whether subjective, like labour, or objective, like objects for the satisfaction of natural or historical needs, initially appears as common to all epochs of production. This material therefore appears initially as mere presupposition, lying quite outside the scope of political economy, and falls within its purview only when it is modified by the formal relations or appears as modifying them.'[32]

III.

Regarded in this way, the question of the difference between Marx and Ricardo on the role of use-value in economics no longer presents any difficulties. It cannot be related to their basic theories of value since both subscribed to the labour theory of value. From

[30] *Theories* I, p.92 and *Capital* I, p.682 (542); *Capital* III, p.323.

[31] 'What distinguishes Jones from the other economists (except perhaps Sismondi) is that he emphasises that the essential feature of capital is its socially determined form, and that he reduces the whole difference between the capitalist and other modes of production to this distinct form.' (*Theories* III, p.424.)

[32] *Grundrisse*, p.852. Cf. the parallel section on p.881. 'The first category in which bourgeois wealth presents itself is that of the commodity. The commodity itself appears as the unity of two aspects. It is use-value, i.e. object of the satisfaction of any system whatever of human needs. This is its material side, which the most disparate epochs of production may have in common, and whose examination therefore lies beyond political economy. Use-value falls within the realm of political economy as soon as it becomes modified by the modern relations of production, or as it in turn intervenes to modify them.'

The problem of use-value · 81

the standpoint of the labour theory of value the utility or use-value of the products of labour cannot be granted any influence in the creation of value; their use-value must rather appear as a simple presupposition of their exchangeability. However, it in no way follows from this that use-value has no economic significance at all, and that it should simply be excluded from the sphere of economics.

In Marx's view this is only correct in the case of simple commodity circulation (the exchange form C-M-C). Simple circulation 'consists at bottom[33] only of the formal process of positing exchange-value, sometimes in the role of the commodity, at other times in the role of money'.[34] How exactly the commodities to be exchanged were produced (i.e. whether they originated in a capitalist or pre-capitalist economy), and how they will be consumed after exchange is incidental to the economic study of simple commodity circulation. The protagonists here are simply buyers and sellers, or rather the commodities put up for sale by them, which establish their social connection on their behalf. The real aim of exchange – the mutual satisfaction of the needs of the commodity producers – can only be fulfilled if the commodities simultaneously prove themselves to be values, if they are successfully exchanged for the 'universal commodity', money. Consequently the social change of matter takes place in the change of form of the commodities themselves.

And in this situation the change of form is the only social relationship between the commodity owners – 'the indicator of their social function, or their social relation to each other'.[35] However, as far as the content outside the act of exchange is concerned, this 'content can only be . . . 1) the natural particularity of the commodity being exchanged 2) the particular natural need of the exchangers or both together, the different *use-values* of the commodities being exchanged'.[36] However the content as such does not determine the character of the exchange relation. In fact, use-value simply constitutes 'the material basis in which a specific economic relation presents itself' and 'it is only this specific relation which stamps the use-value as a commodity . . . Not only does the exchange-value not appear as determined by use-value, but rather, furthermore, the commodity only becomes a commodity, insofar as its owner does not relate to it as use-value.'[37] Hence in this situation, where exchange 'takes place

[33] In original, 'au fond'.
[34] *Grundrisse*, p.256.
[35] *ibid.* p.241.
[36] *ibid.* p.242.
[37] *ibid.* p.881.

only for the reciprocal use of the commodity, the use-value . . . the natural peculiarity of the commodity as such, has no standing as an economic form', – is not 'a content of the relation as a social relation'.[38] Consequently only the change of form of the commodity and money has economic significance, and the presentation of simple commodity exchange has to be confined to this change of form alone.[39]

However, although this is correct for simple commodity exchange, nothing would be more erroneous, states Marx, than to conclude 'that the distinction between use-value and exchange-value, which falls outside the characteristic economic form in simple circulation, . . . falls outside it in general . . . For example, Ricardo, who believes that the bourgeois economy deals only with exchange-value, and is concerned with use-value merely exoterically, derives the most important determinations of exchange-value precisely from use-value, from the relation between the two of them: for instance, *ground-rent, the minimum level of wages, and the distinction between fixed and circulating capital*, to which he imputes precisely the most significant influence on the determination of prices; likewise in the relation of demand and supply etc.'[40] Ricardo was indeed right to say that 'exchange-value is the predominant aspect. But of course use does not come to a halt because it is determined only by exchange; although of course it obtains its direction thereby'.[41] 'To use is to consume, whether for production or consumption. Exchange is the mediation of this act through a social process. Use can be posited' through exchange 'and be a mere consequence of exchange; then again exchange can appear merely as a moment of use, etc. From the standpoint of capital (in circulation), exchange appears as the positing of use-value, while on the other hand its use (in the act of production) appears as positing for exchange, as positing its exchange-value. Similarly with production and consumption. In the bourgeois economy (as in any) they are posited in specific distinctions and specific unities. The point is to understand precisely these specific distinguishing characteristics . . . and not, as Ricardo does, to completely abstract from them, or like the dull Say, to make a pompous fuss about nothing more than the presupposition of the word "utility".' For 'Use-value itself plays a role as an economic category.

[38] *ibid.* p.267.
[39] 'If we want to examine the social relation of individuals within their economic process, we must keep to the characteristic form of this process itself.' (*Grundrisse*, German edn. p.914.)
[40] *Grundrisse*, pp.646–47.
[41] *ibid.* p.267.

Where it plays this role ... the degree to which use-value exists outside economics and its determinate forms and not merely as presupposed matter ... is something which emerges from the development itself.'[42]

IV.

So when, according to Marx, does use-value as such become modified by the formal relations of bourgeois economy, and when, in its turn, does it intervene to modify these formal relations – that is, as a 'determinate economic form' itself?

In the *Marginal Notes on A.Wagner*, which have already been cited, Marx points out that even in simple commodity circulation, with the development of the money-form of the commodity, the value of a commodity must be represented in 'use-value, i.e. in the natural form of the other commodity'. In Marx's view this does not only mean that money must be a commodity as a matter of course, i.e. possess use-value in its material, but also, that this use-value is connected to quite specific physical properties of the money-commodity which make it capable of fulfilling its function. We read in the *Rough Draft* : 'The study of the precious metals as subjects of the money relation, as incarnations of the latter, is therefore by no means a matter lying outside the realm of political economy, as Proudhon believes, any more than the physical composition of paint, and of marble lie outside the realm of painting and sculpture. The attributes possessed by the commodity as exchange-value, attributes for which its natural qualities are not adequate, express the demands made upon those commodities which are the material of money par excellence. These demands at the level at which we have confined ourselves up until now [i.e. the level of pure circulation of metals] are most completely satisfied by the precious metals.'[43]

The commodities which fulfil the function of the universal equivalent, can double their use-value precisely because of their specific attributes, which make them the only material for money. They contain 'besides their particular use-value as a particular commodity', a 'universal' or 'formal' use-value.[44] 'This latter use-value is itself a characteristic form, i.e. it arises from the specific role, which it [the money-commodity] plays as a result of the all-sided action exerted on it by the other commodities in the process of exchange.'[45]

---

[42] *ibid*. pp.646, 267.
[43] *ibid*. p.174.
[44] 'The formal use-value [of money] unrelated to any real individual need.' (*Contribution*, p.89.)
[45] *Contribution*, p.47.

With this, the 'material change and the change of form coincide, since in money the content itself is part of the characteristic economic form.'[46]

The second example which Marx refers to in the *Marginal Notes* is of decisive importance – the exchange between capital and labour. If we look, for example, at simple commodity circulation, as it occurs 'on the surface of the bourgeois world', in retail trade, 'a worker who buys a loaf of bread, and a millionaire who buys the same thing, seem, in this act, to be simply buyers, as the grocer who confronts them is simply a seller. The content of these purchases, like their extent, here appears as completely irrelevant compared with the formal aspect.'[47]

However the matter looks quite different if we proceed from this exchange on the surface, to the exchange which determines the essence of the capitalist mode of production – that between capital and labour. For, if in simple circulation, 'commodity A is exchanged for money B, and the latter then for the commodity C, which is destined for consumption – the original object of the exchange for A – then the use of commodity C, its consumption, falls entirely outside circulation; is irrelevant to the form of the relation . . . is of purely physical interest, expressing no more than the relation of the individual in his natural quality to an object of his individual need. What he does with commodity C is a question which belongs outside the economic relation.'[48] In contrast to this, in the exchange between capital and labour, it is precisely the use-value of the commodity purchased by the capitalist (i.e. labour-power) which constitutes the presupposition of the capitalist production process and the capital relation itself. In this transaction the capitalist exchanges a commodity whose consumption 'coincides directly with the objectification (*Vergegenständlichung*) of labour i.e. with the positing of exchange-value'.[49] Consequently, if 'the content of use-value was irrelevant in simple circulation' here, by contrast, 'the use-value of that which is exchanged for money appears as a particular economic relation . . . falls within the economic process because the use-value here is itself determined by exchange-value'.[50]

Hence if the creation of surplus-value, as the increase in the exchange-value of capital, is derived from the specific use-value of the commodity labour-power, then political economy must in turn

---

[46] *Grundrisse*, p.667.
[47] ibid. p.251.
[48] ibid. p.274.
[49] *Grundrisse*, German edn. p.944.
[50] *Grundrisse*, pp.274-75, 311.

restrict the share of the value-product accruing to the worker to the equivalent of the goods necessary to maintain him, and consequently must allow this share to be determined at bottom by means of use-value.[51] In this instance, too, the category of use-value has an impact on the economic relations of the capitalist mode of production.

We can also confirm now use-value constantly influences the forms of economic relations in the circulation process of capital. We disregard here the many ways in which the material nature of the product affects the duration of the working period and the circulation period,[52] and proceed directly to the distinction which is basic to the circulation process – that between fixed and circulating capital, which Marx refers to in his polemic against Ricardo, which we have already cited.

As far as fixed capital is concerned, it only circulates 'as value to the degree that it is used up or consumed as use-value in the production process. But the time in which it is consumed and in which it must be reproduced in its form as use-value depends on its relative durability. Hence its durability, or its greater or lesser perishability – the greater or smaller amount of time during which it can continue to perform its function within the repeated production processes of capital – this aspect of its use-value here becomes a form-determining moment i.e. a determinant for capital as regards its form, not as regards its substance. The necessary reproduction of fixed capital, together with the proportion of the total capital consisting of it, here modify, therefore, the turnover time of the total capital and thereby its valorisation.'[53]

Thus, in the categories of fixed and circulating capital, 'the distinction between the [three] elements [of the labour process] as use-values . . . appears as a qualitative distinction within capital itself, and as the determinant of the complete movement (turnover).'[54] This therefore represents yet another instance where use-value enters into the process of capital as an economic factor.[55]

[51] 'Ricardo regards the product of labour in respect of the worker only as use-value – only the part of the product which he needs to be able to live as a worker. But how it comes about that the worker suddenly only represents use-value in the exchange, or only draws use-value from the exchange is by no means clear to him.' (*ibid.* p.551.)
[52] Cf. especially Chapters V, XII and XIII of *Capital* II.
[53] *Grundrisse*, p.685. Cf. *Capital* II, pp.170-71.
[54] *Grundrisse*, p.692.
[55] In this regard we should refer to the instruments of labour which, 'as capital united with the land', function in the form of factory buildings, railways, bridges, tunnels, docks etc. The fact that such instruments of labour are 'localised, attached to the soil by their roots, assigns to this portion of fixed

However, the role of use-value is seen most clearly in the reproduction process of aggregate social capital, as it is presented in Part III of Volume II of *Capital*. At the beginning of this section Marx points out that as long as the analysis was simply one of the reproduction process of an individual capital (i.e. as in Volume I), 'the natural form of the commodity-product was completely irrelevant to the analysis . . . whether it consisted of machines, corn or mirrors'. In Volume I it was simply 'presupposed on the one hand that the capitalist sells the product at its value, and on the other that he finds within the sphere of circulation the objective means of production for restarting the process'. For, 'the only act within the sphere of circulation on which we have dwelt was the purchase and sale of labour-power as the fundamental condition of capitalist production'.[56] However, 'This merely formal[57] manner of presentation is no longer adequate in the study of the aggregate social capital', in the reproduction of which the problem is not merely the replacement of value, but also the replacement of material, and consequently everything depends on the material shape, on the use-value of the value-product.[58]

The same point is made in the *Theories*, the difference being that Marx expressly refers to the significance of use-value as an economic category: 'In considering surplus-value as such, the original form of the product, hence of the surplus-product, is of no consequence. It becomes important when we consider the actual process of reproduction, partly in order to understand its forms, and partly in order to grasp the influence of luxury production etc. on reproduction.'[59] 'Here', Marx stresses, 'is another example of how use-value as such acquires economic significance.'[60]

capital a peculiar role in the economy of nations. They cannot be sent abroad, cannot circulate as commodities in the world market. Title to this fixed capital may change, it may be bought and sold, and to this extent may circulate ideally. These titles of ownership may even circulate in foreign markets, for instance, in the form of stocks. But a change of the persons owning this class of fixed capital does not alter the relation of the immovable, materially fixed part of the national wealth to its movable part.' (*Capital* II, p.166.)

[56] *ibid.* pp.356-57.
[57] i.e. bearing in mind the form of the process.
[58] *Capital* II, p.398. The well-known schemes of reproduction of Tugan-Baranovsky and Otto Bauer suffer precisely from not having observed this methodological postulate.
[59] *Capital* II, p.407.
[60] *Theories* III, pp.251-52. In another passage in the same work Marx examines the question as to whether 'a part of the surplus-value can be directly transformed into constant capital . . . without first having been alienated'. He writes: 'In industrial areas there are machine-builders who build whole

The problem of use-value · 87

We now proceed to those subjects dealt with in Volume III of *Capital*. We can also find numerous examples here of the significance of use-value as an economic category. This is obvious in the case of ground-rent, which Marx (like Ricardo) derives ultimately 'from the relation of exchange-value to use-value'. The importance of use-value is also shown in relation to the rate of profit, insofar as this is dependent on fluctuations in the value of raw materials. For, 'it is especially agricultural produce proper, i.e. the raw materials taken from organic nature, which . . . is subject to fluctuations of value in consequence of changing yields etc. Owing to uncontrollable natural conditions, favourable or unfavourable seasons etc. the same quantity of labour may be represented in very different quantities of use-values, and a definite quantity of these use-values may therefore have very different prices.'[61] Such variations in price, 'always affect the rate of profit, even if they leave the wage untouched and hence the rate and amount of surplus-value too'.[62] We should also devote special attention to the influence of use-value on the accumulation of capital.

Grossmann writes: 'In marxist literature up till now stress has been laid merely on the fact that the *mass of the value* of the constant capital grows both absolutely, and in relation to the variable capital in the course of capitalist production and the accumulation of capital, with the increase in the productivity of labour, and the transition to a higher organic composition of capital. However this phenomenon only constitutes one side of the process of accumula-

factories for the manufacturers. Let us assume one-tenth is surplus-product, unpaid labour, whether this tenth, the surplus-product, consists of factory buildings which are built for a third party and are sold to them, or of factory buildings which the producer builds for himself – sells to himself – clearly makes no difference. The only thing that matters here is whether the kind of use-value in which the surplus labour is expressed can re-enter as means of production into the sphere of production of the capitalist to whom the surplus belongs. This is yet another example of how important is the analysis of use-value for the determination of economic phenomena.' (*Theories* II, pp.488-89.)

[61] *Capital* III, pp.117-18.

[62] *ibid.* p.115. Another example is provided by the uneven development of the different spheres of production in the capitalist economy. We read in Volume III: 'The fact that the development of productivity in different lines of industry proceeds at substantially different rates and frequently even in opposite directions, is not due merely to the anarchy of competition and the peculiarities of the bourgeois mode of production. Productivity of labour is also bound up with natural conditions, which frequently become less productive as productivity grows – inasmuch as the latter depends on social conditions. Hence the opposite movements in these different spheres – progress here, retrogression there. Consider only the influence of the seasons, for instance, which determines the available quantity of the bulk of raw materials, the exhaustion of forest lands, coal and iron mines etc.' (*ibid.* p.260.)

tion, in that it is regarded from the aspect of value. In fact, it cannot be repeated too often that the reproduction process is not merely a process of valorisation but also a labour process – it produces not merely values, but also use-values'. And, 'looked at from the aspect of use-value, the increase in productive capacity does not only operate in the direction of the devaluation of existing capital, but also in the direction of a quantitative increase in objects of use.'[63] The effect that this has on the accumulation of capital can be read in Volume III of *Capital*.[64]

It states there: 'The increase in productive power can only directly increase the value of the existing capital, if by raising the rate of profit it increases that portion of the value of the annual product which is reconverted into capital ... Indirectly however, the development of the productivity of labour contributes to the increase of the value of existing capital by increasing the mass and variety of use-values[65] in which the same exchange-value is represented and which form the material substance i.e. the material elements of capital, the material objects making up the constant capital directly and the variable capital at least indirectly. More products which may be converted into capital, whatever their exchange-value, are created with the same capital and the same labour. These products may serve to absorb additional labour, hence also additional surplus labour and therefore create additional capital.' For 'the amount of labour which a capital can command does not depend on its value, but on the mass of raw and auxiliary materials, machinery and elements of fixed capital and necessities of life, all of which it comprises whatever their value may be. As the mass of labour employed and that of surplus labour increases, there is also a growth in the value of the reproduced capital and in the surplus-value newly added to it.'[66]

V.

The problem of supply and demand is dealt with in particular detail in Volume III of *Capital*. This problem is closely related to

---

[63] Grossmann, *Das Akkumulations- und Zusammenbruchsgesetz des kapitalistischen Systems*, pp.326-28.
[64] Cf. in addition *Capital* I, pp.752-53 (604-05).
[65] 'If one has more elements of production (even of the same value) the technical level of production can be expanded; then, at the same mass of value of capital more workers can be employed in the production process, who, will therefore produce more value in the next cycle of production.' (Grossmann, *op. cit.* p.330.)
[66] *Capital* III, p.248.

The problem of use-value · 89

that of the much discussed question of socially necessary labour-time, which has already been broached in Chapter 2 above.[67]

Right at the beginning of Volume I we read, 'Socially necessary labour-time is the labour-time required to produce any use-value under the conditions of production normal for a given society and with the average degree of skill and intensity prevalent in that society.' And, that 'which determines the magnitude of the value of any article is therefore the amount of labour socially necessary or the labour-time socially necessary for its production'.[68]

We encounter this 'technological' meaning of the concept of socially necessary labour-time again and again in *Capital*, and in other of Marx's works. However, we also encounter another meaning, according to which labour can only count as 'socially necessary' if it corresponds to the aggregate requirements of society, for a particular use-value.

In Volume I of *Capital* we read, 'Let us suppose that every piece of linen in the market contains nothing but socially necessary labour-time. In spite of all this all these pieces taken as a whole may contain superfluously expended labour-time. If the market cannot stomach the whole quantity at the normal price of 2 shillings a yard this proves that too great a portion of the total social labour-time has been expended in the form of weaving. The effect is the same as if each individual weaver had expended more labour-time upon his particular product than was socially necessary. As the German proverb has it : caught together, hanged together. All the linen on the market counts as one single article of commerce, and each piece of linen is only an aliquot part of it. And in fact the value of each single yard is also nothing but the materialisation of the same socially determined quantity of homogeneous human labour.'[69]

Marx expresses the same idea in numerous other passages. And Engels even combined both meanings in one definition when he stated in the course of an attack on Rodbertus, 'If he had investigated by what means and how labour creates value and therefore also determines and measures it, he would have arrived at socially necessary labour, necessary for the single product, both in relation to other products of the same kind, and also in relation to society's total demand.'[70]

The amalgamation of these two meanings of 'socially necessary

---

[67] Cf. p.51.
[68] *Capital* I, p.129 (39).
[69] *ibid.* p.202 (107).
[70] Engels's Preface to Marx's *Poverty of Philosophy*, p.20.

labour' has been seen as an intolerable contradiction by numerous writers.[71] In reality the contradiction is only apparent; it is in fact a question of different levels of analysis, which require operating with two different, but mutually complementary concepts.

Volume III of *Capital* states on this : 'To say that a commodity has a use-value is merely to say that it satisfies some social need. So long as we dealt with individual commodities only, we could assume that there was a need for a particular commodity – its quantity already implied by its price – without inquiring further into the amount of the need which has to be satisfied. This quantity is, however, of essential importance, as soon as the product of an entire branch of production is placed on one side, and the social need for it on the other. It then becomes necessary to consider the extent i.e. the amount of this social need.'[72]

In other words : The analysis so far has proceeded from a series of simplifying assumptions. First it was assumed that commodities are exchanged at their values, and second, that they always find a buyer. Only in this way was it possible to outline the production and circulation process of capital in pure form, without the influence of disturbing 'accompanying circumstances'. Now is the time, however, to bring into the economic analysis the moment of supply and demand which has so far been neglected, but which must at last be given its due.

As far as supply is concerned, this means, in the first instance, that instead of one individual commodity (or the amount of commodities produced by a single capitalist), we now have to posit the aggregate product of an entire branch of production. For the individual commodity the determination of socially necessary labour-time proceeds from the fact that 'the individual value of the commodity (and what amounts to the same under the present assumption, its selling price) should coincide with its social value'.[73] However, the matter is quite different when it is a question of the aggregate product of a branch of production. Here the requirement of socially necessary labour-time can only apply for the entire mass of commodities; and so consequently the individual value of commodities has to be distinguished from their social value. Social value assumes the form of

---

[71] See the review of the relevant literature in the instructive study by T.Grigorovici. *Die Wertlehre bei Marx und Lassalle. Beitrag zur Geschichte eines wissenschaftlichen Misverständnisses* 1908. Cf., also Diehl's *Sozialwissenschaftliche Erläuterungen zu D.Ricardos Grundgesetzen*, I, 1905, pp.125-28.

[72] *Capital* III, p.185. The same line of thought can also be found in the *Rough Draft* pp.404-05.

[73] *Capital* III, p.182.

market value, which represents the average value of the sum of commodities, from which, consequently, the individual values of some commodities must always diverge : they must either stand above or below the stated market value. This is because we can generally distinguish three categories of producers in each branch of production : producers who produce under above-average, average, or below-average conditions. 'Which of the categories has a decisive effect on the average value, will in particular depend on the numerical ratio or the proportional size of the categories.'[47] As a rule this will be the average category. In this case that part of the total amount of commodities produced under the poorer conditions will have to be sold off below their individual value, whereas the commodities produced under the above average can secure an extra amount of profit. However, it may be the case that either the class producing under the better conditions, or that under the worse conditions will predominate. In the first instance the commodities produced under the better conditions will determine the market value; in the second instance, those produced under the poorer conditions.

The determination of market value appears in this way if we look exclusively at the mass of commodities thrown on to the market, ignoring the possibility of an imbalance between supply and demand. Hence, 'provided that the demand is large enough . . . to absorb the whole mass of the commodities at the values which have been fixed [by competition among the buyers] . . . the commodity will still be sold at its market value, no matter which of the three above-mentioned cases regulates that market value. The mass of commodities not only satisfies a need but satisfies it to its full social extent.'[75] However, we know that in the capitalist mode of production, 'there exists an accidental rather than a necessary connection between the total amount of social labour applied to a social article . . . on the one hand, and the extent of the demands made by the society for the satisfaction of the need gratified by the article in question, on the other. Every individual article, or every definite quantity of a commodity may, indeed, contain no more than the social labour required for its production, and from this point of view the market value of this entire commodity represents only necessary labour, but if this commodity has been produced in excess of the existing social needs, then so much of the social labour-time is squandered and the mass of the commodity comes to represent a much smaller quantity of

[74] *Theories* II, p.204.
[75] *Capital* III, p.185.

social labour in the market than is actually incorporated in it ... the reverse applies if the quantity of social labour employed in the production of a certain kind of commodity is too small to meet the social need for that commodity.'[76]

In both cases the 'determination of market value which we [previously] outlined abstractly' is modified, in the sense that 'if the supply is too small, the market value is always regulated by the commodities produced under the least favourable circumstances and if the supply is too large, always by the commodities produced under the most favourable conditions; that therefore it is one of the extremes which determines the market value, in spite of the fact that if we proceed only from the relation between the amounts of the commodity produced under different conditions, a different result should obtain.'[77]

So it can be seen that which of the categories (of producers) determines market value depends not only on their proportional strength, but also, in a certain sense, on the relation of supply and demand. But doesn't this completely invalidate Marx's theory of value? Not at all. This would only be true if each time demand outweighed supply, or vice versa, this led to a proportional increase or fall in market value itself. However, in this case the market value would be identical with market price, or it would – as Marx expressed it – 'have to stand higher than itself'.[78] For, according to Marx's conception, market value can only move within the limits set by the conditions of production (and consequently by the individual value) of one of the three categories.

We read in the section of the *Theories* devoted to ground-rent that: 'A difference between market value and individual value arises in general not because products are sold absolutely above their value, but only because the value of the individual product may be different from the value of the product of a whole sphere ... The difference between the market value and the individual value of a product can therefore only be due to the fact that the definite quantities of labour with which different parts of the total product are manufactured have different degrees of productivity. It can never be due to the value being determined irrespective of the quantity of labour altogether employed in this sphere.'[79]

Thus, if as a consequence of the market situation, the mass of

[76] ibid. p.187.
[77] ibid. p.185.
[78] *Theories* II, p.271.
[79] ibid. pp.270-71.

commodities is sold above the individual value of the commodities produced under the worst conditions, or alternatively below the individual value of those produced under the best conditions, the market price would indeed diverge from the market value.[80] This regulation of the occasional fluctuations of market price is, of course, the main function allotted to the relation of supply and demand in the system of bourgeois economics.

It is evident that our interpretation of Marx's theory of market value diverges very considerably from that normally presented in marxist literature. The following passage by Grigorovici could serve as an example. ' "If the demand is large enough to absorb commodities at their market value", says Marx, "this commodity will be sold at its market value, no matter which of the three aforementioned cases regulates it. This mass of commodities does not merely satisfy a need, but satisfies it to its full social extent. Should their quantity be smaller or greater, however, than the demand for them, the market price will diverge from the market value", i.e. the market price will exceed or fall below the market value; market price and market value will not coincide.' The author concludes, 'Thus, what affects the relation of supply and demand, or in other words the demand-moment is not a change in market value, but simply a divergence of market price from the market value of the commodity, although in both the first and second cases it seems as if the market value itself has changed, as a result of the change in the relation of supply and demand; because in the first case the commodity produced under the poorer conditions seems to regulate market value, and in the second the commodity produced under the better.'[81]

This then is Grigorovici's view. However, what does the passage from Volume III, which we have already cited in part, actually say on this point?

'Should demand for this mass now also remain the same, this commodity will be sold at its market value, no matter which of the three aforementioned cases regulates this market value . . . Should their quantity be smaller or greater, however, than the demand for them, there will be divergencies between the market price and the market value. And the first divergence is that if the supply is too small, the market value is always regulated by the commodities produced under the least favourable circumstances, and, if the supply

[80] Cf. *ibid.* p.268. 'This market value itself can never be greater than the value of the product of the least fertile class' (the coal-mine). 'If it were higher this would only show that the market price stood above the market value. But the market value must represent real value.'
[81] Grigorovici, *op. cit.* p.37.

is too large, always by the commodities produced under the most favourable conditions; that therefore it is one of the extremes which determines the market value, in spite of the fact that if we proceed only from the relation between the amounts of the commodity produced under different conditions, a different result should obtain.'[82]

The formulation is not at all clear, and consequently can give rise to uncertainties. However, Marx expresses himself more precisely on p.179 of Volume III. He writes: 'At a certain price, a commodity occupies just so much place on the market. This place remains the same in case of a price change only if the higher price is accompanied by a drop in the supply of the commodity, and a lower price by an increase of supply. And if the demand is so great that it does not contract when the price is regulated by the value of commodities produced under the least favourable conditions, *then these determine* the *market value*. This is only possible if demand is greater than usual, or if supply drops below the usual level. Finally, if the mass of the commodities produced exceeds the quantity disposed of at average market values, *the commodities produced under the most favourable conditions regulate the market value.*'

We in no way want to deny that there are passages in Marx which seem to prove the opposite of what has just been said.[83] What is important, however, is not to 'explain' these unclarities away on the basis of a falsely conceived marxist orthodoxy, but rather to understand and interpret the true meaning of Marx's explanations in terms of their 'inner logic'. And we consider that our interpretation of the passages on market value corresponds better with Marx's theory as a whole, in particular with his theory of ground-rent, than the interpretations which are to be found in Grigorovici and others.

However, this is not the place to go into this special problem in detail. Our point was only to show that Marx, in strictly logical fashion, deals with the problem of 'socially necessary labour-time' on two different levels, and that his aim in doing this was to place the moment of social demand, i.e. use-value, in its true light.

In another passage in Volume III we read: 'It continues to be a necessary requirement that the commodity represent use-value. But if the use-value of individual commodities depends on whether they themselves satisfy a particular need, then the use-value of the mass of the social product depends on whether it satisfies the quantitatively determined social need for each particular kind of product

---

[82] *Capital* III, p.185.
[83] It should not be forgotten, as Engels remarked, that the manuscript for Volume III only represents a 'first extremely incomplete draft'.

in an adequate manner, and whether the labour is therefore proportionately distributed among the different spheres in keeping with these social needs, which are quantitatively circumscribed. . . . The social need, that is the use-value on a social scale, appears here as a determining factor for the amount of total social labour-time which is expended in various specific spheres of production. But it is merely the same law which is already applied in the case of single commodities, namely that the use-value of a commodity is the basis of its exchange-value and thus of its value . . . This quantitative limit to the quota of social labour-time available for the various spheres of production is but a more developed expression of the law of value in general, although the necessary labour-time assumes a different meaning here. Only just so much of it is necessary for the satisfaction of social needs. It is use-value which brings about this limitation.'[84]

And so we can see again how use-value operates as such in the relations of the bourgeois economy, which is based on exchange-value, and consequently how it becomes an economic category itself.

With this last example, we come to the end of our analysis. Future research into Marx will decide whether the extracts which we have cited from the *Rough Draft* prove us correct, and actually lead to a partial revision of previous interpretations of Marx's economic theory, as we believe they must. We can, however, allow ourselves one final remark; that it was clearly Marx's own unique method of analysis which enabled him to elaborate his opposition to Ricardo in such an original and logical fashion. Engels was surely right when he perceived in Marx's treatment of use-value, and its role in political economy, a classic example of the use of the 'German dialectical method'.[85]

[84] *Capital* III, pp.635-36. Cf. *Theories* I, p.204.
[85] See his review of Marx's *Contribution* (1859) in *MEW* Vol.13, p.476.

PART TWO
The First Formulation of Marx's Theory of Money

Preliminary Note

(The relation of the 'Rough Draft' to the 'Contribution' and to Part I of Volume I of 'Capital')

As we have already remarked, Marx himself only managed to publish a relatively small part of the 1857-58 manuscript; in fact, only the Chapter on Money (pp.115-239 of the *Grundrisse*), which was published, after a fundamental re-working, in the *Contribution*. The remainder was left on his writing-desk and was used only sporadically in *Capital* and in the *Theories*.[1]

From the point of view of the subject matter, therefore, the first part of the *Rough Draft* coincides both with the text of the *Contribution*, and with Part I of Volume I of *Capital*. It should therefore be regarded as the first draft of these texts. However, this is not to be taken literally, since, firstly, there is no presentation of the theory of value in the *Rough Draft* (except for a small fragment on pages

[1] We shall refer to examples of this at appropriate points in the present work.

[2] It is of course present in an implicit sense, as the whole of the presentation of the *Rough Draft* is based on Marx's theory of value. One can see how right Marx was to write to Kugelmann on 11 July 1868 in the following terms: 'The unfortunate fellow' (Marx means the reviewer of *Capital* Volume I in *Centralblatt*) 'does not see that even if there were no chapter on "value" at all in my book, the analysis of the real relations which I give would contain the proof and demonstration of the real value relation.' (*Selected Correspondence*, p.196. The reference is to the *Literarisches Centralblatt für Deutschland*, Leipzig where a review of *Capital* was published in July 1 1868.)

881-882);[2] and secondly, the chapter on money in the *Rough Draft* diverges so clearly from later presentations of the theory of money that Marx considered it necessary to rewrite it completely, and take the reworked text as the basis for his 1859 work.[3] As a result, we possess four versions of Marx's chapter on money. These differ in many details, and a comparison between them can therefore contribute vitally to the understanding of this fundamental – but also difficult – section of his work.

[3] See the fragment of the original text (the *'Urtext'*) for the *Contribution* which in our opinion should also include pp.666-69, 675-701, 745-62, as well as pp.871-901 (German edition) of the *Grundrisse*. This excludes the beginning of the Chapter on Money.

4.
Critique of the Labour-Money Theory

In contrast to the later versions of Marx's theory of money, the theory as it appears in the *Rough Draft* does not confront us in its finished form; we are able to observe it rather in the process of its formation, as Marx, initially, develops his own conception by means of a critique of the Proudhonist Darimon, and Proudhon's own version of the so-called labour-money theory. As a result this critique requires forty pages in the *Rough Draft*, whereas in his 1859 work[1] Marx confined himself to a short resumé, and in *Capital*[2] to a few footnotes. From a formal standpoint this separation of the actual theory of money from the critique of the labour-money utopia was completely justified; since this utopia still haunts us even today in the form of the doctrine of free credit, the pages from the *Rough Draft*, which were later eliminated, are particularly interesting for us.

The Proudhonists declared that the principal evil of our social organisation sprang from the 'privilege' of money, from the hegemony which the precious metals enjoyed in the circulation of commodities and economic life as a whole. Here lay the real source of the unequal exchange between capital and labour, of usury, and of general economic crises. Consequently, the main task was to break the mastery usurped by gold and silver, bring them down to the level of the rabble, the ordinary commodities, and thus restore the 'natural' equality and proportionality of exchange.

Of course the Proudhonists were far from suggesting a return to direct barter. They knew that present-day commodity production requires a general means of exchange. However, couldn't money be robbed of its privileges, they asked, or rather, couldn't all commodities be made directly exchangeable, that is, be made into money?

The dethroning of money could be conceived of in many ways;

---

[1] See *Contribution*, pp.85-86.
[2] Cf. *Capital* I, note 26 p.161 (note 1 p.68); note 4 p.181 (note 1 p.87); note 1 pp.188-89 (note 1 pp.94-95).

first, gold and silver could be retained as money, but in such a way that they directly represent the labour-time embodied in them. 'Suppose for example that the sovereign were not only called a sovereign, which is a mere honorific for the xth fraction of an ounce of gold (accounting name), in the same way that a metre is the name for a certain length, but were called say x hours of labour-time. 1/x ounce of gold is in fact nothing more than 1/x hours of labour-time, materialised, objectified. But gold is labour-time accumulated in the past, labour-time defined. Its title would make a given quantity of labour as such into its standard. The pound of gold would have to be convertible into x hours of labour-time, would have to be able to purchase it at any given moment; as soon as it could buy a greater or lesser amount it would be appreciated or depreciated; in the latter case its convertibility would have ceased. What determines value is not the amount of labour-time incorporated in products, but rather the amount of labour-time necessary at a given moment. Take the pound of gold itself; let it be the product of 20 hours' labour-time. Suppose that for some reason it later requires only 10 hours to produce a pound of gold. The pound of gold whose title advises it that it equals 20 hours' labour time would now merely equal 10 hours' labour-time, since 20 hours' labour-time are equal to 2 pounds of gold. Ten hours of labour are in practice exchanged for 1 pound of gold; hence 1 pound of gold cannot any longer be exchanged for 20 hours' labour-time . Gold money with the plebeian title "x hours of labour" would be exposed to greater fluctuations than any other sort of money and particularly more than the present gold money, because gold cannot rise or fall in relation to gold (it is equal to itself), while the labour-time accumulated in a given quantity of gold, in contrast, must constantly rise or fall in relation to present living labour-time. In order to maintain its convertibility, the productivity of labour-time would have to be kept stationary. Moreover, in view of the general economic law that the costs of production constantly decline, that living labour constantly becomes more productive, hence that the labour-time objectified in products constantly depreciates, the inevitable fate of this golden labour-money would be constant depreciation.'[3]

However, Marx continues, in order to control this evil, paper labour-money could be introduced instead of gold ('as Weitling suggested, and before him the English, and after him the French'). 'The labour-time incorporated in the paper itself would then have as little relevance as the paper value of banknotes . . . If the hour

[3] *Grundrisse*, pp.134-35.

of labour becomes more productive then the chit of paper which represents it would rise in purchasing power and vice versa – exactly as a £5 note at present buys more or less depending on whether the relative value of gold in comparison to other commodities rises or falls. According to the same law which would subject golden labour-money to a constant depreciation, paper labour-money would enjoy constant appreciation!' But that does not matter, exclaim the Proudhonists, 'that is exactly what we are after; the worker would reap the joys of the rising productivity of his labour, instead of creating proportionately more alien wealth and devaluing himself as at present ... Unfortunately there arise some small scruples. First of all; if we once presuppose money, even if it is only time-chits, then we must also presuppose the accumulation of this money, as well as contracts, obligations, fixed burdens etc. which are entered into in the form of this money. The accumulated chits would constantly appreciate together with the newly issued ones, and thus on the one hand the rising productivity of labour would go to the benefit of non-workers, and on the other hand the previously contracted burdens would keep step with the rising yield of labour.'[4] In this way the exploitation of living labour through accumulated labour, interest, crises – in short all the evils which the Proudhonists wanted to overcome by means of their reform of money, would arise again in new forms!

Thus, the substitute-money of the Proudhonists – considered as a social panacea – would come to grief on the law of the increasing productivity of labour.[5] It is of course true that the appreciation of the time-chits 'would be quite irrelevant, if the world could be re-started from the beginning every instant', and therefore, if the obligations which had been entered into never survived the changing value of the labour-money. But since this isn't the case, the labour-money is purely utopian. What its advocates want is to eliminate the overvaluation of money which occurs in crises,[6] and secure for each small

---

[4] ibid. pp.135-36.
[5] Cf. Marx's polemic against the labour-money proposal of the English utopian socialist Bray, in *Poverty of Philosophy*, pp.69-74.
[6] We read in the *Rough Draft* that the Proudhonists in fact 'see only one aspect which surfaces during crises: the appreciation of gold and silver in relation to nearly all other commodities; they do not see the other side, the *depreciation* of gold and silver or of *money* in relation to all other commodities (labour perhaps, not always, excluded) in periods of so-called *prosperity*, periods of a temporary general rise of prices. Since this depreciation of metallic money ... always precedes its appreciation, they ought to have formulated the problem the other way around: how to prevent the periodic depreciation

commodity producer and commodity seller a 'just' price for his commodity. It should be possible not only to convert money into commodities at any time, but also commodities into money – which is naturally only possible if prices coincide exactly with values, that is, with the amounts of labour embodied in the commodities. We come here to the second fundamental error of the advocates of the labour-money theory, or – as Marx named them – the 'time-chitters'; namely, that they lump together value and price, and fail to understand the necessary antagonism of these two forms.

In fact, 'the value (the real exchange-value) of all commodities . . . is determined by their cost of production, in other words by the labour-time required to produce them. Their *price* is this exchange-value of theirs, expressed in money.' So, in the first instance, the distinction between value and price appears purely nominal. 'But such is by no means the case. The value of commodities as determined by labour-time is only their average value. This average appears as an external abstraction if it is calculated out as the average figure of an epoch e.g. 1 lb of coffee equals 1s. if the real average price of coffee is taken over 25 years; but it is very real if it is at the same time recognised as the driving force and the moving principle of the oscillations which commodity prices run through in a given epoch[7] . . . The market value[8] is always different, is always below or above this average value of a commodity. Market value equates itself with real value by means of its constant oscillations, never by means of an equation with real value as if the latter were a third party, but rather by means of a constant non-equation of it-

---

of money (in their language, to abolish the privileges of commodities in relation to money). In this latter formulation the problem would have reduced itself to: how to overcome the rise and fall of prices. The way to do this: abolish prices. And how? By doing away with exchange-value. But this problem arises: exchange corresponds to the bourgeois organisation of society. Hence one last problem: to revolutionise bourgeois society economically. It would then have been self-evident from the outset that the evil of bourgeois society is not to be remedied by "transforming" the banks or by founding a rational "money system".' (*Grundrisse*, p.134.)

[7] Marx adds: 'This reality is not merely of theoretical importance; it forms the basis of mercantile speculation, whose calculus of probabilities depends both on the median price averages which figure as the centre of oscillation, and on the average peaks and troughs of oscillation above or below this centre.' (*Grundrisse*, p.137.)

[8] The concept of market value here means something different from its meaning in *Capital* III – here it is identical with price. (See pp.91-95 above.)

self⁹ . . . Price therefore is distinguished from value not only as the nominal from the real; not only by way of the denomination in gold and silver, but because the latter appears as the law of the motions which the former runs through. But the two are constantly different and never balance out, or balance only coincidentally and exceptionally. The price of a commodity constantly stands above or below the value of a commodity, and the value of the commodity itself exists only in this up-and-down movement of commodity prices. Supply and demand constantly determine the prices of commodities; never balance, or only coincidentally; but the cost of production, for its part, determines the oscillations of supply and demand. . . . On the assumption that the production costs of a commodity and the production costs of gold and silver remain constant, the rise or fall of its market price means nothing more than that a commodity equals x labour-time, constantly commands more or less than x labour-time on the market, that it stands above or beneath its average value as determined by labour-time.' And it is precisely for this reason that the time-chit representing average labour-time would 'never correspond to or be convertible into actual labour-time.'[10]

Thus, whereas the previous objection to the labour-money theory proceeded from the fact that the law of rising productivity has to lead to the continual depreciation of commodities against time-chits, and as a consequence must result in the inconvertibility of the time-chits, this same inconvertibility, about which Marx is now talking, 'is nothing more than another expression for the inconvertibility between real value and market value, between exchange-value and price. In contrast to all other commodities, the time-chit would represent an ideal labour-time which would be exchanged sometimes against more and sometimes against less of the actual variety, and which would achieve a separate existence of its own in the time-chit, an existence corresponding to this non-equivalence. The general equivalent, medium of circulation and measure of commodities would again confront the commodities in an individual[11] form, following its own laws, alienated,[12] i.e. equipped with all the properties of

---

[9] Marx remarks here 'as Hegel would say, not by way of abstract identity, but by constant negation of the negation, i.e. of itself as negation of real value'.

[10] *Grundrisse*, pp.137-39.

[11] Cf. *ibid.* p.218. 'With money, general wealth is not only a form, but at the same time the content itself. The concept of wealth, so to speak, is realised, individualised in a particular object.'

[12] In any kind of money, 'the exchange relation establishes itself as a power external to and independent of the producers'. *ibid.* p.146.

money as it exists at present but unable to perform the same services. The medium with which commodities – these objectified quantities of labour-time – are compared would not be a third commodity but would rather be their own measure of value, labour-time itself; as a result the confusion would reach new heights altogether.' For it is precisely 'the difference between price and value, between the commodity measured by labour-time whose product it is, and the product of the labour-time against which it is exchanged ... [which] ... calls for a third commodity to act as a measure in which the real exchange-value of commodities is expressed. Because price is not equal to value ... the value-determining element – labour-time – cannot be the element in which prices are expressed, as labour-time would then have to express itself simultaneously as the determining and the non-determining element, as the equivalent and non-equivalent of itself.' (Marx adds here: 'at the same time it becomes clear how and why the value relation obtains a separate material existence in the form of money',[13] in other words, why the circulation of commodities must lead on to the development of money.) The time-chitters naturally imagine 'that by annulling the nominal difference between real value and market value, between exchange-value and price – that is, by expressing value in units of labour-time itself instead of in a given objectification of labour time, say gold and silver – that in doing so they also remove the real difference and contradiction between price and value. Given this illusory assumption it is self-evident that the mere introduction of the time-chit does away with all crises, all faults of bourgeois production. The money price of commodities = their real value; demand = supply; production = consumption; money is simultaneously abolished and preserved; the labour-time of which the commodity is the product, which is materialised in the commodity, would need only to be measured in order to create a corresponding mirror-image in the form of a value-symbol, money, time-chits. In this way every commodity would be directly transformed into money; and gold and silver, for their part, would be demoted to the rank of all other commodities.'[14]

---

[13] ibid. p.140.
[14] ibid. p.138. Cf. ibid. p.126, 'This is the last analysis to which Darimon reduces the antagonism. His final judgement is; abolish the privilege of gold and silver, degrade them to the rank of other commodities. Then you no longer have the specific evils of gold and silver, or of notes convertible into gold and silver. You abolish all evils. Or better elevate all commodities to the monopoly position now held by gold and silver. Let the Pope remain, but make everybody Pope.'

Critique of the labour-money theory · 105

We can now see how much of the 'Degradation of Money and the Exaltation of the Commodity' propagated by Proudhon and others, was based on an 'elementary misunderstanding of the inevitable correlation existing between commodity and money'.[15] They failed to understand that any circulation of commodities is bound to lead to the development of money, and therefore that it is impossible 'to abolish money itself as long as exchange-value remains the social form of products'.[16] Perhaps it is possible, however, to overcome the drawbacks of labour-money, which have already been described, by means of the establishment of a 'central exchange bank', so that an element of social planning steps into the place of the anarchic forces of the market?

Indeed, Marx answers: 'If the preconditions under which the price of commodities = their exchange-value are fulfilled, and if we assume the following : balance of supply and demand; balance of production and consumption; and, what this amounts to in the last instance, proportionate production . . . then the money question becomes entirely secondary, in particular the question whether the tickets should be blue or green, paper or tin, or whatever other form social accounting should take. In that case it is totally meaningless to keep up the pretence that an investigation is being made of the real relations of money.'[17]

Let us then imagine a bank which issues time-chits, which at the same time buys – at their cost of production – the commodities of individual producers. The bank would then be the 'general buyer, the buyer not only of this or that commodity but of all commodities', because only in this way could labour-money gain general acceptance. 'But if it is the general buyer then it also has to be the general seller; not only the dock where all the wares are deposited, not only the general warehouse, but also the owner of the commodities, in the same sense as every merchant.' Accordingly, 'a second attribute of

---

[15] *Contribution*, p.86.
[16] *Grundrisse*, p.144.
[17] *ibid*. p.153. Cf. *Capital* I, p.188 (94) note 1 'On this point I will only say further that Owen's "labour-money", for instance, is no more "money" than a theatre ticket is. Owen presupposes directly socialised labour, a form of production diametrically opposed to the production of commodities. The certificate of labour is merely evidence of the part taken by the individual in the common labour, and of his claim to a certain portion of the common product which has been set aside for consumption. But Owen never made the mistake of presupposing the production of commodities, while, at the same time, by juggling with money, trying to circumvent the necessary conditions of that form of production.'

the bank would be necessary; it would need the power to establish the exchange-value of all commodities i.e. the labour-time materialised in them, in an authentic manner'[18] ('which incidentally isn't as simple as testing the fineness and weight of gold and silver,' adds Marx). However, 'its functions could not end here. It would have to determine the labour-time in which commodities could be produced, with the average means of production available in a given industry ... but even that would not be sufficient. It would not only have to determine the time in which a certain quantity of goods had to be produced, and place the producers in conditions which made their labour equally productive (i.e. it would have to balance and arrange the distribution of the instruments of labour), but it would also have to determine the amounts of labour-time to be employed in the different branches of production. (The latter would be necessary because in order to realise exchange-value and make the bank's currency really convertible, social production in general would have to be stabilised and arranged so that the needs of the partners in exchange were always satisfied.)' However, 'this is not all. The biggest exchange process is not that between commodities, but between commodities and labour ... the workers would not be selling their labour to the bank' but rather, according to the dogma of the Proudhonists, 'they would receive the exchange-value for the entire product of their labour etc. Viewed precisely then, the bank would not only be the general buyer and seller, but also the general producer. In fact, it would be either a despotic ruler of production and a manager of distribution, or indeed nothing more than a board which keeps the books and accounts for a society producing in common',[19] (that is, a socialist planning agency). But in that case the Proudhonist ideal of a 'just exchange of commodities' would be turned into its opposite.

Marx concludes, 'Here we have reached the fundamental question ... Can the existing relations of production and the relations of distribution which correspond to them be revolutionised by a change in the instrument of circulation, in the organisation of circulation? Further question : Can such a transformation of circulation be undertaken without touching the existing relations of production and the social relations which rest on them? If every such transformation of circulation presupposes changes in the other conditions of

---

[18] Rodbertus also presupposes, for his 'constituted value' and his labour-money, 'a correct calculation, balancing and fixing of the quantities of labour contained in the products to be exchanged'. C.Rodbertus-Jagetzow, *Schriften*, Vol.II, p.65.
[19] *Grundrisse*, pp.154-56.

production and social upheavals, there would naturally follow from this the collapse of the doctrine which proposes tricks of circulation as a way of, on the one hand, avoiding the violent character of these social changes and, on the other, of making these changes appear not to be a presupposition but a gradual result of the transformations in circulation.'[20] 'It must by now have become entirely clear that this is a piece of foolishness as long as exchange-value is retained as the basis, and that, moreover, the illusion that metallic money allegedly falsifies exchange arises out of a total ignorance of its nature. It is equally clear on the other hand that to the degree to which opposition against the ruling relations of production grows, and these latter themselves push ever more forcibly to cast off their old skin—to that degree polemics are directed against metallic money or money in general, as the most striking, most contradictory and hardest phenomenon which is presented by the system in a palpable form. One or another kind of artful tinkering with money is then supposed to overcome the contradictions of which money is merely the perceptible appearance. Equally clear that some revolutionary operations can be performed with money, insofar as an attack on it seems to leave everything else as it was, and only to rectify it.[21] Then one strikes a blow at the sack, intending the donkey. However as long as the donkey does not feel the blow on the sack one hits in fact only the sack and not the donkey. As soon as he feels it one strikes the donkey and not the sack. As long as these operations are directed against money as such, they are merely an attack on consequences whose causes remain unaffected; i.e. disturbance of the productive process, whose solid basis then also has the power, by means of a more or less violent reaction ... to dominate these.'[22]

So much, then, on Marx's critique of the labour-money utopia.[23]

---

[20] *ibid.* p.122.
[21] Cf. a similar judgement by Marx on Proudhon's theory of interest. He wrote to Schweitzer on 24 January 1865, saying: 'That under certain economic and political conditions the credit system can be used to accelerate the emancipation of the working class, just as, for instance, at the beginning of the nineteenth century in England, it facilitated the transfer of wealth from one class to another, is unquestionable and quite self-evident. But to regard interest-bearing capital as the main form of capital and to try to make a particular form of the credit system, comprising the alleged abolition of interest, the basis for a transformation of society, is an out-and-out petty-bourgeois fantasy.' (*Selected Correspondence*, p.147.)
[22] *Grundrisse*, p.240.
[23] We have left out of account Marx's critique of Proudhon's theory of crises, which he also makes in this context.

It can be seen that the objections he makes to it are already contained, for the most part, in his own theory of money. In fact they form a very important element of it – namely his theory of the development of money. We should therefore turn to the study of this theme as it is set out in detail in Marx's manuscript.

5.
'Transition from Value to Money'*

1. The necessity of the formation of money

'The difficulty', wrote Marx in *Capital*, 'lies not in comprehending that money is a commodity, but in discovering how, why and by what means a commodity becomes money.'[1] The problem is, therefore, that of unearthing the hidden seed of the development of money in the most simple, elementary exchange relation of the commodity.

Those readers who are acquainted with Marx's *Capital* will know that it is precisely this problem which constitutes the main theme of the analysis of the 'simple', total' and 'general' value-form in Volume I of the work. However, the answer to this question can already be found, in essence, in the *Rough Draft*.[2]

Let us recall the stumbling-blocks which, in Marx's view, stand in the way of any form of labour-money. First, the law of the rising productivity of labour, which would lead to a constant depreciation of all commodities in relation to the 'time-chits'. Second, the necessary incongruence 'of real value and market value' of 'value and price'; i.e. the fact that the actual labour-time objectified in the individual commodity cannot directly coincide with general or average labour-time, which is inherent in the concept of value. At this point we have to pick up the thread of Marx's argument once again.

We know that the products of labour are only values insofar as they count as embodiments of the same social substance, general human labour. However, labour 'does not exist in the form of a general object of exchange which is independent of and separate from the particular natural characteristics of commodities'.[3]

---

* See Marx's *Index zu den 7 Heften* in *Grundrisse*, German edn. p.855.
[1] *Capital* I, p.186 (92).
[2] Marx already pointed out that 'money is the first real form of exchange of value as value', and consequently that 'exchange had to individualise exchange-value through the creation of a particular means of exchange' in his first economic writings of 1844. (*MEGA* III, p.532), and also in the *Poverty of Philosophy*, p.81. However this line of reasoning was not developed in detail and firmly established until the *Rough Draft*.
[3] *Grundrisse*, p.168.

110 · *The Making of Marx's 'Capital'*

It is the labour of individuals, exhibiting different degrees of intensity and skill, definite concrete labour, 'which assimilates particular natural materials to particular human requirements'.[4] As such it is objectified 'in a definite particular commodity, with particular characteristics, and particular relations to needs'; whereas as general human labour, as value, it should be embodied 'in a commodity which expresses no more than its quota or quantity, which is indifferent to its own natural properties, and which can therefore be metamorphosed into – i.e. exchanged for – every other commodity which objectifies the same labour-time'.[5] In other words: 'The commodity, as it comes into being, is only objectified individual labour-time of a specific kind, and not *universal* labour-time. The commodity is thus *not* immediately exchange-value, but has still to *become* exchange-value.' However, 'how is it possible to present a particular commodity directly as *objectified universal* labour-time, or – which amounts to the same thing – how can the individual labour-time objectified in a particular commodity directly assume a universal character?'[6]

And what applies to living labour also applies to objectified labour, i.e. to the commodity itself. 'Two commodities, e.g. a yard of cotton and a measure of oil, are different by nature, have different properties, are measured by different measures, are incommensurable.' On the other hand, as values 'all commodities are qualitatively equal and differ only quantitatively, hence can be measured against each other and substituted for one another in certain quantitative relations. Value is their social relation,[7] their economic quality.' It 'presupposes social labour as the substance of all products, disregarding their natural qualities . . . 'A book which possesses a certain

[4] *Capital* I, p.133 (42).
[5] *Grundrisse*, p.168.
[6] *Contribution*, pp.43, 46.
[7] It does not of course follow from the fact that the 'objective character' of commodities 'as values is purely social', *Capital* I, p.138 (4) that they have no material existence independently of the knowledge or volition of men. Thus, in *Theories* III, p.163, Marx says, 'These same circumstances, independent of the mind, but influencing it, which compel the producers to sell their products as commodities . . . provide their products with an exchange-value which (also in their mind) is independent of their use-value. Their "mind", their consciousness, may be completely ignorant of, unaware of the existence of what in fact determines the value of their products or their products as values. They are placed in relationships which determine their thinking but they may not know it. Anyone can use money as money without necessarily understanding what money is. Economic categories are reflected in the mind in a very distorted fashion.'

value and a loaf of bread possessing the same value are exchanged for one another, are the same value but in a different material.' Hence, as value, 'the commodity is an equivalent . . . the general measure, as well as the general representative, the general medium of exchange of all other commodities. As value it is money.'

However, precisely 'because commodities as values are different from one another only quantitatively . . . the natural distinctness of commodities must come into contradiction with their economic equivalence', and so their value has to achieve 'an existence which is qualitatively distinguishable' from them. For, 'as a value every commodity is divisible; in its natural existence this is not the case. As a value it remains the same no matter how many metamorphoses and forms of existence it goes through; in reality, commodities are exchanged only because they are not the same and correspond to different systems of needs. As a value the commodity is general; as a real commodity it is particular. As a value it is always exchangeable; in real exchange it is exchangeable only if it fulfils particular conditions. As a value, the measure of its exchangeability is determined by itself; exchange-value expresses precisely the relation in which it replaces other commodities; in real exchange it is exchangeable only in quantities which are linked with its natural properties and which correspond to the needs of the participants in exchange. (In short, all properties which may be cited as the special qualities of money are properties of the commodity as exchange-value;[8] of the product as value as distinct from the value as product.)'[9]

Hence, what originally appeared as a contradiction between general and individual labour-time, now confronts us as a con-

---

[8] Marx often used the expression 'exchange-value' in the *Grundrisse* (and also, as we have just seen, in the *Theories*), where later he would have simply spoken of 'value'. What he wrote in *Capital* I therefore also applies here: 'When, at the beginning of this chapter, we said in the customary manner that a commodity is both a use-value and an exchange-value, this was, strictly speaking, wrong. A commodity is a use-value or object of utility, and a "value". It appears as the twofold thing it really is as soon as its value possesses its own particular form of manifestation, which is distinct from its natural form. This form of manifestation is exchange-value and the commodity never has this form when looked at in isolation, but only when it is in a value relation or an exchange relation with another commodity of a different kind. Once we know this, our manner of speaking does no harm; it serves rather as an abbreviation.' (*Capital* I, p.152 (60).)

[9] *Grundrisse*, pp.141-42. Cf. Marx's letter to Engels, 2 April 1858. 'From the contradiction between the general character of value and its material existence in a particular commodity etc. – these general characteristics are the same that later appear in money – arises the category of money.' (*Selected Correspondence*, p.98.)

E

tradiction between the general character of the commodity as value, and its particular character as use-value. And Marx goes on to say that this open contradiction 'can only be solved through itself becoming *objectified*'; by the commodity 'doubling itself' in the course of real exchange, i.e. by obtaining 'in *money*, a form of social existence separated from its natural existence'.[10]

Note well, however, this only happens in real exchange. For, as long as all that is required is the determination of value, the only problem is to discover the general value-substance of commodities, the 'immanent measure of value', which forms the basis of the exchange relation.[11] When I exchange two commodities with each other 'I equate each of the commodities with a third i.e. not with themselves. This third which differs from them both . . . since it expresses a relation' is their value; the commodity, 'has first to be converted into labour-time, as something qualitatively different from it' before it can be compared at all with other commodities.

'On paper, in the head, this metamorphosis proceeds by means of mere abstraction; but in the real process of exchange a real *mediation*[12] is required . . . this abstraction has in its turn to be objectified.'[13] However, this can only occur in the relation of commodity to commodity, since the owners of commodities do not stand in some form of communal association as producers, but can only relate to one another through the medium of their products. Consequently the only thing which can become the expression of the value of a commodity is another commodity (similarly the weight of a sugar-loaf can only be expressed through the weight of another solid, for example, iron[14]). Hence, it is not sufficient for the commodity to 'possess a double existence [merely] in the head'. This 'doubling in the idea proceeds (and must proceed) to the point where the commodity appears as double in real exchange; as a natural product on one side, as exchange-value on the other. That is, the commodity's

---

[10] *Grundrisse*, p.145.
[11] The 'immanent measure of value' should in no way be confused with the 'invariable measure of value', which some of the Classical economists looked for in vain. This is because the commodity which serves as an external measure of value must, as Marx showed, be able to vary its value since, 'only as a materialisation of labour-time can it become the equivalent of other commodities, but as a result of changes in the productivity of concrete labour the same amount of labour-time is embodied in unequal volumes of the same type of use-value'. *Contribution*, p.67; Cf. *Theories* III, pp.133-34.
[12] On the category of 'mediation', borrowed from Hegel, see Lukacs, *History and Class Consciousness*, pp.162-64.
[13] *Grundrisse*, pp.142, 143-44.
[14] Cf. *Capital* I, pp.148-49, (56-57).

'Transition from value to money' · 113

exchange-value obtains a material existence separate from the commodity', i.e. it achieves independence in the shape of money.[15]
As consistent as this derivation of money may seem, it involved, initially, certain hesitations which are evident in the *Rough Draft*. For Marx, as also for Lassalle, who had learnt from Hegel, it was an obvious step to take to view money as the embodiment of value in the sense of 'the Ideal, the Universal, the One', in contrast to commodities, which in Hegelian terms represented 'the Real, Particularity, the Many'.[16] And, like Lassalle, Marx too was at first inclined, for just this reason, to regard money as a mere sign of value, 'simply the ideal unity or expression of value of all the real products in circulation'.[17] (We may also detect here the influence of Ricardo's theory of money, with its one-sided emphasis on the function of money as a means of circulation, where it does in fact appear as a mere sign of value.) Hence we can find numerous passages in the *Rough Draft*, especially Notebooks I and II, which treat money in general (and not just paper money), as a mere sign of value or a 'symbol'. We can read there for example : 'The product becomes a commodity i.e. a mere moment of exchange. The commodity is transformed into exchange-value. In order to equate it with itself as an exchange-value, it is exchanged for a symbol which represents it as exchange-value as such. As such a symbolised exchange-value, it can then in turn be exchanged in definite proportions for every other commodity.'[18] Of course, even in this part of the text Marx repeatedly emphasises that 'even if only a sign' money 'must consist of a particular commodity', and that consequently paper money can in no way directly express the value of commodities, but must rather function constantly as the representative of gold currency.[19] However the way he expressed himself in Notebook I of the *Rough Draft*,

[15] *Grundrisse*, p.145.
[16] See Marx's letter to Engels, 1 February 1858, where he comments on Lassalle's book on Heraclitus. (*Selected Correspondence*, pp.94-95.) Cf. Hegel's *Philosophy of Right*: 'If we consider the concept of value, we must look upon the thing itself only as a symbol; it counts not as itself but as what it is worth.' (Cited in *Capital* I, p.185 (91).)
[17] Lassalle, *Die Philosophie Herakleitos des Dunklen von Ephesos*, 1858, Vol.I, p.224, cited by Lenin in *Collected Works*, Vol.38, p.325. On the previous page of Lenin's *Philosophical Notebooks* we read: 'In this connection Lassalle writes about value . . . expounding it in the Hegelian manner (as "separated abstract unity") and adding: . . . "that this unity, money, is not something *actual* but something *merely* ideal (Lassalle's italics) is evident from the fact" etc . . .' Lenin notes in the margin: 'Incorrect (Lassalle's idealism)'.
[18] *Grundrisse*, p.145.
[19] *ibid.* p.167ff.

114 · *The Making of Marx's 'Capital'*

saying that money not only 'represents', but also 'symbolises'[20] the value of commodities, stands in glaring contrast to the real meaning of Marx's theory of money, and as a consequence had to be dropped later. This took place in the *Contribution*,[21] and after that we can find no trace of this 'symbol theory' in Marx's work.

So much then on the dialectical derivation of money from value as it exists in the *Rough Draft*. To the reader who is not acquainted with Marx's theory this derivation might appear 'contrived' – an example of an empty 'dialectic of concepts', which endows economic categories with a life of their own, and, in truly Hegelian fashion, lets them originate from and pass over into one another. One interesting incidental remark in the *Rough Draft* illustrates how easily such an impression can arise, and also shows that Marx himself allowed for the possibility of such a misinterpretation. He writes: 'It will be necessary later, before this question is dropped, to correct the idealist manner of its presentation, which makes it seem as if it were merely a matter of conceptual determinations and of the dialectic of these concepts. Above all in the case of the phrase: product (or activity) becomes commodity; commodity, exchange value; exchange-value, money.'[22] In other words: the reader should not imagine that

---

[20] Cf. *ibid.* p.167. 'From the fact that the commodity develops into general exchange-value, it follows that exchange-value becomes a specific commodity: it can do so only because a specific commodity obtains the privilege of representing, symbolising, the exchange-value of all other commodities; i.e. of becoming money.' (The error here is clearly that of equating the concepts 'representing' and 'symbolising'.)

[21] Cf. the following passage where Marx remarks (in a polemic against himself as it were): 'Money is not a symbol, just as the existence of a use-value in the form of a commodity is no symbol. A social relation of production appears as something existing apart from individual human beings, and the distinctive relations into which they enter in the course of production in society appear as the specific properties of a thing – it is this perverted appearance, this prosaically real, and by no means imaginary, mystification that is characteristic of all social forms of labour positing exchange-value. This perverted appearance manifests itself merely in a more striking manner in money than it does in commodities.' (*Contribution*, p.49.) See also the polemical note in *Capital* I, p.200 (105), according to which Lassalle 'erroneously makes money a mere symbol of value', and *ibid.* pp.185-86 (91-92).

[22] *Grundrisse*, p.151. In our opinion the necessity for such a 'correction' prompted Marx to begin his analysis in the *Contribution* with the commodity, and not with value, as he originally intended (i.e. his plan of 2 April 1858). Cf. Marx's marginal note on Kaufmann's *Theorie der Preisschwankungen* published in Kharkov: 'The mistake generally is to proceed from value as the highest category instead of from the concrete, the commodity ... Yes, but not the single man, and not as abstract being ... The error – to proceed from man as a thinker, and not as an actor ...' *Karl Marx Album*, 1953, p.115.

economic categories are anything other than the reflections of real relations, or that the logical derivation of these categories could proceed independently of their historical derivation. On the contrary – the logical method of approach (as Engels wrote in his review of the *Contribution* in 1859), 'is indeed nothing other than the historical method, only stripped of the historical form and of disturbing accidental occurrences. The point where this history begins must also be the starting-point of the train of thought, and its further progress will be simply the reflection, in abstract and theoretically consistent form, of the course of history. Though the reflection is corrected, it is corrected in accordance with laws provided by the actual course of history, since each factor can be examined at the stage of development where it reaches its full maturity, its classical form.'[23] That this was Marx's method from the outset can be seen best of all in the numerous passages in the *Rough Draft*, in the *Contribution* and in *Capital* which provide – parallel to the logical derivation of value and money – a historical derivation of these same concepts, in which Marx confronts the results of his abstract analysis with actual historical development.

Naturally, Marx could not share Adam Smith's naively ahistorical conception which derived exchange relations from a supposedly innate 'propensity to consume'.[24] He rejects the 'unimaginative notion' of an individual producer of bows in a primitive hunting tribe, who makes it his principal task to exchange bows and arrows for cattle and game, and thus lays the foundation stone of the social division of labour.[25] For Marx, the individual producer of commodities is rather the end result of a very long process of historical development. Exchange was certainly 'one of the principal agents of this individualisation', but it presupposes a certain level of the productivity of labour which by no means existed from the outset.

Our starting point should be natural communities, 'as they originally emerged from the animal kingdom – still powerless before the forces of nature, and as yet unconscious of their own; hence as poor as the animals, and hardly more productive' (Engels). The human being produces here 'no more than he immediately requires. The limit of his needs is the limit of production ... in this case no exchange takes place or exchange is reduced to the exchange of his

---

[23] Engels, *MEW* Vol.13, p.475.
[24] Adam Smith, *An Inquiry into the Nature and Causes of the Wealth of Nations* [1776], New York 1937, p.13.
[25] Notebooks on Smith, in *Collected Works*, Vol.3, London: Lawrence & Wishart 1975.

labour for the product of his labour, and this exchange is the latent form, the germ, of real exchange.'[26]

The turning point comes as soon as people are able to produce more than they need for their daily subsistence, as soon as their labour provides a 'surplus-product'. Now an exchange of products can take place, not, in the first instance, within the confines of natural communities themselves, 'but on their margins, on their borders, the few points where they come into contact with other communities'.[27] But this primitive barter is still far removed from real exchange, with money as its medium. In fact it represents – even where exchange encompasses an entire range of products – 'much more the beginning of the transformation of use-values into commodities than the transformation of commodities into money'. In this situation exchange-value has not acquired an independent form, 'but is still directly tied to use-value. This is manifested in two ways. Use-value, not exchange-value, is the purpose of the whole system of production, and use-values accordingly cease to be use-values and become means of exchange or commodities, only when a larger amount of them has been produced than is required for consumption. On the other hand, they become commodities only within the limits set by their immediate use-value, even when this function is polarised so that the commodities to be exchanged by their owners must be use-values for both of them, but each commodity must be a use-value for its non-owner.'[28]

This is therefore the point at which the '*contradiction between use-value and exchange-value* which is contained in the commodity' clearly emerges. 'For example, commodities as use-values are not divisible at will, a property which as exchange-values they should possess. Or it may happen that the commodity belonging to A may be a use-value required by B; whereas B's commodity may not have any use-value for A. Or the commodity owners may need each other's commodities but these cannot be divided and their relative exchange-

[26] See *Collected Works*, Vol.3, p.224. The last sentence should be understood in the sense that in the actual exchange of goods (to the extent that it is an exchange of equivalents), each partner receives as equivalent for his goods only an amount corresponding to the product of his own labour.
[27] *Contribution*, p.50. Inherent in the concept of exchange is that each of the participants purchases, in return for his own product, one in someone else's possession. 'But this relationship of reciprocal isolation and foreignness does not exist for the members of a primitive community of natural origin.' Only later, 'as soon as products become commodities in the external relations of a community do they also, by reaction, become commodities in the internal life of the community'. (*Capital* I, p.182 (87).)
[28] *Contribution*, p.50.

values are different.'²⁹ (Or, we could add, they may not need them at the same time.) In all such instances no exchange will take place, since the natural characteristics of the commodities contradict their general character as value. In order to overcome this difficulty the product, as exchange-value, has to free itself from its natural incommensurability with other products and acquire a 'value-form independent of its own use-value, or of the individual need of the exchanger'.

Marx continues : 'The problem and the means for its solution arise simultaneously. Commercial intercourse, in which the owners of commodities exchange and compare articles with various other articles, never takes place unless different kinds of commodities belonging to different owners are exchanged for, and equated as values with, one single further kind of commodity. This further commodity, by becoming the equivalent of various other commodities, directly acquires, though within narrow limits, the form of a universal or social equivalent. The universal equivalent form comes and goes with the momentary social contacts which call it into existence. It is transiently attached to this or that commodity in alternation. But with the development of exchange it fixes itself firmly and exclusively onto particular kinds of commodity i.e. it crystallises out into the *money-form*.'³⁰

'At the beginning that commodity will serve as money ... which is most frequently exchanged and circulated as an object of consumption ... i.e. which represents within the given social organisation wealth *par excellence* ... Thus salt, hides, cattle,³¹ slaves ... It is the particular usefulness of the commodity, whether as a particular object of consumption (hides) or as a direct instrument of production (slaves), which stamps it as money in these cases. In the case of further development precisely the opposite will occur i.e. that commodity which has the least utility as an object of consumption or instrument of production will best serve the needs of *exchange as*

---

²⁹ *ibid.* p.51.
³⁰ *Capital* I, pp.182-83 (103).
³¹ 'Nomadic peoples are the first to develop the money-form, because all their worldly possessions are in a movable, and therefore directly alienable form; and because their mode of life, by continually bringing them into contact with foreign communities, encourages the exchange of products.' (*ibid.* p.183 (88).)

In his review of L.H.Morgan's famous book *Ancient Society*, written much later, Marx called attention to Morgan's idea that 'the possession of domesticated animals – which are capable of infinite multiplication – gave the first idea of wealth to the human mind'.

such. In the former case, the commodity becomes money because of its particular use-value; in the latter case it acquires its particular use-value from its serviceability as money. The *precious metals* last, they do not alter, they can be divided and then combined together again, they can be transported relatively easily owing to the compression of great exchange-value in little space – for all these reasons they are especially suitable in the latter stage.'[32]

This is enough to illustrate the procedure which Marx employed in the first – and as is recognised, the most abstract – part of his work. It is all here : the derivation of money from direct barter; the succession of the three stages of exchange (which we know from *Capital* as the 'simple', the 'total' and the 'general' form of value); the antithesis of use-value and exchange-value; and finally the doubling of the commodity into commodity and money, which proceeds from this antithesis. 'Control by the facts ... takes place at every step of the analysis', which proceeds simultaneously, both 'deductively', and 'inductively', 'logically' and 'historically'. Lenin (whom we have just quoted) was correct in claiming that Marx's *Capital*, in its *deepest meaning*, is a work which explains and elucidates the history of capitalism (here, the commodity-producing society), by means of an 'analysis of the concepts which *sum up* this history'.[33] From this standpoint surely there could be no other economic work more realistic than *Capital*, despite the occasional apparent abstruseness of its method of presentation.

2. *The quantitative and the qualitative aspects of the problem of value (the magnitude of value and the form of value)*

We have seen how the creation of money proceeds from the 'contradiction between the particular nature of the commodity as a product and its general nature as exchange-value'. In contrast to bourgeois economists, who see in money simply 'a cunningly con-

---

[32] *Grundrisse*, pp.165-66. Marx adds there: 'At the same time, they [the metals] form the natural transition from the first form of money. At somewhat higher levels of production and exchange, the instrument of production takes precedence over products; and the metals (prior to that, stones) are the first and most indispensable instruments of production. Both are still combined in the case of copper, which played such a large role as money in antiquity: here is the particular use-value as an instrument of production together with other attributes which do not flow out of the use-value of the commodity but correspond to its function as use-value.'

[33] Lenin, *Collected Works*, Vol.38, p.320.

ceived expedient' designed to overcome the difficulties of simple barter, Marx derives it from the basic contradiction 'which is contained in the existence of the commodity as the *direct unity of use-value and exchange-value*'. However, what is the real meaning of this contradiction, and why does Marx attribute such significance to it? Was it because (as Bortkiewicz thinks) he had the 'perverse' desire to 'project' every conceivable contradiction and antithesis onto capitalism?[34] To accept this would mean blocking the way, from the outset, to any understanding of Marx's theory of value. This contradiction, far from being a contrived 'metaphysical' construction, represents, in fact, the most general form in which the real conditions of existence and developmental tendencies of the bourgeois social order are condensed. It is, in fact, only another expression for the fact that in a society of atomised private producers the labour of the individual is not directly social (nor can it be), but must prove itself as such by negating itself, by negating its own original character. For, although the universal dependence of producers on one another first becomes a fact in this mode of production, it lacks any form of unified social planning, and is subject to the blind forces of the market.[35] *'The total movement of this disorder is its order.'*[36]

[34] 'In addition we find in Marx the perverse desire to project logical contradictions onto the objects themselves, in the manner of Hegel. The determination of prices, as it takes place in a capitalist economy, contradicts the law of value. And why not? The capitalist economic order is filled and permeated with contradictions of all kinds. It would only seem right to Marx to enter one more contradiction into capitalism's account.' (L.v.Bortkiewicz, 'Value and Price in the Marxian System', *International Economic Papers*, no.2, 1952. Originally published in German in 1907.)

[35] Cf. *Capital* III, p.881. 'Whereas on the basis of capitalist production, the social character of production confronts the mass of direct producers in the form of strictly regulating authority and a social mechanism of the labour process organised as a complete hierarchy ... among the bearers of this authority, the capitalists themselves, who confront one another only as commodity owners, there reigns the most complete anarchy, within which the social framework of production asserts itself only as an overwhelming natural law vis-à-vis the arbitrary will of the individual.'

But what about the modern, powerful monopolies? Or the tendencies towards *étatisme* in the present-day economy? These are factors which Marx could not study, because they did not exist in his time (1864-65). Do they not prove that capitalism itself has overcome its characteristic anarchy of production, or is on the verge of doing so? Those who argue in this way overlook the fact that they prove too much. If capitalism were really able to eliminate free competition and the anarchy of production, it would eliminate itself at the same time. They forget that, 'the repulsion of capitals from one another' is inherent in the concept of capital, and that a 'universal capital, without any

But how, then, are the interconnections within society established in such a mode of production? At first it seems to be simply a quantitative problem. Every society must satisfy the needs of its members. Consequently it is of great importance for every society that the labour-power at its disposal should not, in the long-term, be squandered or incorrectly employed; and further, that all the branches of production receive the required amounts of labour, and that in none of these is labour employed under poorer than average conditions. As a consequence of its anarchic character, a society of independent commodity producers has no means of regulating this in advance. It knows only one form of social connection – the market. The producer in this society only finds out, *post festum*, 'after exchange is completed ... whether his commodity actually satisfies a social need and whether his labour-time has been properly employed'.[37]

Only in this way can the amount of labour to be performed by the society be ascertained, and the work of the individual brought into conformity with the requirements of the economy as a whole. Hilferding considered that Marx's concept of 'abstract', 'general social' labour had to be primarily interpreted from this standpoint, as meaning 'socially necessary labour'. 'Inside commodity production', says Hilferding, 'one objective social moment underlies the exchange relation, and rules the exchange relation; the socially necessary labour which is embodied in the objects to be exchanged.' And 'they become commensurable only as an expression' of socially necessary labour-time of this kind.[38]

From Marx's polemic against Bailey and Ricardo in Part III of *Theories of Surplus-Value*, we can see just how one-sided (and hence inadequate) this interpretation of Marx's concept of value is.

other, independent capitals with which it could exchange would therefore be a non-thing'. (*Grundrisse*, p.421.)
In another section of the *Rough Draft* we read: 'The autonomisation of the world market ... increases with the development of monetary relations ... and vice versa, since the general bond and all-round interdependence in production and consumption increase together with the independence and indifference of the consumers and producers to one another; since this contradiction leads to crises etc., hence together with the development of this alienation, and on the same basis, efforts are made to overcome it.' The real historical significance of these attempts lies, however, elsewhere: 'Although on the given standpoint, alienation is not overcome by these means, nevertheless relations and connections are introduced thereby which include the possibility of suspending the old standpoint' i.e. capitalism. (*ibid.* pp.160-61.)
[36] K.Marx, *Wage-Labour and Capital*, in *Selected Works*, p.78.
[37] R.Hilferding, *Das Finanzkapital*, 1st edition, p.8.
[38] *ibid.* pp.3-4, 6.

'In order that the commodities may be measured according to the quantity of labour embodied in them . . . the different kinds of labour contained in the different commodities must be reduced to uniform simple labour . . . this reduction to simple average labour is not however the only determinant of the quality of this labour to which as a unity the values of the commodities are reduced. That the quantity of labour embodied in a commodity is the quantity socially necessary for its production – the labour-time being thus necessary labour-time – is a definition which concerns only the magnitude of value.[39] But the labour which constitutes the substance of value is not only uniform, simple, average labour; it is the labour of a private individual represented in a definite product. However, the product as value must be the embodiment of social labour, and as such, be directly convertible from one use-value into all others. . . . Thus the labour of individuals has to be directly[40] represented as its opposite, social labour . . .'[41]

This glaring contradiction can clearly only be resolved by equating the labour of individuals in exchange, by means of its reduction to abstract, universal human labour. 'The labour-time of the individual can produce exchange-value only if it produces universal equivalents, that is to say, if the individual's labour-time represents universal labour-time . . .' 'It becomes social labour by assuming the form of its direct opposite, of abstract universal labour.' The issue is not that of its social nature pure and simple, but rather 'the specific manner in which that labour . . . which posits exchange-value, and thus produces commodities is social labour'.[42]

This becomes clear as soon as we turn to pre-capitalist conditions, where production for exchange either played no role or only a minimal one. For example: 'Under the rural-patriarchal system of production, when spinner and weaver lived under the same roof – the women of the family spinning and the men weaving, let us say for the requirements of the family – yarn and linen were social products, and spinning and weaving social labour within the framework of the family. But their social character did not appear in the form of yarn becoming a universal equivalent exchanged for linen as a universal equivalent, i.e. of the two products exchanging for each other as equal and equally valid expressions of the same universal

[39] Ricardo overlooked this very point (as did most of the popularisers of Marx's theory as well).
[40] Since this direct representation is impossible a 'mediation' has to take place, i.e. the formation of money.
[41] *Theories* III, p.135.
[42] *Contribution*, pp.32-35.

labour-time. On the contrary, the product of labour bore the characteristic social imprint of the family relationship with its naturally evolved division of labour.'

'Or let us take the services and dues in kind of the Middle Ages,' continues Marx. 'It was the distinct labour of the individual in its original form, the particular features of his labour and not its universal aspect that formed the social ties at that time. Or finally let us take communal labour in its spontaneously evolved form as we find it among all civilised nations at the dawn of their history. In this case the social character of labour is evidently not mediated by the labour of the individual assuming the abstract form of universal labour or his product assuming the form of a universal equivalent. The communal system on which this mode of production is based prevents the labour of an individual from becoming private labour and his product the private product of a separate individual; it causes individual labour to appear rather as the direct function of a member of the social organisation.'[43] (The same applies, *mutatis mutandis* of course, to the socialist society of the future.)[44]

In contrast to this, the labours of individuals in a society of 'isolated individuals' i.e. of private producers, only operate 'as an element of the total labour of society through the relations which the act of exchange establishes between the products, and through their mediation, between the producers'.[45] 'The labour of different persons is equated and treated as universal labour only by bringing one use-value into relation with another one in the guise of exchange-value.'[46] Hence it appears ('something which only applies for this particular form of production, commodity production') that 'the specific social character of private labours carried on independently of each other consists in their equality as human labour' . . . and this social character must therefore assume 'in the product, the *form* of value'.[47]

It is clear that we are dealing here with one of the cardinal principles of Marx's theory of value – a principle which distinguishes this theory of value from all its predecessors in radical fashion. Ricardo too was naturally aware of the fact that the labour of the individual has to be reduced to 'socially necessary labour' in order to serve as the basis of value. (He points this out in Section 2 of the first chapter of his book.) However, this only concerns the quantita-

[43] *ibid.* pp.33-34.
[44] Cf. Chapter 30 below, 'The Historical Limits of the Law of Value.'
[45] *Capital* I, p.165 (73).
[46] *Contribution*, p.34.
[47] *Capital* I, p.167 (74).

tive, not the qualitative side of the problem. But the point is, 'not only that the different magnitudes of commodity values are measured by expressing the values in the use-value of one exclusive commodity, but at the same time that they are all expressed in a form in which they exist as the embodiment of social labour and are therefore exchangeable for every other commodity, that they are translatable at will into any use-value desired.' The labour contained in the commodities 'must be represented as social labour, as alienated individual labour'.[48] However, this is only necessary in a commodity-producing society. Only in such a society does the labour of the individual have to represent itself 'as its opposite, impersonal, abstract, general – and only in this form social' labour.[49] Of course even a socialist society would have to 'keep accounts' of the labour-power at its disposal, and would therefore have to reduce individual labour to 'simple average labour'. However, it would not occur to it 'to express the simple fact that the hundred square metres of cloth required one thousand hours of labour for their production ... in the oblique and meaningless way that they have a *value* of one thousand hours of labour'.[50] And it is precisely because Ricardo mistakenly saw the value-form as the 'eternal, natural form of social production' that he restricted himself to the magnitude of value in his analysis.[51] Hence also his 'incorrect theory of money', his failure to understand 'the connection between the determination of the exchange-value of the commodity by labour-time and the fact that the development of commodities necessarily leads to the *formation of money*'.[52]

3. The formation of money and commodity fetishism

The phenomenon of commodity fetishism is closely tied up with the formation of money. We saw that real exchange produces the doubling of the commodity, its separation into commodity and money. It selects 'from the common mass of commodities one sovereign commodity in which the value of all other commodities can be expressed once and for all; a commodity which serves as the direct incarnation of social labour, and is therefore directly and unconditionally exchangeable for all other commodities – namely money.'[53]

[48] *Theories* III, pp.130-31.
[49] *Contribution*, p.69.
[50] Engels, *Anti-Dühring*, 1969, p.367.
[51] Cf. *Capital* I, p.174 note 74 (p.80 note 1).
[52] *Theories* II, p.164.
[53] *Anti-Dühring*, p.427.

However, in order that 'a particular commodity may become, as it were, the general substance of exchange-value', the exchange-value of all commodities has to be identifiable with this particular commodity; one of the commodities has to acquire 'an existence independent of the commodity, an existence based in an autonomous material of its own, in a particular commodity'.[54] 'The exchange-value of a thing is nothing other than the quantitatively specific expression of its capacity for serving as a medium of exchange. In money the medium of exchange becomes a thing, or the exchange-value of the thing achieves an independent existence apart from the thing.'[55] This is a development which already demonstrates unequivocally the fetishism bound up with commodity production, its own special 'personification of objects, and reification of the relations of production'.

Let us go back to Marx's comparison between the value of commodities and the weight of objects. Since sugar is heavy, its weight can be expressed by comparing it with the weight of another body. 'However it would be absurd to make the assumption that the sugar weighs 10 lbs, for example, because I placed ten pound-weights on the other side of the scales.'[56] It would be no less absurd, in fact it would be insane, to suppose further that since the weight of the sugar is expressed in iron-weights, it is something 'ferrous'; that the iron signifies the weight as such, and embodies it. However, it is exactly this insanity which characterises the form in which the relations of exchange appear to the owners of commodities. We know that in exchange, the value of a commodity cannot be expressed except in the use-value of another commodity, let us say, the value of linen in the use-value of a coat. This is true even in the most elementary exchange relation : x Commodity A = y Commodity B (which Marx called the 'simple, isolated or accidental form of value'). Commodity B (the coat) therefore counts 'as a thing in which value is manifested, or which represents value in its tangible natural form'.[57] Nevertheless the coat, in relation to the linen, 'cannot represent value, unless value for the latter, simultaneously assumes the form of a coat',[58] unless, in other words, it appears that 'the coat, just as it is, expresses value and is endowed with the form of value by Nature

---

[54] *Grundrisse*, pp.168, 188.
[55] *ibid.* pp.199-200.
[56] K.Kautsky, *K.Marx' Ökonomische Lehren*, 1906, p.27.
[57] *Capital* I, p.143 (51).
[58] Marx adds : 'An individual, A, for instance, cannot be "your majesty" to another individual, B, unless majesty in B's eyes assumes the physical shape of A, and, moreover changes facial features, hair and many other things, with every new "father of his people".' (*ibid.* p.143 (51-52).)

itself', just as much as 'its property of being heavy or its ability to keep us warm' is provided by Nature.[59] 'As a use-value, the linen is something palpably different from the coat; as value it is identical with the coat, and therefore looks like the coat.'[60] Hence the most simple exchange relation reveals that in a society based on private property, in which the producers can only relate to each other by means of their commodities, 'the social characteristics of their own labour' must appear 'as objective characteristics of the products of labour themselves'.[61]

However, the value-form x Commodity A = y Commodity B only applies to a sporadic and hence transient exchange relation, that solely between two particular commodities. In such a situation it is still very difficult to grasp the reification of the social relations of production. It does not take on a distinct and tangible shape until the money-form. Then, all commodities express their value in the same equivalent, in the same money-commodity. The 'false semblance' consequently becomes firmly established, i.e. that 'the thing in which the magnitude of the value of another thing is represented [has] . . . the equivalent form independently of this relation, as a social property inherent in its nature'.[62] 'The form of direct and universal exchangeability . . .' finally becomes 'entwined with the specific natural form of the commodity gold' (or silver.)[63] This commodity 'does not seem to become money, because all other commodities express their value in it, but, on the contrary, all other commodities universally appear to express their values in gold, because it is *money*. The movement through which this process has been mediated vanishes in its own result, leaving no trace behind. Without any initiative on their part, the commodities find their own value-configuration ready to hand, in the form of a physical commodity existing outside but also alongside them. This physical object, gold or silver in its crude state, becomes, immediately on its emergence from the bowels of the earth, the direct incarnation of all human labour.'[64] Hence the complete inversion and reification of the social relations of production, 'which only impinges on the crude bourgeois vision of the political economist when it . . . confronts him in the shape of money.' (Marx adds : 'He does not suspect that even the

[59] ibid. p.149 (57).
[60] ibid. p.143 (51).
[61] ibid. pp.164-65 (72).
[62] ibid. p.187 (92).
[63] ibid. p.162 (70).
[64] ibid. p.187 (92).

simplest expression of value, such as 20yds. of linen = 1 coat, already presents the riddle of the equivalent form for us to solve.')[65]

However, what is the real source of this unique inversion? Why, in a commodity-producing society, do the mutual relations of human beings 'always have *to be bound to objects*', and why must they '*appear as things*'?[66] The reason is simply that the producers in such a society cannot relate to their labour as direct social labour since they have lost control over their own relations of production. Hence, 'the *social* character of labour appears as the *money-existence* of the commodity, and consequently as *a thing* outside actual production'.[67] 'Objects of utility become commodities only because they are the *products of the labour of private individuals* who work independently of each other ... Since the producers do not come into social contact until they exchange the products of their labour, the specific social characteristics of their private labours appear only within this exchange.' And they appear to them 'as what they are ... i.e. not as direct social relations between persons in their work ... but *as material relations between persons and social relations between things*'.[68]

We have confined ourselves here to passages from Volume I of *Capital* because the analysis of the form of value in this work provides the proof that the 'riddle of the money fetish' is in fact 'simply the riddle of the commodity fetish, now become visible and dazzling to our eyes'.[69] However, this should not be taken to mean that Marx's famous concept of 'commodity fetishism' was first developed in the mid-1860s. It was already in evidence in his earliest economic works. For example, we read in Marx's notes on Mill of 1844: 'The nature of money ... is in the first place ... that the *mediating* activity of

---

[65] *ibid.* pp.149-50 (57-58).
[66] Engels, *MEW* Vol.13, pp.475-76. 'The product which enters into exchange is the commodity. However, it is only a commodity in that a relation between two people or communities attaches itself to the thing, the product, namely the relationship between the producer and the consumer, who are not one and the same person here. This is immediately an example of a quite unique state of affairs which penetrates the whole of economics and has prompted awful confusion in the minds of bourgeois economists: economics does not deal with things, but with relations between people, and in the final analysis between classes; these relations are, however, always connected to things and appear as things. Marx was the first to have uncovered the general validity of this for all economics, and thus rendered the most difficult questions so simple and clear.'
[67] *Capital* III, pp.516-17.
[68] *Capital* I, pp.165-66 (72).
[69] *ibid.* p.187 (93).

human social action by which man's products reciprocally complete each other is alienated, and becomes the characteristic of a material thing, money, which is external to man. When man exteriorises this mediating activity he is active only as an exiled and dehumanised being; the *relation* between things, and human activity with them, becomes the activity of a being outside and above man. Through this *alien intermediary* – whereas man himself should be the intermediary between men – man sees his will, his activity, and his relations to others as a power which is independent of him and of them. His slavery therefore attains its peak. That this intermediary becomes a real god is clear, since the intermediary is the real power over that which he mediates to me.[70] His cult becomes an end in itself. The objects separated from this intermediary have lost their value. Thus they only have value insofar as they represent it, whereas it seemed originally that it only had value in so far as it represented *them*.'[71]

And elsewhere; 'Why must private property develop into the money system? Because man, as a social being, must proceed to exchange, and because exchange – private property being presupposed – must evolve into *value*. The mediating process between the exchangers is not a *human relation*; it is the *abstract relation* of private property and the expression of this abstract relationship is *value*, whose real existence as value is *money*. The object loses the meaning of human personal property, because those who exchange do not relate to each other as people.' Consequently, in money 'the complete domination of the estranged object *over* people makes its appearance. What was the domination of person over person is now the universal domination of *things* over *people*, of the product over

---

[70] Cf. *Grundrisse*, p.331, where we find this entirely Hegelian passage: 'This intermediary situation always appears as the economic situation in its completeness, because it comprises the opposed poles, and ultimately always appears as a one-sidedly higher power vis-à-vis the extremes themselves; because the movement or the relation, which originally appears as mediatory between the extremes, necessarily develops dialectically to where it appears as mediation with itself, as the subject for whom the extremes are merely its moments, whose autonomous presupposition it suspends in order to posit itself, through their suspension, as that which alone is autonomous.' Cf. the echo of this passage in *Capital* I, Chapter 32.

[71] *MEGA* III, p.531. Translated in Bottomore and Rubel, *Karl Marx: Selected Writings in Sociology and Social Philosophy*, Harmondsworth: Penguin 1961, p.179. Also in *Collected Works*, Vol.3, p.212. Cf. *Grundrisse*, p.149, 'Money is originally the representative of all values; in practice this situation is inverted, and all real products and labours become the representatives of money.'

the producers.[72] In the same way that the equivalent, value, formed the basis of the alienation (*Entäusserung*) of private property, so money is the sensuous, objective existence of this alienation.'[73]

All the elements of the later theory of commodity are already present here, even if they appear in philosophical guise. Although this theory did not obtain its real economic basis until the publication of *Capital*, the *Rough Draft*, written ten years before, already demonstrates why all products, and the results of all labour in a commodity-producing society, first have to be exchanged for a 'third, *material* thing', in order to obtain proper social validity and recognition, and further, why this 'material medium' has to become independent of the world of commodities. This provides the basis both for the supremacy of money and money relations and for the inverted reflection of the social relations of production in the consciousness of the participants, i.e. it provides a foundation for commodity fetishism.

This is what we may read in the *Rough Draft* : 'The reciprocal and all-sided dependence of individuals who are indifferent to one another forms their social connection. This social bond is expressed in exchange-value, by means of which alone each individual's own activity or his product becomes an activity and a product for him; he must produce a general product – exchange-value or . . . money' in order to be able to transform his product, 'into a *means of life* for himself'.[74] 'On the other side, the power which each individual exercises over the activity of others or over social wealth exists in him as the owner of exchange-values, of money. The individual carries his social power, as well as his bond with society, in his pocket.'[75] And 'the more production is shaped in such a way that every producer becomes dependent on the exchange-value of his commodity' the more 'the power of *money* grows[76] i.e. the exchange relation establishes itself as a power external to and independent of the producers. What originally appeared as a means to promote production becomes a relation alien to the producers.' Consequently in exchange-value 'the social connection between persons is transformed into a social

---

[72] 'Rob the thing, the completed money system, of its social power, and you must give it to persons to exercise over persons.' *Grundrisse*, p.158.
[73] *Collected Works*, Vol.3, pp.212-13. (Cf. *German Ideology*, p.445.)
[74] Marx states in another passage: 'For the person who creates an infinitesimal part of a yard of cotton, the fact that this is value, exchange-value is not a formal matter. If he had not created an exchange-value, money, he would have created nothing at all.' (*Grundrisse*, p.252.)
[75] *ibid.* pp.156-57.
[76] Later we read of the 'transcendental power of money'.

relation between things; personal capacity into objective wealth'.[77] In this sense money is the 'objective bond of society',[78] the 'real community' which takes the place of the old community, which was held together by natural ties and relations of personal dependence, and which can tolerate 'none other standing above it'.[79] We can see from this that commodity fetishism and the formation of money are simply two different aspects of one single situation (a fact often overlooked in textbooks on marxist economics): namely, that in a commodity-producing society, 'the exchangeability of the commodity' exists 'as a thing beside it . . . as something different from it', 'something no longer directly identical with it',[80] and hence that value must achieve autonomy in relation to commodities.[81] It further follows from this that both phenomena are inseparable from commodity production and that a commodity-producing society is incapable either of freeing itself from money, or of tearing away the 'mystical veil' which obscures the real nature of the material process of production. This will only be possible when the process of production 'becomes production by freely associated producers, and stands under their conscious and planned control. This, however, requires that society possess a material foundation, or a series of material conditions of existence, which in their turn are the natural and spontaneous product of a long and tormented historical development.'[82]

[77] ibid. pp.146, 157.
[78] *Grundrisse*, German edn. p.866. Reference to a heading in the *Index zu den 7 Heften*.
[79] *Grundrisse*, pp.225, 223. It should be further emphasised here that the reification of the social relations of production reaches its peak with capital, especially interest-bearing capital. 'Just as exchange-value . . . appears in money to be a thing, so do all aspects of the activity which creates exchange-values, labour, appear in capital.' (*ibid.* p.254.) This is a theme with which we shall be concerned later.
[80] ibid. p.147.
[81] Marx remarks in the *Theories* that the autonomisation of value might be regarded as a 'scholastic invention' or a 'paradox' (just as Marx's conception of capital as 'independent value' or 'value-in-process' appears paradoxical to bourgeois critics). However, 'it goes without saying that the paradox of reality is also reflected in paradoxes of speech which are at variance with common sense, i.e. with what vulgarians think and believe. The contradictions which arise from the fact that on the basis of commodity production the labour of the individual presents itself as general social labour, and the relations of people as relations between things and as things – these contradictions are innate in the subject matter, not in its verbal expressions.' (*Theories* III, p.137.)
[82] *Capital* I, p.173 (80). A fine comparison between money and the state can be found in Trotsky's *The Revolution Betrayed*, New York 1945, pp.65-66. 'These two problems, state and money, have a number of traits in common, for they both reduce themselves in the last analysis to the problem: pro-

4. The unfolding of the internal contradictions of the money form

Up until now we were concerned to prove that 'the exchange-value relation – of commodities as mutually equal and equivalent objectifications of labour-time – comprises *contradictions* which find their objective expression in a *money which is distinct* from labour time'.[83] Because the commodity has to prove itself simultaneously as both use-value and exchange-value, and because the private labour contained in it must prove itself directly as social labour, the world of commodities must single out one exclusive commodity, in which these contradictions appear to be dissolved. Only this commodity can be the universal equivalent; only the labour incorporated in this commodity represents 'labour in its directly social form . . . although, like all other commodity-producing labour, it is the labour of private individuals',[84] whilst all other commodities sink down to the level of the 'common mass of commodities', as mere use-values. The question then is raised : Is this a definitive solution? Does it really overcome the contradictions of commodity production?

Marx's answer is, no. In the first place : 'The same contradiction between the particular nature of the commodity as product and its

ductivity of labour. State compulsion like money compulsion is an inheritance from the class society, which is incapable of defining the relations of man to man except in the form of fetishes, churchly or secular, after appointing to defend them the most alarming of all fetishes, the state, with a great knife between its teeth. In a communist society the state and money will disappear. Their gradual dying away ought consequently to begin under socialism. We shall be able to speak of the actual triumph of socialism only at that historical moment when the state turns into a semi-state, and money begins to lose its magic power. This will mean that socialism, having freed itself from capitalist fetishes, is beginning to create a more lucid, free and worthy relation among men. Such characteristically anarchist demands as the "abolition of money", "abolition of wages", or "liquidation" of the state and family, possess interest merely as models of mechanical thinking. Money cannot be arbitrarily "abolished", nor the state and the old family "liquidated". They have to exhaust their historic mission, evaporate and fall away. The deathblow to money fetishism will be struck only upon that stage when the steady growth of social wealth has made us bipeds forget our miserly attitude toward every excess minute of labour, and our humiliating fear about the size of our ration. Having lost its ability to bring happiness or trample men into the dust, money will turn into mere book-keeping receipts for the convenience of statisticians and for planning purposes. In the still more distant future, probably these receipts will not be needed. But we can leave this question entirely to posterity who will be more intelligent than we are.'

[83] *Grundrisse*, p.169.
[84] *Capital* I, p.150 (58).

general nature as exchange-value, which created the necessity of positing it doubly, as this particular commodity on the one side, and as money on the other . . . contains from the beginning the possibility that these two separated forms in which the commodity exists are not convertible into one another.[85] . . . As soon as money has become an external thing alongside the commodity, the exchangeability of the commodity for money becomes bound up with external conditions which may or may not be present . . . The commodity is demanded in exchange because of its natural properties, because of the needs for which it is the desired object. Money, by contrast, is demanded only because of its exchange-value, as exchange-value. Hence whether or not the commodity is convertible into money . . . depends on circumstances which initially have nothing to do with it as exchange-value and are independent of that . . . There thus arises the possibility that the commodity, in its specific form as product, can no longer be exchanged for, equated with, its general form as money.'[86]

But not only this. 'Just as the exchange-value of the commodity leads a double existence, as the particular commodity and as money, so does the act of exchange split into two mutually independent acts: exchange of commodities for money, exchange of money for commodities; purchase and sale. Since these have now achieved a spatially and temporally separate and mutually indifferent form of existence, their immediate identity ceases. They may correspond or not; they may balance or not; they may enter into disproportion with one another. They will of course always attempt to equalise one another; but in the place of the earlier immediate equality there now stands the constant movement of equalisation, which evidently presupposes constant non-equivalence. It is now entirely possible that consonance may be reached only by passing through the most extreme dissonance.'[87] For 'the commodity . . . is exchanged for a commodity; at the same time, and equally, it is not exchanged for a commodity, inasmuch as it is exchanged for money . . . Thus already in the quality of money as a medium, in the splitting of exchange into two acts, there lies the germs of crises . . .'[88]

Thirdly, Marx continues, 'Just as exchange itself splits into two mutually independent acts, so does the overall movement of exchange

---

[85] This point was already anticipated in the previous chapter (Marx's discussion of the 'convertibility of the time-chits').
[86] *Grundrisse*, pp.147-48.
[87] *ibid.* p.148.
[88] *ibid.* pp.197-98. Cf. *Capital* I, p.209 (112-14), and in particular *Theories* II, pp.507ff.

itself become separate from the exchangers, the producers of commodities. Exchange for the sake of exchange separates off from exchange for the sake of commodities. A mercantile estate steps between the producers – an estate which only buys in order to sell and only sells so as to buy again, and whose aim in this operation is not the possession of commodities as products but merely the obtaining of exchange-values as such, of money . . . This doubling of exchange – exchange for the sake of consumption and exchange for the sake of exchange – gives rise to a new disproportion. In his exchange, the merchant is guided merely by the difference between the purchase and sale of commodities; but the consumer who buys a commodity must replace its exchange-value once and for all. Circulation, i.e. exchange within the mercantile estate, and the point at which circulation ends, i.e. exchange between the mercantile estate and the consumers – as much as they must ultimately condition one another – are determined by quite different laws and motives, and can enter into the most acute contradiction with one another.' (And consequently another possibility of crises![89]). 'But since production works directly for commerce and only indirectly for consumption, it must not only create but also and equally be a product of this inconsistency between commerce and exchange for consumption.'[90]

Finally, Marx points to the contradictions which reveal themselves in the separation of financial operations from actual trade. 'Money comes into contradiction with itself and with its characteristic by virtue of being itself a *particular* commodity . . . and of being subject, therefore, to particular conditions of exchange in its exchange with other commodities, conditions which contradict its universal unconditional exchangeability.' It is 'determinable by demand and supply; splits into different kinds of money etc.' 'Despite its universal character it is one exchangeable entity among other exchangeable entities. It is not only the universal exchange-value, but at the same time a particular exchange-value alongside other particular exchange-values. Here is a new source of contradictions which make themselves felt in practice.'[91]

'We see then,' Marx concludes, 'how it is an inherent property of money to fulfil its purposes by simultaneously negating them; to achieve independence from commodities; to be a means which becomes an end; to realise the exchange-value of commodities by

---

[89] The possibility of crises should, of course, be distinguished from their necessity; (see the exhaustive exposition of this point in *Theories* II, p.513).
[90] *Grundrisse*, pp.148-49.
[91] *ibid.* p.151.

separating them from it; to facilitate exchange by splitting it; to overcome the difficulties of the direct exchange of commodities by generalising them; to make exchange independent of the producers in the same measure as the producers become dependent on exchange.'[92] The contradiction hidden away in the commodity, between private and social labour, between use-value and exchange-value, between money and commodity is overcome, only to be reproduced simultaneously on another level. Or, as we read in *Capital*: 'The further development of the commodity' into commodity and money 'does not abolish these contradictions, but rather provides the form within which they have room to move. This is, in general, the way in which real contradictions are resolved. For instance, it is a contradiction to depict one body as constantly falling towards another, and at the same time constantly flying away from it. The ellipse is a form of motion within which this contradiction is both realised and resolved.'[93]

With this we have arrived at one of the most important, but at the same time most neglected and misunderstood, aspects of Marx's economics. How often has the thesis of the 'contradiction between use-value and exchange-value' been repeated? (For example, in a superficial and naive form by Kautsky and in a dogmatic and pedantic fashion by Soviet economics of the Stalinist school of thought.) On the other hand, how often has anyone really taken the trouble to develop this thesis or regard it as something more than a survival of the time when Marx 'coquetted with the Hegelian manner of expression'? In reality we are dealing here with one of the most fundamental discoveries of Marx's economics, the neglect of which makes his conclusions in the theory of value and money appear utterly distorted. But not only that. As Lenin wrote: 'In his *Capital* Marx first analyses the simplest, most ordinary and fundamental, most common and everyday *relation* of bourgeois (commodity) society, a relation encountered billions of times, viz. the exchange of commodities. In this very simple phenomenon (in the "cell" of bourgeois society) analysis reveals *all* the contradictions (or the germs of all the contradictions) of modern society. The subsequent exposition shows us the development (both growth *and* movement) of these contradictions and of this society in the sum of the individual parts, from its beginning to its end.'[94]

[92] *ibid.* p.151.
[93] *Capital* I, p.198 (103).
[94] *Collected Works*, Vol.38, p.36. Cf. *Contribution*, p.96: '. . . because the contradiction of commodity and money is the abstract and general form of all contradictions inherent in the bourgeois mode of labour.'

Our investigation of Marx's analysis of the 'Transition from Value to Money' has illustrated how accurately these sentences capture the real meaning of marxist economics. We must now test the validity of this analysis as we proceed further in our investigation.

6.
The Functions of Money

A. Money as measure of value

1. Preliminary note

Before we proceed with our investigation it will be necessary to look briefly at Marx's concept of the 'functional form of existence'.

We have seen that Marx's major concern was to grasp the characteristic forms of economic relations. From this standpoint the entire science of political economy can be characterised as a history of the forms of social production and intercourse.

Each form of production and intercourse has a definite function to fulfil: only after an economic relation 'has performed the function corresponding to each particular form ... does it ... acquire the form in which it may enter a new transformation phase'.[1] Therefore what an economic form actually represents can only be derived from the function which is allotted to it, and which underlies it. In this context Marx speaks repeatedly of 'functional' (or 'functionally or conceptually determined') 'forms of existence', which money and capital continually assume and shed, and in which the dialectical development of these categories finds its expression.[2]

As far as the functions of money in particular are concerned, it is sufficient to cite here the words of H.Block, a bourgeois critic with some insight into Marx. 'The strict division of these functions from the substance of money (social value) and likewise the separation of the functions from one another, is a striking feature of Marx's theory of money. Other theoreticians define money as a means of commerce, a unit of account, a means of exchange or a means of payment, i.e. they elevate one particular function to the position of being the defining feature of money, and then somehow derive all the remaining functions from the main one. In contrast to this Marx strictly separates the essence of money from the services which it is able to perform, owing to its particular character. The individual functions, on the other hand, stand separately and equally beside each

---

[1] *Capital* II, p.50.
[2] Cf. pp.31-32 above.

other.'[3] (Which naturally does not prevent them from interlocking, or from being closely connected genetically.)

2. Money as measure of value

Marx writes in the *Contribution* : 'The principal difficulty in the analysis of money is surmounted as soon as it is understood that the commodity is the origin of money. After that it is only a question of clearly comprehending the specific form peculiar to it. This is not so easy because all bourgeois relations appear to be gilded i.e. they appear to be money relations, and the money-form therefore seems to possess an infinitely varied content, which is quite alien to this form.'[4]

The first of these specific forms of money – the first because it emerges directly from the process of the formation of money itself – is its function as a measure of value.

'Money necessarily crystallises out of the process of exchange, in which different products of labour are in fact equated with each other, and thus converted into commodities. The historical broadening and deepening of the phenomenon of exchange develops the opposition between use-value and value which is latent in the nature of the commodity. The need to give an external expression to this opposition for the purposes of commercial intercourse produces the drive towards an independent form of value, which finds neither rest nor peace until an independent form has been achieved by the differentiation of commodities into commodities and money.'[5] It is no longer necessary for the value of each commodity to be expressed in an infinite series of value equations, as in the direct exchange of products (Marx's 'expanded form of value'); one single equation : x Commodity A = y Money commodity, is sufficient to represent this value in a socially valid form. 'After money has been posited as independent exchange-value', the commodities themselves are 'posited in their particularity in relation to their subject, money . . . By being equated to money they again become related to one another as they were, conceptually, as exchange-values; they balance and equate themselves with one another in given proportions.' Money 'is the universal material into which they must be dipped, in which they become gilded and silver-plated, in order to win their independ-

[3] H.Block, *Die Marxsche Geldtheorie*, Jena 1926, pp.66-67.
[4] *Contribution*, p.64.
[5] *Capital* I, p.181 (86).

ent existence as exchange-values . . . The particular exchange-value, the commodity, becomes expressed as, subsumed under, posited in the character of the independent exchange-value, of money.'[6]

The *Rough Draft* continues: '*Exchange-value, posited in the character of money, is price* . . . money as price shows first of all the identity of all exchange-values; secondly, it shows the unit of which they all contain a given number, so that the equation with money expresses the quantitative specificity of exchange-values, their quantitative relation to one another.'[7] Money operates here as the common denominator, as the measure of values, 'as the material in which the magnitudes of value of commodities are expressed socially'. In this capacity, money is 'the necessary form of appearance of the *measure of value which is immanent in commodities, namely labour-time*'.[8] One definition which follows automatically from the general law of value is that since objectified human labour is contained both in commodities and money, the value of a commodity whose production involves one day's labour becomes expressed in a quantity of gold or silver, in which, similarly, one day's labour is incorporated. The circulation process makes it appear as if it is money which makes commodities commensurable. In reality the opposite is the case : 'Because all commodities, as values, are objectified human labour, and therefore in themselves commensurable, their values can be communally measured in one and the same specific commodity, and this commodity can be converted into the common measure of their values, that is into money.'[9] The measure of value 'presupposes them as values and refers solely to the expression and size of this value . . . to the transformation of values into prices'. It 'already presumes value'.[10]

Prices represent only an ideal transformation of commodities into money. The doubling of the commodity into commodity and money, the formation of money, does not imply that the commodity has become money as such, or that the commodity only possesses universal exchangeability because it has been given a price. 'The concrete form in which commodities enter the process of exchange is as use-values. The commodities will only become universal equivalents as a result of their alienation. The establishment of their price is merely their nominal conversion into the universal equivalent, an

[6] *Grundrisse*, pp.188-90.
[7] *ibid.* p.189.
[8] *Capital* I, p.188 (94).
[9] *ibid.* Cf. *Contribution*, pp.66-67.
[10] *Theories* III, p.40.

equation with gold which still has to be put into practice.'[11] Hence the price of the commodity appears as 'an *external* relation of exchange-values or commodities to money; the commodity *is not* price, in the way in which its social substance stamped it as exchange-value; this quality is not immediately co-extensive with it; but it is mediated by the commodity's comparison with money; the commodity is exchange-value, but it *has* a price.'[12]

We thus return to the question of the non-identity of price and value, which we already touched on in the previous chapter. At first sight this might appear to be a mere terminological difference; in reality it is 'so far from being simply a nominal difference that all the storms which threaten the commodity in the actual process of circulation centre upon it'.[13] For, although the commodity, e.g. iron, 'possesses in price an *ideal* value-shape or an imagined gold-shape', it naturally cannot 'at one and the same time, and in reality, be both iron and gold. To establish its price it is sufficient for it to be *equated* with gold in the imagination.' However, in actual exchange 'it must be actually replaced by gold . . . to render to its owner the service of a universal equivalent'. And in actual exchange, 'price may express both the magnitude of value of the commodity and the greater or lesser quantity of money for which it can be sold under the given circumstances. The *possibility of a quantitative incongruity* between price and magnitude of value . . . is therefore inherent in the *price-form itself*. This is not a defect but, on the contrary, it makes this form the adequate form for a mode of production whose laws can only assert themselves as blindly operating averages between constant irregularities.'[14]

Since prices only represent ideal sums of money, no real money is necessary for establishing a price. That is : 'The ideal transformation of commodities into money is *prima facie* independent of, and unrestricted by the mass of real money. Not a single piece of money is required in this process, just as little as a measuring rod (say a yardstick) really needs to be employed before, for example, the ideal quantity of yards can be expressed. If, for example, the entire national wealth of England is appraised in terms of money, i.e. expressed as a price, everyone knows that there is not enough money in the world to realise this price. Money is needed here only as a category, as a *mental* relation.'[15] Nevertheless, it cannot become an

[11] *Contribution*, p.68.
[12] *Grundrisse*, p.190.
[13] *Contribution*, p.69.
[14] *Capital* I, pp.197, 196 (103, 102).
[15] *Grundrisse*, p.191.

imaginary measure of value, with no connection with the determination of value by means of labour-time, for this reason : 'If say a pound of cotton is worth 8d then I am saying that 1 pound of cotton = 1/116 oz. of gold. . . . This expresses at the same time its particularity as exchange-value against all other commodities, which contain the ounce of gold this or that many times – since they are all in the same way compared to the ounce of gold. This original relation of the pound of cotton with gold . . . is fixed by the quantity of labour-time realised in one and the other, the real common substance of exchange-values'[16] – 'Money as measure, as element of price-determination . . . thus presents the following phenomena : (1) it is required only as an imagined unit once the exchange-value of an ounce of gold compared to any one other commodity has been determined; its actual presence is superfluous, along with, even more so, its available quantity . . . (2) while it thus only needs to be posited ideally and, indeed, in the form of the price of a commodity is only ideally posited *in* it; at the same time, as a simple amount of the natural substance in which it is represented, as a given weight of gold, silver etc . . . it also yields the point of comparison, the unit, the measure.'[17] In this sense, the 'material substance of money is essential' for money's function as a measure of value, 'although its availability and even more its quantity, the *amount* of the portion of gold or silver which serves as a unit, are entirely irrelevant for it in this quality and it is employed in general only as an imaginary non-existent [at least not materially existent] unit.'[18]

The above confirms what we already knew; namely that only a real commodity, a real product of labour, can function as the measure of value. 'Money is a *measure* only because it is labour-time materialised in a specific substance, hence itself *value*.'[19] It does not follow from this either that it always has to be embodied[20] in the same substance, or that it has to be of an 'invariable value'.[21] What follows is only that – 'as in the representation of the exchange-value of any commodity in the use-value of another' – so similarly in the estimation of commodities in gold or silver, it is presupposed that 'at a given

[16] *Grundrisse*, pp.203-204.
[17] *ibid*. pp.207-208.
[18] *ibid*. p.203.
[19] *ibid*. p.791.
[20] 'If the values of all commodities were measured in silver or wheat or copper, and accordingly expressed in terms of silver, wheat or copper prices, then silver, wheat or copper would become the measure of value and consequently universal equivalents.' (*Contribution*, p.66.)
[21] See note 11 of the previous chapter.

moment gold represents a definite quantity of labour-time'. 'If the value of an ounce of gold falls or rises in consequence of a change in the labour-time required for its production, then it will fall or rise *equally* in relation to all other commodities and will thus for all of them continue to represent a *definite* volume of labour-time. The same exchange-values will now be estimated in quantities of gold which are larger or smaller than before but they will retain the same relative value to one another. . . . The fact that, because of the changing value of gold, exchange-values are represented by varying quantities of gold does not prevent gold from functioning as the measure of value, any more than the fact that the value of silver is one fifteenth of that of gold prevents it from taking over this function.'[22]

Thus we have arrived at the question of the double standard of currency. We read in *Capital*: 'If therefore two different commodities, such as gold and silver, serve simultaneously as measures of value, all commodities will have two separate price-expressions, the price in gold and the price in silver, which will quietly co-exist as long as the ratio of the value of silver to that of gold remains unchanged . . . However, every alteration in this ratio disturbs the ratio between the gold-prices and the silver-prices of commodities, and thus proves in fact that a duplication of the measure of value contradicts the function of that measure.'[23]

One thing which is only intimated in the *Rough Draft* is the function of money as measure of prices.[24] As prices, the values of all commodities are transformed into *imaginary* quantities of different magnitudes. 'They are now capable of being compared with each other and measured, and the course of development produces the need to compare them, for technical reasons, with some fixed quantity of gold[25] as their unit of measurement. This unit, by subsequent division into aliquot parts, becomes itself the standard of measure-

---

[22] *Contribution*, pp.67-68. Cf. *Capital* I, pp.192-93 (128-29). The fact that – as H.Block considers (*op. cit.* p.73) – 'Fluctuations in the value of gold, when they reach a certain height, also make the value-measuring function of gold impossible', (think of the paper Mark in the German inflation of the 1920s), is naturally no objection to Marx's theory of gold as measure of value.

[23] *Capital* I, p.190 (96). (The question of a double standard of currency is not dealt with in this context in the *Rough Draft*.)

[24] 'The fact that money is the measure of prices, and hence that exchange-values are compared with one another, is an aspect of the situation which is self-evident.' (*Grundrisse*, p.189.)

[25] Both in the *Contribution* and in *Capital* Marx assumes that gold is the money-commodity, 'for the sake of simplicity'.

ment. Before they become money, gold, silver and copper already possess such standards in their weights . . .'[26]

The money-commodity is thus transformed from the measure of values into the standard of prices. These are two entirely different functions: since 'it is the measure of value as the social incarnation of human labour, and it is the standard of price as a quantity of metal with a fixed weight. As the measure of value it serves to convert the values of all the manifold commodities into prices, into imaginary quantities of gold; as the standard of price it measures those quantities of gold . . . For the standard of price, a certain weight of gold must be fixed as the unit of measurement. In this case, as in all cases where quantities of the same denomination are to be measured, the stability of the measurement is of decisive importance.' On the other hand, 'gold can only serve as a measure of value because it is itself a product of labour, and therefore potentially variable in value'.[27] (The confusion of these two specific forms 'has given rise to the wildest theories,' remarks Marx in *Capital*.)[28]

So much then on the process of the formation of prices, which precedes[29] the circulation of commodities ('precedes' in the sense that any circulation of commodities presupposes definite exchange-values as prices).[30] In the course of this process money acquires certain specific forms, which characterise it only in its function as the measure of value (or standard of price). Let us now look at how money behaves in the actual exchange of commodities, and whether the characteristics which it acquires there contradict those with which we are already acquainted.

[26] *Capital* I, p.191 (97).
[27] *ibid.* p.192 (97-98).
[28] *ibid.* p.190 (96). A detailed discussion of these theories can be found both in the *Contribution* (the chapter on 'Theories of the Standard of Money') and in the *Grundrisse*, pp.789-805, the first version of this chapter.
[29] 'The first phase of circulation is, as it were, a theoretical phase preparatory to real circulation.' (*Contribution*, p.64.)
[30] *Grundrisse*, p.188.

7.
The Functions of Money
B. Money as medium of circulation

Like every economic relation, commodity circulation also presents two different aspects (which are, nevertheless, closely connected to each other). Insofar as it 'transfers commodities from hands in which they are non-use-values to hands in which they are use-values', circulation is simply 'the appropriation of natural objects for human needs', and hence a *process of social metabolism (Stoffwechsel)*. However, to the extent that this replacement of use-values takes place through private exchange, mediated by money, and that the relations of the commodities to one another are crystallised as different forms *(Bestimmung–)* of money, it 'simultaneously gives rise to definite social relations of production', and is therefore a change of form *(Formwechsel)*.[1] Only this second aspect is analysed by Marx.[2]

At first sight the circulation of commodities simply appears as an enormous number of ongoing exchanges of commodity and money, from hand to hand and from place to place. It 'begins from an infinite number of points and returns to an infinite number', without 'the actual beginning also being the point of return'. 'The commodity is exchanged for money; money is exchanged for the commodity' and 'this constant renewal of the same process . . . is repeated endlessly'.[3] However, looked at more precisely, commodity circulation 'reveals other phenomena as well; the phenomena of completion, or the return of the point of departure into itself'. Circulation (as it appears in its two elements, commodity and money), can therefore be conceived of equally well as either a movement of money, or a movement of commodities. 'If I sell in order to buy, then I can also buy in order to sell . . . looking at it as mere circulation, the

[1] *Capital* I, p.198 (104).
[2] Cf. pp.80-83 above.
[3] Marx adds that from this standpoint commodity circulation can be regarded as a 'simply infinite process', in the Hegelian sense. *Grundrisse*, p.197 and *Grundrisse*, German edn. p.865. See Engels, *Anti-Dühring*, pp.61-67 on the Hegelian concept of 'bad infinity'. [Translator's Note: In both cases the term under consideration is the same, viz. *unendlichkeit*.]

point at which I intervene in order to declare it the point of departure has to be a matter of indifference.' However, in both instances, two different circuits take place : C-M-C and M-C-M.

'In the former case money only a means to obtain the commodity, and the commodity the aim; in the second case the commodity only a means to obtain money, and money the aim.'[4] At the same time the second circuit where the extremes M-M are only quantitatively different (consequently where the second M must be larger than the first) presupposes the exchange of non-equivalents; hence 'money and commodity in the circuit M-C-M imply more advanced relations of production, and within simple circulation the circuit is merely a reflexion of a movement of a more complex character'.[5] So for the present we shall confine ourselves to the form of circulation C-M-C (selling in order to buy).

What role does money play in the circuit C-M-C?

If, a short while ago, money served to provide the world of commodities with the material for expressing price, it is clear that in actual exchange its primary task must be to realise the price of commodities, i.e. act as the 'realiser (*Verwirklicher*) of prices'.

We should however remember that not every exchange of commodities amounts to a circulation of commodities. This circulation of commodities not only requires a 'circuit of exchanges, and a totality of them, in constant motion, and more or less present throughout society'.[6] It also presupposes, as we already know, 'that commodities enter into the process of exchange with *definite prices*', and that consequently the equivalent commodity already possesses its money-character.[7]

Indeed : 'At the place where gold is produced, it is a commodity like any other commodity. Its relative value . . . and that of any other commodity is reflected there in the quantities in which they are exchanged for one another. But this transaction is presupposed in the process of circulation, the value of gold is already given in the prices of commodities. It would therefore be entirely wrong to assume that within the framework of circulation the relation of gold and commodities is that of direct barter and that consequently their

[4] *Grundrisse*, pp.197, 201.
[5] *Contribution*, p.123.
[6] In this sense circulation, as 'the first totality among economic categories . . . is also the first form in which the social relation appears as something independent of the individuals, but not only as, say, in a coin or in exchange-value, but extending to the whole of the social movement itself'. (*Grundrisse*, p.197.)
[7] *Contribution*, p.88.

F

relative value is determined by their exchange as simple commodities.'[8] If we cling to this conception 'we overlook the very thing we ought to observe, namely what has happened to the *form* of the commodity. We do not see that gold, as a mere commodity, is not money, and that the other commodities, through their prices, themselves relate to gold as the medium for expressing their own shape in money.'[9] In other words: in circulation commodities are not only actually transformed into money, and exchanged for real money, they are also realised as prices. Hence, the establishment of price is the precondition of commodity circulation, and not its result.

From the fact that money can only circulate commodities with definite prices, it follows that the quantity of gold and silver required for circulation is determined in the first instance by the sum-total of the prices of the commodities which are to be realised. However, this sum total of prices is itself 'determined: firstly, by the prices of the individual commodities; secondly by the quantity of commodities at given prices which enter into circulation . . . Thirdly, however, the quantity of money required for circulation depends not only on the sum total of prices to be realised, but on the rapidity with which money circulates . . . If 1 thaler in one hour makes 10 purchases at 1 thaler each, if it is exchanged 10 times, then it performs quite the same task that 10 thalers would do if they made only one purchase per hour. Velocity is the negative moment; it replaces quantity; by its means a single coin is multiplied.'[10] In fact the circulation of money 'does not begin from a single centre, nor does it return to a single centre from all points of the periphery (as with banks of issue and partly with state issue);[11] but it begins from an infinite number of points and returns to an infinite number. The velocity of the circulating medium can therefore replace the quantity of the circulating medium only up to a certain point.' For this

---

[8] *ibid.* p.90.
[9] *Capital* I, p.199 (104).
[10] *Grundrisse*, p.194. Marx says in a later passage (p.519): 'We have already encountered the law of the substitution of velocity for mass and mass for velocity in money circulation. It holds in production just as in mechanics. It is a circumstance to return to when we consider the equalisation of the rate of profit, price etc.'
[11] Marx distinguishes in just this sense between the simple circuit and the higher 'bent back' circuit of money. 'It is clear that simple money circulation, regarded in itself, is not bent back into itself [but] consists of an infinite number of indifferent and accidentally adjacent movements.' However, 'insofar as it bends back into itself money circulation appears as the mere appearance of a circulation going on behind it and determining it, e.g. when we look at the money circulation between manufacturer, worker, shop-

reason 'a certain mass of payments must be made *simultaneously* ... A definite quantity of money is therefore necessary for circulation, a sum which will always be engaged in circulation, and which is determined by the sum total which starts from the simultaneous points of departure in circulation, and by the velocity with which it runs its course... No matter how many ebbs and flows this quantity of the circulating material is exposed to, an average level nevertheless comes into existence – since the permanent changes are always very gradual, take place over longer periods and are constantly paralysed by a mass of secondary circumstances.'[12]

Presupposing a certain velocity of circulation, it follows from the fact that the mass of the circulating medium is determined by price, and not the other way around, not that 'prices are high or low because much or little money circulates, but rather that much or little money circulates because prices are high or low'.[13] (The above does not apply to paper money issued by the state.) Marx adds: 'This is one of the principal economic laws, and the detailed substantiation of it based on the history of prices is perhaps the only achievement of the post-Ricardian English economists.'[14]

So much on the role which money plays as the medium for the realisation of prices. It should not be overlooked that in the circuit C-M-C the realisation of the price of the commodity primarily serves to facilitate (*vermittlen*) the exchange of this commodity for another commodity. If the result of the entire circuit is looked at, and not merely the isolated C-M or M-C, this result breaks down into the interchange of matter, C-C. 'The commodity is exchanged for

keeper and banker.' *ibid.* p.790. 'The development of money as universal means of payment goes hand in hand with the development of a higher circulation, mediated, bent back into itself and already taken under social control, in which the exclusive importance which it possessed on the basis of simple metallic circulation is annulled.' (*Grundrisse*, German edn. pp.875-76.) And cf. *Contribution*, pp.101-103.

[12] *Grundrisse*, p.195.

[13] *ibid.* pp.194-95. Elsewhere in the text (p.814) we find the remark: 'With the proposition that prices regulate the quantity of currency and not the quantity of currency prices, or in other words, that trade regulates currency (the quantity of the medium of circulation), and currency does not regulate trade, [it] is of course ... supposed that price is only value translated into another language. Value and value as determined by labour-time is the presupposition. It is clear, therefore, that this law is not equally applicable to the fluctuations of prices in all epochs; e.g. in antiquity, e.g. in Rome, where the circulating medium does not itself arise from circulation, from exchange, but from pillage, plunder etc.' Cf. *Contribution*, pp.157-65, and *MEW* Vol.29, p.316.

[14] *Contribution*, pp.105-106.

money; money is exchanged for the commodity. In this way commodity is exchanged for commodity, except that this exchange is a mediated one.' Therefore basically money has simply served 'to exchange the first commodity for the second one.'[15] Consequently if the entire circuit C-M-C is considered, money appears 'as a mere *medium of exchange* of commodities, not however as a medium of exchange adapted to the process of circulation i.e. a *medium of circulation*'.[16] If this new function of money is to be clearly understood, it must be set against its previous functions.

'Insofar as it [money] realises the price of commodities, the commodity is exchanged for its real equivalent in gold and silver . . . but insofar as this process takes place only in order to transform this money back into a commodity, i.e. in order to exchange the first commodity for the second, then money appears only fleetingly, or its substance consists only in this constant appearance as disappearance, as this vehicle of mediation. Money as medium of circulation is *only* medium of circulation. The only attribute which is essential to it in order to serve in this capacity is the attribute of quantity, of amount, in which it circulates.'[17]

From this standpoint, Marx continues, 'it is only a semblance, as if the point were to exchange the commodity for gold or silver as particular commodities : a semblance which disappears as soon as the process is ended, as soon as gold and silver have again been exchanged for a commodity, and the commodity, hence, exchanged for another. The character of gold and silver as mere media of circulation . . . is therefore irrelevant to their make-up as particular natural commodities.' This appears in the fact that in the course of circulation 1 thaler can represent a mass of silver one hundred times greater than it really contains, although in each particular exchange it only represents the silver weight of 1 thaler.[18] 'In circulation as a whole, the 1 thaler thus represents 100 thalers, a weight of silver a hundred times greater than it really contains. It is in truth only a symbol for the weight of silver contained in 100 thalers. Insofar as the price of a commodity of 1 thaler is paid . . . it is of decisive importance that the 1 thaler really contains x weight of silver. If it were

---

[15] *Grundrisse*, pp.197, 208.
[16] *Contribution*, p.96. As a medium of circulation, money functions as a means of purchase, since, in sale and purchase, commodity and money 'confront each other in the same way; the seller represents the commodity, the buyer the money'. (*ibid.* p.98.)
[17] *Grundrisse*, pp.208-209.
[18] All the monetary examples are expressed in thalers, for the sake of consistency, though the original uses both pounds sterling and thalers.

a counterfeit thaler, alloyed with non-precious metals . . . then indeed the price of the commodity would not be realised; in order to realise it, it would have to be paid for in as great a quantity of the non-precious metals as equals x weight of silver. Looking at this moment of circulation in isolation, it is thus essential that the unit of money should really represent a given quantity of gold or silver. But when we take circulation as a totality, as a self-enclosed process, C-M-M-C, then the matter stands differently. In the first case the realisation of price would be only apparent; only a part of the price [of the commodity] would be realised . . . But if a fake thaler were to circulate in the place of a real one, it would render absolutely the same service in circulation as a whole as if it were genuine . . . The genuine thaler is, therefore, in this process, nothing more than a symbol, insofar as the moment in which it realises prices is left out, and we look only at the totality of the process in which it serves only as a medium of exchange and in which the realisation of prices is only a semblance, a fleeting mediation.'[19]

Further on in the text we read this: 'As a mere medium of circulation, in its role in the constant flow of the circulatory process, money is neither the measure of prices,[20] because it is already posited as such in the prices themselves; nor is it the means for the realisation of prices, for it exists as such in one single moment of circulation but disappears as such in the totality of its moments; but is, rather, the mere representative of the price in relation to all other commodities, and serves only as a means to the end that all commodities are to be exchanged at equivalent prices . . . In this relation it is the symbol of itself . . . From this it follows that money as gold or silver, insofar as only its role as means of exchange and circulation is concerned, can be replaced by any other symbol which expresses a given quantity of its unit, and that in this way symbolic money can replace the real, because material money as mere medium of exchange is itself symbolic.'[21]

The medium of circulation obtains its most characteristic form in coin. As coin, money 'has lost its use-value; its use-value is identical with its quality as medium of circulation . . . That is why coin is also only a symbol whose material is irrelevant. But as coin it also loses its universal character, and adopts a national local one. It decomposes into coin of different kinds, according to the material of which it consists, gold, copper, silver etc. It acquires a political

[19] *Grundrisse*, pp.209-10.
[20] Should read 'measure of values'.
[21] *Grundrisse*, pp.211-12. Here the symbol theory is reduced to its correct proportions.

title, and talks, as it were, a different language in different countries.'[22]

What Marx has to say in the *Rough Draft* on coin and on paper money issued by the state at uniform exchange rates does not go beyond a few scattered remarks.[23]

He does, however, stress that, in this matter too, his conclusions 'are deduced in just the opposite way to the usual doctrine. Money can be replaced because its quantity is determined by the prices which it circulates. Insofar as it itself has value – as in the subsidiary medium of circulation [coin], its quantity must be so determined that it can never accumulate as an equivalent, and in fact always figures as an auxiliary cog of the medium of circulation proper. Insofar, however, as it is to replace the latter' – paper money issued by the state – 'it must have no value whatsoever i.e. its value must exist apart from itself'.[24] Therefore the value of money can 'exist separately from its matter, its substance . . . without therefore giving up the privilege of this specific commodity' i.e. of gold or silver, 'because the separated form of existence must necessarily continue to take its denomination from the specific commodity.'[25]

It can be seen that whereas in money's function as medium of circulation 'its material existence, its material substream of a given quantity of gold and silver is irrelevant, and where by contrast its amount is the essential aspect' (since it is only in this way that it can be a 'symbol of itself'), 'in its role as measure . . . where it was introduced only ideally, its material substratum was essential but its quantity and even its existence as such were irrelevant'. Marx remarks, in addition, that it is precisely this conflict between the functions of money[26] which 'explains the otherwise inexplicable phenomenon that the debasement of metallic money, of gold, silver, through admixture of inferior metals, causes a depreciation of money and a rise in prices; because in this case the measure of prices[27] is no longer the cost of production of the ounce of gold, say, but rather of an ounce consisting of $2/3$ copper etc.' But 'on the other hand, if the substratum of money . . . is entirely suspended and replaced by paper

---

[22] *ibid.* p.226.
[23] These remarks occur on p.814 of the *Grundrisse*.
[24] *ibid.* p.814.
[25] *ibid.* p.167.
[26] 'But it is at variance with common sense that in the case of purely imaginary money everything should depend on the physical substance, whereas in the case of the corporeal coin everything should depend on a numerical relation that is nominal.' (*Contribution*, p.121.)
[27] Once again, this should read 'measure of values'.

bearing the symbol of given quantities of real money, in the quantity required by circulation,[28] then the paper circulates at the full gold and silver value. In the first case because the medium of circulation is at the same time the material of money as measure, and the material in which prices are definitively realised; in the second case because money only [operates] in its role as medium of circulation.'[29]

Those readers who are well versed in marxism will immediately notice the difference between the presentation in the *Rough Draft* and the presentation in the *Contribution* and *Capital*. Not only is there no investigation in the former into coin and paper money, but also no detailed analysis of the circuit C-M-C, which can be found in the chapters on the medium of circulation in both of the later works.[30] What the *Rough Draft* offers, therefore, is hardly more than a cursory sketch of this subject. Nevertheless by focussing directly on the functions which money fulfils in the realisation of commodity prices it provides a welcome supplement to the later works, and thus contributes to our understanding of the later presentations, a point which also applies to the next chapter.

[28] Thus in Marx's view the 'quantity theory of money' only applies to paper money issued by the state. (Cf. also *Contribution*, pp.119-20.)
[29] *Grundrisse*, pp.212-13.
[30] *Contribution*, pp.87ff. *Capital* I, pp.198-209 (94ff).

8

The Functions of Money
C. 'Money as money'

1. General comments

Up until now we have become acquainted, in the main, with two functions of money; money as measure of value, and as medium of circulation. In the first function it operates only as ideal money, and in the second only as symbolic money. However, we now come to those forms which are either dependent on the actual presence of money in its 'own golden person', or where it appears, on the other hand, 'as the *sole form of value*, or in other words, the *only adequate form of existence of exchange-value*, in the face of all the other commodities which are here use-values pure and simple'.[1] Marx speaks here of 'money as money', or the 'third function of money'.

What this means is that money '*becomes independent* in relation both to society and to individuals'.[2] This attainment of an independent position, which was already inherent in the concept of money is, however, first of all a product of the process of exchange, and therefore has to be expressed in the development of the various specific forms of money. It achieves temporary independence, for example, in its function as medium of circulation. Whenever the sale C-M takes place, gold or silver, 'which, as measure of values were only ideal money . . . get transformed into actual money'. Thus, the chrysalis state of the commodity as money 'forms an independent phase in its life, in which it can remain for a shorter or longer period'.[3] However, if we look at the act C-M in the context of the circuit C-M-C, this money-chrysalis only serves the change of matter (*Stoffwechsel*) C-M, and therefore has only a temporary and fleeting character. As a fixed crystal of value, as value, become independent, money first appears where it no longer serves as a mere intermediary of exchange, but rather confronts commodities as something other than a medium of circulation.

According to Marx, money appears in three forms in its third

---

[1] *Capital* I, p.227 (130).
[2] *German Ideology*, p.445.
[3] *Contribution*, pp.89, 91.

'Money as money' · 151

function. 1) as hoard, 2) as means of payment and 3) as world coin or world money. In the first form, money remains outside circulation, withdraws from it; in the second it does in fact enter it, but not as a medium of circulation; and finally in the third it breaks through the barriers of internal circulation, as circumscribed by national borders, in order to function as the universal equivalent in international trade, on the world market.[4] Only by studying all these forms can we arrive at the real meaning of the category 'money as money'.

It should also be noted that the *Rough Draft* diverges noticeably from the *Contribution* and from *Capital* on this point (the derivation of the 'third function'). In the *Rough Draft* the category 'money as money' is conceived of essentially as the development of the form M-C-M.[5] Indeed the study of this circuit demonstrates most clearly that here 'money functions neither only as measure, nor only as medium of exchange, nor only as both; but has yet a third quality', that it 'has an independent existence outside circulation, and that in this new character it can be withdrawn from circulation just as the commodity must constantly be definitively withdrawn'.[6] However, since, as we have already emphasised,[7] 'money and commodity in the circuit M-C-M imply *more advanced* relations of production', i.e. the circuit M-C-M suggests the dominance not of simple commodity production but of capitalist production, Marx decided in the *Contribution* to develop the third function of money from C-M-C, 'the immediate form of commodity circulation',[8] and not from the circuit M-C-M, and we must follow this corrected version here. This is all the more essential as we can already see from the *Rough Draft* that the third function of money is already in evidence in the form of circulation C-M-C, insofar as money does not function as a mere medium of circulation.[9]

2. Money as hoard

The hoard is the most striking form of money's autonomy. We saw that the circulation of commodities, 'bursts through all the temporal, spatial and personal barriers imposed by the direct

[4] *ibid.* pp.144ff.
[5] This is also confirmed by Marx's letter to Engels of 2 April 1858, *Selected Correspondence*, pp.97-101.
[6] *Grundrisse*, p.203.
[7] See previous chapter p.143.
[8] *Contribution*, p.123.
[9] *MEW* Vol.29, p.317.

exchange of products ... by splitting up the direct identity ... between the exchange of one's own product and the acquisition of someone else's into the two antithetical segments of sale and purchase ... No one can sell unless someone else purchases. But no one directly needs to purchase because he has just sold.'[10] 'The fact that gold as money assumes an independent existence is thus above all a tangible expression of the separation of the process of circulation or of the metamorphosis of commodities into two discrete and separate transactions which exist side by side.'[11] The splitting of the circuit C-M-C therefore makes it possible for the seller of commodities to deliberately isolate the transaction C-M, to prevent it from proceeding to M-C, in order to get hold of the money-form of the commodity. In this case money petrifies into a hoard, and the seller of commodities becomes a hoarder.

We should preface this by saying that, although the process of hoarding is 'common to all commodity production', 'it figures as *an end in itself* only in the undeveloped, pre-capitalist forms of commodity production'.[12] This is because 'the less products assume the character of commodities, and the less intensively and extensively exchange-value has taken hold of production, the more does money appear as actual wealth as such, as wealth in general – in contrast to its restricted manner of presentation in use-values'.[13] Hence the great significance of hoarding in primitive societies, where it is only the surplus use-values which are transformed into commodities and where 'the traditional mode of production is aimed at satisfying the individual's own requirements, and corresponds to a fixed and limited range of needs'.[14] Gold and silver are the adequate form of existence of the surplus in such societies, and at the same time 'the first form in which wealth, as abstract social wealth, can be held'. This explains why 'the accumulation of all other commodities is less ancient than that of gold and silver'. In the first place this is related to the natural property the precious metals possess, of being imperishable. 'Accumulation is essentially a process which takes place in time.' Every use-value, as such, 'is of service in that it is consumed i.e. destroyed', and this at the same time signifies the destruction of its exchange-value. 'With money on the other hand, its substance, its materiality, is itself its form, in which it represents wealth'. Consequently if money

---

[10] *Capital* I, pp.209, 208 (112).
[11] *Contribution*, p.125.
[12] *Capital* II, p.85.
[13] *Capital* III, p.598.
[14] *Capital* I, p.228 (130).

'appears as the general commodity in all places, so also does it in all times. It maintains itself as wealth at all times . . . it is the treasure "which neither moth nor rust doth corrupt". All commodities are only transitory money; money is the permanent commodity.'[15] Secondly, 'The commodity, as a use-value, satisfies a particular need and forms a particular element of material wealth. But the value of a commodity measures the degree of its attractiveness for all other elements of material wealth, and therefore measures the social wealth of its owner. To the simple owner of commodities among the barbarians . . . value is inseparable from the value-form, and therefore to him the increase in his hoard of gold and silver is an increase in value. It is true that the value of money varies, either as a result of a change in its own value, or of a change in the values of commodities. But this on the one hand does not prevent 200 ounces of gold from continuing to contain more value than 100 ounces, nor on the other hand does it prevent the metallic natural form of this object from continuing to be the universal equivalent form of all other commodities, and the directly social incarnation of all human labour.'[16]

Although hoarding as such is characteristic of pre-capitalist conditions it does at the same time reveal tendencies which eventually lead to the dissolution of these primitive conditions and the decline of the communities which correspond to them.[17] This is because every form of natural wealth, 'before it is replaced by exchange-value . . . presupposes an essential relation between the individual and the objects in which the individual in one of his aspects objectifies himself in the thing, so that his possession of the thing appears at the same time as a certain development of his individuality; wealth in sheep, the development of the individual as shepherd, wealth in grain his development as agriculturist etc. Money, however, as the individual of general wealth[18] . . . as a merely social result, does not at all presuppose an individual relation to its owner; possession of it is not the development of any particular essential aspect of his individuality . . . since this social relation exists at the same time as a sensuous, external object which can be mechanic-

[15] *Grundrisse*, p.231.
[16] *Capital* I, p.230 (133).
[17] In this sense Marx speaks of the 'dissolving effect' of money (and trade) on the primitive communities. However, in the *Rough Draft* the 'dissolving effect of money' is sometimes understood to mean something else, namely that money is the means 'of cutting up property . . . into countless fragments and consuming piece by piece through exchange . . . (Without money, a mass of inexchangeable, inalienable objects)'. (*Grundrisse*, p.871.)
[18] See note 11 on p.103 above.

ally seized, and lost in the same manner. Its relation to the individual thus appears as a purely accidental one; while this relation to a thing having no connection with his individuality gives him, at the same time, by virtue of this thing's character, general power over society, over the whole world of gratifications, labours etc.' (Marx adds: 'The possession of money places me in exactly the same relationship towards wealth [social] as the philosophers' stone would towards the sciences'.)[19]

'Thus the social power becomes the private power of private persons.'[20] However, whatever 'surrenders itself to everything, and is yielded in return for anything, appears as the *universal means of corruption and prostitution*'.[21] For, 'just as everything is alienable for money, everything is obtainable by money ... and it depends on chance what the individual can appropriate and what not, since it depends on the money in his possession ... There is nothing inalienable, since everything is alienable for money. There is no higher or holier, since everything is appropriable by money. The *"res sacrae"* and *"religiosae"*, which may be *"in nullius bonis"*, *"nec aestimationem recipere nec obligari alienarique posse"*, which are exempt

---

[19] *Grundrisse*, pp.221-22. As one can see, Marx follows on here from his critique of money in the *Economic and Philosophical Manuscripts of 1844*, p.167: He writes there, commenting on a passage from Goethe's *Faust*: 'That which is for me through the medium of *money* – that for which I can pay (i.e. which money can buy) – that am I, the possessor of the money. The extent of the power of money is the extent of my power. Money's properties are my properties ... Thus what I am and am capable of is by no means determined by my individuality. I am ugly, but I can buy for myself the most beautiful of women. Therefore I am not ugly, for the effect of ugliness – its deterrent power – is nullified by money. I, as an individual, am lame, but money furnishes me with 24 feet. Therefore I am not lame. I am bad, dishonest, unscrupulous, stupid; but money is honoured, and hence its possessor. Money is the supreme good, therefore its possessor is good. Money saves me the trouble of being dishonest, I am therefore presumed honest. I am stupid, but money is the real mind of all things, and how then should its possessor be stupid? Besides, he can buy talented people for himself, and is he who has power over the talented not more talented than the talented? Do not I, who thanks to money am capable of all that the human heart longs for, possess all human capacities? Does not my money, therefore, transform all my incapacities into their contrary?' One is reminded of Henry Ford who parried the charge of ignorance during court proceedings by saying that he could send for people with the requisite knowledge within five minutes (K.Sward, *Legend of Henry Ford* p.105.)

[20] *Capital* I, p.230 (132).

[21] *Grundrisse*, German edn. p.895. (Cf. the numerous passages in Marx and Engels which deal with the 'universal venality', which is bound up with the money relation.)

from the "*commercio hominum*", do not exist for money – just as all men are equal before God.'[22] ('Things sacred and religious, which cannot be in the possession of anyone, and cannot either receive a valuation or be mortgaged or alienated, which are exempt from the commerce of man.') And it is precisely for this reason that money, in its third quality, must lead to the disintegration of the ancient communities, which are based on use-values – insofar as it is not 'itself the community', as in bourgeois society.[23]

This is all the more so as the drive to accumulate hoards is, by its nature, limitless. 'In gold and silver I possess general wealth in its pure form; the more of it that I pile up, the more general wealth I appropriate. If gold and silver are general wealth, then as particular quantities they only represent it to a particular extent, i.e. inadequately. The whole is impelled constantly to push out beyond itself.'[24] Marx continues, in the *Rough Draft* : 'Money is therefore not only *an* object, but *the* object of greed. It is essentially *auri sacra fames* (the accursed hunger for gold). Greed as such, as a particular form of the drive i.e. as distinct from the craving for a particular kind of wealth e.g. for clothes, weapons, jewels, women, wine etc. is possible only when general wealth, wealth as such, has become individualised in a particular thing i.e. as soon as money is posited in its third quality. Money is therefore not only the object but also the fountainhead of greed . . . The underlying reason is in fact that exchange-value as such becomes the goal, and consequently also an

---

[22] *Grundrisse*, p.839. (Cf. *Capital* I, p.229 (132) where Marx speaks of the 'alchemy' of money circulation, which 'not even the bones of saints, still less the more delicate *res sacrosanctae* . . . are able to withstand . . .')

[23] *Grundrisse*, p.224. We also read this in the *Rough Draft*: 'In antiquity, exchange-value was not the *nexus rerum* : it appears as such only among the mercantile peoples, who had, however, no more than a carrying trade and did not themselves produce. At least this was the case with the Phoenicians, Carthaginians etc. But this is a peripheral matter. They could live just as well in the interstices of the ancient world, as the Jews in Poland, or in the Middle Ages. Rather, this world itself was the precondition for such trading peoples. That is why they fall apart every time they come into serious conflict with the ancient communities. Only with the Greeks, Romans etc. does money appear unhampered in both of its first two functions, as measure and as medium of circulation, and not very far developed in either. But as soon as either their trade etc. develops, or, as in the case of the Romans, conquest brings them money in vast quantities – in short, suddenly, and at a certain stage of their economic development, money necessarily appears in its third role, and the further it develops in that role, the more the decay of their community advances.' (*ibid*. p.223.)

[24] *Grundrisse*, German edn. p.872.

expansion of exchange-value.'[25] 'The metamorphosis C-M, takes place, then, for its own sake, for the purpose of transforming particular physical wealth into general social wealth. *Change of form – instead of exchange of matter – becomes an end in itself.* Exchange-value, which was merely a form, is turned into the content of the movement.'[26] Therefore the cult of money 'has its asceticism, its self-denial, its self-sacrifice – economy and frugality, contempt for mundane temporal and fleeting pleasures; the chase after the *eternal* treasure. Hence the connection between English Puritanism, or also Dutch Protestantism, and money-making.'[27]

If one gets down to the root of the matter the comically appealing figure of the hoarder[28] appears in a different light, for 'the accumulation of money for the sake of money is in fact the barbaric form of production for the sake of production. i.e. the development of the productive powers of social labour beyond the limits of customary requirements'.[29] And therefore, 'The less advanced is the production of commodities the more important is hoarding – the first form in which exchange-value assumes an independent existence as money.'[30]

So much for hoarding proper, which seeks 'to preserve and maintain money as abstract wealth', independently of the social framework and in which 'the independence, the appropriate form of existence of exchange-value, is still only perceived in its directly material form as gold'.[31] As Marx repeatedly stressed, this form disappears 'more and more in bourgeois society', to make room for

[25] *Grundrisse*, p.222, and *Contribution*, p.132.
[26] *Contribution*, pp.127-28.
[27] *Grundrisse*, p.232. This idea was later written about by bourgeois sociologists and economists as if it was something entirely new.
[28] *Contribution*, p.140.
[29] ibid. p.134. We read in the *Rough Draft* (p.225): 'Money as individualised exchange-value and hence as wealth incarnate was what the alchemists sought; it figures in this role within the Monetary (Mercantilist) System. The period which precedes the development of modern industrial society opens with general greed for money on the part of individuals as well as of states. The real development of the sources of wealth takes place as it were behind their backs, as a means of gaining possession of the representatives of wealth . . . The hunt for gold in all countries leads to its discovery; to the formation of new states; initially to the spread of commodities, which produce new needs, and draw distant continents into the metabolism of circulation, i.e. exchange.' In this respect, therefore, money in its third function was 'doubly a means for expanding the universality of wealth, and for drawing the dimensions of exchange over the whole world; for creating the true generality of exchange-value in substance and in extension.'
[30] *Contribution*, p.134.
[31] *Grundrisse*, German edn. p.886.

other forms of the accumulation of money, 'which proceed from the mechanism of circulation itself and which are really mere resting places in it.'[32]

For example, the simple fact of the division of labour and the separation of sales from purchases leads to the temporary piling up of the means of circulation:

'Everybody sells the particular commodity he produces, but he buys all other commodities he needs for his social existence. How often he appears on the market as a seller depends on the labour-time required to produce his commodity, whereas his appearance as a buyer is determined by the constant renewal of his vital requirements. In order to be able to buy without selling, he must have sold something without buying.' From this it follows 'that M-C, the second member of the circuit C-M-C, splits up into a series of purchases, which are not effected all at once but successively over a period of time, so that one part of M circulates as coin, while the other part remains at rest as money. In this case, the money is in fact only *coin in suspension* and the various component parts of the coinage in circulation constantly change, appearing now in one form, now in another.'[33]

Thus reserve funds of coin arise at all points in commerce, and their 'formation, distribution, dissolution and reformation constantly changes'; at the same time they serve as channels for adding to or subtracting from the constantly expanding and contracting mass of money in circulation.[34] In addition to this, reserve funds develop out of the functions of money as means of payment[35] and world currency,[36] which will be dealt with later. The necessity for all these funds is already a product of the mechanism of simple commodity circulation, although they first acquire a significant magnitude within capitalist production. What is specific to this form of production is the accumulation of money which is conditioned by the turnover of capital, i.e. the stockpiling 'of ideal, temporarily unemployed capital, in the shape of money, including newly accumulated and not yet

---

[32] *ibid.*
[33] *Contribution*, pp.125-26.
[34] *ibid.* p.128 and *Capital* I, p.231 (134).
[35] 'The development of money as a means of payment makes it necessary to accumulate it in preparation for the days when the sums which are owing fall due. While hoarding, considered as an independent form of self-enrichment vanishes with the advance of bourgeois society, it grows at the same time in the form of the accumulation of a reserve fund of the means of payment.' (*Capital* I, p.240 (142).)
[36] *ibid.* pp.240-44 (142-44) and *Contribution*, p.149.

158 · *The Making of Marx's 'Capital'*

invested money-capital'.³⁷ Apart from this, in countries with developed capitalist production 'hoards strikingly above their average level . . . indicate stagnation in the circulation of commodities . . . i.e. an interruption in the flow of their metamorphoses'.³⁸

3. Money as means of payment

The second function in which money appears as the absolute form of value, is as means of payment. This function is discussed in two different sections of the *Grundrisse*; first – very briefly – at the end of the 'Chapter on Money' of the *Rough Draft* proper (pp. 235-36) and then in the so-called *Urtext: Zur Kritik*.* Both passages admittedly offer no more than fragments of an examination of the problem, but we shall mention here those points which are essential to our present theme.

Previously we proceeded from the assumption that when money circulates it continues to act at the same time as a real means of purchase, that, hence both poles of exchange, the commodity and money have to be present at one and the same time. 'But a *difference of time* may appear between the existence of the commodities to be exchanged. It may lie in the nature of reciprocal services that a service is performed today, but the service in return can be performed only after a year etc.'³⁹ In such cases the original character

---

³⁷ *Capital* III, p.319.
³⁸ *Capital* I, p.244 (145) cf. *Capital* II, p.353 : 'On the basis of capitalist production the formation of a hoard as such is never an end in itself but the result either of a stagnation of the circulation – larger amounts of money than is generally the case assuming the form of a hoard – or of accumulations necessitated by the turnover; or, finally, the hoard is merely the creation of money-capital existing temporarily in latent form and intended to function as productive capital.'

* Translator's Note : This is the original draft of the *Contribution to the Critique of Political Economy*, which has not been translated into English and is to be found in the German edition of the *Grundrisse* on pp.872-946. The section referred to here appears on pp.873-78 of that edition.

³⁹ *Grundrisse*, p.235. Cf. *Capital* I, 232-33 (134-35): 'With the development of circulation, conditions arise under which the alienation of the commodity becomes separated by an interval of time from the realisation of its price . . . One sort of commodity requires a longer, another a shorter time for its production. Again, the production of different commodities depends on different seasons of the year. One commodity may be born in the market-place, another must travel to a distant market. One commodity owner may therefore step forth as a seller before the other is ready to buy . . . the seller sells an existing commodity, the buyer buys as the mere representative of money, or, rather, as the representative of future money.'

'Money as money' · 159

of the metamorphosis of commodities is changed; the relation of debtor and creditor[40] replaces that of buyer and seller, and the money itself takes on the new quality of being a means of payment. Money can only appear in this function insofar as it represents 'the *only appropriate existence of exchange-value*' or the '*absolute form of the commodity*' i.e. has already developed into its third quality. 'Hard money' also 'lurks' in the function of means of payment.[41]

However, this does appear to be contradicted by the fact that with 'the development of the credit system capitalist production continually strives to *overcome* this metallic barrier, which is simultaneously a material and imaginative barrier to wealth and its movement'.[42] For, as Marx says in the *Rough Draft* : 'insofar as payments are equalised, money appears as a disappearing form, a merely ideal, imagined measure of the magnitudes of value which have been exchanged. Its physical intervention is confined to the settlement of relatively insignificant balances.' And further in the text: 'The development of money as universal means of payment goes hand in hand with the development of a higher circulation, mediated, bent back into itself,[43] and already taken under social control, in which the exclusive importance which it possessed on the basis of simple metallic circulation is annulled.'[44] However, 'if the flow of the equalisation of payments is interrupted by sudden upheavals in credit . . . money is suddenly required as a universal means of payment, and the demand is made that wealth in its entirety should exist doubly – first as commodity, and second as money, so that both these forms of existence cover one another. In such

[40] Cf. *Contribution*, pp.138-39. 'In the course of the metamorphosis of commodities the keeper of commodities changes his skin as often as the commodity undergoes a change or as money appears in a new form. Commodity owners thus faced each other originally simply as commodity owners; then one of them became a seller, the other a buyer; then each became alternately buyer and seller; then they became hoarders, and finally rich men. Commodity owners emerging from the process of circulation are accordingly different from those entering the process. The different forms which money assumes in the process of circulation are in fact only crystallisations of the transformation of commodities, a transformation which is in its turn only the objective expression of the changing social relations in which commodity owners conduct their exchange. New relations of intercourse arise in the process of circulation, and commodity owners, who represent these changed relations, acquire new economic characteristics.'
[41] 'For beneath the invisible measure of value lurks hard money.' (*Contribution*, p.70.)
[42] *Capital* III, p.574.
[43] Cf. above, note 11, pp.144-45.
[44] Cf. Chapter 22 below.

moments of crisis money appears as the exclusive form of wealth, which manifests itself in the active devaluation of all real physical wealth, and not in purely imaginary devaluation as in the Monetary System. Value exists in relation to the world of commodities only in its adequate, exclusive form as money.'

Thus 'the inherent contradictions of the development of money as universal means of payment' become evident here. 'Money is not demanded as measure in such circles, since its physical presence as such is irrelevant; nor as coin, since it does not figure as coin in payments. It is rather required as independent exchange-value, as the physically existing universal equivalent, the materialisation of abstract wealth, in short, precisely in the form in which it is the object of hoarding, as money. Its development as the universal means of payment hides the contradiction, that [on the one hand] exchange-value has assumed forms independent of its mode of existence as money, and on the other, that its mode of existence as money is posited as the definitive and only adequate one.'[45]

The same contradiction is revealed in yet another respect: 'As means of payment – money for itself – money should represent value as such; however it is in fact only an identical quantity of variable value.'[46] We have seen 'that changes in the value of gold and silver do not affect their functions as measure of value and money of account'. However, 'these changes are of decisive importance with regard to hoarded money, since with the rise or fall in the value of gold and silver the value of the hoard of gold or silver will rise or fall. Such changes are of even greater importance for money as means of payment.'[47] For 'what is to be paid is a definite quantity of gold or

---

[45] *Grundrisse*, German edn. pp.875-76. Cf. *Capital* III, p.573. 'But how are gold and silver distinguished from other forms of wealth? Not by the magnitude of their value, for this is determined by the quantity of labour incorporated in them; but by the fact that they represent independent incarnations, expressions of the social character of wealth . . . This social existence of wealth therefore assumes the aspect of a world beyond, of a thing, matter, commodity, alongside of and external to the real elements of social wealth. So long as production is in a state of flux this is forgotten. Credit, likewise a social form of wealth, crowds out money and usurps its place. It is faith in the social character of production which allows the money-form of products to assume the aspect of something that is only evanescent and ideal, something merely imaginative. But as soon as credit is shaken – and this phase of necessity always appears in the modern industrial cycle – all the real wealth is to be actually and suddenly transformed into money, into gold and silver – a mad demand, which, however, grows necessarily out of the system itself.'

[46] *Grundrisse*, German edn. p.871.

[47] *Contribution*, p.148.

silver, in which a definite value i.e. a definite amount of labour-time, was objectified at the time when the contract was concluded. However, gold and silver, like all commodities, change the magnitude of their value with the labour-time required for their production – falling or rising' in value 'as labour-time falls or rises'. 'Consequently it is possible that the realisation (*Realisation*) of the sale from the side of the buyer follows some time after the alienation of the commodity which was sold, that the same quantities of gold or silver contain different, larger or smaller, amounts of value than at the time when the contract was made. Gold and silver retain their specific quality, as money, of being the constantly realised and realisable universal equivalent, of being constantly exchangeable against all commodities in proportion to their own value, independently of any change in the magnitude of their value. However, this magnitude is potentially subject to the same fluctuations as that of every other commodity. Hence whether the payment is made in a real equivalent, i.e. at the magnitude of value originally intended, depends on whether or not the labour-time required for the production of a given amount of gold or silver has stayed the same. The nature of money, as incarnated in a particular commodity, here comes into collision with its function as exchange-value become independent'.[48] 'The total objectification, exteriorisation (*Ausserlichwerdung*) of the social change of matter on the basis of exchange-value appears strikingly in the dependence of all social relations on the production costs of metallic natural objects, which are completely without significance as instruments of production, or agents in the creation of wealth.'[49]

The development of the function of money as means of payment is clearly illustrated in the way in which the forms of commerce, for their part, react upon the relations of production. 'Originally,' we read in the *Contribution*, 'the conversion of products into money in the sphere of circulation appears simply as an individual necessity for the commodity owner when his own product does not constitute use-value for himself, but has still to become a use-value through alienation. In order to make payment on the contractual settlement day, however, he must already have sold commodities. The evolution of the circulation process thus turns selling into a social necessity for him, quite irrespective of his individual needs. As a former buyer of commodities he is forced to become a seller of other commodities so as to obtain money, not as a means of purchase, but as a means of payment... The conversion of commodities into money... or the

[48] *Grundrisse*, German edn. p.877.
[49] *ibid.* p.878.

first metamorphosis of commodities as the ultimate goal, which in hoarding appeared to be the whim of the commodity owner, has now become an economic function. The motive and the content of selling for the sake of payment constitutes the content of the circulation process, a content arising from its very form.'[50]

4. Money as world money

Finally we come to the role which money plays as the international means of payment and purchase, as world money.

The reader should remember that according to Marx's first outline this subject was to have been analysed in the fifth *Book* of the work, the *Book on Foreign Trade*. However, a section of a chapter devoted to this subject, can already be found in the fragment of the original text to the *Contribution*, the *Urtext*.[51] It is clear that the category of 'money as money' could not be fully elaborated, without at the same time investigating the role of money in international trade. Marx was therefore already obliged to diverge from his original outline as early as 1859.

A reading of the section on world money, which is to be found in the *Urtext*, the *Contribution* and in *Capital* (i.e. three different versions), shows how logical this was.

The role which money is required to play in international exchange 'is not a new quality ... which comes in addition to that of being money generally, universal equivalent – and therefore both hoard and means of payment'.[52] In fact money, 'when it leaves the domestic sphere of circulation loses the local functions it has acquired there as the standard of prices, coin, and small change, and as a symbol of value, and falls back into its original form as precious metal in the shape of bullion.'[53] It does not assume any special functions on the world market which might distinguish it from those which we already know. Rather, 'as world money', it regains 'its original natural form in which it played a role in barter originally'.[54] In other words: 'In the sphere of international commodity circulation gold and silver appear not as means of circulation but as universal means

---

[50] *Contribution*, pp.141-42.
[51] *Grundrisse*, German edn. pp.878ff.
[52] *ibid.* p.881.
[53] *Capital* I, p.240 (142).
[54] *Contribution*, p.149. *Grundrisse*, German edn. p.881.

of exchange.'⁵⁵ However, money can only function as the universal means of exchange in the form of means of purchase and means of payment.⁵⁶ Nevertheless, on the world market the relation of these two forms is reversed.

In the sphere of internal circulation, money (to the extent that it was coin) operated exclusively as means of purchase. On the world market, in contrast to this, 'the function [of money] as a means of payment in the settling of international balances is the chief one'. However, gold and silver function as international means of purchase chiefly when 'the customary equilibrium in the interchange of products between different nations is suddenly disturbed', for example, 'when a bad harvest compels one of them to buy on an extraordinary scale'.⁵⁷ In either case, 'money must always exist in its form of a hoard, in its metallic state; in the form in which it is not merely a form of value, but value itself, whose money-form it is'.⁵⁸ And finally, money functions on the world market 'as the universally recognised materialisation of social wealth, whenever it is not a matter of buying or paying, but of transferring wealth from one country to another, and whenever its transfer in the form of commodities is ruled out, either by the conjuncture of the market, or by the purpose of the transfer itself (for instance, in subsidies, money loans for carrying on wars or for enabling banks to resume cash payments, etc.)'⁵⁹

Thus, money's form as international means of exchange and payment is not in fact a 'particular form for that purpose'; rather, it fulfils, as such, only functions in which it appears 'most obviously in its simple, and at the same time, concrete form, as money'.⁶⁰ In contrast, what really marks out the entry of money onto the world market is 'the universality of its appearance, which corresponds to the universality of its concept'.

For it is on the world market that money first becomes 'the uni-

---

⁵⁵ *Contribution*, p.150. In this sense world-money can also be characterised as 'world coin'. However, as such, it is distinguished from coin proper by the fact that 'it is indifferent to its formal character' as means of circulation and is 'essentially commodity as such, omnipresent commodity'. To the extent, therefore, that gold and silver function in international trade 'as mere means of exchange, they in fact carry out the function of coin, but coin which has lost its stamp', so that they 'are only valued according to their metallic weight, do not only represent value, but rather *are* it simultaneously'. (*Grundrisse*, p.227; *Grundrisse*, German edn. pp.871, 879.)
⁵⁶ *Contribution*, p.150.
⁵⁷ ibid. p.150, and *Capital* I, p.242 (144).
⁵⁸ *Capital* III, p.451.
⁵⁹ *Capital* I, p.243 (144).
⁶⁰ *Grundrisse*, German edn. p.883.

versal commodity, not only according to its concept, but also its mode of existence,' and is 'posited as the commodity as such, the *universal* commodity, which retains its character as wealth in all places'.[61] It is there that 'money first functions to its full extent as the commodity whose natural form is also the directly social form of realisation of human labour in the abstract'.[62] In this sense money first becomes realised in 'its third function' as 'world money' – the 'universal world market commodity'.[63]

5. Concluding remarks

Our analysis of the role of money in the circuit C-M-C has shown that the process of exchange is simultaneously the process of the formation of money, and that the independence of the universal means of exchange itself represents 'the product of the process of exchange, of the development of the contradictions contained in the commodity'. But note how far removed the final form of money is from its original state! It unexpectedly developed from a modest mediator in the process of exchange into a factor standing outside it, and independent of it. Whereas originally it simply represented commodities, now the situation is the reverse, and the commodities themselves have become representatives of money. 'Every particular commodity, insofar as it is exchange-value, has a price, expresses a certain quantity of money in a merely imperfect form, since it has to be thrown into circulation in order to be realised, and since it remains a matter of chance, owing to its particularity, whether or not it is realised.' To the extent that we regard it not as value, but in its natural property 'it is only a moment of wealth by way of its relation to a particular need which it satisfies, and expresses in this relation 1. only the wealth of uses, 2. only a quite particular facet of this wealth'.

---

[61] *ibid.* pp.878 and 881.

[62] *Capital* I, p.242 (142). Cf. *Theories* III, p.253: 'But it is only foreign trade, the development of the market to a world market which causes money to develop into world money and abstract labour into social labour. Abstract wealth, value, money, hence abstract labour, develop in the measure that concrete labour becomes a totality of different modes of labour embracing the world market. Capitalist production rests on value, i.e. on the transformation of the labour embodied in the product into social labour. But this is only possible on the basis of foreign trade and of the world market. This is at once the pre condition and the result of capitalist production.'

[63] Therefore Marx repeatedly stresses that 'real money', 'money in the eminent sense of the term' only exists as 'world market money' in the 'universal world market commodity'. (*Capital* III, pp.430, 534.)

By contrast money is on the one hand 'the adequate reality of exchange-value . . . as general wealth itself, concentrated in a particular substance . . . individualised . . . as an individuated, tangible object';[64] on the other hand, it satisfies 'every need, insofar as it can be exchanged for the desired object of every need'. Consequently, money is not only the universal form of social wealth 'in contrast to all the substances of which it consists', but at the same time also its material representative, 'which in its unalloyed metallic shape, contains all the physical wealth evolved in the world of commodities in a latent state'.[65] 'Functioning as a medium of circulation, gold suffered all manner of injuries, it was clipped and even reduced to a purely symbolic scrap of paper. Its golden splendour is restored when it serves as money. The servant becomes the master. The mere underling becomes the god of commodities.'[66]

In another passage Marx writes: 'The special difficulty in grasping money in its fully developed character as money . . . is that a social relation, a definite relation between individuals, here appears as a metal, a stone, as a purely physical, external thing which can be found, as such, in nature, and which is indistinguishable in form from its natural existence . . . It is not at all apparent on its face that its character of being money is merely the result of social processes; it *is* money. This is all the more difficult since its immediate use-value for the living individual stands in no relation whatsoever to this role, and because, in general, the memory of use-value, as distinct from exchange-value, has become entirely extinguished in this incarnation of pure exchange-value. Thus the fundamental contradiction contained in exchange-value, and in the social mode of production corresponding to it, here emerges in all its purity.'[67]

However: 'Money in its final, completed character now appears in all directions as a contradiction which dissolves itself, drives towards its own dissolution. As the general form of wealth the whole world of real riches stands opposite it.' But 'where wealth as such seems to appear in an entirely material, tangible form, its existence is only in my head, a pure fantasy . . . On the other side, as material representative of general wealth, it is realised only by being thrown back into circulation, to disappear in exchange for the singular, particular modes of wealth.' If one wants 'to cling to it, it evaporates in the hand to become a mere phantom of real wealth'; but if one

---

[64] *Grundrisse*, pp.218, 221, and cf. note 11, p.103 above.
[65] *Grundrisse*, p.221, and *Contribution*, p.124.
[66] *Contribution*, pp.124-25.
[67] *Grundrisse*, pp.239-40.

dissolves it into individual gratifications 'it becomes lost to the accumulating individual'. However 'accumulating to increase it . . . turns out again to be false. If the other riches do not accumulate, then it loses its value in the measure in which it is accumulated. What appears as its increase is in fact its decrease. Its independence is a mere semblance; its independence of circulation exists only in view of circulation, exists as dependence on it. It pretends to be the general commodity, but because of its natural particularity it is again a particular commodity, whose value depends both on supply and demand, and on variations in its specific costs of production . . . As absolutely secure wealth, entirely independent of my individuality, it is at the same time, because it is something external to me, the absolutely insecure, which can be separated from me by accident . . . It therefore suspends itself as completed exchange-value.'[68]

The resolution of this glaring contradiction will first emerge in the chapter on capital in the *Rough Draft*. Only this much is intimated here : 'To develop the concept of capital it is necessary to begin not with labour, but with value, and, indeed, with exchange-value as already developed in the movement of circulation . . . The first quality of capital is, then, this; that exchange-value deriving from circulation and presupposing circulation preserves itself within it and by means of it; does not lose itself by entering into it; that circulation is not the movement of its disappearance, but rather the movement of its self-positing as exchange-value, its self-realisation as exchange-value.'[69] Hence the fundamental contradiction of money, as the final product of simple commodity circulation, of the circuit C-M-C, can only be overcome through the process of capitalist production, i.e. in the circuit M-C-M.

[68] *ibid*. pp.233-34.
[69] *ibid*. pp.259-60.

PART THREE
The Section on the Production Process

9.
Introductory Remarks
(On the actuality of the law of value in the capitalist economy)

The result of the analysis up until now can be summarised most succinctly by the order of development: Commodity – Value – Money – Capital. Marx himself gave us timely warning that this is by no means simply a question of concepts and their dialectic,[1] and that the logical succession of the categories simultaneously reflects real historical development. With this proviso our series of stages of development states nothing more than that each of the categories mentioned leads out beyond itself, and that none of them could be completely understood without the preceding ones. However, the converse also seems to be true; namely, each of the categories presupposes the succeeding ones, and could only fully develop on their basis. It is clear, for example, that the category of capital cannot be elaborated without those of the commodity, value and money; but it is equally true that these most general categories can only become fully developed on the basis of capital and the capitalist mode of production. How can this 'contradiction' be solved, and which of the two interpretations of the order of development is the correct one?

Here we come to an old, but continually reappearing objection to Marx's conception of the capitalist mode of production.[2]

[1] Cf. Chapter 5 above.
[2] This objection goes back as far as Tugan-Baranovsky.

The object of the attack is the close connection between Marx's theory of value and his theory of capital – the fact that, in order to arrive at the laws of the capitalist mode of production, Marx proceeds from the analysis of simple commodity production,[3] which presupposes the social equality of the participants in exchange, and therefore disregards the inequality which characterises capitalist production. Or, as we read in one of the most recent of Marx's critics, Rudolf Schlesinger : 'The fact that even great men occasionally make logical mistakes is not important for us, but it is important that Marx derived laws valid for a certain model [i.e. for the capitalist economic order] from those valid in the model which was simpler in structure and earlier in historical succession', i.e. from the 'model' of the simple commodity economy.[4]

As in many other instances, it was Marx himself who first formulated these 'misgivings'. Thus, writing in the *Rough Draft* against Adam Smith and the economists who followed him, Marx stated : 'All the modern economists declare that . . . the individual's own labour is the original title to property, be this in a more economic or a more juristic manner, and that property in the result of the individual's own labour is the basic presupposition of bourgeois society . . . This presupposition is itself based on the assumption *that exchange-value is the economic relation governing the entire relations of production and commerce*, and is therefore itself a historical *product* of bourgeois society, the society of developed exchange-value. On the other hand, since contradictory laws seem to emerge in the study of more concrete economic relations than are presented by simple circulation, all classical economists, up to Ricardo, prefer to allow that conception which springs from bourgeois society itself to count as a general law, but to banish its actual reality to a golden age, *where no property yet existed*. To the age before the economic Fall of Man, as it were, like Boisguillebert for example. *So that the peculiar result emerges, that the true operation of the law of appropriation of bourgeois society has to be transferred to a time when this society did not yet exist, and the basic law of property to the age of propertylessness.*'[5]

Although it is the law of appropriation which is under discussion here, exactly the same can be said in relation to the law of value. We read in the *Theories* : 'Ricardo sought to prove that, apart from certain exceptions, the separation between capital and wage-labour

---

[3] F.Oppenheimer, *Wert und Kapitalprofit*, pp.176ff.
[4] R.Schlesinger, *Marx, His Time and Ours*, 1950, pp.96-97.
[5] *Grundrisse*, German edn. pp.903-04.

does not change anything in the determination of the value of commodities. Basing himself on the exceptions noted by Ricardo, Torrens rejects the law. He reverts to Adam Smith (against whom the Ricardian demonstration is directed) according to whom the value of commodities was determined by the labour-time embodied in them in "that early period" when men confronted one another simply as owners and exchangers of goods, but not when capital and property in land have been evolved. This means ... that the law which applies to commodities qua commodities no longer applies to them once they are regarded as capital or products of capital, or as soon as there is, in general, an advance from the commodity to capital. On the other hand, the product first wholly assumes the form of a commodity – both in the sense that the entire product has to be transformed into exchange-value and in the sense that all the ingredients necessary for its production enter it as commodities – it first wholly becomes a commodity with the development of, and on the basis of, capitalist production. Thus the law of value is supposed to be valid for a type of production which produces no commodities (or produces commodities only to a limited extent) and not to be valid for a type of production which is based on the product as a commodity. The law itself, as well as the commodity as the general form of the product, is abstracted from capitalist production and yet it is precisely in respect of capitalist production that the law is held to be invalid.'[6] Thus what Torrens concludes is 'that here, within capitalist production, the law of value suddenly changes. That is, that the law of value, which is abstracted from capitalist production, contradicts capitalist phenomena. And what does he put in its place? Absolutely nothing but the crude, thoughtless expression of the phenomenon which is to be explained.'[7]

Marx therefore emphatically rejects the conceptions held by Smith and Torrens; it does not occur to him to transfer the operation of the law of value to the 'Golden Age' of pre-capitalist society, since this 'Golden Age', as the bourgeois economists visualise it, is a 'pure fiction' which arises from the surface appearance of the capitalist circulation of commodities, and which Adam Smith, 'in the true eighteenth-century manner puts in the prehistoric period, the period preceding history'.[8] In reality, 'the earliest form of production was

[6] *Theories* III, p.74. Schlesinger refers to just this passage when he speaks of Marx's 'stubborn attempts to save for "value", in a stage when commodities are exchanged at production prices, a meaning which cannot be upheld except by tautologies'. (The real meaning of the passage escapes him.)
[7] *Theories* III, pp.72-73.
[8] *Grundrisse*, p.156.

based on native communities within which private exchange only appears as a quite superficial and secondary exception. However with the historical dissolution of these communities relations of dominance and servitude appear, relations of force, which stand in glaring contradiction to the mild circulation of commodities, and the relations which corresponded to it.'[9] In contrast to these attempts to transfer the reality of the law of value to 'pre-Adamite' times, to the 'paradise lost of the bourgeoisie, where people did not confront one another as capitalists, wage-labourers, landowners, tenant farmers, usurers and so on, but simply as persons who produced commodities and exchanged them',[10] Marx repeatedly stresses that, as on the one hand, the capitalist mode of production 'presupposes above all the circulation of commodities, and hence of money as its basis',[11] so on the other hand commodity production 'does not become the normal, dominant type of production . . . until capitalist production serves as its basis'; that consequently commodity production, 'in its general, absolute form' is precisely the capitalist production of commodities.[12] For 'only where wage-labour is its basis does commodity production impose itself upon society as a whole',[13] and only then can the law of value emerge from the embryonic form, which it possessed under pre-capitalist conditions, to become one of the moving and ruling determinants in the totality of social production. For Marx, therefore, the law of value, far from belonging to the past, is particularly characteristic of capitalist society, and first attains its full validity within it. But how can this be reconciled with the fact (continually emphasised by Marx) that in a developed capitalist society the centre 'around which market prices oscillate' is not the value of a commodity but the price of its production, which diverges from its value? Thus, if Marx asked (in his polemic against Torrens) how it is that the law of value, which was abstracted from capitalist production, should not apply to this very form of production, it could equally be asked how this same law could in fact be abstracted from a mode

[9] *Grundrisse*, German edn. p.904.
[10] *Contribution*, p.59.
[11] *Capital* III, p.324.
[12] *Capital* II, pp.33, 141. Cf. *Theories* III, p.313: 'That it is only on the basis of capitalism that commodity production or the production of products as commodities becomes all-embracing and affects the nature of the products themselves'.
[13] *Capital* I, p.733 (587). Cf. *Capital* II, p.119: 'As a matter of fact capitalist production is commodity production as the general form of production. But it is so, and becomes so more and more in the course of its development, only because labour itself appears here as a commodity, because the labourer sells his labour, that is, the function of his labour-power.'

of production, whose immediately given phenomena *prima facie* contradict it? This is not, however, the place to go into the so-called contradiction between Volumes I and III of *Capital*, i.e. the problem of the 'transformation of values into prices of production'. (We shall come back to this later.) Our sole concern here is the methodological aspect of the problem – the question as to whether, from Marx's standpoint, one can speak of two different 'models', that of the simple commodity economy and that of the capitalist economy, and whether, in fact, Marx derived the laws of the latter from the former?

The answer can be found in Marx's Introduction to the *Rough Draft*, in fact in the famous section on the 'Method of Political Economy'. Marx demonstrates how the method of 'rising from the abstract to the concrete is only the way in which thought appropriates the concrete, reproduces it as the concrete in thought. But this is by no means the process by which the concrete itself comes into being.' Thus, 'the simplest economic category, e.g. exchange-value' in its completed form, 'can never exist other than as an abstract, one-sided relation within an already given, concrete living whole' (that is, capitalist society), although 'as a category' exchange-value seems to lead 'an antediluvian existence'. And consequently : 'In the succession of the economic categories, as in any other historical, social science, it must not be forgotten that their subject – here modern bourgeois society – is always what is given, in the head as well as in reality, and that these categories therefore express the forms of being, the characteristics of existence, and often only individual sides of this specific society, this subject, and that therefore this society by no means begins only at the point where one can speak of it *as such*; this holds for *science as well.*'[14] (For us it began with the analysis of the commodity and of money.)

After demonstrating in this way the abstract character of the 'simplest categories', Marx asks further : 'But do not these simpler categories also have an independent historical or natural existence predating the more concrete ones? That depends.' For example, money can exist 'and did exist historically, before capital existed, before banks existed, before wage-labour existed etc.' However : 'Although money everywhere plays a role from very early on, it is nevertheless a predominant element, in antiquity, only within the confines of certain one-sidedly developed nations, trading nations. And even in the most advanced parts of the ancient world, among

[14] *Grundrisse*, pp.101, 106.

the Greeks and Romans, the full development of money, which is presupposed in modern bourgeois society, appears only in the period of their dissolution.' Thus 'although the simpler category may have existed historically before the more concrete, *it can achieve its full (intensive and extensive) development* [only] *... in the most developed conditions of society!*'[15]

Labour provides another example: 'Labour seems a quite simple category. The conception of labour in this general form – as labour as such – is also immeasurably old. Nevertheless, when it is economically conceived in this simplicity, "labour" is as modern a category as are the relations which create this simple abstraction.' This is because, 'Indifference towards any specific kind of labour presupposes a very developed totality of real kinds of labour, of which no single one is any longer predominant ... On the other side, this abstraction of labour as such is not merely the mental product of a concrete totality of labours. Indifference towards specific labours corresponds to a form of society in which individuals can with ease transfer from one labour to another, and where the specific kind is a matter of chance for them, hence of indifference.'

However, such a situation is encountered for the first time in a developed capitalist society.[16] Marx concludes: 'This example of labour shows strikingly how even the most abstract categories, despite their validity – precisely because of their abstractness – for all epochs, are nevertheless, in the specific character of this abstraction, themselves likewise a product of historical relations, and *possess their full validity only for, and within these relations*.'[17]

What Marx says here on the category of labour also applies of course to the category of value as determined by labour. This category also had an 'antediluvian existence', it too existed historically long before capitalist production, although only in an immature and embryonic form, and by no means 'penetrated all economic relations'. To this extent, 'it is quite appropriate to regard the values of commodities as not only theoretically, but also historically prior to

---

[15] *ibid.* pp.101-04.
[16] Cf. *Capital* I, p.152 (60): 'The secret of the expression of value, namely the equality and equivalence of all kinds of labour because and insofar as they are human labour in general, could not be deciphered until the notion of human equality had already acquired the permanence of a fixed popular opinion. This however becomes possible only in a society where the commodity-form is the universal form of the product, hence the dominant social relation is the relation between men as possessors of commodities.'
[17] *Grundrisse*, pp.103, 104, 105.

the prices of production'.[18] However, the category of value only appears in its developed form in capitalist society, since only in this society does commodity production become the general form of production.[19]

In fact, products become commodities in a capitalist society, to the same degree that all commodities also become the products of capital. For this reason a modification of the law of value must take place. Hence the law of value only operates as an abstract determinant here, expressing only one aspect of capitalist society – although a fundamental one; namely the fact that all economic subjects have to relate to one another as exchangers of commodities (including the mutual relation of worker and capitalist).[20] However, abstract determinants cannot be applied directly to 'further developed concrete relations'; they have first to be mediated. And this mediation is established by the category of prices of production. Consequently the 'inversion of the law of value', the dialectical transition from labour-value (or the simple commodity economy) to prices of production (or capital) is not a historical deduction, but a method of comprehending the concrete, i.e. capitalist society itself. In other words (to go back to Marx's critics) it is not a question of two different 'models', but of one and the same model – that of the modern capitalist mode of production – which can only be apprehended by uncovering the internal laws of its movement, hence by means of the 'ascent from the abstract to the concrete'. In order to understand the prices of production, which appear on the surface, we must go back to their hidden cause, value. And those who do not agree to this must confine themselves to mere empiricism, and therefore abandon any attempt to give a real explanation of the processes of the capitalist economy.

So much then on the way in which Marx solved the question of the 'actuality of the law of value'. This chapter was included to make it easier to understand what comes later. The reader should realise in advance why Marx begins with the analysis of simple commodity circulation, and the role allotted to this analysis in his theory. And he should not overlook the fact that this is a question of the most abstract sphere of capitalist production; of a sphere behind

---

[18] *Capital* III, p.177.
[19] Cf. Chapter 4 of Rubin's work referred to previously.
[20] As far as this relation is concerned Marx's critics cannot deny that the most important exchange of all – the purchase and sale of labour-power – conforms, primarily, to the law of value, i.e. the 'first model', despite the modifications indicated by Marx himself. (See *Capital* III, pp.159-60.)

which 'yet another world conceals itself, the world of the interconnections of capital',[21] in which a radical inversion (*Umschlag*) of both the law of value and the law of appropriation becomes unavoidable.

[21] *Grundrisse*, p.639.

10.
The Law of Appropriation in a Simple Commodity Economy

The 'Chapter on Capital'[1] which follows the 'Chapter on Money' opens with an illuminating study of the 'law of appropriation, as it appears in simple circulation'.[2] This is a welcome complement to Volume I of *Capital*, where this theme is only touched on incidentally.[3]

Up until now Marx's presentation has not gone beyond the sphere of simple circulation. In simple commodity circulation the exchangers initially confront each other as persons who can only acquire each other's commodities on the basis of a voluntary agreement to exchange, and who must therefore acknowledge each other as the owners of private property. The exchange relation itself does not tell us how they became commodity owners, and how the original appropriation of the commodities came about. However, since the commodity as value simply represents objectified labour, and since from the standpoint of circulation 'alien commodities, i.e. other people's labour, can only be appropriated through the *alienation* of one's own, it follows that the property in the commodity which precedes exchange appears [as] . . . arising directly from the labour of its owner, and labour appears as the original mode of appropriation . . . as the legal title to property.' It was in this sense that the classical

---

[1] The entire 'Chapter on Capital' was (as we learn from the editorial note on p.150 of the German edition of the *Grundrisse*) originally designated as the 'Chapter on Money as Capital', and it is therefore incomprehensible why the publishers of the work use this original title as the contents guide on the top edge of pp.151-62, which are devoted to the analysis of the 'law of appropriation'. The Soviet economist Leontiev takes this erroneous guide at its face value and struggles to prove to his readers that 'although, at first sight the content of pp.151-62 does not appear to correspond to the heading provided by Marx' this is, in reality, merely an 'apparent contradiction'. (*O pervonatshalnom nabroske 'Kapitala'* Marksa, Moscow, 1946, p.27.)

[2] So designated in the *Index zu den 7 Heften*, in both versions. (pp. 151-62 and 901-18, *Grundrisse*, German edn.)

[3] Cf. *Capital* I, pp.178-79 (85-86), 279-80 (176).

economists pronounced '*property in the result of the individual's own labour to be the basic presupposition of bourgeois society*'.[4]

The 'law of appropriation through one's own labour' which characterises the simple commodity economy gives rise to 'a realm of bourgeois freedom and equality based on this law [which] spreads out, on its own accord in circulation'. The principle of reciprocity, 'the pre-established harmony between the owners of commodities', is also a consequence of this law.[5]

In fact, 'although individual A feels a need for the commodity of individual B, he does not appropriate it by force', and neither does the commodity owner B, but rather, 'they recognise one another reciprocally as proprietors, as persons whose will penetrates their commodities'. In this way, the 'juridical moment of the Person and of *Freedom*, insofar as it is contained in the former', enters the relation of the commodity owners. (Marx remarks in this connection : 'In Roman Law the slave is therefore correctly defined as one who may not enter into exchange for the purpose of acquiring anything for himself.') Admittedly, a certain element of compulsion is contained in the fact that the partners in exchange are driven to exchange by their needs. Looked at in this way, however, 'it is only my own nature, this totality of needs and drives, which exerts a force on me; it is nothing alien ... But it is after all, precisely in this way that I exercise compulsion over the other person and drive him into the system of exchange'.[6] In this way the circulation of commodities reveals itself directly as the realisation of the freedom and independence of the owners of commodities.

In exchange, individuals confront each other merely as the owners of commodities, and each of these individuals 'has the same social relation towards the other as the other has to him. As subjects of exchange, their relation is that of *equality*. It is impossible to detect any trace of distinction, not to speak of contradiction, between them.'[7] Of course the exchangers represent different needs and different use-values. This situation, 'far from endangering the social equality of the individuals, rather makes their natural difference into the basis of their social equality. If individual A had the same need as individual B, and if both had realised their labour in the same object, then no relation whatever would be present between them; considering only their production, they would not be different indi-

---

[4] *Grundrisse*, German edn. pp.902, 903.
[5] *ibid.* p.904.
[6] *Grundrisse*, pp.243-46.
[7] *ibid.* p.241.

Appropriation in a simple commodity economy · 177

viduals at all. Both have the need to breathe; for both the air exists as atmosphere; this brings them into no social contact; as breathing individuals they relate to one another only as natural bodies, not as persons. Only the differences between their needs and between their production give rise to exchange and to their social equation in exchange; these natural differences are therefore the precondition of their social equality in the act of exchange, and of this relation in general, in which they relate to one another as productive.'[8]

On the other hand, 'The commodities which they exchange are, as exchange-values, also equivalents . . . which not only are equal but are expressly supposed to be equal'; and 'if one individual, say, cheated another this *would happen not because of the nature of the social function in which they confront one another* . . . but only because of natural cleverness, persuasiveness etc., in short only the purely individual superiority of one individual over another'.[9] Here therefore, both the exchanging subjects and the objects exchanged seem subject to the law of equality.

Finally, in exchange, in addition to the quality of freedom and equality comes that of reciprocity: 'Individual A serves the needs of individual B by means of the commodity "a" only insofar as and because individual B serves the needs of individual A by means of the commodity "b", and vice versa. Each serves the other in order to serve himself; each makes use of the other, reciprocally, as his means.' Consequently, it is also 'present in the consciousness of the exchanging subjects that each arrives at his end only insofar as he serves the other as means; that each is a means for the other; and finally that the reciprocity in which each is simultaneously means and end, and in fact only attains his end through becoming a means for the other, and only becomes means by attaining his end, is a necessary fact, presupposed as a natural precondition of exchange, but that as such it is irrelevant to each of the two subjects of the exchange and is only of interest to him to the extent that it satisfies *his* interest.'[10]

Marx says in another passage that the economists 'express this as follows: each pursues his private interest and only his private interest;

[8] *ibid.* p.242.
[9] *ibid.* p.241.
[10] *ibid.* pp.243-44, and *Grundrisse*, German edn. pp.911-12. 'The common interest', we read further on in the text, 'is indeed recognised as a fact by both sides, but it is not a motive as such; rather it exists, so to speak, only behind the backs of these self-reflected individual interests . . . At most the individual can have the consoling awareness that the satisfaction of his most selfish individual interests is precisely the realisation of the superseded antithesis, of the general social interest . . . The general interest is precisely the generality of self-seeking interests.'

and thereby serves the private interests of all, the general interest, without willing or knowing it.' However : 'The real point is not that each individual's pursuit of his private interest promotes the totality of private interests, the general interest. One could just as well deduce from this abstract phrase that each individual reciprocally blocks the assertion of the others' interests so that, instead of a general affirmation, this war of all against all produces a general negation. The point is rather that private interest is itself already a socially determined interest, which can be achieved only within the conditions laid down by society, and with the means provided by society ... It is the interest of private persons; but its content, as well as the form and means of its realisation, is given by social conditions independent of all of them.'[11]

Marx further examines how the commodity owners' conceptions of equality, freedom and reciprocity, which arise from commodity exchange, are consolidated and perfected through the money system. This is related primarily to money's role as 'equaliser'. As a 'radical leveller'[12] it extinguishes all natural differences and makes 'a worker who buys commodities for 3s ... appear in the same function, in the same equality ... as the king who does the same'.[13] And even accumulation, the petrification of money into a hoard, only abolishes the equality of the commodity owners in appearance. For 'if one individual accumulates and the other does not, then none does it at the expense of the other ... He can only take in the form of money, what is there in the form of the commodity ... One enjoys the content of wealth, the other takes possession of wealth in its general form. If one grows impoverished and the other grows wealthier, this is a question of their own discretion, their thrift, industry,[14] morality etc., and by no means emerges of itself from the economic relations ... in which the individuals in circulation confront one another.'

Furthermore; 'even *inheritance*, and similar legal relations, which might prolong any such inequalities, do not detract from this social equality. If individual A's relation was not in contradiction with equality originally, then such a contradiction can surely not arise from the fact that individual B steps into the place of individual A, thus perpetuating him. Inheritance is rather an assertion of the social law beyond the natural life-span, and a reinforcement of it against the chance influences of nature; the intervention of the latter tends

[11] *Grundrisse*, p.156.
[12] *Capital* I, p.229 (132).
[13] *Grundrisse*, p.246.
[14] i.e. industriousness.

Appropriation in a simple commodity economy · 179

rather to do away with the freedom of the individual. Moreover, since the individual in this relation is merely the individuation of money, *he is therefore as such as immortal as money itself*.'[15] So much then for the 'harmonies of freedom and equality' which necessarily arise from the real conditions of commodity exchange, and which make it appear as 'a very Eden of the innate rights of man'.[16] It is not at all surprising that the apologists of capitalism, right up to the present day, prefer to retreat to the realm of simple commodity exchange, when they wish to conjure away the contradictions of the capitalist economic order! Because of the fact that capitalist relations are also relations of exchange, they are now regarded merely as such. Marx remarks: 'What all this wisdom comes down to is the attempt to stick fast at the simplest economic relations, which, conceived by themselves, are pure abstractions; but these relations are in reality mediated by the deepest antitheses, and represent only one side, in which the full expression of the antitheses is obscured.'[17] Consequently, if bourgeois economists hold up the relations of simple commodity exchange as a refutation of 'the more developed economic relations in which individuals relate to one another no longer merely as buyers or sellers but in specific relations ... then it is the same as if it were asserted that there is no difference, to say nothing of antithesis and contradiction, between natural bodies, because all of them, when looked at from e.g. the point of view of their weight, have weight, and are therefore equal; or are equal because all of them occupy three dimensions.' The economists forget here that even the presupposition with which they begin 'by no means arises either out of the individual's will, or out of the immediate nature of the individual, but that it is rather historical' and that in developed commodity circulation, 'the individual has an existence only as a producer of exchange-value, hence the whole negation of his natural existence is already implied'.[18] And on the other hand they forget that the sphere of commodity circulation merely represents the surface of bourgeois society beneath which, however, 'in the depths, entirely different processes take place', giving rise to 'different, more involved' economic relations 'which collide to a greater or lesser extent with the freedom and independence of the individuals'.
    In order to demonstrate the completely unhistorical character of

[15] *Grundrisse*, p.247 and *Grundrisse*, German edn. p.915.
[16] *Capital* I, p.280 (176).
[17] 'What is overlooked ... is that already the simple forms of exchange-value and of money latently contain the opposition between labour and capital etc.' (*Grundrisse*, p.248.)
[18] *Grundrisse*, pp.247-48.

this 'infantile abstraction' of bourgeois apologetics, Marx turns to the social division of labour, which constitutes the precondition of commodity production. The classical economists (from Petty to Smith) understood the division of labour as being 'correlative with exchange-value' since the products which assume the form of commodities and values are in fact nothing other than labour realised in different ways and in different use-values, nothing other than 'the objective existence of the division of labour'. This division simply expresses, 'in active form, as the particularisation of labour . . . what the different use-values express in material form'. In commodity exchange the division of labour only appears 'in the result'; it merely expresses the fact 'that the subjects of exchange produce different commodities, which correspond to different needs, that if each individual depends on the production of all, all depend on his production in that they mutually complement each other, and that in this way the product of each individual, through the circulation process and to the extent of the amount of value he possesses, is a means of participating in social production as a whole.'[19] However, this obscures the more complex economic relations which are comprised in the social division of labour. It is clear, though, that commodity production 'does not merely presuppose the division of labour in a general sense, but a specifically developed form of it',[20] which is manifested in the isolation of the individual, 'the assertion of the individual's independence at each particular point'[21] and the private character of the commodity producers.[22] And it is this specific form of the division of labour which is the crucial issue! For, if we look only at the exchange relation as such, 'an English tenant farmer and a French peasant stand in the same economic relation. But the French peasant only sells the small amount of surplus left over from the production of his family. He consumes most of the product himself, and hence does not relate to the bulk of it as exchange-value, but as use-value, a direct means of subsistence. In contrast, the English tenant farmer is completely dependent on the sale of his product, thus on its sale

---

[19] *Grundrisse*, German edn. pp.907-09.
[20] *ibid.* p.905.
[21] *'punktuelle Verselbständigung'* (*ibid.* p.906.) A concept drawn from Hegel.
[22] Thus the social division of labour – and often in a rather developed form – also existed in the primitive communist communities, although this did not mean that the products they produced assumed the form of commodities. But though it is correct 'to say that individual exchange presupposes the division of labour, it is wrong to maintain that division of labour presupposes individual exchange'. (*Contribution*, p.60.)

as a commodity, and hence on the social use-value of his product. His entire production is therefore determined and seized on by exchange-value.'

Marx concludes that this shows 'what a very different development of the productive forces of labour, and its division, what different relations between individuals within production, are required so that grain, for example, may be produced as simple exchange-value, and thus enter in its entirety into circulation; and what economic processes are required to make an English farmer out of a French peasant.'[23] However, it is not the peasant, living in a semi-natural economy, who is a characteristic figure of developed commodity production, but the capitalist farmer – since production for the market is of decisive importance in the latter case. The analysis of the form of the division of labour, as the basis of commodity exchange, therefore leads to the result (already known to us) that we must presuppose 'the entire system of bourgeois production in order that exchange-value may appear, on the surface of things, as the simple point of departure', and in order that the members of society 'may confront each other in the circulation process as *free producers in the simple relation of buyers and sellers*, and figure as its independent subjects'.[24] It is therefore no accident that the ideas peculiar to developed commodity production, summed up in the 'trinity of property, freedom and equality', were first theoretically formulated by the Italian, English and French economists of the seventeenth and eighteenth centuries. These ideas thus merely anticipated the realisation of this trinity in modern bourgeois society. Far from expressing certain eternal characteristics of human nature, these ideas are rather mere reflections of the capitalist process of exchange, which constitutes their real basis. 'As pure ideas they are idealised expressions of its different moments; as developed in legal, political and social relations they are simply reproduced in other planes.'[25]

So much for the bourgeois-apologist misinterpretation of simple commodity circulation and the laws arising from it.[26] Marx saw a counterpart to this 'in the foolishness of those socialists (in particular the French, who want to depict socialism as the realisation of the

[23] *Grundrisse*, German edn. p.906.
[24] *ibid.* p.907.
[25] *ibid.* pp.915-16. Marx adds: 'And so it has been in history. Equality and freedom as developed to this extent are exactly the opposite of the freedom and equality in the world of antiquity, where developed exchange-value was not their basis, but where rather the development of that basis destroyed them.' (*Grundrisse*, p.245. Cf. Engels, *Anti-Dühring*, p.124.)
[26] Cf. the short sketch 'Bastiat and Carey' in the *Grundrisse*, pp.883-93.

ideals of bourgeois society articulated by the French Revolution) who maintain that exchange and exchange-value etc. are originally (in time) or essentially (in their adequate form) a system of universal freedom and equality, but have been perverted by money, capital, etc.' The answer to these socialists (Marx is thinking above all of Proudhon[27]) is that 'exchange-value or, more precisely, the money system, is in fact the system of equality and freedom, and that the disturbances which they encounter in the further development of the system are disturbances inherent in it, are precisely the realisation of equality and freedom, which turn out to be inequality and unfreedom.'[28]

An extremely important methodological conclusion follows from what has been said: since the production process 'as it *appears* on the *surface* of society' knows no other mode of appropriation than the 'appropriation of the product of labour by labour, and of the product of alien labour by the individual's own labour', based on the equality, freedom and reciprocity of the producers, it follows that the contradictions which emerge in the course of the development of commodity production 'must be derived just as much as this law of the original appropriation of labour, *from the development of exchange-value itself*'.[29] Simple commodity circulation only seems to allow the acquisition of property in alien labour by the surrender of the individual's own labour i.e. only through the exchange of equivalents. The theory now has to demonstrate how this changes in the course of further development, and how it eventually comes about that 'private property in the product of one's own labour is identical with the separation of labour and property, so that labour will create alien property and property will command alien labour'.[30]

[27] Cf. *Capital* I, pp.178-79 n.1 (84-85 n.2).
[28] *Grundrisse*, pp.248-49.
[29] *Grundrisse*, German edn. p.904.
[30] *Grundrisse*, p.238.

11.
The Transition to Capital

('The development of capital out of money')[1]

We now come to the main subject of Marx's analysis – the category of capital. The first question is naturally: What is capital? How is its concept to be developed?
We read in the *Rough Draft* that the Classical economists often conceive of capital as 'accumulated (properly speaking objectified[2]) labour, which serves as the means for new labour'. However, 'it is just as impossible to proceed directly from labour to capital, as it is to go from the different human races directly to the banker, or from nature to the steam-engine'. The usual definition says basically nothing more than that capital is a means of production, 'for, in the broadest sense, every object, including those furnished purely by nature e.g. a stone, must first be appropriated by some sort of activity before it can function as an instrument, as means of production. According to this, capital would have existed in all forms of society, and is something altogether ahistorical. Hence every limb of the body is capital, since each of them not only has to be developed through activity, labour, but also nourished, reproduced, in order to be active as an organ. The arm, and especially the hand, are then capital. Capital would be only a new name for a thing as old as the human race, since every form of labour, including the least developed, hunting, fishing etc. presupposes that the product of prior labour is used as means for direct, living labour.'
Thus the above definition only 'refers to the simple material of

---

[1] The chapter 'The Transition to Capital' is present in two versions in the *Grundrisse*, as was the previous chapter. These are in the main manuscript itself (pp.239ff of the English edition of the *Rough Draft*) and also in the fragment of the *Urtext: 'Zur Kritik'* (original text of the *Contribution*) to be found on p.919ff of the German edition. Both versions are used here.

[2] 'Already in *accumulated* labour, something has sneaked in, because, in its essential characteristic, it should be merely *objectified* labour, in which, however, a certain amount of labour is accumulated. But accumulated labour already comprises a quantity of objects in which labour is realised.' (*Grundrisse*, p.258.)

capital without regard to the formal character without which it is not capital'. 'If then the specific form of capital is abstracted away, and only the content is emphasised, as which it is a necessary moment of all labour, *then of course nothing is easier than to demonstrate that capital is a necessary condition for all human production.* The proof of this proceeds precisely by abstraction from the specific aspects which make it the moment of a specifically developed *historic* stage of human production. The catch is that if all capital is objectified labour which serves as means for new production, it is not the case that all objectified labour which serves as means for new production is capital. *Capital is conceived as a thing, not as a relation.*'[3]

At first sight another explanation seems to be more promising, namely that which conceives of capital as a 'sum of values' or 'self-reproducing exchange-value'. At least this 'contains the *form* wherein exchange-value [4] is the point of departure',[5] instead of an accumulation of the material products of labour. However: 'Every sum of values is an exchange-value, and every exchange-value is a sum of values. I cannot get from exchange-value to capital by means of mere addition.'[6] On the other hand, 'while all capital is a sum of commodities, that is, of exchange-values, not every sum of commodities, of exchange-values, is capital'.[7] Thus the second explanation is of no more use than the first.

In fact, the economists help themselves out of their predicament by defining as 'capital' any value 'which produces a *profit* or which is at least employed with the intention of producing a profit'. But in this case they simply assume what has to be explained, 'since profit

---

[3] *ibid.* pp.257-59. Cf. the well-known passage from Marx's *Wage-Labour and Capital* (1847): 'Accumulated labour which serves as a means of new production is capital. So say the economists – What is a Negro slave? A man of the black race. The one explanation is as good as the other. A Negro is a Negro. He only becomes a slave in certain relations. A cotton-spinning Jenny is a machine for spinning cotton. It becomes *capital* only in certain relations. Torn from these relationships it is no more capital than gold in itself is money or sugar the price of sugar.' And further: '*Capital*, also, is a social relation of production. *It is a bourgeois production relation*, a production relation of bourgeois society. Are not the means of subsistence, the instruments of labour, the raw materials of which capital consists, produced and accumulated under given social conditions, in definite social relations? Are they not utilised for new production under given social conditions, in definite social relations? And is it not just this definite social character which turns the products serving for new production into *capital*?' (*Selected Works*, pp.79-80.)
[4] Cf. Note 8 on p.111 above.
[5] *Grundrisse*, p.258.
[6] *ibid.* p.251.
[7] *Wage-Labour and Capital* (*Selected Works*, p.81.)

is a specific relation of capital to itself'.[8] It is clear that this does not answer the question. Capital must be understood as self-augmenting value, and hence as a process. And for this purpose it is necessary to proceed, not from a mere sum of values, or products of labour, but from 'exchange-value *as it is already developed in the movement of circulation*'. Marx's analysis therefore begins here.

However, which of the two forms of circulation which we already know (C-M-C and M-C-M) is involved here? In which can value become capital?

Clearly not in the circuit C-M-C (simple circulation) since here the exchange of value (*Wertwechsel*) of the commodity and money merely has the role of a 'fleeting mediation' : 'One commodity is ultimately exchanged for another commodity . . . and the circulation itself only served, on the one hand to allow use-values to change hands according to need, and on the other to allow them to change hands to the extent to which labour-time is contained in them . . . and to the extent to which they are factors of equal weight in general social labour-time.'[9] As such, simple commodity circulation, the form C-M-C, does not therefore carry 'the principle of self-renewal within itself', it cannot 'ignite itself anew from its own resources'; the repetition of the process 'does not follow from the conditions of circulation itself . . . Commodities constantly have to be thrown into it anew from the outside, like fuel into a fire. Otherwise it flickers out in indifference.'[10]

In other words, consumption, use-value, constitutes the ultimate

[8] *Grundrisse*, p.258. We read a little further on in the Rough Draft: 'It is damned difficult for Messrs. the economists to make the theoretical transition from the self-preservation of value in capital to its multiplication; and this in its fundamental character, not only as an accident or result . . . Admittedly, the economists try to introduce this into the relation of capital as an essential aspect, but if this is not done in the brutal form of defining capital as that which brings profit, where the increase of capital itself is already posited as a special *economic* form, profit, then it happens only surreptitiously and very feebly . . . Drivel to the effect that nobody would employ his capital without drawing a gain from it amounts either to the absurdity that the good capitalists will remain capitalists even *without* employing their capital; or to a very banal form of saying that gainful investment is inherent in the concept of capital. Very well. In that case it would have to be demonstrated.' (*ibid.* pp.270-71.)

[9] *Grundrisse*, German edn. p.925: 'Regarded in itself, circulation is the mediation of presupposed extremes. But it does not posit these extremes. Therefore, as the entirety of mediation, as a total process itself, it must be mediated. Its immediate existence is therefore pure semblance. It is the phenomenon of a process going on behind its back.' (*ibid.* p.920.)

[10] *Grundrisse*, p.255 and, in German edn. p.920.

aim and the real content of simple commodity circulation. Marx concludes: 'Therefore it is not in this aspect of the content (of the material) that we must look for the attributes which lead further.' We should rather stay with the formal aspect, where 'exchange-value as such becomes further developed and receives more profound qualities through the process of circulation itself. With the aspect, that is to say, of the development of money', as it appears as the result of the circulation process.[11] Thus we come to the category of 'Money as Capital', 'which goes beyond its simple quality as money'[12] and in so doing, establishes a transition from value and money to capital.

Naturally this can only apply to money in its 'third quality or function',[13] since it is only in this form that money is 'no longer a merely mediating form of commodity exchange . . . It is a product of circulation which has, as it were, grown out of it contrary to agreement', and in which value 'becomes independent' of circulation. And simultaneously it is a form in which the only sensible movement appears to be the enlargement of value, its continual multiplication.[14]

In fact, as long as we remain in the sphere of simple commodity circulation, the independence of money must in the last analysis prove to be chimerical, since even money in its third quality is only 'suspended medium of circulation', which owes its formation to a deliberate or an involuntary interruption of the circulation process. If it 're-enters circulation this is the end of its immortality, the value contained in it is dissipated in the use-values of the commodities for which it is exchanged, and it becomes a mere medium of circulation once more.' On the other hand, if money remains withdrawn from circulation 'it is as valueless as if it lay buried in the depths of a mine'; it 'collapses into its material, which is left over as the inorganic ash of the process as a whole'.[15] And even if the money which has been withdrawn from circulation is hoarded, no real increase or creation of value takes place in the movement C-M-C. 'Value does not emerge from value; rather, value is thrown into circulation in the

---

[11] *Grundrisse*, German edn. p.925.

[12] '*Money as capital* is an aspect of money which goes beyond its simple character as money. It can be regarded as a higher realisation; as it can be said that man is a developed ape. However, in this way the lower form is posited as the primary subject, over the higher', which would be incorrect. 'In any case, *money as capital* is distinct from *money as money*. The new aspect is to be developed.' (*Grundrisse*, p.251.) Cf. *Capital* I, Chapter 4, where the discussion centres on 'Money as Capital'.

[13] Cf Chapter 8 above.

[14] *Grundrisse*, German edn. pp.928, 935.

[15] *ibid*. pp.929, 925, (p.263 in the English edn.).

form of the commodity, in order to be withdrawn from it in the unusable form of the hoard. . . . The same magnitude of value which previously existed in the form of the commodity, now exists in the form of money; it becomes stored up in the latter form, since it is dispensed with in the other . . . thus enrichment appears in its content as voluntary impoverishment.'[16] Consequently, in simple circulation the increase of money 'can only appear in the form of hoarding, mediated by C-M, the constantly renewed sale of the commodity, since money is not permitted to run its full course', by which it transforms itself into the commodity again.[17] Hence in the form C-M-C neither the entry nor the non-entry of money into circulation can protect it from the eventual loss of its independence and immortality.[18]

Where then is the real solution to the problem to be found? What are the conditions under which money can go beyond the stage of primitive hoarding, for it – without being absorbed as a mere medium of circulation or petrifying into a hoard – to preserve and augment itself as independent value? (For 'as the universal form of wealth . . . money is only capable of a quantitative movement : that of increasing itself . . . it only preserves itself as distinct from use-value, as value in its own right, by constant self-multiplication.'[19]) It is clear that these conditions first obtain in the circuit M-C-M (buying in order to sell). Because in order for money to 'preserve itself as money, it must return to circulation just as often as it leaves it, but not as a mere medium of circulation . . . [It must] still remain money in its existence as commodity, and exist only as a temporary form of the commodity in its existence as money . . . Its entry into circulation must be itself as a moment of its remaining at home with itself, and its remaining at home with itself[20] an entry into circulation.' (In other words : it is only in the form of money as capital that the limitless drive for the enlargement of exchange-value can turn from a mere 'chimera' into a living, actual reality.[21]) On the other hand,

[16] *Grundrisse*, German edn. pp.929, 935.
[17] *ibid.* p.930.
[18] Cf. *Capital* I, p.268 (166): 'Capital cannot therefore arise from circulation and it is equally impossible for it to arise apart from circulation. It must have its origin both in circulation and not in circulation.'
[19] *Grundrisse*, German edn. p.936.
[20] *Beisichbleiben* – once more reminiscent of Hegelian terminology.
[21] 'However, as representative of the general form of wealth – money – capital is the endless and limitless drive to go beyond its limiting barrier. Every boundary (*Grenze*) is and has to be a barrier (*Schranke*) for it. Else it would cease to be capital – money as self-reproductive. If ever it perceived a certain boundary not as a barrier, but became comfortable within it as a

circulation itself has to appear 'as a moment in the production of exchange-values', as a link in the process by which they are preserved and augmented. To this end exchange-value has to be 'in fact exchanged for use-value and the commodity consumed as use-value, but it must preserve itself as exchange-value in this consumption'.[22] Hence the consumption of this commodity must be productive consumption, directed not at immediate use, but rather at the reproduction and new production of values.[23] Only under these conditions i.e. if the circuit C-M-C turns into the circuit M-C-M, can money become self-preserving and self-augmenting value, become capital.

However we must define more precisely the use-value, whose consumption should show itself as the production both of value and of surplus-value at one and the same time. As already noted, capital is, by its nature, a 'surplus-value breeding' value.[24] 'The only use-value i.e. usefulness, which can stand opposite capital as such is that which increases, multiplies, and hence preserves it as capital ... not an article of consumption, in which it loses itself, but rather in which it preserves and increases itself.' Only such a use-value can be confronted by capital as 'independent value' and capital can only be realised in such a value.

From this aspect, the commodity, as such, cannot be the opposite of capital, since money which has become capital 'is indifferent to the particularities of all commodities, and can take on any form of the commodity which is desired. It is not this or that commodity, but it can be metamorphosed into any commodity ... Instead of excluding it, the entire range of commodities, all commodities, appear as an equal number of incarnations of money', since they — just like

boundary, it would itself have declined from exchange-value to use-value, from the general form of wealth to a specific, substantial mode of the same ... The quantitative boundary of the surplus-value appears to it as a mere natural barrier, as a necessity which it constantly tries to violate and beyond which it constantly seeks to go.' (*Grundrisse*, pp.334-35.) The conceptual distinction between 'boundary' and 'barrier' is taken from Hegel. (See *Science of Logic*, Vol.I, pp.129-51.)

[22] *Grundrisse*, German edn. pp.931-32. This is not possible in simple commodity circulation: 'The use-value existing in the commodity disappears (for its owner) as soon as its price is realised in money; the exchange-value which is fixed in money disappears (for the owner of money) as soon as it is realised in the commodity as use-value ... By the simple act of exchange each can only become lost in its characteristic against the other, when it is realised in it. None can remain in the one characteristic, in that it passes over into the other.' (*ibid.* pp.919-20.)

[23] *ibid.* pp.932-33.

[24] 'Active value is simply value which posits surplus-value.' (*Grundrisse*, German edn. p.936.)

money – only count in exchange as objectified labour. In this respect there is no difference in principle between commodities and the money which has been transformed into capital.[25] 'The only antithesis to *objectified* labour is *unobjectified* . . . labour as subjectivity. (Or objectified labour, i.e. labour which is present in space, can also be opposed, as past labour, to labour which is present in time.)' However, as such it can 'be present only as the *living subject*, in which it exists as capacity, as possibility; hence as *worker*'.[26] Thus the only use-value which '*can constitute an opposition and a complement to money as capital, is labour*' as a use-value '*from which exchange-value itself develops, is produced and increased*'. And the 'only exchange by which money can become capital is when its owner enters into exchange with the owner of the living capacity to work[27] i.e. the worker'.[28] In this sense living labour can be characterised as the use-value of capital – as the 'real *not-capital*' which confronts capital as such.[29]

It can be seen that this is the same solution to the problem which we have already encountered in Volume I of *Capital*;[30] except there the solution is present in its finished form, with the intermediary stages left out, whereas here, we can observe it, as it were, *in statu nascendi*. In both instances, however, the transformation of money into capital – as Marx himself notes in one passage – 'is developed from the relation of independent exchange-value to use-value'.[31] It would therefore be pointless to counterpose the later, 'more realistic' seeming version of the solution in *Capital* to the more 'metaphysical' one in the *Rough Draft*. Both are the product of Marx's dialectical

---

[25] ibid. p.941.
[26] *Grundrisse*, p.272 and cf. p.942 of the German edition.
[27] In the *Rough Draft* Marx uses throughout the expression 'capacity to work' (*Arbeitsvermögen*) in the place of the later expression 'labour-power' (*Arbeitskraft*).
[28] *Grundrisse*, German edn. pp.942, 943, 944.
[29] *Grundrisse*, p.274. 'Labour posited as *not-capital* as such is: (1) *not-objectified labour, conceived negatively* . . . it is not-raw-material, not-instrument of labour, not-raw-product: labour separated from all means and objects of labour, from its entire objectivity.' . . . (2) but in this quality labour is 'the living source of value' (for the capitalists), and thereby is 'the general possibility of wealth', 'which proves itself as such in action'. Both statements 'are reciprocally determined and follow from the essence of labour, such as it is *presupposed* by capital as its contradiction and as its contradictory being, and such as it, in turn, presupposes capital'. (*ibid.* pp.295-96.) In this context we have to confine ourselves to an – admittedly very meagre – summary of this important, but difficult, aspect of the *Rough Draft*.
[30] See *Capital* I, pp.270ff (167ff).
[31] *Grundrisse*, German edn. p.952.

method, and should therefore be accepted or rejected by the same token. The difference lies only in the method of presentation.

It would definitely be quite wrong to regard this solution as merely a dialectical elaboration of concepts! It is based just as much on an exhaustive analysis of the concrete historical conditions which led to the formation of the capitalist mode of production. In both *Capital* and the *Rough Draft*, the first presupposition of the capital relation is the fact that the owner of money, the capitalist, 'can exchange his money for another's ability to work, as a commodity'; hence that 'firstly the worker disposes as a free proprietor of his ability to work (i.e. he relates to it as a commodity)' and secondly, 'that he can no longer exchange his labour in the form of another commodity, as objectified labour, but rather the only commodity which he has to offer, to sell, is his living capacity to work, present in his living bodily existence' . . . However, the fact that the capitalist 'finds the ability to work as a commodity on the market, within the boundaries of circulation – the presupposition from which we set out and which forms the starting point of the production process of bourgeois society – is clearly the result of a long historical development, the *resumé* of numerous economic changes, and presupposes the decline of other modes of production . . . and a particular development of the productive powers of social labour.'[32]

Marx takes this opportunity to note: 'This point definitely shows how the dialectical form of presentation is only correct when it knows its own limits.' But these limits are determined by the actual course of historical development. 'The general concept of capital can be derived from the study of simple circulation, because within the bourgeois mode of production simple circulation itself exists only as a presupposition of capital and presupposing it. The emergence of its general concept does not make capital into the incarnation of an eternal idea; it shows rather the way in which in reality and only as a *necessary* form, it must first issue into exchange-value-positing labour, onto production based on exchange-value.'[33] Thus, what at first sight might appear to be a mere 'dialectic of concepts' is in reality only the reflection of the fact that simple commodity circulation, which only becomes the general form which penetrates the entire economic organism under the rule of capital, represents no more than an 'abstract sphere' within this mode of production, 'which establishes itself as a moment, a mere form of appearance of a deeper

---

[32] *ibid.* p.945. Cf. *Capital* I, p.273 (169).
[33] *Grundrisse*, German edn. pp.945-46.

The transition to capital · 191

process – that of *industrial capital* which lies behind it, and which both produces it and results from it'.[34]

Marx stresses 'that it is vitally important to keep this point in mind', that the exchange relation between the capitalist and the wage-labourer is, at first, 'simply a relation of money and commodity, a relation of simple circulation'. For what takes place within circulation 'is not the exchange between *money* and *labour*, but the exchange between *money* and the *living capacity to work*'.[35] However what drives this exchange beyond the limits of simple circulation in the course of further development is the specific use-value of what has been exchanged, the use-value of the capacity to work.

As we already know, in simple circulation the content of use-value is economically irrelevant 'and is no concern of the form of the relation'. In the exchange between capital and labour, however, 'the use-value of that which is exchanged for money appears as a particular economic relation', as an 'essential economic moment' of the exchange.[36] Consequently in reality, 'there take place *two* processes, which are different and opposed to each other not only formally but also qualitatively', namely 1. the exchange of the capacity to work for wages (an act which belongs to simple circulation) and 2. the use of the capacity to work by the capitalists. 'Since the capacity to work exists in the *life* of the subject himself and is only manifested as his life expression . . . the appropriation of the title to its use during the act of its use naturally puts buyer and seller in a different relation from that which prevails in the case of objectified labour, which is present as an object external to the producer.'[37] For this reason, 'the difference between the second act and the first – note that the particular process of the appropriation of labour by capital is the second act – is exactly the difference between the exchange of capital and labour, and exchange between commodities as it is mediated by money. *In the exchange between capital and labour, the first act is an exchange, falls entirely within circulation; the second is a process qualitatively different from exchange*, and only by misuse could it have been called any sort of exchange at all. It stands directly

---

[34] *ibid.* pp.922-23.
[35] *ibid.* p.946.
[36] *Grundrisse*, p.274.
[37] 'This', adds Marx, 'does not impinge upon the exchange relation . . . As use-value, the capacity to work is only realised in the activity of labour itself, but in the same way [as the use-value of a bottle of wine] is only realised in drinking the wine. Labour itself falls as little into the process of simple circulation as drinking.' (*Grundrisse*, German edn. p.946.)

opposite the exchange' of commodities; it is an 'essentially different category'.[38]

In the course of the transformation from C-M-C to M-C-M money has become capital. 'The immortality which money strove for, in positing itself negatively against circulation, in withdrawing from it, is attained by capital, in that it is preserved precisely by being abandoned to circulation. Capital, as the exchange-value which presupposes circulation, is in turn presupposed by it, and preserves itself in it, alternately takes on both the aspects which are contained in simple circulation', namely C and M, 'and indeed, not in the manner characteristic of simple circulation, where one form passes over into the other, but rather in this way : in each of its aspects it is simultaneously the relation to its contrary aspect'.[39] 'Just as simple circulation itself, money and commodity as such exist for capital as only particular abstract moments of its existence, in which it just as often appears, passes over from one moment into the other, as it disappears.' Thus, 'in capital money has lost its fixedness and from a tangible thing it has become a process'.[40] Hand in hand with this a profound change occurs in the mode of production as a whole : whereas previously, at the stage of simple commodity circulation, value-creating production was only of significance to the extent that the commodities which entered circulation were embodiments of social labour-time, and therefore, as such, had to be values, 'now circulation itself returns back into the activity which posits or produces exchange-value . . . as into its ground' (and at the same time 'as its result').[41] And whereas previously all that was required for

---

[38] *Grundrisse*, p.275.

[39] *Grundrisse*, German edn. p.938 : 'Capital posits the permanence of value . . . by incarnating itself in fleeting commodities and taking on their form, but at the same time changing them just as constantly; alternates between its eternal form in money and its passing form in commodities; permanence is posited as the only thing it can be, a passing passage – process – life. But capital obtains this ability only by constantly sucking in living labour as its soul, vampire-like.' (*Grundrisse*, p.646.) Cf. *Capital* I, p.342 (234): 'Capital is dead labour which, vampire-like, lives only by sucking living labour, and lives the more, the more labour it sucks.'

[40] *Grundrisse*, German edn. p.937.

[41] *Grundrisse*, p.255. At first sight this seems to be a question of a purely Hegelian construction, since the 'return to the foundation', is one of the most fundamental features of the Hegelian dialectic. (See note 107 on p.38 above.)

However, one can see from the following passage from the *Rough Draft* how realistically Marx conceived of this 'return': 'Thus circulation [i.e. simple commodity circulation] presupposed a production which was only acquainted with exchange-value in the form of surplus, excess; but it returned

circulation was a form of production which only 'created exchange-value as a surplus', the production of value now becomes the decisive social form which rules the entire system of production. A historical process, which is theoretically expressed in the category 'money as capital'.

to a production which took place only with a relation to circulation, to a production which posited exchange-value as its immediate object (*Objekt*). This is an example of the historical return of simple circulation to capital, to exchange-value as the form governing production.' (*Grundrisse*, German edn. p.922.)

12.
Exchange between Capital and Labour-Power

In the previous chapter we pointed to two different processes in the exchange between capital and labour. For the worker this exchange simply represents the sale of his labour-power for a particular sum of money, for wages; what the capitalist gains by means of this exchange is labour itself, 'the productive power which capital obtains and multiplies' which does not arise from the value of the commodity which capital purchases, but from its use-value. The worker's exchange is an act of simple commodity circulation in which his commodity (labour-power) passes through the circulation form C-M-C; whereas capital represents the moment opposed to this, the form M-C-M. Finally, for the worker the matter is one of an exchange of equivalents (labour-power for the price of labour), whilst on the other hand one can only speak of an apparent exchange (or a 'non-exchange') on the side of capital since, through that exchange, the capitalist 'has to obtain more value than he has given'.

We want to start by looking at the first of these processes, the exchange between capital and labour-power.

As in any exchange, the worker appears here as the owner of his commodity, labour-power, which does not however exist as a thing external to him, but as part of his living body. It is therefore evident that he can only hand over the disposition over his capacity to work to the owner of money, to the capitalist, if this disposition 'is restricted to a *specific* labour and is *restricted in time* (so much labour-time)'.[1]

It follows from this that the worker 'can always begin the exchange anew as soon as he has taken in the quantity of substances required in order to reproduce the externalisation of his life'; and that labour constitutes 'a constant new source of exchange with

---

[1] *Grundrisse*, p.282. We read in *Capital*, that if the worker were to sell his labour-power, 'in a lump, once and for all, he would be selling himself, converting himself from a free man into a slave, from an owner of a commodity into a commodity'. (*Capital* I, p.271 (168).)

capital for the worker as long as he is capable of working'. The periodic recurrence of the act of exchange is merely the expression of the fact that the worker 'is not a *perpetuum mobile*', and must first sleep and eat his fill 'before he is capable of repeating his labour and his exchange with capital'.[2] Besides this, the repetition is only apparent. 'What he exchanges with capital is his entire labouring capacity, which he spends, say, in 20 years. Instead of paying for it in a lump sum, capital pays him in small doses', which naturally changes nothing in the basic nature of the relation.[3]

However, the fact that the worker is the owner of his labour-power and only grants temporary disposal over it to capital in exchange is of decisive importance, since it counts as one of those features of the relation of wage-labour which raise it historically above earlier modes of exploitation. For example, in the slave-relation the actual direct producer 'belongs to the *individual particular* owner and is his labouring machine. As a totality of *force-expenditure* as labour capacity, he is a thing belonging to another, and does not relate as subject to his particular expenditure of force, nor to the act of living labour.' In the serf-relation 'he [the direct producer] appears as a moment of property in land itself, is an appendage of the soil, exactly like draught-cattle'. By contrast the wage-labourer 'belongs to himself and has disposition over the expenditure of his forces through exchange'. What he sells 'is always nothing more than a specific, particular measure of force-expenditure; labour capacity as a totality is greater than every particular expenditure'.[4] (Which means, in fact, that the worker is recognised as a person, as a human being, 'who is something for himself apart from his labour and who alienates his life-expression only as a means towards his own life'.[5]) In addition, the wage-labourer sells his expenditure of force 'to a particular capitalist, whom he confronts as an independent individual. It is clear that this is not his relation to the existence of capital as capital, i.e. to the capitalist class.[6] Nevertheless in this way, as far as

[2] Marx says further: 'Instead of aiming their amazement in this direction – and considering the worker to owe a debt to capital for the fact that he is alive at all, and can repeat certain life processes every day . . . these whitewashing sycophants of bourgeois economics should rather have fixed their attention on the fact that, after constantly repeated labour, he always has *only* his living direct labour itself to exchange.' (*Grundrisse*, pp.293-94.)
[3] *ibid.* p.294.
[4] *ibid.* pp.464-65.
[5] *ibid.* p.289.
[6] Cf. *Capital* I, p.719 (573): 'From the standpoint of society, then, the working class . . . is just as much an appendage of capital as the lifeless instruments of labour are . . . The Roman slave was held by chains; the wage-

the individual real person is concerned, there is a wide field of choice, of arbitrary will, and hence of formal freedom'[7] which the producers of other class societies lacked and without which the worker's struggle for liberation would be simply inconceivable.

Thus, the labour-power of the worker appears to him 'as his property, as one of his moments, over which he, as subject, exercises domination, and which he maintains by expending it'. In this situation he acts simply as a commodity owner, and it is clear 'that the use which the buyer makes of the purchased commodity is as irrelevant to the *specific form* of the relation here as it is with any other commodity . . . Even if the capitalist were to content himself merely with the capacity of disposing, without actually making the worker work, e.g. in order to have his labour as a reserve, or to deprive his competitor of this capacity of disposing[8] . . . [nevertheless] the exchange would still have taken place in full.'

Admittedly the piecework system 'introduces the semblance that the worker obtains a specified share of the product. But this is only another form of measuring time[9] (instead of saying, you *will* work for 12 hours, it is said, you get so much per piece; i.e. we measure the time you have worked by the number of products)', and this form in no way alters the fact that the worker simply receives an equivalent to his labour-power from the capitalist, in accordance with the law of commodity exchange.[10]

With regard to the amount of this equivalent, to the value of labour-power, is clear that it cannot be determined 'by the manner in which its buyer *uses* it, but only by the amount of objectified labour contained in it'.[11] ('The use-value of a thing does not concern its seller as such, but only its buyer. The property of saltpetre, that it can be used to make gunpowder, does not determine the price of saltpetre; this price is determined rather by the cost of production of saltpetre . . .'[12] Similarly labour-power 'has a use-value for the worker himself only insofar as it is *exchange-value*, not insofar as it

---

labourer is bound to his owner by invisible threads. The appearance of independence is maintained by a constant change in the person of the individual employer, and by the legal fiction of a contract.'

[7] *Grundrisse*, p.464.

[8] Marx uses the example of theatre directors, who 'buy singers for a season not in order to have them sing, but so that they do not sing in a competitor's theatre'.

[9] Cf. Note 12 on p.60 above.

[10] *Grundrisse*, p.282.

[11] *ibid.* pp.282, 466.

[12] *ibid.* p.306.

produces exchange-values'.[13] However, this exchange-value is determined by the cost of production of labour-power, i.e. of the worker himself. The commodity which he offers 'exists only as an ability, a capacity of his bodily existence' : accordingly the value of his labour-power is measured by the quantity of labour which is necessary to maintain the life of the worker and reproduce him as a worker. This, 'in general terms ... is the measure of the amount of value, the sum of money which he obtains in exchange'.[14]

Like every exchange of commodities, the exchange between labour-power and capital is mediated by money. 'Because the worker receives the equivalent in the form of money, the form of general wealth, he is in this exchange an equal vis-à-vis the capitalist, like every other party in exchange.' Of course, this equality is 'only a semblance and a deceptive semblance', and it is rendered null and void in reality by the fact that capital appropriates a part of the worker's labour-time *without exchange* by means of the *form* of exchange', hence that the worker stands 'in another economically determinate relation' to the capitalist 'than that of exchange' ... 'This semblance exists, nevertheless, as an illusion on his part and to a certain degree on the other side, and thus essentially modifies his relation by comparison to that of workers in other social modes of production.'[15]

But not only that! Since the worker exchanges his labour-power for money, 'for the general form of wealth, he becomes a co-participant in general wealth up to the limit of his equivalent – a quantitative limit which, of course, turns into a qualitative one, as in every exchange'. Although it is true that this limit is as a rule very narrowly defined, on the other hand the worker is 'neither bound to a particular manner of satisfaction [of his needs] ... nor to particular objects.[16] The extent of his consumption is not qualitatively, but rather quantitatively restricted[17].' This also serves to 'distinguish him from slaves, serfs etc'.[18]

---

[13] *ibid.* p.307.
[14] *ibid.* pp.282-83.
[15] *ibid.* pp.284, 465, 674.
[16] And Marx adds that it is precisely by these means that it becomes possible for the worker to participate 'in the higher, even cultural satisfactions, agitation for his own interests, newspaper subscriptions, attending lectures, educating his children, developing his tastes etc ... his only share of civilisation which distinguishes him from the slave'. (*ibid.* p.287.)
[17] In the original: *'ausgeschlossen'*.
[18] *ibid.* p.283. Marx adds that the fact that the circle of satisfactions is only quantitatively limited gives the modern workers, 'also as consumers an

The exchange between labour-power and capital also falls into the realm of simple commodity circulation because for the worker it is the satisfaction of his immediate needs, rather than value as such, which constitutes the aim of exchange. 'He does obtain money, it is the satisfaction of his immediate needs, rather than value as transient mediation. What he obtains from the exchange is therefore not exchange-value, not wealth, but a means of subsistence, objects for the preservation of his life, the satisfaction of his needs in general, physical, social etc.'[19] However, we have seen in our study of the circuit C-M-C that money can be withdrawn from circulation and become a hoard. In this sense the worker might then be theoretically in the position to save a part of the money which has come into his possession, keep it in the general form of wealth, and consequently 'enrich' himself. However, this is only possible 'through his sacrificing substantial satisfaction to obtain the *form* of wealth – i.e. through *self-denial*, saving, cutting corners in his *consumption* so as to withdraw less from circulation than he puts goods into it'. Or also by 'denying himself more and more rest' and 'more frequently renewing the act of exchanging' his labour-power, 'or extending it quantitatively, hence through *industriousness*'.

Marx sarcastically comments, that it is in fact the workers who, in the present society, are treated to sermons on 'industriousness'; the demand is raised 'that he for whom the object of exchange is subsistence should deny himself, not he for whom it is wealth . . .'[20] 'Still, no economist will deny that if the workers generally, that is, as workers (what the individual worker does or can do, as distinct from his genus, can only exist just as exception, not as rule, because it is not inherent in the character of the relation itself), that is if they acted according to this demand *as a rule*' they would – apart from the enormous losses to general consumption – 'be employing means which absolutely contradict their purpose . . . If all or the majority are too industrious (to the degree that industriousness in modern industry is in fact left to their own personal choice, which is

entirely different importance . . . from that which they possessed e.g. in antiquity or in the Middle Ages, or now possess in Asia'. (*ibid.*)

[19] *ibid.* p.284. (As the reader can see, it never occurred to Marx to limit the value of labour-power to the physical 'minimum of existence'!)

[20] *ibid.* p.284. (In the following sentence Marx says: 'The illusion that the capitalists in fact practised "self-denial" – and became capitalists thereby – a demand and a notion which only made sense at all in the early period when capital was emerging from feudal etc. relations – has been abandoned by all modern economists of sound judgement.' The author of *Capital* was certainly too optimistic in this respect.)

Exchange between capital and labour-power · 199

not the case in the most important and most developed branches of production), then they increase not the value of their commodity, but only its quantity . . . [and] a general reduction of wages will bring them back to earth again.'[21] Consequently, the best that the workers can achieve through saving is a more expedient distribution of their expenditure, so that 'in their old age, or in the case of illness, crises etc. they do not become a burden on the poor-houses, the state, or on the proceeds of begging . . . and on the capitalists, vegetating out of the latter's pockets'. And this is also 'what the capitalists actually demand. The workers should save enough at the times when business is good to be able more or less to live in the bad times, to endure short-time or the lowering of wages etc.' They should make it easier for capital to overcome crises, and on the other hand ensure that 'the capitalists can extract high interest rates out of their savings, or the state eat them up . . . that is, save in every way for *capital* and not for himself'![22]

The fact that the average worker cannot enrich himself by saving, cannot lift himself out of his class position, is simply the result of the fact that 'he finds himself in a relation of simple circulation' in his exchange with capital, and thus as equivalent for his labour-power 'obtains not wealth, but only subsistence, use-values for immediate consumption . . . If the point of departure in circulation is the commodity, use-value as the principle of exchange, then we

[21] *ibid.* pp.285-86.
[22] *ibid.* p.287. Incidentally, adds Marx, 'each capitalist does demand that his workers save, but only *his own*, because they stand toward him as workers; but by no means the remaining *world of workers*, for these stand toward him as consumers. In spite of all "pious" speeches he therefore searches for means to spur them on to consumption, to give his wares new charms, to inspire them with new needs by constant chatter etc. It is precisely this side of the relation of capital and labour which is an essential civilising moment, and on which the historic justification, but also the contemporary power of capital rests.' (*ibid.* p.287.)
Cf. Marx's essay *Wages* (1847): 'The purpose – at least in the strict economic sense, of savings banks is supposed to be that the workers, by their own foresight and intelligence, balance out the good periods of work with the bad; i.e. distribute their wages in the cycle which the movement of industry makes, so that they actually do not spend more than the minimum of wages indispensable to life. But we have seen that not only do the fluctuations in wages revolutionise the workers, but that without their momentary increase above the minimum they would remain excluded from all progress in production, public wealth, civilisation, i.e. the possibility of emancipation. He is supposed to turn himself into a bourgeois calculating machine, to systematise niggardliness, and give meanness a stationary, conservative character.' (*Collected Works*, Vol. 6, p.426.)

necessarily arrive back at the commodity', which 'after having described its circle is consumed as the direct object of need'. In this process money simply has the role of the means of exchange, 'vanishing mediation'.[23] However, if the money saved by the worker 'does not remain merely the product of circulation', then sooner or later 'it would itself have to become capital i.e. buy labour'. The consequence of this would be 'the establishment at another point of the contradiction it is supposed to overcome'. Therefore if the product of exchange from the workers' side were not 'use-value, subsistence, satisfaction of direct needs . . . then labour would confront capital not as labour, not as not-capital, but as capital. But capital, too, cannot confront capital if capital does not confront labour, since capital is only capital as not-labour; in this contradictory relation. Thus the concept and the relation of capital itself would be destroyed.'[24]

In simple commodity exchange the seller has no rights whatsoever to the fruits of the commodity which he has put up for sale; this applies also to the wage-labourer, who, for the price of his ability to work, *'surrenders his creative power*, like Esau his birthright for a mess of pottage'. His exchange with capital is, for him, the same as *'the renunciation of all fruits of labour'*[25] (as Cherbuliez, the follower of Sismondi, expressed it). What 'appears paradoxical *as result* is already contained in this presupposition'. Since in the capitalist mode of production the worker only disposes of his ability to work, which coincides with his own personal existence, whereas on the other hand all the means for the objectification of his labour belong to capital, the benefits of his productive power can accrue only to capital, and not to him. 'The worker therefore sells labour as a simple, predetermined exchange-value, determined by a previous process – he sells labour itself as *objectified labour* . . . capital buys it as living labour, as the general productive force of wealth; activity which increases wealth. It is clear therefore that the worker *cannot become rich* in this exchange. Rather he necessarily *impoverishes himself* . . . because the creative power of his labour establishes itself as the power of capital, as an *alien power* confronting him. He divests himself of labour as the force productive of wealth; capital appropriates it as such.'[26] 'The separation between labour and property in the product

---

[23] *Grundrisse*, pp.289, 295.
[24] *ibid.* p.288.
[25] *ibid.* p.308.
[26] Marx notes elsewhere that even the bourgeois economists admit this, in that they do not regard the wage, the *'Salär'*, as productive. 'For them of course, to be productive means to be productive of wealth. Now, since wages are the product of the exchange between worker and capital – and the only

Exchange between capital and labour-power · 201

of labour, between labour and wealth, is thus posited in this act of exchange itself.'[27]

The last point Marx goes into in his representation of the exchange between labour-power and capital is that of the abstract character of the labour which confronts capital. 'Since capital *as such* is indifferent to every particularity of its substance . . .' the labour which confronts it is also 'absolutely indifferent to its *particular specificity*, but capable of all specificities . . . That is to say that labour is of course in each single instance a specific labour, but capital can come into relation with every specific labour; potentially it confronts the *totality* of all labours, and the particular one it confronts at a given time is an accidental matter.' Correspondingly the worker, too, 'is absolutely indifferent to the specificity of his labour; it has no interest for him as such, but only in as much as it is in fact *labour*; and as such a use-value for capital. It is therefore his economic character that he is the carrier of labour as such – i.e. of labour as *use-value* for capital; he is a *worker*, in opposition to the capitalist.' It is precisely this which distinguishes him from 'craftsmen and guild-members etc. whose economic character lies precisely in the *specificity* of their labour and in their relation to a *specific master*'.[28] The wage relation 'therefore develops more purely and adequately in proportion as labour loses all the characteristics of art; as its particular skill becomes something more and more abstract and irrelevant and as it becomes more and more a *purely abstract activity*, a purely mechanical activity, hence indifferent to its particular form . . . Here it can be seen once again', Marx concludes, 'that the

product posited in this act itself – they therefore admit that the worker produces *no wealth* in this exchange, neither for the capitalist, because for the latter the payment of money for a use-value – and this payment forms the only function of capital in this relation – is a sacrifice of wealth, not creation of the same, which is why he tries to pay the smallest amount possible; nor for the worker, because it brings him only subsistence, the satisfaction of individual needs, more or less – *never* the general form of wealth, never wealth. Nor can it do so, since the content of the commodity which he sells rises in no way above the general laws of circulation: [his aim] is to obtain for the value which he throws into circulation its equivalent, through the coin, in another use-value, which he consumes. Such an operation, of course, can never bring wealth, but has to bring back him who undertakes it exactly to the point at which he began.' (*ibid.* p.294.)

[27] *ibid.* p.307.

[28] 'In guild and craft labour, where capital itself still has a limited form, and is still entirely immersed in a particular substance, hence is not yet capital as such, labour, too, appears as still immersed in its particular specificity, not in the totality and abstraction of labour *as such* in which it confronts capital.' (*ibid.* p.296.)

particular specificity of the relation of production, of the category – here capital and labour – becomes real only with the development of a *particular material mode of production* and of a particular stage in the development of the *industrial productive forces*' i.e. of capitalism.[29]

So much then on the first aspect of the process which takes place between capital and labour; the exchange of labour-power which belongs in the realm of simple commodity circulation. 'The *transformation of labour* (as living, purposive activity) into capital is, in itself, the result of the exchange between capital and labour, insofar as it gives the capitalist the title of ownership of the product of labour.' However, this transformation only becomes real 'through the *consumption of labour*, which initially falls outside this exchange and is independent of it', hence only in the capitalist production process.[30] Therefore this must now be described.

[29] *ibid.* pp.296-97.
[30] *ibid.* p.308.

13.
Labour Process and Valorisation Process

We can be quite brief here; firstly because the analysis of the labour process and the valorisation process appears in a more complete and illuminating form in *Capital* than in the *Rough Draft*; and secondly, because the *Rough Draft* contains fewer ideas on this subject which offer anything new in comparison to the later work, or which might serve to complement it (and this is what is decisive as far as this work is concerned). The distinction lies chiefly in the manner of presentation; this seems important enough, however, to justify a separate treatment of the relevant section of the *Rough Draft*.[1]

We have seen that living labour, in its immediate existence, separated from capital in the bodily shape of the worker, is only potentially a source of value: 'it is made into a real activity only through contact with capital' (it cannot do this by itself, Marx adds, because it lacks an object); 'then it becomes a really value-positing productive activity'. The first phase of the process is now concluded 'insofar as we are dealing with the process of exchange as such'; equivalents have been exchanged, and the capitalist is now in possession of the labour-power which must go on to prove itself as formative of capital, as the productive power of wealth, by means of its activity, labour. The further process must therefore comprise the consumption of labour, 'the relation of capital to labour as capital's use-value'.[2]

In the final product of the exchange between capitalist and worker, capital was able to incorporate living labour into itself; it became one moment of capital – alongside its material moments which exist in the form of means of production and simply embody objectified labour. In order to maintain and expand itself, capital as objectified labour now has to enter into a process with non-objectified labour: 'On the one side the objectivity in which it exists has to be worked on, i.e. consumed by labour; on the other side the mere subjectivity of labour ... has to be suspended and labour has to be

[1] See *Grundrisse*, pp.297-318, 321-26.
[2] *ibid.* p.298.

objectified in the material of capital.' This can only occur in the production process by means of the subjection of the objectified element of capital, as passive material, to the forming activity of labour. For this reason : 'the relation of capital in its content, to labour – of objectified to living labour – can, in general, be nothing more than the relation of labour to its objectivity, its material.' However, as mere material of labour the substance of capital can only appear in two qualities; that of raw material 'i.e. of the formless matter, the mere material for the form-positing, purposive activity of labour', and that of the instrument of labour, 'the objective means which subjective activity inserts between itself as an object, as its conductor'.[3] By consuming the raw material and the instruments of labour, labour 'changes its own form' and 'undergoes a transformation, from the form of unrest into that of being, from the form of motion into that of objectivity'.[4] The outcome of the process is the product, in which the elements of capital consumed in production (raw material, instrument, labour) reappear as in a neutral result.[5] The entire process can therefore be designated as productive consumption, that is, consumption which 'is not simply consumption of the material', but rather 'consumes the given form of the object in order to posit it in a new objective form . . . It consumes the objective character of the object – the indifference towards the form – and the subjective character of the activity; forms the one, materialises the other. But as *product*, the result of the production process is use-value.'[6]

Note that the analysis up until now has been confined to the material aspect of the production process. However, this material aspect not only seems to conceal the specific movement of capital but also the quality of value. 'Cotton which becomes cotton yarn, or cotton yarn which becomes cloth, or cloth which becomes the material for printing and dyeing, exist for labour only as available cotton, yarn, cloth. As products of labour . . . they themselves do not enter any process but rather [operate] as material existences with certain natural properties. *How* these were posited in them makes no difference to the relation of living labour towards them; they exist for it only insofar as they exist as distinct from it, i.e. as material for

---

[3] *ibid.* p.298-99.
[4] *Capital* I, p.296 (189).
[5] In the sense that the distinction between the subjective and objective factors of the production process disappears in the product.
[6] *Grundrisse*, p.301.

Labour process and valorisation process · 205

labour.'[7] This means, therefore : 'To the extent that we have examined the process so far, capital in its being-for-itself – i.e. the capitalist[8] – does not enter at all. It is not the capitalist who is consumed by labour as raw material and instrument of labour. And it is not the capitalist who does this consuming, but rather labour.' The production process 'does not appear as the production process of capital, but as the production process in general' (as it is equally 'characteristic of all forms of production') 'and capital's distinction from labour appears only in the material character of raw material and instrument of labour' in which 'all relation . . . to labour itself as the use-value of capital . . . is extinguished'. (Marx adds : 'It is this aspect . . . on which the economists seize in order to represent capital as a necessary element of every production process. Of course, they do this only by forgetting to pay attention to its conduct as capital during this process.')[9]

We read further on in the text : 'Nothing can emerge at the end of the process which did not appear as a presupposition and precondition at the beginning. But on the other hand, everything also has to come out.' Thus, if the analysis up until now has not led any further than to the concept of the simple production process 'posited in no particular *economic* form', then this must be due to the fact that it was confined to the material aspect of the process, without this being conceived of as the process of the preservation and multiplication of values, i.e. according to its particular form. Seen as such, this process is the process of the self-preservation of capital.[10]

'Capital as form [i.e. looked at as a social relation] consists not of objects of labour and labour, but rather of *values*, and still more precisely of *prices*.' The fact that the constituent parts of capital undergo material changes in the course of the labour process, that 'out of the form of unrest – of the process – they again condense themselves into a resting, objective form, in the product . . . does not affect their character as values . . . Earlier, they appeared as elemental, indifferent preconditions of the product. Now they are the product. The value of the product can therefore only = the sum of

---

[7] ibid. p.302. Cf. *Capital* I, p.289 (182) : 'It is by their imperfections that the means of production in any process bring to our attention their character of being the products of past labour. A knife which fails to cut, a piece of thread which keeps on snapping, forcibly remind us of Mr. A, the cutler, or Mr. B, the spinner. In a successful product, the role played by past labour in mediating its useful properties has been extinguished.'
[8] See p.210 below.
[9] *Grundrisse*, p.303.
[10] ibid. p.304.

the values which were materialised in the specific material elements of the process... The value of the product is equal to the value of the raw material plus the value of the part of the instrument of labour which has been destroyed... plus the value of labour.'[11] (Or, the price of the product is equal to the cost of its production.[12])

Looked at in this way, the value of capital would not have changed at all and would have merely assumed another physical shape. The material transformation is of course an absolute necessity, since without it the self-preservation of capital would not be possible. However, the fact that the material process of production proceeds to an end-product 'is already contained in the first precondition, that capital really becomes use-value', is the presupposition of the capitalist mode of production. 'The statement that the necessary price [value] = the sum of the prices of the costs of production, is therefore purely analytical.' It simply states that the original value of the capital decomposes in the production process into particular quantitative elements (value of labour-power, value of raw material, value of the instruments of labour), in order to reappear in the product as the simple sum of values. 'But the sum is equal to the original unity... If capital was originally equal to 100 thalers, then afterwards, as before, it remains equal to 100 thalers, although the 100 thalers existed in the production price[13] as 50 thalers of cotton, 40 thalers of wages + 10 thalers of spinning machines, and now exist as cotton yarn to the price of 100 thalers. This reproduction of the 100 thalers is a simple retention of self-equivalence, except that it is mediated through the material production process.'[14] The only movement which takes place here with value is 'that it sometimes appears as a whole, unity; then as a division of this same unity into different amounts; finally appears as a sum.' (One could 'just as well have regarded the original 100 thalers as a sum of 50+40+10 thalers, but equally as a sum of 60+30+10 thalers etc.' The value of the whole would not have changed in the slightest.) 'The character of being a sum, of being added up, arose only out of the subdivision which took place in the act of production; but does not exist in the product as such. The statement thus says nothing more than that the price of the product = the price of the costs of production, or that the value of capital = the value of the product, that the value of

---

[11] Even in the *Rough Draft* the expression 'value of labour' is often used instead of the value of the capacity to work.
[12] *ibid.* p.313.
[13] What is understood by 'production price' here is the same thing which Marx later characterised as 'cost price', in Volume III of *Capital*.
[14] *Grundrisse*, pp.313-14.

the capital has preserved itself in the act of production . . . With this mere identity of capital, or reproduction of its value throughout the production process, we would have come no further than we were at the beginning.'[15]

Marx adds: 'It is clear that it is not in fact this to which the economists refer when they speak of the determination of price by the cost of production. Otherwise a value greater than that originally present could never be created (no greater exchange-value, although perhaps a greater use-value)' which would contradict the concept of capital itself.[16] Capital 'would not remain outside circulation, but would rather take on the form of different commodities; however it would do so for nothing; this would be a purposeless process, since it would ultimately represent only the same sum of money, and would have run the risk of suffering some damage in the act of production.' As a consequence the participation of the capitalist in the production process would be confined to advancing the worker his wages, 'paying him the price of the product in advance of its realisation'. He would have given him credit 'and free of charge at that, *pour le roi de Prusse*'.

However: 'The capitalist has to eat and drink too; he cannot live from this change in the form of money.' He has no option but to continually employ a part of the original capital for his own personal requirements, and eventually his capital will have disappeared.[17] On

---

[15] *ibid*. p.315. In fact, 'in addition to the simple division and re-addition, the production process also adds the formal element to value . . . that its elements now appear as *production costs*, i.e. precisely that the elements of the production process are not preserved in their material character, but rather as values . . .' (*ibid*. p.316.)

[16] *ibid*. p.315.

[17] 'But', say the apologetic economists, 'the capitalist is paid for the *labour* of throwing the 100 thalers into the production process as capital, instead of eating them up. But with what is he to be paid? And does not his labour appear as absolutely useless, since capital includes the wage; so that the workers could live from the simple reproduction of the cost of production, which the capitalist cannot do? He would thus appear among the *faux frais de production*. But, whatever his merits may be, reproduction would be possible without him, since, in the production process, the workers only transfer the value which they take out, hence have no need for the entire relation of capital in order to begin it always anew; and secondly, there would then be no fund out of which to pay him what he deserves, since the price of the commodity = the cost of production. But, if his labour were defined as a particular labour alongside and apart from that of the workers, e.g. as the labour of superintendence etc., then he would, like them, receive a certain wage, would thus fall into the same category as they, and would by no means relate

H

the other hand, 'it is equally clear ... that capital, even as conventionally defined, would *not* retain its *value* if it could retain nothing but its value. The risks of production have to be compensated. Capital has to preserve itself through the fluctuations of prices. The constantly ongoing devaluation of capital, resulting from the increase in the force of production, has to be compensated etc. The economists therefore state flatly that if no gain, no profit were to be made, everybody would eat up his money instead of throwing it into production and employing it as capital. In short, if this not-realisation i.e. not-multiplication of the value of capital, is presupposed, then what is presupposed is that capital is not a real element of production, that it is not a *specific relation of production*; then a condition is presupposed in which the production costs do not have the form of capital and where capital is not posited as the condition of production.'[18]

Consequently, what political economists understand by 'production costs' is in fact something quite different. They calculate thus: 'Original capital = 100 (e.g. raw material = 50; labour = 40; instruments = 10) + 5% interest + 5% profit. Thus the production cost = 110, not 100 : the production cost is thus greater than the cost of production.'[19] However, this creates a new difficulty: how can this 10% addition to the costs of production be explained? Using arguments which we already know from *Capital*,[20] Marx demonstrates that surplus-value – which is 'generally value beyond the equivalent' – can be derived neither from the higher use-value of the product,[21] nor from the commercial transaction ('profit upon aliena-

---

to labour as a capitalist; and he would never get rich, but receive merely an exchange-value which he would have to consume via circulation. The existence of capital *vis-à-vis* labour requires that capital in its being-for-itself, the capitalist, should exist and be able to live as *not-worker*.' (*ibid.* p.317.)
   [18] *ibid.* pp.316-17.
   [19] *ibid.* p.315. Cf. *Theories* III, pp.79ff.
   [20] See *Capital* I, pp.261-67 (161-66).
   [21] Marx notes at this juncture that, 'in order to construct a legitimation, an apology for capital', the economists explain it, 'with the aid of the very process which makes its existence impossible. In order to demonstrate it, they demonstrate it away. You pay me for my labour, you exchange it for its product and deduct from my pay the value of the raw material and instrument which you have furnished. That means we are *partners* who bring different elements into the process of production and exchange according to their values. Thus the product is transformed into money, and the money is divided in such a way that you, the capitalist, obtain the price of your raw material and your instrument, while I, the worker, obtain the price which my labour added to them. The benefit for you is that you now possess raw material and

tion'[22]), and that any attempted explanation along these lines will lead nowhere. It states in the *Rough Draft*: 'It is easy to understand how labour can increase use-value; the difficulty is, how it can create exchange-values greater than those with which it began.'[23] Otherwise 'the statement that the price = the cost of production . . . would have to read; the price of a commodity is always greater than its cost of production.'[24]

What follows is the solution which we already know, in which surplus-value originates from the difference between the labour materialised in the wage and the living labour performed by the worker. That is to say: 'If one day's work were necessary in order to keep one worker alive for one day, then capital would not exist, because the working day would then exchange for its own product, so that capital could not valorise itself and hence could not maintain itself as capital . . . If capital [i.e. the capitalist] also had to work in order to live, then it would maintain itself not as capital but as labour. Property in raw materials and instruments of labour would be purely nominal; economically they would belong to the worker as much as to the capitalist, since they would create value for the capitalist only insofar as he himself were a worker. He would relate to them therefore not as capital, but as simple material and means of labour, like the worker himself does in the production process. If, however, only half a working day is necessary in order to keep one worker alive one whole day, then the surplus-value of the product is self-evident, because the capitalist has paid the price of only half a working day but has obtained a whole day objectified in the product; thus has exchanged nothing for the second half of the working day . . . No matter that for the worker the exchange between capital and labour . . . is a simple exchange; as far as the capitalist is concerned it must be a not-exchange. He [the capitalist] has to obtain more value than he gives. Looked at from the capitalists' side, the exchange must be only apparent; i.e. belong to an economic category other than exchange, or capital as capital and labour as labour in opposition to it would be impossible . . . The only thing which can

---

instrument in a form in which they are capable of being consumed (circulated); for me, that my labour has realised itself. Of course, you would soon be in the situation of having eaten up all your capital in the form of money, whereas I, as worker, would enter into the possession of both.' (*Grundrisse*, p.322.)

[22] *ibid.* p.315.
[23] *ibid.* pp.317-18.
[24] *ibid.* p.316.

make him into a capitalist is not exchanged, but rather a process through which he obtains objectified labour-time i.e. value, without exchange.'[25]

We should draw attention here to one moment, which as Marx repeatedly stressed 'is posited itself in the economic relation', i.e. in the capital-relation. This is : 'In the first act, in the exchange between capital and labour, labour as such, existing *for itself*,[26] necessarily appeared as the *worker*. Similarly here in the second process ... capital in its being-for-itself is the *capitalist*. Of course, the socialists' (from whom Marx wants to distinguish himself as a scientific communist) 'sometimes say, we need capital, but not the capitalist. Then capital appears as a pure thing, not as a relation of production which, reflected in itself, is precisely the capitalist. I may well separate capital from a given individual capitalist, and it can be transferred to another. But in losing capital he loses the quality of being a capitalist. Thus capital is indeed separable from an individual capitalist, but not from *the* capitalist who as such confronts *the* worker. (Thus also the individual worker can cease to be the being-for-itself of labour; he may inherit or steal money etc. But then he ceases to be a worker. As a worker he is nothing more than labour in its being-for-itself).'[27]

But let us return to the proper subject of this chapter. As we have seen, the *Rough Draft* differs considerably in this respect from Volume I of *Capital*. The *Rough Draft* lacks not only the strict conceptual distinctions between raw material and object of labour, labour process and production process and between the process of value-formation and the process of valorisation – in addition the mode of presentation itself has an abstract character and exhibits traces of a 'coquetting with the Hegelian mode of expression'. In fact, though, the results of the analysis are the same in both texts, so that the presentation in the *Rough Draft* in this instance can be more or less regarded as the first version of Chapter 7 of Volume I of *Capital*.[28] However, what makes this presentation especially attractive (which applies to the *Rough Draft* in general) is that it takes us

---

[25] ibid. pp.324, 322.
[26] This terminology is borrowed from Hegel.
[27] *Grundrisse*, pp.303-04. This passage is directed against Bray, Gray, Proudhon *et al.*, but applies just as well to the present-day advocate of the theory of 'state capitalism'. They too forget that the capitalist is contained within the concept of capital, and that 'capitalism' without the capitalist class would be a contradiction in terms.
[28] See *Capital* I, pp.283-306 (177-98).

Labour process and valorisation process · 211

into Marx's scientific workshop, and allows us to witness the process by which his economic theory develops. The next chapter will show even more clearly that this does not take place without experiment and terminological approximations.

14.
Creation of Value and Preservation of Value in the Production Process

('Variable' and 'Constant' Capital)

In the previous chapter our main concern was that part of production costs in which the expansion of value, surplus-value, originates. This is living labour, directly exchanged for capital.[1] However, what happens to those parts of the value of capital which represent the labour embodied in raw materials and in the means of labour? For example, if the capitalist has a capital of 100 thalers and lays out 50 for cotton, 10 for the instruments of labour[2] and 40 for wages (four hours' labour being contained in the wage), then he reckons – after letting the worker work for eight hours – to have preserved his capital, 'reproduced', with a profit of 40 thalers, so that he would be in the possession of a commodity equal to 140 thalers. But how is the worker supposed to accomplish this 'since one half of his working day, as his wages show, creates only 40 thalers out of the instrument and material; the other half only the same; and he disposes of only one working day, cannot work two days in one?' Since his actual product equals 80 thalers he can only reproduce 80, not 140; the capitalist would therefore suffer a loss of 20 on his original capital, instead of making a profit of 40 thalers.[3] If this is so, how can labour be regarded as the sole source of value, as value-creating?[4]

Once more we have to distinguish between value and use-value.

---

[1] 'What in this transaction is *directly* sold is not a commodity in which labour has already realised itself, but *the use of the labour-power itself* and therefore in fact the *labour itself*, since the use of the labour-power is its activity – labour. It is therefore not an exchange of labour mediated through an exchange of commodities.' (*Theories* I, p.397.)

[2] Of course, here the 10 thalers only represent the portion of the instruments of labour which is entirely consumed in one period of production.

[3] *Grundrisse*, p.354. Of course, this example is somewhat inept, since an employer who only employed one worker cannot count as a capitalist. But this is of no concern here.

[4] Marx says: 'Such objections were heaped on Ricardo; that he regarded profit and wages only as components of production costs, not the machine and the material.' (*ibid.* p.354.)

Creation and preservation of value · 213

If we look at the production process from the standpoint of the simple labour process, the above question presents no difficulties. In the labour process 'labour presupposes the existence of an instrument which facilitates the work, and of a material in which it presents itself, which it forms'. It is clear that, 'if the cotton did not already have the form of yarn and wood and iron the form of the spindle', the worker 'could produce no fabric, no higher use-value. For him himself, the 50 thalers and the 10 thalers in the production process are nothing *but yarn and spindle, not exchange-values*'.[5] In the course of production 'the transitoriness of the form of things is used to posit their usefulness. When cotton becomes yarn, yarn becomes fabric, fabric becomes printed etc., or dyed etc. fabric, and this becomes, say, a garment, then (1) the substance of cotton has preserved itself in all these forms . . . (2) in each of these subsequent processes, the material has obtained a more useful form, a form making it more appropriate to consumption; until it has obtained at the end the form in which it can directly become an object of consumption, when, therefore the consumption of the material and the suspension of its form satisfies a human need, and its transformation is the same as its use'.[6]

Thus it is inherent in the simple labour process, 'that the earlier stage of production is preserved through to the later', that the material of labour and the means of labour can only be protected from uselessness and decay, by becoming the object of new living labour. 'As regards *use-value*, labour has the property of preserving the existing use-value by raising it, and it raises it by making it into the object of new labour as defined by an ultimate aim; by changing it in turn from the form of its indifferent consistency into that of objective material, the body of labour.'[7] But 'this *preservation of the old use-value* is not a process taking place separately from the increase or the completion of the use-value by new labour'; – and the

---

[5] ibid. pp.354, 355.
[6] ibid. p.361.
[7] ibid. p.362 (where Marx also writes: 'A spindle maintains itself as a use-value only by being used up for spinning. If it is not, the specific form, which is here posited in iron and wood, would be spoiled for use, together with the labour which posited it and the material in which it did the positing. The use-value of wood and iron, and of their form as well, are preserved only by being posited as a means of living labour, as an objective moment of the existence of labour's vitality. As an instrument of labour, it is their destiny to be used up, but used up in the process of spinning. The increased productivity which it lends to labour creates more use-values and thereby replaces the use-value eaten up in the consumption of the instrument.')

fact that the worker preserves it 'by using the instrument as instrument and by giving the raw material a higher use-value . . . lies in the nature of work itself'.[8]

So much on the preservation and increase of the use-value of the means of production effected by the labour process. As elements of capital, however, these means of production are simultaneously values, definite amounts of objectified labour-time. As such they reappear in the value of the product. But, how does this occur? We saw that the worker added nothing in value to the product apart from his working day (For example: 'If in addition to the fabric, the worker also had to create the yarn and the spindle in the same working day, then the process would in fact be impossible.') Hence, if the values of the means of production reappear in the product this is only because they already existed previously, before the process of production. They are not 'reproduced'[9] or newly created in this process, but simply preserved 'in that their quality is preserved as use-value for further labour, through the contact with living labour. The use-value of cotton, as well as its use-value as yarn, are preserved by being woven; by existing as one of the objective moments (together with the spinning wheel) in the weaving process. *The quantity of labour-time contained in the cotton and the cotton yarn are therefore also preserved thereby.* The preservation of the quality of previous labour in the simple production process – hence of its material as well – becomes, in the realisation process, the preservation of the quantity of labour already objectified.'[10] However, this preservation does not require any additional effort by the worker. Assuming that the means of production come from nature, without any human assistance, then the value of the product is reduced to the value added by the worker, and will equal one objectified working day. Insofar as the means of production 'are products of previous labour . . . the product contains, in addition to its new value, the old as well.'[11] The worker, therefore, 'replaces the old labour-time by the act of working itself, not by the addition of special labour-time for this purpose. He replaces it simply by the addition of the *new*, by means of which the old is preserved in the product and becomes an element of a new product.'[12]

[8] ibid. pp.362-63.
[9] Marx remarks on this: 'It can therefore only be said that he reproduces these values insofar as *without* labour they would rot, be useless; but *without them, labour* would be equally useless.' (ibid. p.355.)
[10] ibid. pp.355, 363.
[11] ibid. p.356.
[12] ibid.

It can be seen that it is not the quantity of living labour but rather its quality which preserves the labour-time already present in the raw material and instrument of labour. Here we come to a point where the presentation in the *Rough Draft* diverges from that of *Capital*. Thus we read in the *Rough Draft* : 'That the labour-time contained in the raw material and instrument is preserved at the same time is a result *not of the quantity of labour*, but of its *quality of being labour as such*; and there is no special payment for this, its general quality, for the fact that *labour, as labour is labour* – leaving aside all special qualifications, all specific kinds of labour – because capital has bought this quality as part of its exchange with the worker.'[13]

In *Capital*, in contrast to this, the twofold nature of the results of labour (namely the 'addition of new value to the object of labour' on the one hand, and the 'preservation of the old value in the product' on the other) is derived from the twofold nature of labour itself, from its double character as concrete useful labour which creates use-values, and abstract human, value-creating labour.

We read there : 'We saw, when we were considering the process of creating value, that if a use-value is effectively consumed in the production of a new use-value, the quantity of labour expended to produce the article which has been consumed, forms a part of the quantity of labour necessary to produce the new use-value; this portion is therefore labour transferred from the means of production to the new product. Hence the worker preserves the values of the already consumed means of production, or transfers them to the product as portions of its value, not by virtue of his *additional labour as such*, but by virtue of the *particular useful character of that labour*, by virtue of its *specific productive* form.'[14] And further : 'On the one hand, it is by virtue of its *general character* as expenditure of human labour-power in the abstract that spinning adds new value to the values of the cotton and the spindle; and on the other hand, it is by virtue of its special character as a concrete, useful process that the same labour of spinning both *transfers* the values of the means of production to the product and *preserves* them in the product. Hence a *twofold* result emerges *within the same period of time*.'[15]

A comparison of the two presentations shows why Marx had to

---

[13] ibid. p.359.
[14] *Capital* I, p.308 (200).
[15] ibid. pp.308-09 (200-01).

correct his original formulation. Labour, in its abstract character as 'labour in general', represents value-creating labour and is capable of merely quantitative distinction only. Consequently it cannot be used to explain the preservation of value.[16]

We pointed out previously that the value-preserving capacity of labour costs the worker nothing; the same applies to the capitalist who pockets it *'for nothing, as surplus labour'*. 'But he obtains it free of charge because ... the material and the instrument of labour are already in his hands as presupposition, and the worker cannot work, therefore, without making this already objectified labour, now in the hands of capital, into the material of his own labour, thereby also preserving the labour objectified in this material.'[17] 'Like every other natural or social power of labour, or of such previous labour as does not need to be repeated (e.g. the historical development of the worker), this natural animating power of labour – namely that, by using the material and instrument, it preserves them in one or another form, including the labour objectified in them, their exchange-value becomes a *power of capital*, not of labour. Hence not paid for by capital. As little as the worker is paid for the fact that he can think etc.'[18] Therefore if this natural gift of active labour-power brings benefits only to the capitalist, this is 'already posited in the *relation of capital and labour*, which in itself is already the former's profit and the latter's wage'.[19] Or, expressed in another way: 'Within the production process the separation of labour from its objective moments of existence – instruments and material – is *suspended*. *The existence of capital and labour rests on this separation*. Capital does not pay for the suspension of this separation which proceeds in the real production process – for otherwise work would

---

[16] We read, besides, in another passage from the *Rough Draft*: 'Living labour *adds a new amount of labour*; however, it is not this *quantitative addition* which preserves the amount of already objectified labour, but rather its *quality as living labour*, the fact that it relates as labour to the use-values in which the previous labour exists.' (*Grundrisse*, p.363.) But what is the 'relation of labour to use-values' apart from concrete, useful labour?

[17] ibid. p.356.

[18] ibid. p.358.

[19] ibid. p.357. This connection only occurs to the capitalist in periods of crisis. 'If the capitalist employs labour only in order to create surplus-value – to create value in addition to that already present – then it can be seen as soon as he orders work to stop that his already present capital, as well, becomes devalued; that living labour hence not only adds new value, but, by the very act of adding new value to the old one, maintains, eternises it.' (*ibid.* p.365.)

Creation and preservation of value · 217

not go on at all ... If it had to pay for this quality also, then it would just cease to be capital.'[20]

In contrast to the means of production, whose value is merely preserved and transferred to the product, the subjective factor of the production process, labour-power, is itself a source of new value, since its activity represents 'the objectification of new labour-time in a use-value'. It is important to distinguish between necessary and surplus labour at this point. As long as the worker merely produces an equivalent for the value of his own labour-power 'he only *replaces* the money advanced by the capitalist in purchasing labour-power, and spent by the worker on the means of subsistence'. With regard to the amount of wages spent, this part of the newly created value 'appears merely as *reproduction*. Nevertheless, it is a *real* reproduction, not, as in the case of the value of the means of production, simply an *apparent* one. The replacement of one value by another is here brought about by the creation of new value.'[21] By contrast, what the worker produces beyond this is 'not reproduction, but the addition of value, surplus-value' – hence a creation of value which represents a fundamentally different category and which alone gives capitalist production the reason for its existence.

The consequences of this are as follows: as far as their value is concerned, the different factors of the production process behave completely differently. The objectified factors (raw material, instrument of labour) cannot add more value to the product than they possess themselves; their value is simply preserved, and therefore remains unchanged.[22] The situation is quite different with the subjective factor, labour-power, which not only reproduces its own value, but adds new value, surplus-value, to the product. It is the only element of production which undergoes an alteration in value in the course of the valorisation process. We thus come to the concepts of constant and variable capital, which correspond to the dif-

[20] *ibid.* p.364. Marx adds: 'This is part of the material role which labour plays by its nature in the production process; of its use-value. But as use-value, labour belongs to the capitalist; it belongs to the worker merely as exchange-value. Its living quality of preserving objectified labour-time by using it as the objective condition of living labour in the production process is none of the worker's business. *This appropriation, by means of which living labour makes instruments and material in the production process* into the body of its soul and thereby resurrects them from the dead, does indeed stand in antithesis to the fact that labour itself is objectless, is a reality only in the immediate vitality of the worker – and that instrument and material, in capital, exist as beings-for-themselves.' (*ibid.* p.364.)
[21] *Capital* I, p.316 (208). Cf. *Grundrisse*, pp.359-60.
[22] *Grundrisse*, pp.321-22.

ferent functions of the means of production and labour-power in the valorisation process.[23] This is a conceptual distinction whose importance for Marx's theoretical system is immediately obvious, but which he only came to in the course of his work on the *Rough Draft*.[24] What later turned out to be 'constant' capital is initially characterised as 'unchanged', 'unchangeable' or 'invariable' value, and is counterposed to the 'changed', 'changeable' or 'reproduced value'.[25] It is not until later, towards the end of his analysis of the production process, that he begins to use the denotations 'constant' and 'variable' capital.

Marx used this distinction between value-creating and value-preserving labour to put a stop to those theories expounded by bourgeois apologists which sought to derive the profit of capital from the 'productive services', 'which the means of production perform in the labour process by means of their *use-value*'.[26] 'The individual capitalist may imagine (and for his accounts it serves as well) that, if he owns a capital of 100 thalers, 50 thalers in cotton, 40 thalers to buy labour with, 10 thalers in instrument, plus a profit of 10 per cent counted as part of his production costs, then labour has to replace his 50 thalers of cotton, 40 thalers subsistence, 10 thalers instrument plus 10 per cent of 50, of 40 and of 10; so that in his imagination, labour creates 55 thalers of raw material, 44 thalers subsistence and 11 thalers instrument for him, together = 110. But', Marx adds, 'this is a peculiar notion for economists ... If the worker's working day = 10 hours, and if he can create 40 thalers in 8 hours, i.e. can create his wage, or what is the same, can maintain and replace his labour-capacity, then he needs 4/5 of a day in order to replace his wages for capital, and he gives capital 1/5 in surplus labour, or 10 thalers.' This surplus of 10 thalers then constitutes the total profit of the capitalist. 'The total objectified labour which the worker has created, then,

---

[23] 'The same elements of capital which, from the point of view of the labour process, can be distinguished respectively as the objective and subjective factors, as means of production and labour-power, can be distinguished, from the point of view of the valorisation process, as constant and variable capital.' (*Capital* I, p.317 (209).)

[24] 'This point must, indeed, be examined, because the distinction between the invariable value, the part of capital which is preserved; that which is reproduced. ... and that which is newly produced, is of essential importance.' (*Grundrisse*, p.386.)

[25] Cf. *Grundrisse*, pp.321, 377, 386, 395-96.

[26] 'But the commodity as an exchange-value is always considered solely from the standpoint of the result. What matters is not the service it renders, but the service rendered to it in the course of its production ... It can easily be seen what "service" the category "service" must render to economists of the stamp of J.B.Say and F.Bastiat ...' (*Contribution*, p.37.)

Creation and preservation of value · 219

is 50 thalers, and regardless of the costs of the instrument and of the raw materials, more he cannot add, for his day cannot objectify itself in more labour than that . . .'[27] The illusion 'of the ordinary economist and the even more ordinary capitalist . . . that 10 per cent has been produced in equal proportions by all parts of capital',[28] rests on the one hand on the misinterpretation of the role of the means of production in the valorisation process, and on the other on the confusion of the real rate of surplus-value with this rate, calculated on capital as a whole i.e. the rate of profit.[29] However, the rate of profit on capital in no way expresses the rate 'at which living labour increases objective labour; for this increase is merely = to the surplus with which the worker reproduces his wage i.e. = to the time which he works over and above that which he would have to work in order to reproduce his wages.'[30] The extent of this increase can therefore only be reliably determined from the relation of the new value produced to the variable part of capital.

[27] *Grundrisse*, p.357.
[28] *ibid.* p.376. As often happens in the *Rough Draft*, Marx inadvertently replaced the numerical example in which the worker creates 40 thalers of surplus-value with one in which he only creates 10 thalers of surplus-value.
[29] See Chapter 25 of this work on the categories of profit and rate of profit.
[30] Marx continues, 'If the worker . . . were not a worker for a capitalist, and if he related to the use-values contained in the 100 thalers not as to capital but simply as to the objective conditions of his labour', then he would naturally not be compelled to perform surplus labour. He would, let us say, only work for ¾ of a day. But if he worked the whole day, 'because the material and the instrument were there on hand', it would not occur to him to regard the new gain thus created as a percentage of the total 'capital' of 100. For him, the increase of 25 per cent would simply imply that 'he could buy one fourth additional subsistence . . . and since he is concerned with use-values, these items of subsistence by themselves would be of value for him'. (*Grundrisse*, p.375.)

15.
The General Concept and Two Basic Forms of Surplus-Value

The previous chapter has brought us to the central category of Marx's system; to the category which, (as Engels said) 'was destined to revolutionise all previous economics, and which offered the key to an understanding of all capitalist production'[1] the category of surplus-value.

We saw that the increase in values which takes place in the capitalist process of production could in no way be derived from the 'productive services' of the objectified elements of capital, from the means of production. 'The advances made in the form of material and machine are merely transposed from one form into another . . . Their value is the result of previous production, not of the immediate production in which they serve as instrument and material.' Therefore the only value which is actually produced in the production process 'is that added by the new amount of labour. This value, however, consists of necessary labour, which reproduces wages . . . and of surplus labour, hence surplus-value above and beyond the necessary.'[2] Thus the secret of capitalist 'money-making' is resolved by the fact that the wage-labourer, who owns none of the means of production, is compelled to work beyond the time necessary for the maintenance of his life – that he can only live at all, if he simultaneously sacrifices a part of his life to capital. Only by these means can capital valorise itself, create surplus-value. 'What appears as surplus-value on capital's side appears identically on the worker's side as surplus labour in excess of his requirements as worker, hence in excess of his immediate requirements for keeping himself alive.'[3] In this respect there is no basic difference between the social situation of the wage-labourer and that of the exploited classes of earlier epochs; since '*Where capital rules* (just as where there is slavery and

---

[1] *Capital* II, p.16.
[2] *Grundrisse*, p.595.
[3] *ibid.* pp.324-25.

bondage or serfdom of any sort), *the worker's absolute labour-time*[4] *is posited for him as condition of being allowed to work the necessary labour-time, i.e. of being allowed to realise the labour-time necessary for the maintenance of his labour capacity in use-values for himself.*'[5]

Thus, just as with previous modes of exploitation, capital's mode of exploitation is also based on the surplus labour of the direct producers. It is clear that the capital relation (and also that of serfdom and slavery) would not be possible if human labour merely provided what was necessary to keep the producers alive. 'If the whole labour of a country', wrote an English author in 1821, 'were sufficient only to raise the support of the whole population, there would be no surplus labour, consequently nothing that can be allowed to accumulate as capital.'[6] Consequently, advantageous natural conditions, or a relatively high degree of productiveness of human labour, constitute the preconditions for every form of exploitation, for all forms of class-rule. In this sense, 'it can be said that surplus-value etc. rests on a *natural law*, that is, on the productivity of human labour in its exchange with nature'.[7] However, it does not follow from the fact that all surplus labour presupposes a surplus-product that the converse is true – that the mere possibility of a surplus-product creates the actual fact of surplus labour. Relations have to arise which compel the producers to work beyond their necessary labour-time. Marx cites in this connection a letter from a West Indian plantation owner, printed in *The Times* in November 1857, where the latter complains about the so-called 'Quashees' (the free blacks of Jamaica[8]). He describes, with 'great moral indignation', how the Quashees – instead of hiring themselves out as wage-labourers on the

---

[4] That is labour-time containing surplus-value.
[5] *ibid.* p.533.
[6] Taken from the anonymous pamphlet cited on p.397 of the *Grundrisse* and called *The Source and Remedy of the National Difficulties, deduced from principles of political economy in a letter to Lord John Russell.* (Cf. *Theories* III, p.251.)
[7] *Theories* III, p.332. (Several passages can be found in Marx's economic works which throw light on the question of the 'natural basis of surplus-value', from different aspects. The most important ones are: *Theories* I, pp.49, 151-53; *Theories* II, pp.16-17, 406-07; *Theories* III, pp.332, 449; *Grundrisse*, pp.324-25, 641-42; *Capital* I, pp.647-48 (512-13), 650-51 (514-15); *Capital* III, pp.632-34, 790-92.)
[8] The abolition of slavery took place in the British colony of Jamaica in 1833 – see the 'objective' description (that is, in reality, one which takes the side of the planters) in Sir Alan Burns, *History of the British West Indies*, 1954, pp.525ff.

sugar-plantations – 'content themselves with producing only what is strictly necessary for their own consumption, and alongside this "use-value", regard loafing (indulgence and idleness) as the real luxury good; how they do not care a damn for the sugar and the fixed capital invested in the plantations, but rather observe the planter's impending bankruptcy with an ironic grin of malicious pleasure, and even exploit their acquired Christianity as an embellishment for this mood of malicious glee and indolence.' These blacks 'have ceased to be slaves, not in order to become wage-labourers, but, instead, self-sustaining peasants working for their own consumption.[9] As far as

[9] It is quite obvious that the West Indian planter massively exaggerated in his letter. In fact, the great majority of 'Quashees' did not own their own land, from which they could satisfy 'their own necessary consumption'. They were therefore compelled to work for starvation wages on the plantations of their former masters. Just how desperate their situation was is proved – among other things – by the rebellion of the Jamaican Negroes in October 1865, which was cruelly suppressed by the British government. (See the echoes of this event in the correspondence between Marx and Engels. *MEW* Vol.31, pp.155, 157, 159, 187.)
In this connection it should be remembered that in England itself the former slave-owners found their warmest advocate in the person of the famous 'anti-capitalist romantic', Thomas Carlyle. He wrote in his pamphlet *Occasional Discourse on Negro Slavery*: 'Where a black man by working about half an hour a day (such is the calculation) can supply himself, by aid of sun and soil, with as much pumpkins as will suffice, he is likely to be a little stiff (to) raise into hard work! Supply and demand, which, science says, should be brought to bear on him, have an up-hill task with such a man. Strong sun supplies itself gratis, rich soil in those unpeopled or half-peopled regions almost gratis; these are his "supply"; and half an hour a day, directed upon these, will produce pumpkin, which is his "demand". The fortunate black man, very swiftly does he settle his account with supply and demand :– not so swiftly the less fortunate white man of these tropical localities. He himself cannot work; and his black neighbour, rich in pumpkin, is in no haste to help him. Sunk to the ears in pumpkin, imbibing saccharine juices, and much at his ease in the Creation, he can listen to the less fortunate white man's "demand", and take his own time in supplying it. Higher wages, massa; higher, for your cane-crop cannot wait; still higher, – till no conceivable opulence of cane-crop will cover such wages!' And further: 'If Quashee will not honestly aid in bringing out those sugars, cinnamons, and nobler products of the West Indian islands, for the benefit of all mankind, then I say neither will the Powers' (that is our dear Lord, as whose interpreter Carlyle presents himself) 'permit Quashees to continue growing pumpkins there for his own lazy benefit; but will sheer him out, by-and-by, like a lazy gourd overshadowing rich ground; him and all that partake with him – perhaps in a very terrible manner . . . No, the gods wish besides pumpkins, that spices and valuable products be grown in the West Indies; thus much they have declared in making the West Indies: infinitely more they wish that manful industrious men occupy their West Indies, not indolent two-legged cattle, however

The concept and forms of surplus-value · 223

they are concerned capital does not exist as capital, because autonomous wealth as such can exist only either on the basis of *direct forced labour, slavery, or indirect forced labour, wage-labour*.' Marx adds: 'Wealth confronts direct forced labour not as capital, but rather as *relation of domination* ... for which wealth itself has value only as gratification, not as wealth itself and which can therefore never create *general industriousness*' and universal application in the same way that the capital-relation can.[10]

In the last sentence we referred to the special role which capital plays 'as an agent in producing diligent labour on the part of others, as an extractor of surplus labour and an exploiter of labour-power'.[11] The ruling classes of earlier epochs also managed to squeeze considerable amounts of surplus labour from their subjects. But where the development of the productive forces is still slight the surplus-product must also remain relatively small, and the 'masters themselves do not live much better than the servants'.[12] On the other hand it is clear 'that in any economic formation of society, where the *use-value* rather than the exchange-value of the product predominates, surplus labour will be restricted by a more or less confined set of needs, and that no *boundless thirst for surplus labour* will arise from

---

"happy" over their abundant pumpkins!' 'You are not "slaves" now,' preaches Carlyle, the *laudator temporis acti*, to the Jamaican blacks, 'nor do I wish, if it can be avoided, to see you slaves again; but decidedly you will have to be servants to those that are born wiser than you, that are born lords of you – servants to the whites, if they are, as what mortal can doubt they are? Born wiser than you. That you may depend upon it my obscure Black friends, is and was always the Law of the World, for you and for all men: To be servants, the more foolish of us to the more wise; and only sorrow, futility and disappointment will betide both, till both in some approximate degree get to conform to the same ... I say, no well being and in the end no being at all, will be possible for you or us, if the law of Heaven is not complied with. And if "slaves" means "essentially servant hired for life" – for life, or by a contract of long continuance and not easily dissoluble – I ask whether, in all human things, the "contract of long continuance" is not precisely the contract to be desired, were the right terms once found for it? Servant hired for life, were the right terms once found, which I do not pretend they are, seems to me much preferable to servant hired for the month, or by contract dissoluble in a day. An ill-situated servant, that; servant grown to be nomadic; between whom and his master a good relation cannot easily spring up!' (Cited from the text of the North American, J.Bigelow, *Jamaica in 1850: or, the Effects of Sixteen Years of Freedom on a Slave Colony*, New York 1851, pp.118-22.) For the later development of Carlyle cf. *Capital* I, p.366 (245-51).

[10] *Grundrisse*, p.326.
[11] *Capital* I, p.425 (309-10).
[12] *Theories* II, p.16.

224 · *The Making of Marx's 'Capital'*

the character of production itself.'[13] Only under capitalism does the appropriation of surplus labour become an end in itself, and its continuous expansion become an indispensable condition of the production process. Capital has means and powers[14] at its disposal which far exceed the direct enforced labour of previous societies in terms of 'energy, limitlessness, and efficacy', and which therefore make the capitalist mode of production appear as an 'epoch-making mode of exploitation'.[15] In this context Marx is thinking, above all, of the production of so-called relative surplus-value.

There are two basic methods of expanding surplus labour. Firstly, by the simple prolongation of the labour process. Secondly – with a given length of the working day – by an increase in the productivity of labour, or its intensification.[16] In the first case surplus labour is obtained by the extension of the total amount of time worked by the producers, and in the second by shortening their necessary labour-time. Marx therefore calls the first absolute, and the second relative surplus labour. The foundation of the first is the 'natural fertility of the land, of nature';[17] whereas the second is based 'on the development of the social productive forces of labour'.[18] Correspondingly, the first form of surplus labour is not only the general basis of the second, but also much older than it. In fact it is as old as human exploitation in general, and is therefore a form of exploitation which can be said to be common to all class societies.[19]

[13] *Capital* I, p.345 (235).
[14] Marx states in another section in the *Rough Draft* that not until capitalism does money become the 'means of general industriousness', does the striving for money become the 'urge of all'. 'When the aim of labour is not a particular product standing in a particular relation to the particular needs of the individual, but money, wealth in its general form . . . the individual's industriousness knows no bounds; it is indifferent to its particularity, and takes on every form which serves the purpose.' Admittedly, Marx adds: 'General industriousness is possible only where every act of labour produces general wealth, not a particular form of it; where, therefore, the individual's reward too, is money.' It therefore presupposes labour as wage-labour. (*Grundrisse*, p.224.)
[15] *Capital* II, p.37.
[16] *Capital* I, p.533 (409).
[17] Consequently, the possibility of surplus labour depends on the natural productivity of agricultural labour, and this constitutes, according to Marx, the correct kernel of the Physiocratic doctrine. (*Capital* III, p.784.)
[18] *Theories* III, p.449.
[19] This form of surplus labour played the dominant role in the systems of serfdom and slavery. By contrast, relative surplus labour only crops up sporadically in pre-capitalist conditions. Thus, for example, the feudal lords who produced for export in East and Central Europe in the 17-19th centuries sometimes tried to force upon their serfs the so-called 'measured forced labour'

Absolute surplus labour is also indispensable for capital – especially during the infancy of the capitalist mode of production, when it first 'takes over the labour process *in its given or historically transmitted shape*, and simply prolongs its duration'.[20] Absolute surplus labour thus plays the decisive role here, and consequently 'the distinction between production under capital and earlier stages of production is only formal' at this particular level of development (in the sense that the extraction of surplus labour in previous systems of production is 'posited directly by force', whereas under capital, by contrast 'it is mediated through exchange'). 'Use-values grow here in the same simple relation as exchange-values, and for that reason this form of surplus labour appears in the slave and serf modes of production etc. where use-value is the chief and predominant concern, as well as in the mode of production of capital, which is directly oriented towards exchange-value, and only indirectly towards use-value.'[21] However, regardless of how important and indispensable the appropriation of absolute surplus labour was, and still is, it does not characterise the essence of the capitalist mode of production. (We shall see later that the latter's methods of production are based on the combination of both types of surplus labour.) The essence of the capitalist mode of production consists rather in the continuous revolutionising of the technical and social conditions of the labour process in order to push back the original natural limits of necessary labour-time and thus progressively to extend the domain of surplus labour. It is not therefore in absolute but in relative surplus labour 'that the industrial and distinguishing historic character of the mode of production founded on capital' appears.[22] This is the primary sense in which capital is productive – 'insofar as it is a coercive force on wage-labour . . . spurring on the productive power of labour to produce relative surplus-value'.[23]

('*Gemessene Robot*' – an Austro-Bohemian expression). (Cf. the charters of Maria Theresa and Joseph II forbidding this 'standard forced labour' [*Massrobot*].) However, such attempts by the feudal lords mostly came to grief on the primitiveness of the agricultural technique then prevailing. This situation is referred to by Richard Jones in his *Essay on the Distribution of Wealth and on the Sources of Taxation* (1831, pp.37-38). We read on this in *Theories* III, p.400 : 'Rent can only be increased either by the more skilful and effective utilisation of the labour of the tenantry (relative surplus labour), this however is hampered by the inability of the proprietors to advance the science of agriculture, *or* by an increase in the total quantity of labour extracted.'
[20] *Capital* I, p.432 (315).
[21] *Grundrisse*, p.769.
[22] *ibid*.
[23] *Theories* I, p.93.

In this respect the difference between the mode of production of capital and that of any previous epoch goes much deeper. We stressed that the capitalist mode of production is oriented to exchange-value from the outset, and that the production of use-values is not an end, but only a means to an end – the valorisation of capital. But this means that capital not only has to enforce surplus labour, but also realise it as surplus-value.

Two things result from this. Firstly, 'the surplus-value created at one point requires the creation of surplus-value at *another* point for which it can be exchanged.' 'A precondition of production based on capital is therefore the *production of a constantly widening sphere of circulation*, whether the sphere itself is directly expanded or whether *more points within it are created as points of production* ... Hence just as capital has the tendency on one side to create ever more surplus labour, so it has the complementary tendency to create more points of exchange; i.e., here, seen from the standpoint of *absolute* surplus-value or surplus labour, to summon up more surplus labour as complement to itself; i.e. at bottom, to propagate production based on capital, or the mode of production corresponding to it.'[24] Thus every limit appears to capital 'as a barrier to be overcome', in that it seeks 'to subjugate every moment of production itself to exchange and to suspend the production of direct use-values not entering into exchange i.e. precisely to posit production based on capital in place of earlier modes of production.' Consequently, trade appears 'as an essentially all-embracing presupposition and moment of production itself' and 'the tendency to create the *world market* is directly given in the concept of capital itself.'[25]

On the other hand, we read in the *Rough Draft* that, in order to advance the production of *relative* surplus-value based on the increase and development of the productive forces, capital must seek to ensure 'that the consuming circle within circulation expands as did the productive circle previously'. The capitalist mode of production therefore requires : 'Firstly : quantitative expansion of existing consumption; secondly : creation of new needs by propagating existing

---

[24] Marx also speaks, in this sense, of the 'propagandistic tendency of capital' in other passages in the *Grundrisse* (pp.542, 771). In *Capital* these 'propagandistic tendencies' are mentioned in Volume I, p.649 (514-15).
Cf. Luxemburg's *Accumulation of Capital*, p.467. 'Capitalism is the first mode of economy with the weapon of propaganda – a mode which tends to engulf the entire globe and stamp out all other economies, tolerating no rival at its side.' (Hilferding too, spoke of the 'propagandist power' of the cartels in *Das Finanzkapital*, p.289.)
[25] *Grundrisse*, pp.407-08.

ones in a wide circle; thirdly: production of new needs and discovery and creation of new use-values.' In other words, the main issue is 'that the surplus labour gained does not remain a merely quantitative surplus, but rather constantly increases the circle of qualitative differences within labour . . . makes it more diverse, more internally differentiated.' 'For example, if, through a doubling of productive force, a capital of 50 can now do what a capital of 100 did before, so that a capital of 50 and the necessary labour corresponding to it become free, then, for the capital and labour which have been set free, a new, qualitatively different branch of production must be created, which satisfies and brings forth a new need.[26] The value of the old industry is preserved by the creation of the fund for a new one in which the relation of capital and labour posits itself in a new form. Hence exploration of all of nature in order to discover new, useful qualities in things; universal exchange of the products of all alien climates and lands; new (artificial) preparation of natural objects, by which they are given new use-values . . . the development, hence, of the natural sciences to their highest point; likewise the discovery, creation, and satisfaction of new needs arising from society itself; the cultivation of all the qualities of the social human being, production of the same in a form as rich as possible in needs, because rich in qualities and relations – production of this being as the most total and universal possible social product, for, in order to take gratification in a many-sided way, he must be capable of many pleasures, hence cultured to a high degree – is likewise a condition of production founded on capital.'[27]

Marx goes on to say that, just as capitalist production 'creates universal industriousness on one side . . . so does it create on the other side a system of general exploitation of the natural and human qualities, a system of general utility,[28] utilising science itself just as much as all the physical and mental qualities; while there appears nothing higher in itself, nothing legitimate for itself, outside this circle of social production and exchange. Thus capital creates the bourgeois society, and the universal appropriation of nature as well as of the social bond itself by the members of society. Hence the great civilising influence of capital; its production of a stage of society in comparison

---

[26] One only has to think of the newly-created mass needs for cars, refrigerators, television sets etc.
[27] *Grundrisse*, pp.408-09.
[28] Marx hints here at the 'Doctrine of Utility' developed by the philosophers and economists of the 17th and 18th centuries. One should also look at his sketch of the development of the theory of utility in the *German Ideology*, pp.268ff and note 51, on pp.758-59 of *Capital* I (Note 2, p.609).

to which all earlier ones appear as mere *local developments* of humanity and as *nature-idolatry*. For the first time, nature becomes purely an object for humankind, purely a matter of utility; ceases to be recognised as a power for itself; and the theoretical discovery of its autonomous laws appears merely as a ruse[29] so as to subjugate it under human needs, whether as an object of consumption or a means of production. In accord with this tendency, capital drives beyond national barriers and prejudices as much as beyond nature worship, as well as all traditional, confined, complacent, encrusted satisfactions of present needs, and reproductions of old ways of life. It is destructive towards all of this, and constantly revolutionises it, tearing down all the barriers which hem in the development of the forces of production, the expansion of needs, the all-sided development of production, and the exploitation and exchange of natural and mental forces.'[30]

This is sufficient here on the 'propagandist' and 'civilising' tendencies of capital, as they emerge from its drive for absolute and relative surplus-value. This line of thought – which was first developed in the section of the *Rough Draft* devoted to the circulation process – represents something new. It is not to be found in *Capital* (except for occasional remarks), which is why we have introduced it here. We ought also to draw attention to the structure of the section of Marx's work dealing with the 'production process of capital', as it follows from the distinction between the two basic forms of surplus-value. As long as his concern was simply one of explaining the valorisation of capital in general, Marx was able to disregard, and had to disregard, relative surplus-value and confine himself to the analysis of the absolute form. However, the emphasis of the analysis shifts at this point : it becomes necessary to advance to relative surplus labour and relative surplus-value if we want to explain why capital creates for itself the most adequate form of its existence in the mechanised

---

[29] Marx makes use once again of a Hegelian concept. Lukacs writes : 'It is well known that the "cunning of reason" is the central concept in Hegel's later philosophy. Translated into more prosaic terms the expression refers to the idea that men make their own history themselves and that the actual driving force behind the events of history is to be found in the passions of men and in their individual, egoistic aspirations; but the totality of these individual passions nevertheless ends by producing *something other* than what the men involved had wanted and striven to attain. Nevertheless this other result is no fortuitous product, on the contrary, it is here that the laws of history, the "spirit" (to use Hegel's term) actually makes itself manifest.' (*The Young Hegel*, 1975, p.354.)

[30] *Grundrisse*, pp.409-410. Compare this with the well-known description of this tendency in the *Communist Manifesto* (*Selected Works*, pp.38-40).

factory and why the mass of living labour employed continually falls in relation to that objectified in the means of production during the course of the development of capitalist production, although the proportion of unpaid living labour to paid constantly grows. (This theme will be dealt with mainly in Chapters 17 and 18 of this work.)

16.
Relative Surplus-Value and Productive Force

(On the increasing difficulty of valorising capital with the development of the capitalist mode of production)

At this point there is an analysis in the *Rough Draft* which, although not in *Capital* Volume I, should nevertheless be gone into in some detail.

We have seen that the main distinguishing feature of capital's mode of production, what is specific to it, is its striving for relative surplus-value. Only through this can capital constantly advance the development of the material forces of production, and subjugate social progress itself to the service of wealth.[1]

However, in doing this capital encounters barriers which are inherent in it and make its mode of production appear as merely a transitory, although necessary, period of development.[2]

Capital can develop the productive forces of society only in as much as it valorises itself in doing so, insofar as it creates a surplus-value. However, the expansion of its value is bounded by the limits of the relation between necessary and surplus labour. It follows from this that the valorisation of capital must become more and more difficult as the productive forces are developed and necessary labour approaches its 'lowest' limit.

Let us assume that the proportion of necessary to surplus labour is 1 : 1. That is, the worker works just as long for the capitalist as he works for himself.

'By appropriating the entire day's work and then consuming it in the production process with the materials of which his capital consists, but by giving in exchange only the labour objectified in the worker – i.e. half a day's work – the capitalist creates the surplus-value of his capital; in this case half a day of objectified labour.' Now suppose 'that the productive powers of labour double... i.e. the

---

[1] *Grundrisse*, pp.589-90.
[2] We disregard here those barriers which arise from the necessity of the realisation of capital and its surplus-value. (This question is first dealt with by Marx in the Section of the *Rough Draft* devoted to the circulation process of capital.)

same labour creates double the *use-value* in the same time'.³ Then the worker would only have to work for a quarter of a day in order to live for a whole day. If his labour-time were to be cut by a quarter the capitalist could still appropriate the same amount of surplus labour. Of course he would not be inclined to agree to such a shortening of the working day, since as a capitalist he must aim for a constantly growing valorisation of his capital – even if he is not compelled to do so through competition with other capitalists. He would therefore simply let the worker work the full day. 'The increase in productive force which allows the worker to work for ¼ day and live a whole day now expresses itself simply in that he now has to work ¾ for capital, whereas before he worked for it for only ¾ day. The increased productive force of his labour, to the extent that it is a shortening of the time required to replace the labour objectified in him . . . appears as a lengthening of the time he labours for the valorisation of capital . . .'⁴

But, Marx continues, something striking now takes place; the productivity of labour has doubled, but the surplus labour (or surplus-value) has only grown by a half – from two quarters of the day to three quarters. 'This shows then that surplus labour (from the worker's standpoint) or surplus-value (from capital's standpoint) does not grow in the same numerical proportion as productive force.' By contrast, if the worker had had originally to work for two thirds of a day, in order to live for a whole day, the necessary labour would have fallen from two thirds to one third through the doubling of the productive force, and correspondingly surplus labour would have doubled. The extent to which the increase 'in the productive force of labour increases the value of capital thus depends on the original relation between the portion of labour objectified in the worker and his living labour' (in which the total working day of the worker 'always appears as a limit'). Naturally the capitalist can never annex the entire working day since a definite portion of it always has to be exchanged for the labour objectified in the worker : 'Surplus-value

---

³ Marx adds : 'For the moment' (i.e. at the present stage of the analysis), 'use-value is defined in the present relation as only that which the worker consumes in order to stay alive as a worker : the quantity of the means of life for which, through the mediation of money, he exchanges the labour objectified in his living labouring capacity.' (*ibid.* p.334.) In other words; the increase in productive force is only analysed to the extent that it affects branches of industry, 'whose products, directly or indirectly, enter into the formation of the worker's means of consumption'. A contrary assumption would only complicate the analysis without changing its result. (Cf. *Theories* I, pp.213ff and *Capital* I, p.436 (317-18).)

⁴ *Grundrisse*, pp.334-35.

in general is only the relation of living labour to that objectified in the worker; *one member of the relation must therefore always remain*. A certain relation between increase in productive force and increase of value is already given in the fact that the relation is constant as a relation, although its factors vary'. Because of this relative surplus-value cannot grow 'in the same numerical proportion as the productive force'.[5] Rather its growth must slow down, as the following example shows.

We assume that the doubling of productivity has reduced necessary labour from a half to a quarter of a day, by which the capitalist has gained one quarter of a day's relative surplus-value. Suppose now that productivity doubles again; necessary labour will fall from a quarter to an eighth of a day and surplus labour will merely increase by one eighth of a day. Thus with every further increase in productivity the relative growth in surplus-value becomes smaller. 'If necessary labour had already been reduced to 1/1000, then the total surplus-value would be = 999/1000. Now if the productive force increased a thousandfold, then necessary labour would decline to 1/1,000,000 working day and the total surplus-value would amount to 999,999/1,000,000 of a working day . . . it would have thus grown by 999/1,000,000 . . . i.e. the thousandfold increase in productive force would have increased the total surplus by only a thousandth . . .'[6]

Marx summarises the result of his examination of the relation of the growth of relative surplus-value to the growth of the productivity of labour in the following three points:

'*Firstly* : The increase in the productive force of living labour increases the value of capital (or diminishes the value of the worker)[7] not because it increases the quantity of products or use-values created by the same labour – the productive force of labour is its natural force – but rather because it diminishes *necessary* labour, hence, in the same relation as it diminishes the former, it creates *surplus labour* or, what amounts to the same thing, surplus-value; because the surplus-value which capital obtains through the production process consists only of the excess of surplus labour over *necessary labour*. The increase in productive force can increase surplus labour – i.e. the

---

[5] *ibid.* pp.337-38. (Cf. in addition, the critique of Ricardo on pp.351-52.)
[6] In the original this reads: 'not even by 1/11'. (p.339; see footnote 51.) This is clearly an arithmetical error, like others which can be found both in the *Rough Draft* and in the *Theories*. Engels remarked in a similar context: 'Firmly grounded as Marx was in algebra, he was never entirely at home with numerical calculations . . .' (*Capital* II, p.289.)
[7] That is, labour-power.

excess of labour objectified in the exchange-value of the working day – only to the extent that it diminishes the relation of *necessary labour* to *surplus labour*, and only in the proportion in which it diminishes this relation.'

'*Secondly* : The surplus-value of capital does not increase as does the multiplier of the productive force, i.e. the amount to which the productive force . . . increases; but by the surplus of the fraction of the living work day which originally represents necessary labour, in excess over this same fraction divided by the multiplier of the productive force . . . Thus the *absolute sum* by which capital increases its value through a given increase of the productive force depends on the *given fractional part* of the working day, on the fractional part of the working day which represents *necessary labour*, and which therefore expresses the original relation of *necessary labour* to the living work day. The increase in productive force in a given relation can therefore increase the value of capital differently e.g. in different countries. A general increase of productive force in a given relation can increase the value of capital[8] differently in the different branches of industry, and will do so, depending on the different relation of necessary labour to the living work day in these branches.' (Marx adds : 'This relation would naturally be the same in all branches of business in a system of free competition, if labour were simple labour everywhere, hence necessary labour the same. If it represented the same amount of objectified labour.')[9]

'*Thirdly* : The larger the surplus-value of capital *before the increase of productive force*, the larger the amount of presupposed surplus labour or surplus-value of capital or the smaller the fractional part of the working day which forms the equivalent of the worker, which expresses necessary labour, the smaller is the increase in surplus-value which capital obtains from the increase of productive force. Its surplus-value rises, but in an ever smaller relation to the development of the productive force. Thus the more developed capital already is, the more surplus labour it has created, the more terribly must it develop the productive force in order to valorise itself in only smaller proportions, i.e. to add surplus-value – because its barrier always remains the relation between the fractional part of the day which expresses necessary labour, and the entire working day. It can move only within these boundaries. The smaller already the fractional part falling to *necessary labour*, the greater the *surplus labour*, the less can any increase in productive force perceptibly

[9] *Grundrisse*, pp.339-340.
[8] This refers of course to the surplus-value.

diminish necessary labour; since the denominator has grown enormously.[10] The self-valorisation of capital becomes more difficult to the extent that it has already been valorised.' In fact, at a certain point 'the increase in productive forces . . . valorisation itself . . . would become irrelevant to capital – because its proportions have become minimal and it would have ceased to be capital'.[11]

Marx stresses that these theses are 'only correct in this abstraction for the relation from the present standpoint' (that is, as long as the question is only that of the purely abstract relation between the development of productivity and the growth of surplus-value). 'Additional relations will enter which modify them significantly. The whole, to the extent that it proceeds entirely in generalities, *actually already belongs in the doctrine of profit*.'[12] And this is also the reason why these theses – despite their importance – only exist fragmentarily in Volume I of the later work.[13] However, they will be drawn upon later for the solution of the fundamental problem of the falling rate of profit – and we will have the opportunity to come back to them there.[14]

[10] 'But this happens not' (as the 'harmonisers' Bastiat and Carey suppose) 'because wages have increased, or the share of the labour in the product, but because it has already fallen so low, regarded in relation to the product of labour or the living work day.' (*ibid.* p.341.)
[11] *ibid.* pp.340-41.
[12] *ibid.* p.341.
[13] *Capital* I, p.657 (519).
[14] See the Appendix to Part V of this work.

17.
The Methods of Production of Relative Surplus-Value
(Co-operation, manufacture and machinery)[1]

In contrast to absolute surplus-value, relative surplus-value is not obtained by prolonging the period of work, but by cheapening the labour-power of the worker. 'Capital, therefore, has an immanent drive and a constant tendency . . . to revolutionise the technical and social conditions of the [labour] process and consequently the *mode of production itself* . . . in order to increase the *productivity of labour*, to lower the *value of labour-power* by increasing the productivity of labour and so to *shorten* the portion of the working day necessary for the reproduction of that value.'[2]

What then are the particular methods of production which capital develops in its drive for relative surplus-value?

The principal methods referred to are the capitalist application of co-operation, the division of labour according to manufacture, and, above all, the development of modern machinery. These occupy the whole of Part IV of Volume I of *Capital*, but are only dealt with sketchily in the *Rough Draft*, and then intermingled with other questions.

What first characterises these methods of production is that they subordinate the social productive powers of labour to the service of capital. As already pointed out,[3] it is inherent in the concept of wage-labour itself that the worker relinquishes the use-value of his commodity and consequently the fruits of his labour. The 'separation between labour and property in the product of labour' is therefore already given by the fact of the exchange between capital and labour.[4] However, what the worker sells to the capitalist, and what

---

[1] Up until now we have been able to follow the order of the presentation in the *Rough Draft*. However, from this chapter onwards this becomes impossible as the subjects under study are often dealt with in sections of Marx's manuscript which are scattered throughout the work.
[2] *Capital* I, pp.432, 436-37 (315, 319).
[3] See Chapter 12 above.
[4] *Grundrisse*, p.307.

he is paid for is 'his individual, isolated labour-power'. But in the process of production he is not employed as an individual but as a member of a 'working organism', through which his capacity to work acquires new, social powers.[5]

The reason for this is that even simple co-operation between labour-powers in no way signifies their mere addition; an addition to the productive force comes about, which arises from the very fact of the collective, combined character of labour. (This applies even more to the division of labour within workshops.) However, since the combination of the workers in the production process 'is not posited by them but by capital' it 'is not *their* being but the being of capital. *Vis-à-vis* the individual worker, the combination appears accidental.'[6] Therefore, the increase in productivity which arises from the co-operation of the workers benefits not them, but rather capital. (This is the simple consequence of the fact, 'that the really great development of the productive power of labour starts only from the moment when it is transformed into wage-labour . . . only under conditions in which the worker himself can no longer appropriate its result'.[7]) 'Thus all the progress of civilisation, or in other words every increase in the *powers of social production* . . . enriches not the worker but rather *capital*', becomes monopolised by the capitalist class. But all this progress operates to extend the domain of relative surplus labour, owing to the increase in productivity, and – 'since capital is the antithesis of the worker' – also to increase 'the *objective power* standing over labour', i.e. the power of capital.[8] (Marx states in another passage: 'The worker therefore justifiably regards the development of the productive power of his own labour as hostile to himself . . .')[9]

Thus the development of the specifically capitalist mode of production rests primarily on the social powers of labour. But capital can only place these powers at its service because it is, from the outset, a collective force and as such 'does not have isolated, but combined labour to deal with'.[10] The aim of capitalist production is *not* the creation of use-value, but exchange-value (more precisely: surplus-value). The surplus labour 'must therefore be large enough from the beginning to allow a part of it to be re-employed as capital'; that is, capital must be in the position 'of setting a certain quantity

---

[5] *Capital* I, p.451 (331).
[6] *Grundrisse*, p.585.
[7] *Theories* I, p.70.
[8] *Grundrisse*, p.308.
[9] *Theories* II, p.573.
[10] *Grundrisse*, p.529.

Methods of production of relative surplus-value · 237

of living labour capacities to work simultaneously'.[11] In this sense the accumulation and concentration of labour-powers, the 'grouping of *many* around *one* capital', is contained in the concept of capital (unlike the accumulation and concentration of 'capital in its finished form',[12] which 'occurs by contrast against many capitals', and therefore presupposes the sphere of competition).[13]

In fact, at the beginnings of capitalist production the combination of workers by capital is 'merely *formal*, and concerns only the product of labour, not labour itself'. This combination simply consists in the fact that capital 'employs different hand weavers, spinners etc. who live independently and are dispersed over the land ... Here, then, the mode of production is not yet determined by capital, but rather found on hand by it. The point of unity of all these scattered workers lies only in their mutual relation to capital ... Instead of exchanging with many they exchange only with the one capitalist. The co-ordination of their work exists only *in itself* ... insofar as each of them works for capital – hence possesses a centre in it – without [in fact] working together.'[14] Here, concentration is confined to the

---

[11] *ibid.* p.589. The combination of many workers in one production process is naturally not a form which is peculiar to capitalism. It is sufficient to refer here to the 'sporadic use of co-operation on a large scale' in the industrial enterprises of the ancient world or the Middle Ages, as well as large-scale agriculture carried out by slaves or serfs. 'Certain branches of industry, e.g. mining, already presuppose co-operation from the beginning. Thus, so long as capital does not exist, this labour takes place as forced labour (serf or slave labour) under an overseer. Likewise road building etc. In order to take over these works capital does not create but rather takes over the accumulation and concentration of workers.' However, in contrast to earlier systems of production, capital effects this 'same concentration in another way, through the manner of its exchange with free labour'. Here co-operation on a large scale is 'not compelled through direct physical force ...; it is compelled by the fact that the conditions of production are alien property and are themselves present as objective association which is the same as accumulation and concentration of the conditions of production.' (*ibid.* pp.529, 586, 590.)

[12] Cf. note 129 on p.44 above.

[13] 'Before accumulation by capital, there is presupposed an accumulation which constitutes capital, which is a part of its conceptual determination; we can hardly call it concentration yet, because this takes place in distinction to many capitals; but if one still speaks only of capital generally, then concentration still coincides with accumulation or with the concept of capital. i.e. it does not yet form a particular aspect. However, capital does indeed exist from the outset as One or Unity as opposed to the workers as Many. And it thus appears as the concentration of workers ..., as a unity falling outside of them. In this respect, concentration is contained in the concept of capital ...' (*Grundrisse*, p.590.)

[14] *ibid.* p.586. Cf. *ibid.* pp.510-11.

concentration of exchange through capital. But this stage is rapidly superseded; a situation soon comes about in which capital no longer employs the workers as it finds them, but sets them to work together in one undertaking. 'Now capital appears as the collective force of the workers . . . as well as that which ties them together, and hence as the unity which creates this force' – which at the same time brings about 'the complete severance of the workers from the conditions of production', and their total dependence on capital.[15]

Initially this will merely involve the simple co-operation of a 'large number of workers working together, at the same time, in one place . . . in order to produce the same sort of commodity under the command of the same capitalist'. Such a factory can hardly be distinguished from the mode of production of the guild handicraft industries, 'except by the greater number of workers simultaneously employed by the same individual capital'.[16] But capital cannot confine itself to the mere co-ordination of workers – it must go beyond this stage. Of course, any production on a larger scale presupposes such co-ordination, and in this sense simple co-operation remains the 'basic form of capitalist production'. However, it would be historically incorrect to see it as a particular 'fixed' epoch in the development of the capitalist mode of production.[17]

This is because almost from its very beginning the factory of the early period of capitalism is compelled 'to use the concentration of workers in one place and the simultaneity of their labour in a different way' – so that the entire plant is divided into definite partial operations, and each of these operations is allotted to a particular group of workers. This creates the typical form of capitalist manufacture as an industrial mode of production, whose principle becomes the division of labour within the work-shop, and where, from the outset, what matters is not the quality of the product, as in handicraft, but mass production 'because the objective is exchange-value and surplus-value'.

Consequently manufacture, as the first historical form of capitalist production, initially appears 'where mass quantities are produced for export, for the external market', that is in commercial centres and coastal towns whose industrial production is 'so to speak naturally oriented towards exchange-value'. However, outside these great emporia, manufacture does not initially 'seize hold of the so-called urban trades, but of the rural secondary occupations, spinning

---

[15] ibid. p.587.
[16] *Capital* I, p.439 (322).
[17] ibid. p.453 (335).

Methods of production of relative surplus-value · 239

and weaving – the labour which requires the least guild-level skills, technical training'. Or 'certain branches of production, such as glassworks, metal-works, sawmills etc. which demand a higher concentration of labour-powers from the outset . . . likewise concentration of the means of labour etc.' and therefore 'cannot be operated on guild-principles'.[18]

Nevertheless, however much early capitalist manufacture strives for relative surplus-value through co-operation and the division of labour, its laws are by no means identical with those 'which correspond to large-scale industry'.[19] For its basis remains handicraft skill, despite all the developments of the division of labour – its 'specific machinery' is the 'collective worker, formed out of the combination of a number of individual specialised workers'.[20] Consequently it is still correct to assume that 'necessary labour still takes up a great portion of the entire available labour-time in manufacture, hence that surplus-value per individual worker is still relatively small'. This is compensated for by the fact that in manufacture 'the rate of profit is higher, hence that capital accumulates more rapidly in relation to its already existing amount, than it does in big industry'. However, on the other hand, 'manufacture obtains this higher profit only through the employment of many workers at once . . .' And therefore it is absolute surplus-value which still predominates in manufacture, and gives it its characteristic stamp.[21]

This barrier is not overcome until modern industry, based on the use of machinery. In contrast to manufacture, the revolutionising of the mode of production in large-scale industry does not proceed from labour-power but from the means of labour.[22] This creates a situation in which the original relation between the worker and the means of labour becomes fundamentally changed. Handicraft, which was subject to the worker, is replaced by an 'animated monster' which 'objectifies the scientific idea and is in fact the co-ordinator', so that the individual worker only 'exists as its living isolated accessory'.[23] In contrast to the simple tool, the machine, and even more so, machinery as an automatic system, appears to be 'in no way . . . the individual worker's means of labour. Its distinguishing characteristic is not in the least, as with the means of labour, that it transmits the worker's activity to the object. This activity, rather, is posited in such a way

[18] *Grundrisse*, p.511.
[19] *Theories* II, p.583.
[20] *Capital* I, p.468 (348).
[21] *Grundrisse*, p.588.
[22] *Capital* I, p.492 (371).
[23] *Grundrisse*, p.470.

I

that it merely transmits the machine's work, the machine's action, on to the raw material – supervises it and guards against interruptions. Not as with the instrument, which the worker animates and makes into his organ with his skill and strength, and whose handling therefore depends on his virtuosity. Rather, it is the machine which possesses skill and strength in place of the worker,[24] is itself the virtuoso, with a soul of its own in the mechanical laws acting through it ... The worker's activity, reduced[25] to a mere abstraction of activity, is determined and regulated on all sides by the movement of the machinery, and not the opposite.' Consequently the production process has ceased 'to be a labour process in the sense of a process dominated by labour as its governing unity. Labour appears, rather, merely as a conscious organ, scattered among the individual living workers at numerous points of the mechanical system; subsumed under the total process of the machinery itself, as itself only a link of the system, whose unity exists not in the living workers, but rather in the living (active) machinery ... against which the valorising power of the individual labour capacity is an infinitesimal, vanishing magnitude ...' The full development of capital takes place only when the means of labour 'appear as a machine within the production process, opposite labour; and the entire production process appears as not subsumed under the direct skilfulness of the worker, but rather as the technical application of science. [It is], hence, the tendency of capital to give production a scientific character; direct labour [is] reduced to a mere moment of this process.'[26]

How does this transformation of the means of labour, and the consequent revolutionising of the entire mode of production, affect the valorisation process of capital?

[24] Marx says on pre-capitalist forms of co-operation: 'The greater the extent to which production still rests on mere manual labour, on use of muscle power etc. in short on physical exertion by individual labours, the more does the increase of the productive force consist in their collaboration on a mass scale.' ('Hence the violent rounding up of the people in Egypt, Etruria, India etc. for forced construction and compulsory public works.') The situation is different with 'semi-artistic crafts': here what was important was the 'skilfulness of individual, but uncombined labour'. Capital 'combines mass labour with skill, but in such a way that the former loses its physical power, and the skill resides not in the worker but in the machine and in the scientific combination of both as a whole in the factory. The social spirit of labour obtains an objective existence separate from the individual workers.' (*ibid.* p.529.)
[25] In the sense that the worker's activity 'becomes more and more a ... purely mechanical activity, hence indifferent to its particular form.' (*ibid.* p.297.)
[26] *ibid.* pp.692-94, 699.

Methods of production of relative surplus-value · 241

In another passage Marx comments that political economists often claim that machinery 'saves labour' and that with its help 'human labour performs actions and creates things it would be absolutely incapable of creating without it.' Both points are correct, but only refer to 'the use-value of machinery'[27] and to the labour process as such, not to machinery's role in the valorisation process of capital. Here machinery's main function is to act as a means of increasing the production of surplus-value.

As Marx describes so impressively and in such detail in Volume I of *Capital*, the introduction of the machine system went hand in hand with an excessive lengthening of the working day and with the most ruthless exploitation of the labour of women and children. But this is not the immanent purpose of machinery – it is essentially a means for increasing *relative* surplus-value.

It is inherent in the concept of relative surplus-value that necessary labour is saved by increasing productivity, in order to extend surplus labour.[28] 'The transformation of the means of labour into machinery is the realisation of this tendency.'[29] Therefore 'only in the imagination of economists does [machinery] leap to the aid of the individual worker', by reducing and facilitating his labour! (On the contrary: the capitalist use of machinery robs the activity of the worker of all 'independence and attractiveness', by transforming him not only into a part of a worker, but into a mere segment of a machine.) 'Capital employs machinery, rather, only to the extent that' (through reducing necessary labour) 'it enables the worker to work a larger part of his time for capital, to relate to a larger part of his time as time which does not belong to him. . . . Through this process, the amount of labour necessary for the production of a given object is indeed reduced to a minimum, but only in order to valorise a maximum of labour in the maximum number of objects.'[30] Thus in reality the capitalist use of machinery turns out to be the opposite of that attributed to it by bourgeois apologists; instead of making the worker

---

[27] *ibid.* p.389.
[28] What is characteristic of machinery is 'the saving of necessary labour and the creating of surplus labour'. (*ibid.*)
[29] *ibid.* p.693. Cf. the section of the *Rough Draft* quoted in note 153 on p.49 above where Marx stresses that the 'entrance of machinery' is not to be developed 'from competition' but rather 'from the relation of capital to living labour'. (In *Wage-Labour and Capital* Marx himself derives machinery from the competition of capitalists.)
[30] *Grundrisse*, p.701. Marx notes in addition: 'The first aspect is important, because capital here – quite unintentionally – reduces human labour, expenditure of energy, to a minimum. This will redound to the benefit of emancipated labour, and is the condition of its emancipation.'

more independent and alleviating his exploitation it serves rather to confiscate an increasingly large part of his labour-time as surplus labour, and so strengthens and perpetuates the hostile power of capital over him.

We shall not deal with a further effect of machinery – the development of the so-called industrial reserve army – until the next chapter. But we should refer here to the fact that 'however much the use of machinery may increase surplus labour at the expense of necessary labour by raising the productive power of labour, it is clear that it attains this result only by diminishing the number of workers employed by a given amount of capital. It converts a portion of capital which was formerly variable, i.e. had been turned into living labour, into machinery, i.e. into constant capital which does not produce surplus-value.'[31] . . . Hence there is an immanent contradiction in the application of machinery to the production of surplus-value, since, of the two factors of the surplus-value created by a given amount of capital, one, the rate of surplus-value, cannot be increased except by diminishing the other, the number of workers.'[32] We shall see later how this contradiction is simultaneously resolved and deepened.

So much, then, on the role played by machinery in the valorisation process of capital. The development of machinery does of course present other aspects, if we look at it from the viewpoint of the pure labour process, and disregard its use under capitalism. The *Rough Draft* has the following to say on these other aspects : 'Nature builds no machines, no locomotives, railways, electric telegraphs, self-acting mules etc. These are products of human industry; natural material transformed into organs of the human will over nature, or of human participation in nature. They are organs of the human brain, created by the human hand; the power of knowledge objectified.' The development of machinery 'indicates to what degree general social knowledge has become a direct force of production, and to what degree, hence, the conditions of the process of social life itself have come under the control of the general intellect[33] and been transformed in

---

[31] The result of this is the law of the 'increasing organic composition of capital'; a law which was already stated by the classical economists, but which was first allotted its appropriate place in the system of political economy by Marx. (*Wages, Price and Profit, Selected Works*, pp.224-25.)

[32] *Capital* I, p.531 (407).

[33] Cf. Marx's distinction between 'universal' and 'co-operative' labour in Volume III of *Capital*. 'Both kinds play their role in the process of production, both flow one into the other, but both are also differentiated. Universal labour is all scientific labour, all discovery and all invention. This labour depends

Methods of production of relative surplus-value · 243

accordance with it. To what degree the powers of social production have been produced, not only in the form of knowledge, but also as immediate organs of social practice, of the real life process.'[34] Not only does this signify that 'individual labour as such has altogether ceased to appear as productive, but rather, is so only in those common labours which subordinate the forces of nature to themselves.'[35] In addition, it signifies that the development of machinery as an automatic system taken to its logical extreme (one thinks today of all-embracing 'automation') radically alters the nature of the labour process by allotting to the worker the completely changed function of mere 'watchman and regulator'.[36] But the result of this is that the development of machinery – although leading under capitalism only to the oppression of workers – offers, in fact, the surest prospect for their future liberation, by facilitating that radical reduction of working time, without which the abolition of class society would remain mere words.[37] (We shall come back to this theme in more detail in Chapter 28.) On the other hand it is precisely the development of modern machinery which makes it a 'question of life or death for that monstrosity, the disposable working population held in reserve in misery for the changing requirements of capitalist exploitation to be replaced by the individuals who are absolutely available for the different kinds of labour required of them; the partially developed individual, who is merely the bearer of one specialised social function' (as the wage-labourer is today) 'must be replaced by the totally developed individual, for whom the different social functions are different modes of activity to be taken up in turn.'[38] Naturally each of these can only be realised in a communist society; but capital – against its will – presses forward in this direction! 'On the one side, then, it calls to life all the powers of science and of nature, as of social combination and of social intercourse in order to make the creation of wealth independent (relatively) of the labour-time employed on it.[39] On the other side,

partly on the co-operation of the living, and partly on the utilisation of the labours of those who have gone before.' By contrast, 'co-operative labour is the direct co-operation of individuals' (i.e. the communist organisation of society). (*Capital* III, p.104.)
[34] *Grundrisse*, p.706.
[35] *ibid*. p.700.
[36] *ibid*. p.705.
[37]Cf. Note 30 above.
[38] *Capital* I, p.618 (488).
[39] Marx says in this connection: 'To the degree that labour-time – the mere quantity of labour – is posited by capital as the sole determinant element, to that degree does direct labour and its quantity disappear as the determinant principle of production – of the creation of use-values – and is

it wants to use labour-time as the measuring rod for the giant social forces thereby created, and to confine them within the limits required to maintain the already created value as value. Forces of production and social relations – two different sides of the development of the social individual – appear to capital as mere means, and are merely means for it to produce on its limited foundation. In fact, however, they are the material conditions to blow this foundation sky-high.'[40] However, this is a question which goes far beyond the scope of this chapter, and which we will first deal with in more detail in the chapter on socialist society.

reduced both quantitatively, to a smaller proportion, and qualitatively, as an, of course, indispensable but subordinate moment, compared to general, scientific labour, technological application of natural sciences, on one side, and to the general productive force arising from social combination in total production on the other side – a combination which appears as a natural fruit of social labour (although it is a historic product). Capital thus works towards its own dissolution as the form dominating production.' (*Grundrisse*, p.700.)
[40] *ibid.* p.706.

18.
'Simultaneous Working Days'. The Capitalist Law of Population and the 'Industrial Reserve Army'

(Marx's critique of Malthus)

Until this point in the analysis Marx's primary concern was to investigate the nature of surplus-value, to develop it as the embodiment 'of the absolute or relative labour-time mobilised by capital over and above necessary labour-time.'[1] The number of workers employed by capital was irrelevant to the understanding of this process, since in every case surplus-value was gained either by prolonging the total labour-time of the worker or by reducing necessary labour-time, whether this applied to one hundred, ten or only one working day; in each case the degree of valorisation of capital or the rate of surplus-value simply depended on the division of the working day into necessary and surplus labour. It was possible, therefore, to disregard the number of workers exploited by capital, or, as this is called throughout the *Rough Draft*, the sum of 'simultaneous working days'.[2]

However, as already pointed out in the previous chapter, capital is from the outset a 'collective power', which is based on overcoming the individualisation of the worker, and concentrating many workers under one capitalist. 'There cannot be one capitalist for every worker, but rather there has to be a certain quantity of workers per capitalist, not like one or two journeymen per master.' For, 'if the capitalist employed only one worker in order to live from that one's surplus time, then he would obviously gain doubly if he himself also worked, with his own funds, for then he would gain, in addition to the surplus time, the wage paid the worker.'[3] By restricting himself to one worker he would rather 'lose in the process . . . or the worker would only be his helper, and thus he would not stand in relation to him as capital'. Therefore in order for 'capital to exist as capital', in order that the

---

[1] *Grundrisse*, p.385.
[2] We encounter the same terminology almost throughout Marx's *Theories of Surplus-Value*.
[3] Marx assumes here that the worker works half the day for himself, and half for the capitalist.

capitalist 'can both live from profit as well as accumulate' he must be able 'to set a certain quantity of living labour capacities to work simultaneously . . . his profit must be equal to the sum of the surplus time of many simultaneous living work days'.[4]

How does the number of workers employed by capital affect the valorisation of capital, the production of surplus-value?

We must first of all distinguish between the rate and the mass of surplus-value. For the first, as we have said, the number of workers employed is completely irrelevant. The capital may employ 5 or 50 workers; if the workers all work for the same length of time and if the relation between paid and unpaid labour is the same, then each of the 50 workers will produce just as much surplus-value as each of the 5. However, what will differ is the total mass of the surplus-value produced in each of the two cases – the scale on which capital can valorise itself at one time. In order to determine this mass, one must not only know – as with a single working day – the rate of surplus-value and the length of the working day, but also how often the working day is repeated spatially, that is the number of simultaneously employed workers. Both of the last two factors can nevertheless be summarised in the concept of 'aggregate labour',[5] in which the distinction between several working days and one working day would disappear in relation to the determination of the surplus-value produced. In the same way the labour set in motion by the aggregate capital of a society can also be thought of as one working day (thus for example the aggregate labour of 6 million workers who on average work 8 hours daily, as 1 working day of 48 million hours). If this 'social working day' represents a fixed magnitude, then surplus-value can clearly only 'be increased relatively, by means of a greater productive power of labour'; however, this is given 'only absolutely . . . through transformation of a greater part of the population into workers, and increase of the number of simultaneous working days'.[6] Therefore the growth of the working population appears here as the 'mathematical limit to the production of surplus-value by the total social capital'.[7]

So much on the ways in which the number of labour-powers employed affects the valorisation of capital, the mass of surplus-value which it produces. However, this is by no means the only aspect offered by the study of 'simultaneous working days'.

[4] *Grundrisse*, pp.585, 588.
[5] 'Aggregate labour, i.e. the working day multiplied by the number of simultaneous working days . . .' (*Grundrisse* p.830.)
[6] *ibid*. p.774. (Cf. *Capital* III, pp.243-44.)
[7] *Capital* I, p.422 (307).

The method of production based on capital is only possible because capital can continually appropriate surplus labour. However, surplus labour 'exists only in relation with necessary, hence only insofar as the latter exists. Capital must therefore constantly posit necessary labour, in order to posit surplus labour . . . but at the same time it must suspend it as necessary in order to posit it as surplus labour . . .' It is its tendency, therefore, to create as much labour as possible, just as it is equally its tendency to reduce necessary labour to a minimum. Marx says: 'As long as we regard the single working day, the process is naturally simple : (1) to lengthen it up to the limits of natural possibility (2) to shorten the necessary part of it more and more (i.e. to increase the productive forces without limit).' However, the matter is different if the question is not part of one working day, but of 'many working days alongside one another'. The tendencies which have been mentioned appear here in modified form.

On the one hand it is inherent in the nature of capital to strive for limitless valorisation (it creates only 'a specific surplus-value because it cannot create an infinite one all at once; but it is the constant movement to create more of the same'[8]). However, the living work day, which constitutes the source of its valorisation, is always limited – whether this be a question of a natural limit, or a legal one drawn by society. Consequently if its duration cannot be prolonged, and if the development of the technique of production does not permit any increase in relative surplus labour, then capital can leap over the limit of the working day 'only by positing *another* working day *alongside* the first at the same time – by the spatial addition of more simultaneous working days. E.g. I can drive the surplus labour of A no higher than 3 hours; but if I add the days of B, C, D etc. then it becomes 12 hours. In place of a surplus time of 3, I have created one of 12.'[9] Thus within definite limits the prolongation of the working day can be replaced by increasing the number of workers, and the mass of absolute surplus-value can be increased, despite a constant rate of surplus-value.[10] This therefore explains capital's striving to

[8] *Grundrisse*, p.334.
[9] *ibid.* p.400.
[10] The proposition 'that . . . if the rate of surplus-value is given, the amount of surplus-value depends on the number of workers simultaneously employed by the same capital' appears to be a tautological statement, says Marx elsewhere. 'For if 1 working day gives me 2 surplus hours, then 12 working days give me 24 surplus hours or 2 surplus days. The statement, however, becomes very important in connection with the determination of profit, which is equal to the proportion of surplus-value to the capital advanced, thus depending on the absolute amount of surplus-value . . . If one merely considers the simple law of surplus-value, then it seems tautological to say

employ as many workers as possible; it is in order to be able to squeeze surplus labour from as many as possible.

On the other hand, however, the drive for relative surplus-value compels capital 'to posit as many workers as possible as not necessary, and just as in the case ... of the single working day it was a tendency of capital to reduce the necessary working hours, so now the necessary working days are reduced in relation to the total amount of objectified labour-time. If 6 are necessary to produce 12 superfluous working hours, then capital works towards the reduction of these 6 to 4. Or 6 working days can be regarded as one working day of 72 hours; if necessary labour-time is reduced by 24 hours, then two days of necessary labour fall away – i.e. 2 workers.'[11] 'The ... law of an increase in the number of hours of surplus labour', by means of a reduction in necessary labour 'thus now obtains the form of a reduction in the number of necessary workers'.[12] (However, here the decrease in the number of workers indicates the growth in relative surplus-value, whereas in the previous case their increase expressed itself in the growth of absolute surplus-value).

Capital strives to link 'absolute with relative surplus-value'. What it therefore seeks is the 'greatest stretching of the working day with greatest number of simultaneous working days, together with reduction of necessary labour-time to a minimum, on one side, and of the number of necessary workers to the minimum on the other'.[13] The first process signifies an increase of the working population, the second its relative decrease, although it can remain the same in absolute terms or even grow. 'Both tendencies necessary tendencies of capital. The unity of these contradictory tendencies, hence the

---

that with a given rate of surplus-value and a given length of the working day, the absolute amount of surplus-value depends on the amount of capital employed. For an increase in this amount of capital and an increase in the number of workers simultaneously employed are, on the assumption made, identical, or merely different expressions of the same fact. But when one turns to an examination of profit, where the amount of the total capital employed and the number of workers employed vary greatly for capitals of equal size, then the importance of the law becomes clear.' (*Theories* II, p.410.)

[11] *Grundrisse*, p.400. Since the remaining 4 workers together provide a further 12 hours of surplus labour, each of them now has to perform not 2, but three hours of surplus labour. Thus relative surplus labour has grown; previously its relation to necessary labour was 2 : 10: now it is 3 : 9. However if it were possible for the same capital to employ all 6 workers at the new rate 'then the surplus-value would not only have increased relatively, but also absolutely'. (*ibid*.)
[12] *ibid.* p.768.
[13] *ibid.* p.770.

living contradiction'[14] is given 'only with machinery',[15] which reduces necessary labour only in order to expand surplus labour, and which consequently turns out to be the most potent means for the production of both relative and absolute surplus-value. (And it is precisely for this reason that the capitalist use of machinery – as already pointed out – has to be elaborated and understood primarily from the relation of capital to living labour i.e. from its striving for the appropriation of surplus-value, and not from competition.)[16]

It can be seen that: 'If labour time is regarded not as the working day of the individual worker, but as the indefinite working day of an indefinite number of workers, then all relations of population' enter into the investigation; 'all the contradictions which modern population theory expresses as such, but does not grasp' emerge from the basic forms of surplus-value.[17] It then appears that the two-sided law of capital 'to link up the greatest absolute mass of necessary labour with the greatest relative mass of surplus labour' corresponds to an equally two-sided law, on the one hand to transform the largest possible part of the population into a working population, and on the other 'to constantly posit a part of it as surplus population – population which is useless until such time as capital can utilise it'.[18]

[14] Cf. Hegel's *Science of Logic*, Volume II, pp.68-69. 'But it has been a fundamental prejudice of hitherto existing logic and of ordinary imagination that Contradiction is a determination having less essence and immanence than Identity; but indeed, if there were any question of rank, and the two determinations had to be fixed as separate, Contradiction would have to be taken as the profounder and more essential. For as opposed to it Identity is only the determination of the simple immediate, or of dead Being, while Contradiction is the root of all movement and life, and it is only insofar as it contains a Contradiction that anything moves and has impulse and activity . . . Something therefore only has life insofar as it contains Contradiction, and is that force which can both comprehend and endure Contradiction.'
[15] *Grundrisse*, p.775.
[16] Cf. note 28 on p.241 above.
[17] *Grundrisse*, pp.539-40, 401.
[18] *ibid.* p.399. 'There are two tendencies which constantly cut across one another; [firstly] to employ as little labour as possible, in order to produce the same or a greater quantity of commodities, in order to produce the same or a greater net produce, surplus-value, net revenue; secondly, to employ the largest possible number of workers (although as few as possible in proportion to the quantity of commodities produced by them), because – at a given level of productivity – the mass of surplus-value and of surplus-product grows with the amount of labour employed. The one tendency throws the workers on to the streets and makes a part of the population redundant, the other absorbs them again and extends wage-labour absolutely, so that the lot of the worker is always fluctuating but he never escapes from it.' (*Theories* II, p.573.)

We thus come to the question of the so-called industrial reserve army,[19] which Marx derived directly from the concept of relative surplus-value in the *Rough Draft* (in contrast to *Capital*), without having first described the effect of machinery and capital accumulattion on the development of the working population. (See pages 608-10 of the *Grundrisse*.) However, since this part of his exposition – apart from the point just mentioned – offers little that is new in comparison to the later work, we can easily omit it. We merely indicate here the way in which Marx conceived of the industrial reserve army as a result of the dialectical process of the simultaneous positing and abolition of necessary labour by capital;[20] and the fact that the *Rough Draft* equates the reserve army with the 'sphere of pauperism', whereas according to *Capital* this sphere, populated by impoverished and lumpen proletarian elements, simply forms the 'deepest sediment of relative overpopulation'.

By contrast, the preceding section of the *Grundrisse* (pages 604-08) appears of special interest. This deals with the law of population under capitalism as distinct from earlier stages of production, and contains the only detailed critique of Malthus's theory of population from Marx's pen which is known to us.[21]

This runs as follows : 'In different modes of social production there are different laws of the increase of population and of overpopulation'[22] which – since this is a matter of 'the History of the Nature of Humanity' – 'are *natural* laws, but natural laws of humanity only at a specific historic development, with a development of the

---

[19] In fact this expression is not used in the *Grundrisse*, although in two places (pp.400 and 610) Marx characterises the 'surplus population' of workers in contrast to the 'necessary population' as 'reserve' and as 'reserve for later use'. We should however remember that the expression 'industrial reserve army' had already been coined by Engels in 1845. (See his *Condition of the Working Class in England*, Moscow: Progress Publishers 1973.)

[20] 'Capital, as the positing of surplus labour, is equally and in the same moment the positing and the not-positing of necessary labour; it exists only insofar as necessary labour both exists and does not exist.' (*Grundrisse*, p.401.)

[21] Cf. the analogous (but less profound) critique of this theory in Sismondi's *Nouveaux Principes*, II, 1819, pp.266-78.

[22] Cf. the frequently quoted passage from Volume I of *Capital*: 'The working population therefore produces both the accumulation of capital and the means by which it is itself made relatively superfluous . . . and it does this to an always increasing extent. This is a law of population peculiar to the capitalist mode of production; and in fact every particular historical mode of production has its own special laws of population, which are historically valid within that particular sphere. An abstract law of population exists only for plants and animals and even then only in the absence of any historical intervention by man'. (*Capital* I, pp.783-84 (631-32).)

forces of production determined by humanity's own process of history ... These different laws can simply be reduced to the different modes of relating to the conditions of production or, in respect to the living individual, the conditions of his reproduction as a member of society, since he labours and appropriates only in society. The dissolution of these relations in regard to the single individual, or to part of the population, places them outside the reproductive conditions of this specific basis, and hence posits them as overpopulation'. However, it is 'only in the mode of production based on capital' that overpopulation 'appears as the result of labour itself, of the development of the productive power of labour'. Consequently, nothing is more false than to lump together the different historical laws of population increase, as the followers of Malthus do! For 'overpopulation at one level of social production can be different from what it is at another, and its effect can be different'. Thus for example 'overpopulation among hunting peoples was different from that among the Athenians, in turn different among the latter from that among the Germanic tribes ... An overpopulation of free Athenians who become transformed into colonists is significantly different from an overpopulation of workers who become transformed into workhouse inmates. Similarly the begging overpopulation which consumes the surplus-product of a monastery is different from that which forms in a factory ...'

Marx says further, that since in all pre-capitalist social formations '...the development of the forces of production is not the basis of appropriation, but a specific relation to the conditions of production (forms of property) appears as a *presupposed barrier*, to the forces of production,[23] and is merely to be reproduced, it follows that the development of population, in which the development of all productive forces is summarised,[24] must even more strongly encounter

---

[23] It is exactly this notion, according to which, in all social formations 'where landed property and agriculture constitute the basis of the economic order', the working individual 'has an objective existence in property in the land which presupposes his activity, and does not appear merely as its result', which Marx takes as the basis of his detailed description of the 'epochs in the economic formation of society', which is to be found in the *Grundrisse*, pp.471-514.

[24] Marx stresses the importance of population as the 'source of wealth' in other sections of the *Rough Draft*. For example, on p.608: 'If we further examine the conditions of the development of the productive forces as well as of exchange, division of labour, co-operation, all-sided observation, which can only proceed from many heads, science, as many centres of exchange as possible – all of it identical with growth of population.'

an *external barrier* and thus appear as something to be restricted.' That is, in order for such a society 'to exist in the old mode requires the reproduction of its members in the presupposed objective conditions', but this is only 'reconcilable with a specific amount of population'. At all levels of society however, 'overpopulation posited on the basis of a specific population "appears" just as determinate as the adequate population. Overpopulation and population taken together are *the* population which a specific production basis can create. The extent to which it goes beyond its barrier is given by the barrier itself, or rather by the same base which posits the barrier. Just as necessary labour and surplus labour together [are] the whole of labour on a given base.'[25]

Thus Malthus is certainly not to be reproached for 'asserting the fact of overpopulation in all forms of society'. (Although 'he has not proved it, for there is nothing more uncritical than his motley compilations from historians' and travellers' descriptions.') The chief defect in his 'Doctrine of Population' is that he 'regards overpopulation as being of the same kind in all the different historical phases of economic development'; that he 'does not understand their specific difference, and hence stupidly reduces these very complicated and varying relations to a single relation, two equations, in which the natural reproduction of humanity appears on the one side, and the natural reproduction of edible plants (or means of subsistence) on the other, as two natural series, the former geometric and the latter arithmetic in progression. In this way he transforms the historically distinct relations into an abstract numerical relation, which he has fished purely out of thin air, and which rests neither on natural nor on historical laws.'[26]

Marx continues that according to Malthus there should be 'a natural difference between the reproduction of mankind and e.g. grain. This baboon thereby implies that the *increase of humanity* is a purely natural process which requires *external restraints*, checks, to prevent it from proceeding in geometric progression. This *geometric reproduction* is the natural reproduction process of mankind.' In fact in actual history one finds that 'population proceeds in very different relations and that overpopulation is likewise a historically determined relation, in no way determined by abstract number or by the absolute limit of the productivity of the necessaries of life, but by

---

[25] *ibid.* pp.604-07, 486.
[26] *Grundrisse*, pp.605-06. Cf. *Theories* II, p.115, where Marx calls Malthus's 'nonsense about geometrical and arithmetical progression, borrowed from earlier writers' a 'purely imaginary hypothesis'.

Marx's critique of Malthus · 253

limits *posited rather by specific conditions of production.*' However, Malthus simply brushes aside these specific historical laws of the movement of population. 'Malthusian man, abstracted from historically determined man, exists only in his brain; hence also the geometric method of reproduction corresponding to this natural Malthusian man. Real history thus appears to him in such a way that the reproduction of his natural humanity is not an abstraction from the historic process of real reproduction, but just the contrary, that real reproduction is an application of the Malthusian theory. Hence the inherent conditions of population as well as of overpopulation at every stage of history appear to him as a series of external checks which have *prevented* the population from developing in the Malthusian form.' On the other hand, 'the production of the necessaries of life – as it is checked, determined by human action – appears' to Malthus 'as a check which it posits to itself. The ferns would cover the entire earth. Their reproduction would stop only where space for them ceased. They would obey no arithmetic proportion. It is hard to say where Malthus has discovered that the reproduction of voluntary natural products would stop for intrinsic reasons, without external checks. He transforms the immanent, historically changing limits of the human reproduction process into outer barriers; and the *outer barriers* to natural reproduction into *immanent limits* or *natural laws* of reproduction.'[27]

Secondly, Malthus foolishly relates 'a specific quantity of people to a specific quantity of necessaries.' Ricardo already 'correctly confronted him with the fact that the quantity of grain available is completely irrelevant to the worker if he has no *employment*; that it is therefore the means of employment and not of subsistence which put him into the category of surplus population'.[28] Marx says further that Ricardo's objection 'should be conceived more generally', since this 'relates to the social mediation as such', 'through which the individual gains access to the means of his reproduction and creates them;

---

[27] *Grundrisse*, pp.606-07. 'In his splendid work', (*On the Origin of the Species*), 'Darwin did not realise that by discovering the "geometrical" progression in the animal and plant kingdom he overthrew Malthus's theory. Malthus's theory is based on the fact that he set the geometrical progression of man against the chimerical "arithmetical" progression of animals and plants. In Darwin's work we also find (quite apart from his fundamental principle) the detailed refutation, based on natural history, of the Malthusian theory.' (*Theories* II, p.121.)
[28] Cf. Engels's letter to F.A.Lange of 29 March 1865, *Selected Correspondence*, p.160.

hence it relates to the *conditions of production* and his relation to them. There was no barrier to the reproduction of the Athenian slave other than the producible necessaries. And we never hear that there were *surplus slaves* in antiquity. The call for them increased rather. There was however a surplus population of non-workers (in the immediate sense), who were not too many in relation to the necessaries available, but had lost the conditions under which they could appropriate them.' (Marx adds: 'The invention of surplus workers i.e. of propertyless people who work, belongs to the period of capital.') The surplus population of the feudal period can be just as little deduced from some relation between the number of people and quantity of necessaries: 'The beggars who fastened themselves to the monasteries and helped them eat up their surplus-product are in the same class as the feudal retainers, and this shows that the surplus produce could not be eaten up by the small number of its owners.' And finally 'the overpopulation e.g. among hunting peoples, which shows itself in the warfare between the tribes proves not that the earth could not support their small numbers, but rather that the condition of their reproduction required a great amount of territory for few people.' Thus 'never a relation to a *non-existent* absolute mass of means of subsistence, but rather relation to the conditions of reproduction . . . including likewise the *conditions of reproduction of human beings*, of the total population, of relative surplus population. This surplus purely relative; in no way related to the means of subsistence as such, but rather to the mode of producing them. Hence also only a surplus at this stage of development.'[29]

So much then on Malthus's actual doctrine of population, which Marx elsewhere called a 'lampoon on the Human Race'.[30] In fact Malthus later tried to give this doctrine a direct economic foundation, by basing it on the so-called law of the 'declining yield of the soil'. However Marx does not go into this point in his critique of Malthus's theory of population, since he only intended to take it into consideration in the discussion of Ricardo's theory of rent.[31] Consequently he confines himself in the *Rough Draft* to remarking that the said law is merely to be traced back to the fact that 'in the stage of industry familiar to Ricardo etc. agriculture remained behind

---

[29] *Grundrisse*, pp.607-08.
[30] In a letter to J.B.Schweitzer of 24 January 1865, *Selected Correspondence*, p.143.
[31] 'What is not actually proper to Malthus at all, the introduction of the theory of rent . . . does not belong here.' (*Grundrisse*, p.608.)

industry, which [is] incidentally inherent in bourgeois production although in varying relations'.[32]

Thus the end result of the simple law of surplus-value is the tendency of capital not only to 'drive human labour towards infinity', but also to make it 'relatively superfluous'.[33] In conceptual terms, then, the theory of surplus population and the industrial reserve army is also contained in the theory of surplus-value. How the existence of overpopulation is connected to the formation of surplus capital, and with capital accumulation, will be shown later.

[32] *ibid.* The fact that the 'relatively larger unproductiveness of agriculture' simply represented an historical state of affairs, i.e. can disappear even under capitalism, was pointed out by Marx in the *Theories.* (*Theories* II, pp.105-07, 244. Cf. in addition *Grundrisse,* p.669.)

[33] *Grundrisse,* p.399.

19.
The Reproduction Process and the Inversion of the Law of Appropriation[1]

In the preceding analysis capital has only been regarded in the process of its formation, of its becoming, but not in the continuous flow of its renewal and reproduction. However, as Marx says, this mere repetition, the sheer continuity of the capitalist production process, 'imposes on the process certain new characteristics, or rather, causes the disappearance of some apparent characteristics possessed by the process in isolation'.[2] Thus 'at the first occurrence of capital' its presuppositions appear to be 'external presuppositions; . . . hence not emergent from its inner essence and not explained by it'. It is therefore necessary to grasp the process of the formation of capital in the context of the reproduction process so that these presuppositions 'appear as moments of the motion of capital itself, so that it has itself – regardless how they may arise historically – pre-posited them as its own moments'.[3]

In other words: From the point of view of the analysis up until now it could be, and had to be, assumed 'that the capitalist, once upon a time, became possessed of money by some form of primitive accumulation that took place independently of the unpaid labour of other people' before he could frequent the market as a buyer of labour-power and means of production: that consequently the appropriation of alien labour by the capitalist presupposed the exchange of commodities which are his property and which are thrown into circulation by him – 'of values which do not arise from his exchange

---

[1] This is a summation of two paragraphs from the *Grundrisse* (pp.450-58) which correspond to Chapter 23 and Section I of Chapter 24 of *Capital* Volume I, and which should be regarded as their first draft. The main difference between the two versions (disregarding the much more brilliant method of representation in the later work), is that in *Capital* the question is first examined from the standpoint of 'simple' and then from 'extended' reproduction, whereas only the latter method of observation is to be found in the *Rough Draft*.
[2] *Capital* I, p.712 (567).
[3] *Grundrisse*, p.450.

with living labour, or not from his relation as *capital* to *labour*'.⁴ This is the 'primitive accumulation', which the bourgeois economists favour so much in order to bring the fact that the valorisation of capital consists in the appropriation of unpaid labour 'into harmony with the general laws of property, as they are proclaimed by capitalist society itself'. Regardless of how matters may stand today, they say, the capitalists originally 'worked for' their capital; and so nothing is more natural than that they should receive a reward for their 'productive services'.

But there are numerous difficulties in this argument. In the first place we are only too well acquainted with the role played by robbery, cheating, enslavement – in brief, force – in the actual historical development of capital.⁵ These bear no relation to the peaceful accumulation of what has been 'worked for'. (If capitalism had confined itself merely to these peaceful methods it would never have progressed beyond its infancy.) And secondly, the bourgeois economists are guilty of a confusion here in that they pronounce the conditions of the becoming of capital 'as the conditions of its contemporary realisation i.e. presenting the moments in which the capitalist still appropriates as the non-capitalist – because he is still becoming – as the very conditions in which he appropriates as capitalist'. They forget that the accumulation of capital which precedes labour and which does not spring from it belongs to those conditions which 'lie behind it as historical preludes, just as the processes by means of which the earth made the transition from a liquid sea of fire and vapour to its present form now lie beyond its life as finished earth'. Admittedly 'individual capitals can continue to arise e.g. by means of hoarding. But the hoard is transformed into capital only by means of the exploitation of labour.'⁶ These apologetic attempts to derive the 'eternal right of capital to the fruits of alien labour' from the '*property by labour*' and from the 'simple and "just" laws of the exchange of equivalents' should, as Marx says in *Capital*, be banished to the realm of 'children's primers'. We can see how correct this is as soon as we direct our attention to the process of the reproduction of capital instead of one isolated process of production.

We saw that the outcome of the original process of production was the surplus labour appropriated by the capitalist: this initially exists in the form of a surplus-product and must then be transformed into money. Marx first examines the conditions of the realisation of

---

[4] *Capital* I, p.714 (569) and *Grundrisse*, p.456.
[5] *Grundrisse*, p.460 and *Capital* I, p.874 (714).
[6] *Grundrisse*, p.460.

the surplus-product, and of realisation in general, in the following section of the work which deals with the circulation process of capital. We therefore have to assume here that the capitalist succeeds in putting his commodity up for sale and selling it at its value. Through this, the surplus-value is also realised and transformed into the form of money. But this money 'is now already capital *in itself* and as such *a claim on new labour*'.[7] This new capital (which Marx calls 'surplus capital' or 'additional capital' in distinction to the original type whose fruit it is) must also naturally be valorised, and thus go through the process of production.

But the preconditions of the second process are vastly different from those of the first!

Surplus capital is above all nothing but capitalised surplus-value. 'There is not one single atom of its value that does not owe its existence to unpaid labour.'[8] As a consequence the particular forms which it must assume in order to valorise itself anew, namely those of constant and variable capital, are simply forms of surplus labour itself. Previously, insofar as the original act of production was considered, it appeared as 'an act of capital', that the material conditions of production – raw material, instrument and the means of subsistence for the workers – were 'on hand in the amounts which made it possible for living labour to realise itself not only as necessary, but also as surplus labour'.[9] But now 'it no longer seems, as it still did in the first examination of the production process, as if capital, for its part, brought with it any value whatsoever from circulation ... All moments which confronted living labour capacity and employed it as alien, external powers, and which consumed it under certain conditions independent of itself, are now posited as its own product and result.'[10]

But not just that. The absolute separation between property and labour, which is inherent in the capital-relation,[11] but only represented a historical precondition of it from the previous standpoint, 'now also appears as the product of labour itself, as objectification, materialisation of its own moments'. Up until now it could be assumed that capital became a power ruling over labour, precisely by means of the 'primitive accumulation' of its owners. However, this illusion disappears as soon as we look at the circuit of surplus capital,

---

[7] *ibid.* p.367.
[8] *Capital* I, p.728 (582).
[9] *Grundrisse*, p.452. (Naturally the portion of surplus-value consumed by the capitalists is disregarded here.)
[10] *ibid.* pp.453, 451.
[11] Cf. pp.200-01 above.

Inversion of the law of appropriation · 259

i.e. the process of reproduction. It now becomes clear that it is a result of the action of labour-capacity itself, that the material conditions for production which have been created by it confront it as capital and that the realisation process of labour is simultaneously its de-realisation process.[12] For, by its entry into the production process, labour-capacity 'has not only produced the conditions of necessary labour as conditions belonging to capital; but also the value-creating possibility, the valorisation which lies as possibility within it, now likewise exists as surplus-value, surplus-product, in a word as capital ... The worker has produced not only the alien wealth and his own poverty, but also the relation of this wealth ... to himself as this poverty', thus the capital-relation itself.[13] And 'this social relation, production relation, appears in fact as an even more important result of the process than its material results'.[14]

The result of the previous inquiry was that we have above all to distinguish between the conditions of capital in its becoming, and those of capital as it has become, as 'finished capital'.[15] Once capital has developed historically it goes on to produce the conditions of its existence – 'not as conditions of its arising, but as results of its presence ... It no longer proceeds from presuppositions in order to

---

[12] As an example of the unique mode of presentation of the *Rough Draft* and its often apparently abstruse 'Hegelian' terminology, we quote here the entire passage from which this sentence was taken. 'Living labour therefore now appears from its own standpoint as acting within the production process in such a way that, as it realises itself in the objective conditions, it simultaneously repulses this realisation from itself as an alien reality, and hence posits itself as insubstantial, as mere penurious labour-capacity in face of this reality alienated from it, belonging not to it but to others; that it posits its own reality not as a being for it, but merely as a being for others, and hence also as mere other-being, or being of another opposite itself. This realisation process is at the same time the de-realisation process of labour. It posits itself objectively, but it posits this, its objectivity, as its own not-being or as the being of its not-being – of capital. It returns back into itself as the mere possibility of value-creation or valorisation; because the whole of real wealth, the world of real value and likewise the real conditions of its own realisation are posited opposite it as independent existences.' (*ibid.* p.454.)
[13] Cf. *Capital* I, p.724 (578): 'The capitalist process of production, therefore, seen as a total, connected process, i.e. a process of reproduction, produces not only commodities, not only surplus-value, but it also produces and reproduces the capital-relation itself; on the one hand the capitalist, on the other the wage-labourer.'
[14] *Grundrisse*, pp.453, 458. Cf. *ibid.* p.512. 'The production of capitalists and wage-labourers is thus a chief product of capital's valorisation process. Ordinary economics, which looks only at the things produced, forgets this completely.'
[15] See note 129 on p.44 above.

become, but rather it is itself presupposed, and proceeds from itself to create the conditions of its maintenance and growth.'[16]

In fact, Marx repeats, 'For the formation of surplus capital I, if we give that name to the surplus capital emerging from the original production process . . . it appears as a condition that the capitalist should possess values, of which he formally exchanges one part for living labour-capacity' ('We say formally, because living labour must replace and return to him these exchanged values as well') – 'But let us now think', Marx continues, 'of this surplus capital as having been thrown back into the production process, as realising its surplus-value anew in exchange and as appearing anew as surplus capital at the beginning of the third production process. This surplus capital II has different presuppositions from surplus capital I. The presupposition of surplus capital I was the existence of values belonging to the capitalist and thrown by him into circulation. The presupposition of surplus capital II is nothing more than the existence of surplus capital I; i.e. in other words, the presupposition that the capitalist has already appropriated alien labour without exchange. This puts him into a position where he is able to begin the process again and again . . . *The previous appropriation of alien labour now appears as the simple precondition for the new appropriation of alien labour* . . . The fact that he [i.e. the capitalist] has previously confronted living labour as capital appears as the only condition required in order that he may not only maintain himself as capital, but also, as a growing capital, increasingly appropriate alien labour without equivalent; or that he may extend his power, his existence as capital opposite living labour-capacity,[17] and on the other side constantly

---

[16] *Grundrisse*, p.460. On p.278, *ibid.*, we read : 'It must be kept in mind that new forces of production and relations of production do not develop out of nothing, nor drop from the sky, nor from the womb of the self-positing Idea; but from within and in antithesis to the existing development of production and the inherited, traditional relations of property. While in the completed bourgeois system every economic relation presupposes every other in its bourgeois economic form, and everything posited is thus also a presupposition, this is the case with every organic system. This organic system itself, as a totality, has its presuppositions, and its development to its totality consists precisely in subordinating all elements of society to itself, or in creating out of it the organs which it still lacks. This is historically how it becomes a totality. The process of becoming this totality forms a moment of its process, of its development.'

[17] 'Thus the production by labour of this surplus capital . . . is at the same time the creation of the real necessity of new surplus labour and of new surplus capital. It here becomes evident that labour itself progressively extends and gives an ever wider and fuller existence to the objective world of wealth

Inversion of the law of appropriation · 261

posit living labour-capacity anew in its subjective, insubstantial penury as living labour-capacity.'[18]

We now come to a passage in the *Rough Draft* which was incorporated into Volume I of *Capital* with only slight alterations.[19] It runs: 'Insofar as surplus capital I was created by means of a simple exchange between objectified labour and living labour-capacity – an exchange entirely based on the laws of the exchange of equivalents as measured by the quantity of labour or labour-time contained in them – and *insofar* as the legal expression of this exchange presupposed nothing other than everyone's right of property over his own products, and of free disposition over them[20] – but insofar as the relation of surplus capital II to I is therefore a consequence of this first relation – we see that by a peculiar logic, the right of property undergoes a dialectical inversion, so that on the side of capital it becomes the right to an alien product, or the right of property over alien labour, the right to appropriate alien labour without an equivalent.... The right of property is inverted to become on the one side, the right to appropriate alien labour, and, on the other side, the duty of respecting the product of one's own labour, and one's own labour itself, as values belonging to others. The exchange of equivalents, however, which appeared as the original operation, an operation to which the right of property gave legal expression, has become turned round in such a way that the exchange by one side is now only illusory, since the part of capital which is exchanged for living labour-capacity, firstly is itself *alien labour*, appropriated without equivalent, and, secondly, *has to be replaced with a surplus by living labour-capacity*, is thus in fact not consigned away, but merely changed from one form into another. The relation of exchange has thus dropped away entirely, or is a *mere semblance.* Furthermore, the right of property originally appeared to be based on one's own labour.[21] Property now appears as the right to alien labour, and as the impossibility of

---

as power alien to labour, so that, relative to the values created . . . the penurious subjectivity of living labour-capacity forms an ever more glaring contrast.' (*ibid.* p.455.)

[18] *ibid.* pp.456-57.

[19] See *Capital* I, pp.728-30 (583-84).

[20] In *Capital*: 'presupposes nothing beyond the worker's power to dispose freely of his own capacities, and the money owner or commodity owner's power to dispose freely of the values that belong to him.'

[21] In *Capital* this sentence follows: 'Some such assumption was at least necessary, since only commodity owners with equal rights confronted each other, and the sole means of appropriating the commodities of others was the alienation of a man's own commodities, commodities which, however, could only be produced by labour.'

labour's appropriating its own product. The complete separation between property, and even more so, wealth, and labour, now appears as a consequence of the law which began with their identity.'[22]

The special importance of these sentences is immediately obvious. They mark a point where the fundamental difference between Marx's conception of capital and that of his predecessors emerges most clearly. Naturally, it had been perceived, and stated,[23] before Marx that the transition to the capitalist mode of production corresponded to an inversion in the law of appropriation. But Marx was the first to explain the nature of this inversion and demonstrate its necessity, since the whole problem in understanding capital and its forms consists in discovering how the form of appropriation of labour without equivalent, which characterises capitalism, 'arises from the law of commodity exchange – out of the fact that commodities exchange for one another in proportion to the amount of labour-time embodied in them', and thus 'to start with does not contradict this law'.[24] However, this difficulty could not be resolved as long as the economists thought in terms of the direct exchange of the worker's labour with the capitalist, rather than the exchange of his value-creating capacity, labour-power. The reason why is as follows. As with the exchange of all commodities, that of labour-power is also governed by the cost of its reproduction; that is, by the quantity of labour-time objectified in it – since 'the value as such . . . is always effect, never cause'. 'Hence the exchange which proceeds between capitalist and worker thus corresponds completely to the laws of exchange', in that it is a question of the exchange-value of the commodity which is purchased by the capitalist. 'But the use-value of the value the capitalist has acquired through exchange is itself the element of valorisation and its measure, living labour and labour-time, and, specifically, more labour-time than the reproduction of the living worker costs. Hence, by virtue of having acquired labour-capacity in exchange as an equivalent, capital has acquired labour-time – to the extent that it exceeds the labour-time contained in labour-capacity – in exchange without equivalent; it has appropriated alien labour-time without exchange by means of the *form* of exchange. This is why exchange becomes merely formal . . . and in the further development of capital even the semblance is suspended that capital exchanges for labour-capacity anything other than its

[22] *Grundrisse*, pp.457-58.
[23] By Smith (Cf. *Theories* I, pp.86-87); by Sismondi and Cherbuliez (see *Capital* I, footnote 6 on p.730 (note 1 on p.584) and *Theories* III, pp.377-78). Cf. Marx's critique of Ricardo, *Theories* II, pp.399-407.
[24] *Theories* III, pp.481-82.

[labour-capacity's] own objectified labour; i.e. that it exchanges anything at all for it . . . Thus the exchange turns into its opposite, and the laws of private property – liberty, equality, property (property in one's own labour, and free disposition over it) – turn into the worker's propertylessness, and the dispossession of his labour (i.e.) the fact that he relates to it as alien property, and vice versa.'[25]

This then is the solution to the problem, the solution which Rosa Luxemburg correctly characterised as a 'triumph of historical dialectics'.[26] The unique character of the commodity labour-power, which as value simply represents its cost of production, but which as use-value is itself the source of the creation of new value, makes it possible for the exchange between the worker and the capitalist to simultaneously correspond to, yet contradict, the laws of commodity exchange; that this, the most important of all the acts of exchange, amounts in fact to the appropriation of alien labour, without exchange, although 'under the semblance of exchange'. It is clear, however, as Marx emphasised, that this semblance is a 'necessary semblance', insofar as capitalist production itself is the production of commodities and therefore presupposes the laws of commodity exchange.

It is of course true that this inversion of the law of appropriation only becomes visible 'if we consider capitalist production in the uninterrupted flow of its renewal, and if, in place of the individual capitalist and the individual worker, we view them in their totality, as the capitalist class and the working class confronting each other'.[27] For, looked at in isolation, the transaction between the capitalist and the worker must appear as completely 'just', that is corresponding to the general laws of commodity exchange, and there would be no reason to suppose that it should turn round into its opposite. But if that is the case then all one can see is a falsification or injury to the 'original' right, which was based on the strict equality between the owners of commodities and which did not seem to allow any room for the one-sided appropriation of the products of alien labour, for the exploitation of one of the producers by the other.

This is the sense in which capital's mode of appropriation is criticised by petit-bourgeois socialists (Proudhon, for example[28]), and

[25] *Grundrisse*, pp.673-74.
[26] *Accumulation of Capital*, p.265.
[27] *Capital* I, p.732 (586).
[28] 'We may well, therefore, feel astonished at the cleverness of Proudhon, who would abolish capitalist property – by enforcing the eternal laws of property which are themselves based on commodity production.' (*Capital* I, p.734 (587).)

the political economists who followed Sismondi. Thus Cherbuliez stresses that if the capitalist appropriates the product of the worker's labour this 'is an inescapable consequence of the law of appropriation' whose 'fundamental principle' consists, inversely, in that the producer has 'an exclusive right to the value resulting from his labour'.[29] Marx answers that such a 'right' is a 'pure fiction', a mere reflex of processes of modern commodity circulation looked at in isolation. 'Commodities are exchanged with one another according to their value, that is, according to the labour embodied in them. Individuals confront one another only as commodity owners and can therefore only acquire other individual's commodities by alienating their own. It therefore appears as if they exchanged only their own labour since the exchange of commodities which contain other people's labour, insofar as they themselves were not acquired by the individuals in exchange for their own commodities, presupposes different relations between people than those of (simple) commodity owners, of buyers and of sellers. In capitalist production this semblance, which its surface displays, disappears. What does not disappear however is the illusion that originally men confront one another only as commodity owners and that consequently, a person is only a property owner insofar as he is a worker.' Marx concludes that 'as has been stated, this "originally" is a delusion arising from the surface appearance of capitalist production and has never existed historically', since in real history 'man always comes on to the stage as a property owner before he appears as a worker'.[30]

We read in similar vein in the *Rough Draft*: 'The notion that production and hence society depended in all states of production on the *exchange of mere labour for labour is a delusion.* In the various forms in which labour relates to the conditions of production as its own property, the reproduction of the worker is by no means posited through *mere labour,* for his property relation is not the result but the presupposition of his labour. In landed property this is clear; it must also become clear in the guild-system that the particular kind of property which labour creates does not rest on labour alone or on the exchange of labour, but on an objective connection between the worker and a community and conditions which are there before him, which he takes as his basis. These too are products of labour, of the labour of world history; of the labour of the community – of its historic development, which does not proceed from the labour of individuals or from the exchange of their labours . . . A situation in

---

[29] Cited from *Theories* III, p.377.
[30] *ibid.* p.378.

which labour is merely exchanged for labour . . . presupposes the separation of labour from its original intertwinement with its objective conditions – which is why it appears as mere labour on one side, while on the other side its product, as objectified labour, has an entirely independent existence as value opposite it.'[31] This state of affairs, therefore, presupposes capitalist production, but with it the capitalist mode of appropriation as well.

In other words, the traditional conception of 'property-in-labour' is not only a piece of mythology from political economy. It also fundamentally misconceives the specifically historical character of commodity exchange and commodity production in general. It consequently overlooks the fact that capital's mode of appropriation, which is based on the propertylessness and expropriation of the worker, is neither a complete negation nor a 'falsification' of the laws of free exchange, but is rather 'their highest development'. 'For as long as labour-capacity as a commodity'.[33] 'From then onwards comproduction does not yet rest on exchange, but exchange is rather merely a narrow circle resting on a foundation of non-exchange, as in all stages preceding bourgeois production.'[32]

The inversion of the law of appropriation comes about first of all 'because the ultimate stage of free exchange is the exchange of labour-capacity as a commodity'.[33] 'From then onwards commodity production is generalised and becomes the typical form of production; it is only from then onwards that every product is produced for sale from the outset and all wealth produced goes through the sphere of circulation. Only where wage-labour is its basis does commodity production impose itself upon society as a whole; but it is also true that only there does it unfold all its hidden potentialities.'[34] Hardly surprising then that the full development of commodity production 'according to its inherent laws' drives onwards to results which contradict its mode of appropriation and turn it into its opposite!

Nevertheless the circulation process, 'as it appears on the surface of society . . . knows no other method of appropriation' apart from

[31] *Grundrisse*, p.515.
[32] *ibid.* p.674.
[33] *ibid.*
[34] *Capital* I, p.733 (587). Lukacs states: 'The commodity can only be understood in its undistorted essence when it becomes the universal category of society as a whole.' And it is precisely for this reason that, 'where the commodity is universal, it manifests itself differently from the commodity as a particular, isolated, non-dominant phenomenon'. (*History and Class Consciousness*, pp.86, 85.)

through the exchange of equivalents, and it is for precisely this reason that this mode of appropriation itself, as well as the laws which contradict it, have *'to be derived from the development of exchange-value itself'*.[35] (The same holds true for the law of value, which on the one hand no longer seems to apply to the capitalist mode of production, but on the other hand requires this mode of production in order to attain its full validity.)[36] Of course, bourgeois economics has to sever the connection between the mode of appropriation of the simple commodity economy and that of capitalist production – it is unable to grasp their mutual relation as 'unity of opposites'. In the first place it does not possess the tool of the dialectical method, and in the second it has no theoretical understanding of either the simple commodity economy, or the capitalist mode of production itself, as having a merely relative, historical character.

So much on Marx's analysis of surplus capital, as it is to be found in the *Rough Draft*. This analysis has shown us that 'the true nature of capital emerges only at the end of the second circuit' (i.e. the circuit of surplus capital I), and hence that it is here that the illusion first disappears 'that the capitalist exchanges anything at all with the worker other than a part of the latter's own objectified labour'.[37] Not until this point does labour appear 'as a mere means to realise objectified, dead labour, to penetrate it with an animating soul while losing its own soul to it'; whereas the objective conditions of this labour 'are posited as alien, independent existences . . . as self-sufficient values for themselves, which form wealth alien to labour-capacity, the wealth of capital'.[38] The result of this is the 'most extreme alienation', the separation of labour itself from the conditions of its realisation. 'Once this separation is given, the production

[35] *Grundrisse*, German edn. p.904.
[36] Cf. Chapter 9 above.
[37] *Grundrisse*, pp.514, 516-17.
[38] 'The material on which it [labour-capacity] works is alien material; the instrument is likewise an alien instrument; its labour appears as a mere accessory to their substance and hence objectifies itself in things not belonging to it. Indeed, living labour itself appears as alien vis-à-vis living labour-capacity, whose labour it is, whose own life expression it is, for it has been surrendered to capital in exchange for objectified labour, for the product of labour itself. Labour-capacity relates to its labour as to an alien, and if capital were willing to pay it without making it labour it would enter the bargain with pleasure. Thus labour-capacity's own labour is as alien to it . . . as are material and instrument. Which is why the product then appears to it as a combination of alien material, alien instrument and alien labour – as alien property, and why, after production, it has become poorer by the life forces expended, but otherwise begins the drudgery anew.' (*ibid.* p.462.)

Inversion of the law of appropriation · 267

process can only produce it anew, reproduce it and reproduce it on an expanded scale.'[39] But we know : 'What appears paradoxical as result is already contained in the presupposition', in the act of exchange between the capitalist and the worker, since 'the separation of labour from property in the product of labour, of labour from wealth, is thus posited in this act of exchange itself.'[40] This presupposition is merely realised in the production and reproduction process of capital.

[39] *ibid.* p.462.
[40] *ibid.* p.307. 'What is capital, regarded not as the result of, but as the prerequisite for the process (of production)? What makes it capital before it enters the process so that the latter merely develops its immanent character? The social framework in which it exists. The fact that living labour is confronted by past labour, activity is confronted by the product, man is confronted by things, labour is confronted by its own materialised conditions as alien, independent, self-contained subjects, personifications, in short, as someone else's property and, in this form, as "employers" and "commanders" of labour itself, which they appropriate instead of being appropriated by it . . . Money . . . in the process appropriates surplus-value, no matter what name it bears . . . because it is already presupposed as capital before the production process . . . If it did not enter into the process as capital it would not emerge from it as capital.' (*Theories* III, pp.475, 476.)

20.
Primitive Accumulation and the Accumulation of Capitals

Marx's examination of surplus capital showed us that, 'as soon as capital has become capital as such it creates its own presuppositions i.e. the possession of the real conditions of the creation of new values *without exchange* – by means of its own production process. These presuppositions, which originally appeared as conditions of its becoming . . . now appear as results of its own realisation . . . as posited by it – *not as conditions of its arising, but as results of its presence.*'[1] What follows from this, however, is that the conditions of the becoming of capital are distinct from the capitalist mode of production itself and must be explained outside of it.[2] This is not only of importance in refuting the evasions of the apologists, which were mentioned in the previous chapter. 'What is much more important for us', says Marx, 'is that our method indicates the points where historical investigation must enter in, or where bourgeois economy as a merely historical form of the production process points beyond itself to earlier historical modes of production.'[3] This is because although it was necessary to understand the development of economic categories as the dialectical development of what was already contained in the concept of capital, one must also not overlook the

---

[1] *Grundrisse*, p.460.
[2] 'While, e.g. the flight of serfs to the cities is one of the historic conditions and presuppositions of urbanism, it is not a condition, not a moment of the reality of developed cities, but belongs rather to their past presuppositions, to the presuppositions of their becoming which are suspended in their being.' (*ibid*. p.459.)
[3] *ibid*. pp.460-61. Marx continues: 'In order to develop the laws of bourgeois economy, therefore, it is not necessary to write the real history of the relations of production. But the correct observation and deduction of these laws, as having themselves become in history, always leads to primary equations – like the empirical numbers, e.g. in natural science – which point towards a past lying behind this system. These indications, together with a correct grasp of the present, then also offer the key to the understanding of the past – a work in its own right, which, it is to be hoped, we shall be able to undertake as well.' (*ibid*. pp.460-61.)

fact that this is not merely a question of a dialectic of concepts, and that in general 'the dialectical method of presentation is only correct when it knows its limits'.[4] Thus Marx's method itself leads us to the investigation of the 'antediluvian conditions of capital', which 'belong to the history of its formation, but in no way to its contemporary history', and which find their most distinct expression in the so-called primitive accumulation of capital.

We read in the *Rough Draft* that the conditions of the capital-relation as such 'are themselves posited in the relation as it appears originally'. These are : 1. 'the presence of living labour-capacity as a merely subjective existence, separated from the conditions of living labour as well as from the means of existence . . . the means of self-preservation of living labour-capacity'. 2. the value (capital) to be found on the other side must 'be an accumulation of use-values sufficiently large to furnish the objective conditions not only for the production of the products or values required to reproduce or maintain living labour-capacity, but also for the absorption of surplus labour – to supply the objective material for the latter'; 3. but 'a free exchange relation between both sides' must be present . . . 'i.e. hence, production which does not directly furnish the producer with his necessaries, but which is mediated through exchange, and which cannot therefore usurp alien labour directly, but must buy it, exchange it'; and finally 4. the side which confronts the worker must 'present itself as value, and must regard the positing of value, self-valorisation, money-making, as the ultimate purpose – not direct consumption or the creation of use-value'.[5]

Let us begin with the last two conditions. We have already emphasised that it is impossible to speak of the capital-relation as long as the worker himself does not dispose of his own expenditure of force through exchange. Consequently, the capitalist mode of production presupposes the dissolution of all relations 'in which the *workers themselves*, the living labour-capacities themselves, still belong *directly among the objective conditions of production*, and are appropriated as such – i.e. are slaves or serfs. For capital, the worker is not a condition of production, only work is. If it can make machines do it, or even water, air, so much the better. And it does not appropriate the worker, but his labour – not directly, but mediated through exchange.'[6] (Marx remarks on this : 'The fact that slavery is possible at individual points within the bourgeois system of

[4] *Grundrisse*, German edn. p.945.
[5] *Grundrisse*, pp.463-64.
[6] *ibid.* p.498.

production does not contradict this. However slavery is then possible there only because it does not exist at other points and appears as an anomaly opposite the bourgeois system itself.'[7])

Nevertheless the exchange of living labour for money, for objectified labour, does not yet constitute 'either capital on one side, or wage-labour on the other'. This can also apply in other types of relation. For example, the so-called services. 'If A exchanges a value or money . . . in order to obtain a service from B' then they both 'in fact exchange only use-values with one another'; A gives necessaries (or money), B labour, a service which A wants to consume, either directly – personal service – or by providing B with the material, whereby the latter creates a use-value designed for his consumption by means of the objectification of his labour. 'For example, when the peasant takes a wandering tailor, of the kind that existed in times past, into his house, and gives him the material to make clothes with.[8] Of if I give money to a doctor to patch up my health. What is important in these cases is the service which both do for one another. *Do ut facias* here appears on quite the same level as *facio ut des*, or *do ut des*.* The man who takes the cloth I supplied to him and makes me an article of clothing out of it gives me a use-value. form of activity. I give him a completed use-value; he completes another for me. The difference between previous, objectified labour and living, present labour here appears as a merely formal difference between the different tenses of labour, at one time in the perfect and at another in the present.'[9]

In fact, continues Marx, 'the article of clothing not only con-

---

[7] ibid. p.464. Cf. also p.224. 'Negro slavery – a purely industrial slavery – which is, besides, incompatible with the development of bourgeois society and disappears with it, presupposes wage-labour, and if other, free states with wage-labour did not exist alongside it, if, instead, the Negro states were isolated, then all social conditions there would immediately turn into pre-civilised forms.'

[8] '[T]he tailor and shoemaker, who in my youth still paid their visits to our Rhine peasants, one after another, turning the home-made materials into shoes and clothing.' (Engels, *Supplement to Capital Volume Three, Capital* III, p.897.)

* *Do ut facias*: I give that you may do: *facia ut des*: I do that you may give: *do ut des*: I give that you might give.

[9] *Grundrisse*, pp.465-66. 'In the exchange of money for labour or service, with the aim of direct consumption, a real exchange always takes place; the fact that amounts of labour are exchanged on both sides is of merely formal interest for measuring the particular forms of the utility of labour by compar-But instead of giving it directly in objective form, he gives it in the ing them with each other. This concerns only the form of exchange; but does

tains a specific form-giving labour – a specific form of usefulness imparted to the cloth by the movement of labour – but it also contains a certain quantity of labour – hence not only use-value, but value generally, value as such. But this value does not exist for A, since he consumes the article, and is not a clothes dealer. He has therefore bought the labour not as *value-positing* labour, but as an activity which creates utility, use-value.' In the case of personal services this use-value is even consumed 'as such without making the transition from the form of movement into the form of the object. If, as is frequently the case in simple relations, the performer of the service does not obtain *money*, but direct use-values themselves, then it no longer even seems as if value were being dealt in on one or the other side; merely use-values. But even given that A pays money for the service, this is not a transformation of his money into capital, but rather the positing of his money as mere medium of circulation, in order to obtain an object for consumption, a specific use-value. This act is for that reason not an act which produces wealth, but the opposite, one which consumes wealth.' The owner of money 'sees his money not valorised but *devalued* in its transposition from the form of value into the form of use-value' – and the more often 'he repeats the exchange, the poorer he becomes'.[10] The money which he 'here exchanges for living labour – service in kind, or service objectified in a thing – is not *capital* but revenue, money as a medium of circulation in order to obtain use-value . . . not money which will preserve and valorise itself as such through the acquisition of labour. Exchange of *money as revenue*, as a mere medium of circulation, for living labour, can never posit money as capital, not, therefore, labour as wage-labour in the economic sense. A lengthy disquisition is not required to show that to consume (spend) money is not the same as to produce money.'[11]

not form its content. In the exchange of capital for labour, value is not a measure for the exchange of two use-values, but is rather the content of the exchange itself.' (*ibid.* p.469.)

[10] 'One of the savants of Paul de Kock may tell me that, without this purchase' of service, 'I cannot live, and therefore also I cannot enrich myself; that this purchase is therefore an indirect means, or at least a condition, for my enrichment – in the same way as the circulation of my blood or the process of breathing are conditions for my enrichment. But neither the circulation of my blood nor my breathing in themselves make me any the richer; on the contrary, they both presuppose a costly assimilation of food; if that were not necessary, there would be no poor devils about.' (*Theories* I, pp.402-03.)

[11] *Grundrisse*, pp.466-67. Cf. *ibid.* p.272: 'Labour as mere performance of services for the satisfaction of immediate needs has nothing whatever to do with capital, since that is not capital's concern. If a capitalist hires a wood-

K

Marx concludes: 'It is not, then, simply the exchange of *objectified labour for living labour* ... which constitutes capital and hence wage-labour, but rather, the exchange of objectified labour as value, as self-sufficient value, for living labour as *its* use-value, as use-value not for a specific, particular use or consumption, but as use-value for *value*.'[12]

This is the reason why the free day labourers, who are to be found sporadically in the period of pre-bourgeois relations, cannot be classified as 'wage-labourers'. True, their services were bought 'not for the purposes of consumption, but of production; but, firstly, even if on a large scale, for the production only of *direct use-values*, not of *values*; and secondly, if a nobleman e.g. brings the free worker together with his serfs, even if he re-sells a part of the worker's product, and the free worker thus creates value for him, then this exchange takes place only for the superfluous [product] and only for the sake of superfluity, for *luxury consumption;* is thus at bottom only a veiled purchase of alien labour for immediate consumption or as use-value.'[13] (Marx adds: 'Incidentally, wherever these free workers increase in number, and where this relation grows, there the old mode of production ... is in the process of dissolution, and the elements of real wage-labour are in preparation.' What can also naturally happen as in ancient Poland, is that these free servants 'emerge ... and vanish again without a change in the mode of production taking place'.[14])

The capital-relation can therefore only arise if the commodities put up for sale by the purchaser of labour-power simply serve as a means of preserving and increasing the values in his possession. In order for this to take place, the worker must not only be personally

---

cutter to chop wood to roast his mutton over, then not only does the woodcutter relate to the capitalist, but also the capitalist to the woodcutter, in the relation of simple exchange. The woodcutter gives him his service, a use-value, which does not increase capital; rather, capital consumes itself in it; and the capitalist gives him another commodity for it in the form of money. The same relation holds for all services which workers exchange directly for the money of other persons, and which are consumed by these persons. This is consumption of revenue, which, as such, always falls within simple circulation; it is not consumption of capital.'

[12] *ibid.* p.469. As one can see this is a perspective which was later developed in great detail by Marx in Part I of the *Theories* – 'Adam Smith's Conception of Productive Labour', pp.155-76.

[13] It is on this basis that we should evaluate the attempts of some European economic historians to deduce the 'capitalist' character of eighteenth-century estates from the presence of free day labourers on them.

[14] *Grundrisse*, p.469.

free; he must also be put into the position where it is no longer possible for him to exchange the products which he has produced himself, and where the only commodity which he has to offer is his own labour-power. ('So long as *both* sides exchange their labour with one another in the form of *objectified* labour, the relation is impossible.')[15] Consequently, the owners of labour-power must be propertyless proletarians. Although this precondition may appear simple and self-evident from the vantage point of the present social order, it required centuries of development before a class of such proletarians could come into being. For (apart from slavery, and slave-like situations, 'where the worker himself appears among the natural conditions of production for a third individual or community'[16]), the producers of earlier periods were always either owners of, or at least in possession of, the means of production (soil and land, or the implements of their craft). Consequently the objective conditions of production appear here as 'natural presuppositions, *natural conditions of the producer's existence* – just as his living body, even though he reproduces and develops it, is originally not posited by himself, but appears as the *presupposition* of his self.' Thus the mode of production of earlier epochs was based on the original unity of the producers with the conditions of production[17] – and it is not this unity 'which

[15] *ibid.* p.464.
[16] *ibid.* p.495.
[17] 'The original unity between the worker and the conditions of production . . . has two main forms: the Asiatic communal system (primitive communism) and small-scale agriculture based on the family . . . Both are embryonic forms and both are equally unfitted to develop labour as social labour and the productive power of social labour. Hence the necessity for the separation, for the rupture, for the antithesis between labour and property (by which property in the conditions of production is to be understood). The most extreme form of this rupture, and the one in which the productive forces of social labour are also most powerfully developed, is capital. The original unity can be re-established only on the material foundation which creates it and by means of the revolutions which, in the process of this creation, the working class and the whole society undergo.' (*Theories* III, pp.422-23.) On the subject of the 'Asiatic form of society'; it is evident from all the available texts that Marx regarded the so-called 'Asiatic form of society' as one species of primitive communism, standing at the beginning of the history of culture (which is also confirmed by the above quotation from the *Theories*). This fact also explains why Marx begins his enumeration of the successive periods of economic history (in the *Preface* to the *Contribution*) not with primitive communism, but with the 'Asiatic mode of production'. We read there: 'In broad outline, the Asiatic, ancient, feudal and modern bourgeois modes of production may be designated as epochs marking progress in the economic development of society' (*Contribution*, p.21), although in the same text (and in the previously written *Rough Draft*) he starts the history of culture with primitive

requires explanation or is the result of a historic process, but rather the *separation* . . . a separation which is completely posited only in the relation of wage-labour and capital'.[18]

In other words, the capitalist mode of production presupposes a series of historical changes in which, first of all, the various forms in which the producers were bound to the means of production were destroyed. It thus presupposes, above all : in the first place the 'dissolution of the relation to the earth – land and soil – as natural conditions of production, to which he relates as to his own inorganic being; the workshop of his forces and the domain of his will.' (Consequently 'the formula of capital' above all *'includes not-land-ownership*, or, the negation of the situation in which the working individual relates to land and soil, to the earth, as his own i.e. in which he works, produces, as proprietor of the land and soil'.[19]) Secondly the capitalist mode of production presupposes the dissolution of relations in which the producer 'appears as the *proprietor of the instrument*'. ('Just as the above form of landed property presupposes a real community,[20] so does this property of the worker in the instrument presuppose a particular form of the development of manufacture, namely craft artisan work; bound up with it, the guild-corporation system, etc.') And finally it presupposes 'included in both' the dissolution of the situation in which the producer still 'has in his possession before production the *means of consumption* which are necessary for him to live as a producer – i.e. during production, *before* its completion.' ('As proprietor of land he appears as directly provided with the necessary consumption fund. As master in a craft he has inherited it, earned it, saved it up – and as a youth he is first an apprentice, whereas he does not appear as an actual independent worker at all, but shares the master's fate in a patriarchal way . . .')

---

communism, and stresses that this 'primitive form' existed not only in Asia, but also with the Romans, Germans, Celts and Slavs (*Contribution*, p.33). (This apparent 'contradiction' has never been noticed by the recent advocates of the theory of a specifically 'Asian form of society').

[18] *Grundrisse*, p.489.

[19] 'The first condition for the development of capital is the separation of landed property from labour – the emergence of land, the primary condition of labour, as an independent force, a force in the hands of a separate class, confronting the free worker.' Consequently in the Physiocratic version of economics, 'the landowner appears as the true capitalist, that is, the appropriator of surplus-value . . . In this respect too the Physiocratic system hits the mark . . .' (*Theories* I, pp.51-52.)

[20] In contrast to the social connection based on commodity exchange and money. (Cf. p.128 above.)

Primitive accumulation · 275

The *Rough Draft* continues : 'These are now . . . historic presuppositions needed before the worker can be found as a free worker, as objectless purely subjective labour-capacity confronting the objective conditions of production as his *not-property*, as alien property, as *value* for-itself, as capital. But the question arises, on the other side, which conditions are required so that he finds himself up against a *capital*?'[21]

The answer runs : 'It is inherent in the concept of capital . . . in its origin, that it begins with *money*, and hence with wealth existing in the form of money. It is likewise inherent in it that it appears as coming out of circulation, as the product of circulation. The formation of capital thus does not emerge from landed property (here at most from the *tenant*, insofar as he is a dealer in agricultural products); or from the guild (although there is a possibility at the last point[22]); but rather from merchant's and usurer's wealth.'[23] The former, in particular, constitutes a necessary condition for the development of the capitalist mode of production, since 'this presupposes production for trade, selling on a large scale, and not to the individual customer, hence also a merchant who does not buy to satisfy his personal wants but concentrates the purchases of many buyers in his one purchase.' On the other hand the entire development of merchant's wealth operates in the direction of 'giving production more and more the character of production for exchange-value', thereby undermining the old relations of production. (It is in this sense that Marx spoke of the 'dissolving effect' of trade and merchant's wealth[24].) Yet this effect 'is incapable by itself of promoting and explaining the transition from one mode of production to another'[25] (i.e. from feudal to capitalist). ('Or else', we read in the *Rough Draft*, 'ancient Rome, Byzantium etc. would have ended their history with free labour and capital, or rather begun a new history. There, too, the dissolution of the old property relations was bound up with development of monetary wealth – of trade etc. But instead of leading to

[21] *Grundrisse*, pp.497-98.
[22] Namely to the extent that 'individual guild masters may develop into capitalists with the dissolution of the guilds; but the case is rare, in the nature of the thing as well. As a rule, the whole guild system declines and falls, both master and journeyman, where the capitalist and the worker arise'. (*ibid.* p.506.)
[23] *ibid.* p.505.
[24] For example in the *Grundrisse*, pp.856-57 (see note 17 on p.153 above).
[25] *Capital* III, p.327.

industry this dissolution led in fact to the supremacy of the countryside over the city.'[26])

Thus it was not monetary wealth as such which made capitalists out of the merchants and money owners of the fifteenth to seventeenth centuries. This presupposed rather the historical process of the divorce of the means of production from labour and from the workers. Not until after this process 'had reached a certain level could monetary wealth place itself as a mediator between the objective conditions of life, thus liberated, and the liberated but also *homeless* and *emptyhanded* labour-powers, and buy the latter with the former'.[27] It was only then that the capitalist could engage in 'primitive accumulation' of the conditions of production.

This was by no means a process of creation out of nothing (which is fundamentally how the matter appears to bourgeois economists).[28] 'The process of dissolution, which transforms a mass of individuals of a nation etc. potentially into free wage-labourers – individuals forced solely by their lack of property to labour and sell their labour – presupposes on the other side *not* that these individuals' previous sources of income and in part conditions of property have *disappeared*, but the reverse, that *only* their utilisation has become different...' For 'this much is clear; the same process which divorced a mass of individuals from their previous relations to the objective conditions of labour, relations which were, in one way or another, affirmative, negated these relations, and thereby transformed these individuals into *free workers*, this same process freed – potentially – these objective conditions of labour – land and soil, raw material, necessaries of life, instruments of labour, money or all of these – from their *previous state of attachment* to the individuals now separated from them.' This process 'was the divorce of elements which up until then were bound together; its result is therefore not that one of the elements disappears, but that each of them appears in a negative relation to the other – the (potentially) free worker on the one

---

[26] *Grundrisse*, p.506. Cf. *Capital* III, p.332. 'In the ancient world the effect of commerce and the development of merchant's capital always resulted in a slave economy; depending on the point of departure, it also resulted in the transformation of a patriarchal slave system devoted to the production of the immediate means of subsistence into one devoted to the production of surplus-value. However, in the modern world, it results in the capitalist mode of production. It follows from this that these results spring in themselves from circumstances other than the development of merchant's capital.'

[27] *Grundrisse*, p.509.

[28] Cf. *Capital* II, pp.140-43. (Smith's view of the formation of a reserve stock.)

side, capital (potentially) on the other.' The separation of the objective conditions of labour from the masses, who have become transformed into free workers, necessarily appears also 'at the same time as the achievement of independence by these same conditions at the opposite pole'.[29]

Marx continues: 'There can therefore be nothing more ridiculous than to conceive this *original formation* of capital' (i.e. primitive accumulation) 'as if capital had stockpiled and created the objective conditions of production – necessaries, raw materials, instruments – and then offered them to the worker, *who was bare of these possessions*[30] . . . Rather its original formation is that, through the historic process of the dissolution of the old mode of production, value existing as money-wealth is enabled, on one side, to buy the objective conditions of labour; on the other side, to exchange money for the living labour of the workers who have been set free. All these moments are present;[31] their divorce is itself a historic process, a process of dissolution, and it is the *latter* which enables money to transform itself into *capital*.[32] Money itself, to the extent that it also plays an active role,

---

[29] *Grundrisse*, p.503.

[30] Marx notes in a footnote: 'The first glance shows what a nonsensical circle it would be if on the one hand the workers whom capital has put to work in order to posit itself as capital had first to be created, to be brought to life through its stockpiling if they waited for its command *Let There Be Workers*!; while at the same time it were itself incapable of stockpiling without alien labour, could at most stockpile its own labour, i.e. could exist in the form of not-capital and not-money; since labour, before the existence of capital, can only realise itself in forms such as craft labour, petty agriculture etc., in short all forms which can not stockpile, or only sparingly; in forms which allow of only a small surplus-product and eat up most of it.' (*ibid.* p.506.)

[31] This also applies to the instruments of labour, since 'monetary wealth neither invented nor fabricated the spinning wheel and the loom. But once unbound from their land and soil, spinner and weaver with their stools and wheels came under the command of monetary wealth.' (*ibid.* pp.507-08.)

[32] We read further on in the text: 'The way in which money transforms itself into capital often shows itself quite tangibly in history; e.g. when the merchant induces a number of weavers and spinners, who until then wove and spun as a rural secondary occupation, to work for him, making their secondary into their chief occupation; but then has them in his power and has brought them under his command as wage-labourers. To draw them away from their home towns and to concentrate them in a place of work is a further step. In this simple process it is clear that the capitalist has prepared neither the raw material, nor the instrument, nor the means of subsistence for the weaver and the spinner. All that he has done is to restrict them little by little to one kind of work in which they become dependent on selling, on the buyer, the merchant, and ultimately produce only for and through him. He bought their

does so only insofar as it intervenes in this process as itself a highly energetic solvent, and to that extent assists in the creation of the *plucked*, objectless *free workers*; but certainly not by creating the objective conditions of their existence; rather by helping to speed up their separation from them – their propertylessness.'[33]

At this stage, capital proper '*does nothing but bring together the mass of hands and instruments which it finds on hand. It agglomerates them under its command*. That is its *real stockpiling*; the stockpiling of workers, along with their instruments, at particular points.'[34] In fact, 'from the historical foundation from which this process proceeds' ((manufacture, etc.) 'this concentration can only take place in the form that these workers are assembled together as wage-labourers, that is, as workers who must sell their labour-power because the conditions of labour confront them independently as alien property, as an alien force . . . [because] the disposal of them through the intermediary of money is in the hands of individual owners of money or of commodities, who, thereby, become *capitalists*.'[35] However, it is necessary at this point to distinguish between the capitalist form and the content of this process, since it is a universal condition for labour as such that 'subsistence for the workers must be available, before new necessaries are reproduced', and that 'the products of their labour must constitute the raw material and means of production for their own reproduction.' And it is only under capitalism that this reserve supply of means of subsistence and means of production assumes the form of commodities and capital. 'The properties, the characteristic features of the *capitalist mode of production* and therefore of capital itself insofar as it expresses a definite relation of the producers to one another and to their products, are necessarily, and invariably, described by the economists as the properties of the *objects*.'[36]

---

labour originally only by buying their product; as soon as they restrict themselves to the production of this exchange-value and thus must directly produce exchange-values, must exchange their labour directly for money in order to survive, then they must come under his command, and at the end even the illusion that they sold him products disappears. He buys their labour and takes their property first in the form of the product, and soon after that the instrument as well, or he leaves it to them as sham property in order to reduce his own production costs.' (*ibid.* p.510.)

[33] *ibid.* pp.506-07, 508-09.
[34] *ibid.* p.508.
[35] *Theories* III, p.271.
[36] *ibid.* p.270.

Primitive accumulation · 279

Popularisations of Marx's economics often treat the chapter on primitive accumulation as one which, although important in itself, basically lies outside the scope of economic analysis proper, a mere *historical* digression on Marx's part. This is clearly false.[37]

Of course one precondition for the capitalist mode of production to exist at all is the breaking of the original unity between the producers and the conditions of production, and the loss by the producers of the 'function of accumulating' which accompanies their loss of the conditions of production and their 'labour fund'.[38] Regarded in this way, primitive accumulation is one of those elements which make up the capital-relation itself, and it is therefore 'contained in the concept of capital'.[39] It does not follow from this, however, that we should regard the process of the divorce of the worker from the means of production as being concluded once and for all. Simply as an historical fact! On the contrary: 'Once capital exists, the capitalist mode of production itself evolves in such a way that it maintains and reproduces this separation on a constantly increasing scale until the historical reversal takes place.'[40] This process is accomplished through the continuous conversion of surplus-value into capital, 'as a result of which the increased products of labour which are at the same time its objective conditions, conditions of reproduction, continuously

---

[37] Uncharacteristically, the same incorrect view can also be found in Luxemburg. 'Admittedly, Marx dealt in detail with the process of appropriating non-capitalist means of production as well as the transformation of the peasants into a capitalist proletariat. Chapter 25 of *Capital* Volume I is devoted to describing the origin of the English proletariat, of the capitalist agricultural tenant class and of industrial capital, with particular emphasis on the looting of colonial countries by European capital. Yet we must bear in mind that all this is treated solely with a view to so-called primitive accumulation. For Marx, these processes are incidental, illustrating merely the genesis of capital, its first appearance in the world; they are, as it were, travails by which the capitalist mode of production emerges from a feudal society. As soon as he comes to analyse the capitalist process of production and circulation he reaffirms the universal and exclusive domination of capitalist production.' *Accumulation of Capital*, pp.364-65.

[38] *Theories* III, p.421.

[39] 'But in order to come into being capital presupposes a certain accumulation; which is already contained in the independent antithesis between objectified and living labour: in the independent survival of this antithesis. This accumulation, necessary for capital to come into being, which is already therefore included in its concept as presupposition – as a moment – is to be distinguished essentially from the accumulation of capital which has already become capital, where there must already be capitals.' (*ibid.* pp.319-20; cf. *ibid.* p.590.)

[40] That is, until a communist society is established.

confront labour as *capital* i.e. as forces – personified in the capitalist – which are alienated from labour and dominate it. Consequently, it becomes a specific function of the capitalist to accumulate, that is, to reconvert a part of the surplus-product into means of production.' (The *Rough Draft* speaks in this sense of the 'specific accumulation of capital', by which is meant the 'tendering' by the capitalist of the material for new 'surplus labour', for extended reproduction).[41] However, this accumulation 'merely presents as a *continuous process* what in *primitive accumulation* appears as a distinct historical process, as the process of the emergence of capital and as a transition from one mode of production to the other'.[42]

But this is not all. If on the one hand the transformation of money into capital presupposes the historical process of primitive accumulation, 'it is on the other hand the effect of capital and of its process, once arisen, to conquer all of production and, at all points, to develop and complete the divorce between labour and property, between labour and the objective conditions of labour'.[43] Consequently the further advance of the capitalist mode of production not only has as its consequence the progressive destruction of handicrafts, and of the small-scale landed property of the cultivator himself etc., but also the 'swallowing up of small capitalists by large, and the deprivation of the former of their capital'. We are once again confronted with the identical process of separation, 'which begins with primitive accumulation, appears as a permanent process in the accumulation and concentration of capital and expresses itself finally as centralisation of existing capitals in a few hands and a deprivation

---

[41] This does not of course mean that it is something unique to capital to use parts of the surplus-product for extended reproduction. 'For it is stupid . . . to regard it as a quality specific to capital – that the objective conditions of living labour must be present as such – whether they are furnished by nature or produced in history. Hence the specific accumulation of capital means nothing more 'than that it valorises objectified surplus labour – surplus-product – in a new living surplus labour, instead of investing (spending) it, like, say, Egyptian kings or Etruscan priest-nobles for pyramids etc.' (*Grundrisse*, p.433.) Thus, in capitalism the function of the extension of production is allotted to the capitalists; it is presented as the transformation of the surplus-product into capital. (And it is precisely in this that its extension of production is to be distinguished from previous modes of production.) 'And the stupid economist concludes from this', mocks Marx, 'that if this operation did not proceed in this contradictory specific way, it could not take place at all. Reproduction on an extended scale is inseparably connected in his mind with accumulation, the capitalist form of this reproduction.' (*Theories* III, p.272.)

[42] *ibid.* p.272.
[43] *Grundrisse*, p.512.

of many of their capital'.[44] This is a process which will only reach its conclusion with the removal of capitalism itself, that is, with the re-establishment of the original unity between the producers and their objective conditions of production.

[44] *Capital* III, p.246. (Cf. the identical passage in *Theories* III, pp.271-72.)

Appendix

A Critical Assessment of Marx's Theory of Wages

1. Marx's theory of wages

Like his predecessors, Marx distinguishes between the value and price of labour-power (or to put it in the language of the classical economists, between the 'natural' and 'market price' of 'labour'). The price of labour-power is the wage, insofar as this is simply a function of the relation of supply and demand on the labour market; on the other hand the value of labour-power is that average quantity to which the actual wage paid seeks to adjust itself in the long run, and which is therefore independent of supply and demand.

However, how is the value of labour-power determined? Like that of all commodities – through its cost of production. However, since labour-power 'only exists as a capacity of the living individual',[1] and since it is inseparable from its bearer, the worker himself, the costs of its production clearly break down into those costs which are required to 'maintain the worker as worker' and to 'perpetuate the race of workers'; and these are primarily the necessities which serve for the maintenance of workers and their families, for their nourishment, clothing, housing etc., if we disregard the relatively small costs of training of the great majority of workers. In this sense the value of labour-power is determined by the value of the 'necessary means of subsistence', and in the final analysis by the amount of labour incorporated in them.

To this extent the determination of the value of labour-power coincides with the determination of the value of all other commodities. The difference does not become evident until we investigate the extent of the means of subsistence which are necessary for the maintenance of the worker, or 'the necessary wants' which are their basis.

It is clear that the sum of the 'necessary means of subsistence' must at the least suffice 'to maintain the working individual in his normal state as a working individual'.[2] We therefore have to make a distinction between the energy expended merely in the 'life-process'

[1] *Capital* I, p.274 (171).
[2] *ibid.* p.275 (171).

of the worker, and that expended in the 'labour process' (to adopt O.Bauer's well-chosen terminology[3]). (If only the former is replaced, then the additional expenditure of energy which work itself requires would not be – or would only be insufficiently – compensated for, leading to only a very restricted reproduction of labour-power and the consequent falling of the price of labour-power below its value.) It is also clear that the so-called 'natural needs, such as food, clothing, fuel and housing' can vary a great deal, 'according to the climatic and other physical peculiarities of the country'.[4]

But is it in fact simply a question of 'natural' needs and are these identical with the 'necessary' needs in the sense used in political economy? Political economy is of course a social, not a natural science. As a result it does not ask which needs are necessary 'in themselves', or from the standpoint of physiology, but rather which needs correspond to the 'traditional', socially given, way of life of the worker in a particular country at a particular time. In fact, 'the number and extent of his so-called necessary requirements, as also the manner in which they are satisfied, are themselves products of *history*, and depend therefore to a great extent on the level of civilisation attained by a country; in particular they depend on the conditions in which, and consequently on the habits and expectations with which, the class of free workers has been formed.' And we would add to that that the extent of these needs also naturally depends on the demands which the working class raises and succeeds in achieving in its political and trade-union struggle against the capitalist class, providing that they can be consolidated, and are not merely achievements of a temporary nature. In this sense Marx expressly stresses the 'historical and moral element' which enters into the determination of the value of labour-power.[5]

However, what follows from the fact that – as distinct from all other commodities – 'the value of labour-power is constituted from two elements, one of which is merely physical, the other historical or social'?[6] Nothing other than that the laws of the determination of wages are 'elastic' (as Engels put it), and that the value of labour-power must vary within particular limits. 'Its ultimate limit is determined by the physical element, that is to say, to maintain and reproduce itself, to perpetuate its physical existence, the working class must receive the necessaries absolutely indispensable for living and multi-

---

[3] O.Bauer, *Rationalisierung und Fehlrationalisierung*, pp.170-71.
[4] *Capital* I, p.275 (171).
[5] *ibid.*
[6] *Wages, Price and Profit. Selected Works*, p.222.

plying. The value of those indispensable necessaries forms, therefore, the ultimate limit of the value of labour.'[7] And its upper limit? This cannot be determined by human needs since human needs are very flexible.

We read in Marx on this subject: 'But as to profits, there exists no law which determines their minimum. We cannot say what is the ultimate limit of their decrease. And why cannot we fix that limit? Because, although we can fix the minimum of wages, we cannot fix their maximum. We can only say that, the limits of the working day being given, the maximum of profit corresponds to the physical minimum of wages; and that wages being given, the maximum of profit corresponds to such a prolongation of the working day as is compatible with the physical forces of the labourer. The maximum of profit is, therefore, limited by the physical minimum of wages and the physical maximum of the working day. It is evident that between the two limits of this maximum rate of profit an immense scale of variations is possible. The fixation of its actual degree is only settled by the continuous struggle between capital and labour, the capitalist constantly tending to reduce wages to their physical minimum, and to extend the working day to its physical maximum, while the worker constantly presses in the opposite direction. The matter resolves itself into a question of the respective powers of the combatants.'[8]

This passage should not be understood as meaning that there might be no upper limit at all to the value of labour-power, and wage increases. Such a limit does exist, and is in fact quite narrowly drawn. However, this can be derived neither from the form and extent of the working class's socially given standards of living, nor from some abstractly understood size of national product which is to be distributed, but only from the nature of capital itself. For it is simply not the case that labour and capital represent two autonomous powers, whose respective 'shares' in the national product merely depend on their respective strengths; rather, labour is subject to the economic power of capital in capitalism from the outset, and its 'share' must naturally always be conditional on the 'share' of capital. Therefore the real uppermost limit of wages is given by the size of profit, and, more precisely, by the movements of the rate of profit. Or as Rosa Luxemburg writes: 'The entire capitalist economy, i.e. primarily the purchase of labour-power, has production for profit as its aim. Hence a definite rate of profit as the aim of production pre-

[7] ibid.
[8] ibid. p.223.

cedes the hire of workers as something given, and at the same time constitutes the average upper barrier beyond which wages cannot increase. But it is also an inherent tendency in profit to extend itself without limit at the expense of the worker, i.e. to reduce him to the bare minimum of existence. The wage moves up or down between these extremes, according to the relation between supply and demand, that is, the relation between the disposable labour-powers and the size of the capital which is seeking an outlet in production.'[9]

That this constitutes the real meaning of Marx's theory of wages has already long been recognised by several bourgeois economists. Thus, Werner Sombart wrote in his polemic against Julius Wolf: 'Wolf is evidently caught in the delusion that marxist theory maintains that wages must necessarily remain based on the value of the necessary means of subsistence; he even rediscovers the "eternal law of wages" in Marx, if not literally, at least in terms of its content. A more distorted interpretation could hardly be found. One only needs to read Marx's indignant attacks on the advocates of the eternal law of wages. But, even without taking account of these explicit reservations, Wolf ought to have inferred the conclusion from Marx's theory as a whole, that only one single law is in fact essential to it: "Wages can never rise so high that the capitalist loses interest in production".'[10]

Admittedly, Sombart's essay was written in the 1890s. However, since that time several socialists have 'learnt' so much in addition that they still cannot distinguish between Marx's theory of wages and Lassalle's 'iron law of wages', and interpret Marx's theory, like Julius Wolf, as implying a 'physiological minimum of existence'. For example, one can read in Fritz Sternberg: 'The worker's wage oscillates, as Marx formulated it, around its costs of production i.e. around a standard which enables him to maintain himself.'[11] If a recognised marxist is so ill-informed what can one expect of those who, quite simply, want to destroy Marx?

---

[9] Rosa Luxemburg, *Ausgewählte Reden und Schriften* II, p.99. Cf. Karl Kautsky, *Karl Marx' ökonomische Lehren*, 1906, p.236. 'The wage can never increase so much that it endangers surplus-value itself. In the capitalist mode of production the demand for labour-power is occasioned by capital's need for self-valorisation, for the production of surplus-value. Therefore capital will never buy labour-power at a price which would exclude the production of surplus-value.'
[10] Quoted from K.Diehl, *Sozialökonomische Erläuterungen zu David Ricardos Grundgesetzen der Volkswirtschaft und Besteuerung* II, p.76.
[11] Fritz Sternberg, *Marx und die Gegenwart*, pp.13-14.

2. *Marx on the movement of wages*

A. The general conditions for increases in wages

How should we judge Sternberg's further claim that according to Marx, 'industrial concentration and the accumulation of capital do not lead to an increase in real wages', but to its opposite, their fall?[12] Can we give him credence at least on this point?

Marx's arguments on this subject can be found in Chapter 17 of Volume I of *Capital*, where he examines the 'changes of magnitude in the price of labour-power and in surplus-value'.[13] We discover from this that 'the relative magnitudes of surplus-value and of price of labour-power are determined by three circumstances : 1) the *length of the working day*, or the extensive magnitude of labour; 2) the *normal intensity of labour*, its intensive magnitude, whereby a given quantity of labour is expended in a given time; and 3) the *productivity of labour*, whereby the same quantity of labour yields, in a given time, a greater or a smaller quantity of the product, depending on the degree of development attained by the conditions of production.'[14] And we should remember that according to Marx a change in any one of these three factors can lead to an increase in real wages!

As far as changes in the length of the working day are concerned, it is clear that with a prolongation of the working day both the surplus-value, and the wage which the worker receives for his day's work, can simultaneously increase, 'either equally or unequally'.[15]

We read in the *Theories* : 'If one takes a given magnitude and

---

[12] 'Industrial concentration and accumulation do lead to an increase in the productivity of labour, but not to a subsequent increase in real wages. On the contrary . . .' (*ibid.*).
[13] The fact that Marx confined himself to the price of labour-power had good reasons, as can be seen from the passage in *Theories* quoted on p.70 above. He did so because – in order not to complicate unnecessarily the investigation of the laws of the formation of surplus-value – he had to initially conceive of the value of labour-power as 'something fixed, as a given magnitude'. Marx's *Capital* also proceeds from these methodological premises, i.e. the quantity of the 'means of subsistence habitually required by the average worker' and in this sense too, the value of labour-power, is treated as a 'constant magnitude'. (*Capital* I, p.655 (519).) This does not of course mean that the 'average quantity of necessary means of subsistence' cannot change, or grow for example, in the real capitalist world. Marx would have first dealt with this case in his intended 'special theory of wage-labour' if he had ever reached the point of carrying out this part of his plan.
[14] *Capital* I, p.655 (519-20).
[15] *ibid.* p.661 (525).

divides it into two parts, it is clear that one part can only increase in so far as the other decreases, and vice versa. But this is by no means the case with expanding (elastic) magnitudes. And the working day represents such an elastic magnitude, as long as no normal working day has been won. With such magnitudes, both parts can grow, either to an equal or unequal extent.' (i.e. both the 'paid' part corresponding to the wage, and the 'unpaid' part corresponding to surplus-value).' An increase in one is not brought about by a decrease in the other and vice versa. This is, moreover,' (disregarding any increase in the intensity of labour) 'the only case in which wages and surplus-value, in terms of exchange-value, can both increase and possibly even in equal proportions. (That they can increase in terms of use-value is self-evident).'[16]

At the present time, that is, since the defeat of fascism in 1945, this particular case does not seem to be of particular relevance. It is the reduction of the working day, rather than its prolongation, which is on the agenda in Europe today. But if one considers the enormous amount of overtime put in by workers during the present period of prosperity in most capitalist countries, this particular variant analysed by Marx becomes much more real, since it is undoubtedly true that where increases in real wages have taken place in these countries they can also be traced back to overtime.

Of much greater importance is Marx's second variant which relates to increases in the intensity of labour. This is what he says in *Capital*. 'Increased intensity of labour means increased expenditure of labour in a given time. Hence a working day of more intense labour is embodied in more products than is one of less intense labour, the length of each day being the same. Admittedly, an increase in the productivity of labour will also supply more products in a given working day. But in that case the value of each single product falls, for it costs less labour than before; whereas in the case mentioned here that value remains unchanged, because each article costs the

---

[16] *Theories* II, p.408. However, the increase in the value of labour in such an instance is often only apparent: 'The value of a day's labour-power is . . . estimated on the basis of its normal average duration, or the normal duration of the life of a worker, and on the basis of the appropriate normal standard of conversion of living substances into motion as it applies to human nature. Up to a certain point the increased deterioration of labour-power inseparable from a lengthening of the working day may be compensated for by making amends in the form of higher wages. But beyond this point deterioration increases in geometrical progression, and all the requirements for the normal reproduction and functioning of labour-power cease to be fulfilled.' (*Capital* I, p.664 (527).)

same amount of labour as before. Here we have an increase in the number of products unaccompanied by a fall in their individual prices ... A given working day, therefore, no longer creates a constant value, but a variable one; in a day of 12 hours of ordinary intensity, the value created is, say, 6 shillings, but, with increased intensity, the value created may be 7, 8 or more shillings. It is clear that, *if the value created by a day's labour increases* from, say, 6 to 8 shillings, then *the two parts into which this value is divided*, namely the price of labour-power and surplus-value, may both increase *simultaneously*, and either equally or unequally . . . Here, the rise in the price of labour-power does not necessarily imply that it has risen above the value of labour-power.' (i.e. in this case the value of labour-power can also increase.)

On the other hand, the increase in the price of labour-power 'may [sometimes] be accompanied by a *fall* below its value'. This always occurs 'when the rise in the price of labour-power does not compensate for its more rapid deterioraton.'[17] Whether this has happened or not, whether only the price or also the value of labour-power rises as a consequence of a growing intensity of labour, in both cases growth in real wages can follow. The importance of this variant can be seen by looking at the indubitable fact that the high real wages of workers in the leading capitalist countries can be explained by periodic rises in the intensity of work (as Henryk Grossmann pointed out in his excellent critique of Sternberg's *Imperialism*).[18]

We now come to the most important variant : to changes in the relation between the wage and the surplus-value which are the result of the increasing productivity of labour. We read in Chapter 17 of Volume I of *Capital*. 'The value of labour-power is determined by the value of a certain quantity of the means of subsistence. It is the *value* and not the *mass* of these means of subsistence that varies with the productivity of labour. It is however possible that owing to an increase in the productivity of labour both the worker and the capitalist may *simultaneously* be able to appropriate a greater quantity of these necessaries, without any change in price of labour-power or in surplus-value. Let the value of labour-power be 3 shillings, and let the necessary labour-time amount to 6 hours. Let the surplus-value be, similarly, 3 shillings, and the surplus labour 6 hours. Now, if the productivity of labour were to be doubled without any alteration in the ratio between necessary labour and surplus labour, there would be no change in the magnitude either of the surplus-value or

[17] *Capital* I, pp.660-61 (524-25).
[18] In *Grünbergs Archiv*, 1928.

of the price of labour-power. The only result would be that each of these would represent twice as many use-values as before, and that each use-value would be twice as cheap as before. Although labour-power would be *unchanged* in price, it would have risen *above* its value. However, now assume a fall in the price of labour-power, not as far as 1/6d., the lowest possible point consistent with its new value, but to 2/10d. or 2/6d. This lower price would still represent an increased quantity of means of subsistence. In this way it is possible, given increasing productivity of labour, for the price of labour-power to fall constantly, and for this fall to be accompanied by a constant growth in the mass of the worker's means of subsistence.'[19] (And the extent of this growth clearly would depend 'on the relative weight thrown into the scale by the pressure of capital on the one side, and the resistance of the worker on the other'.)

It is just this latter variant – the case where the wage is only partially adjusted to the fall in the value of labour-power occasioned by growing productivity of labour, thus allowing the workers a certain, smaller or larger, compensation – which seems to be of particular theoretical and practical interest. According to Marx's theory of wages the value of the necessities which are physiologically indispensable only determines the lowest limit of the value of labour-power, whereas its upper limit is fixed by the 'respective powers of the parties to the struggle' i.e. capital and labour. Accordingly Marx stressed in the *Theories* 'that the workers themselves, although they cannot prevent reductions in real wages [resulting from increases in productivity], will not permit them to be reduced to the absolute minimum; on the contrary, they achieve a certain quantitative participation in the general growth of wealth.'[20] And more decisively in Marx's lecture *Wages, Price and Profit*: 'By virtue of the increased productivity of labour, the same amount of the average daily necessaries might sink from three to two shillings, or only four hours out of the working day instead of six, be wanted to reproduce an equivalent for the value of the daily necessaries. The working man would now be able to buy with two shillings as many necessaries as he did before with three shillings. Indeed the *value of labour* would have sunk but that diminished value would command the same amount of commodities as before. . . . Although the labourer's absolute standard of life would have remained the same, his relative wages,

---

[19] *Capital* I, p.659 (523). This is the theoretical formula which lies at the heart of the increases in real wages which have largely taken place in the latter half of the nineteenth century and the twentieth century.
[20] *Theories* III, p.312.

and therewith his *relative social position*, as compared with that of the capitalist would have been lowered.' If however, the worker, 'should resist that reduction of relative wages, he would only try to get some share in the increased productive powers of his own labour, and to maintain his former relative position in the social scale'.[21]

It must therefore follow from this that workers can participate to a certain extent in the development of the productivity of labour. In fact Marx categorically denied the theory already propounded in 1835 by the American political economist, Carey, 'that wages everywhere rise and fall in proportion to the productivity of labour'. He states that 'the whole of our analysis of the production of surplus-value shows the absurdity of this deduction . . .'.[22] For 'the increasing productivity of labour . . . is accompanied by a cheapening of the worker, i.e. a higher rate of surplus-value, even if real wages are rising'. But the latter 'never rise in proportion to the productivity of labour'.[23] (If this were to be the rule, the rate of surplus-value could never rise – and hence the production of 'relative surplus-value', and capitalism itself, would become an impossibility!'[24]) No wonder then that present-day bourgeois economists simply assert that there is a rigid parallelism between real wages and the productivity of labour, without being able to offer any real proof.

So much on the analysis contained in Chapter 17. It is evident that each of the variants mentioned contains the possibility of an increase in real wages. Thus – Sternberg notwithstanding – Marx was far from denying such a possibility. On the contrary, his remarks on

[21] *Wages, Price and Profit*, in *Selected Works*, pp.217-18.
[22] *Capital* I, p.705 (563).
[23] *ibid.* p.753 (604). 'In any case, because in a given country the value of labour is falling relatively to its productivity, it must not be imagined that wages in different countries are inversely proportional to the productivity of labour. In fact exactly the opposite is the case. The more productive one country is relative to another in the world market, the higher will be its wages as compared with the other. In England, not only nominal wages but also real wages are higher than on the continent. The worker eats more meat; he satisfies more needs . . . But in proportion to the productivity of the English workers their wages are not higher.' (*Theories* II, pp.16-17.)
[24] Cf. Natalie Moszkowska's essay directed against A.Braunthal, entitled 'Zur *Verelendungstheorie*' in *Die Gesellschaft*, 1930, p.235: 'Braunthal disputes the relative worsening of the conditions of those without property in comparison to the propertied, or the growing disproportion between the actual, and the technically feasible living standards of workers in the course of capitalist development . . . The meaning of the passage quoted, however, is clearly this: The rate of surplus-value, or of exploitation does not rise in the course of capitalist development (or at any rate, since the organisation of the proletariat); on the contrary, it continues at more or less the same level . . .'

the accumulation of capital in particular, show the extent to which he took such an eventuality into account.

B. The economic cycle and the movement of wages

It is sufficient here to reproduce a long but very important passage from *Capital*, Chapter 25, Section 1, entitled 'A Growing Demand for Labour-Power Accompanies Accumulation if the Composition of Capital Remains the Same'.

'*Growth of capital* implies growth of its variable constituent, in other words the part invested in labour-power . . . Since the capital produces a surplus-value every year, of which one part is added every year to the original capital; since this increment itself grows every year along with the augmentation of the capital already functioning; and since, lastly, under conditions especially liable to stimulate the drive for self-enrichment, such as the opening of new markets, or of new spheres for the outlay of capital resulting from newly developed social requirements, the *scale of accumulation* may suddenly be extended *merely by a change in the proportion in which the surplus-value or the surplus-product is divided into capital and revenue* – for all these reasons the requirements of accumulating capital may exceed the growth in labour-power or in the number of workers; the demand for workers may outstrip the supply, and thus wages may rise. This must indeed ultimately be the case if the conditions assumed above continue to prevail. For since in each year more workers are employed than in the preceding year, sooner or later a point must be reached at which the requirements of accumulation begin to outgrow the customary supply of labour, and a rise of wages therefore takes place.'

It is of course true that 'under the conditions of accumulation assumed so far, conditions which are the most favourable to the workers, their relation of dependence on capital takes on forms which are endurable. . . . Instead of becoming more intensive with the growth of capital, this relation of dependence only becomes more extensive, i.e. the sphere of capital's exploitation and domination merely extends with its own dimensions and the number of people subjected to it. A larger part of the workers' own surplus-product, which is always increasing and is continually being transformed into additional capital, comes back to them in the shape of means of payment, so that they can extend the circle of their enjoyments, make additions to their consumption fund of clothes, furniture etc. and lay by a small reserve fund of money. But these things no more abolish the exploitation of the wage-labour, and his situation of dependence, than do better clothing, food and treatment, and a larger *peculium* in the case of the slave. A rise in the price of labour, as a consequence of the accumulation of capital, only means in fact that the length and weight of the golden chain[25] the wage-labourer has already forged for himself, allow it to be loosened somewhat.' It implies 'at the best of times *a merely quantitative reduction* in the amount of unpaid labour the worker has to supply. This reduction can never go so far as to threaten the system itself.' This is because: 'Either the price of labour keeps on rising, because its rise does not interfere with the progress of accumulation . . . In this case it is evident that a reduction in the amount of unpaid labour in no way interferes with the extension of the domain of capital. Or, the other alternative, accumulation slackens as a result of the rise in the price of labour, because the stimulus of gain is blunted. The rate of accumulation lessens; but this means that the primary cause of that lessening itself vanishes, i.e. the disproportion between capital and exploitable labour-power. The mechanism of the process of capitalist production removes the very obstacle it temporarily creates. The price of labour falls again to a *level corresponding with capital's requirements for self valorisation*, whether this level is below, the same as, or above that which was normal before the rise of wages took place.'

Marx concludes, 'The rise of wages is therefore confined within limits that not only leave intact the foundations of the capitalist system, but also secure its reproduction on an increasing scale. The law of capitalist accumulation . . . in fact expresses the situation that the very *nature* of accumulation excludes every diminution in the degree of exploitation of labour, and every rise in the price of labour, which could seriously imperil the continual reproduction, on an ever larger scale, of the capital-relation.'[26]

The reader will have to excuse this long quotation. It was necessary, in order to show that Marx underlined not only the possibility, but also the necessity of an increase in real wages during the prosperity phase of the industrial cycle. In fact, the 'growing demand for labour-power' is examined in the section quoted under the assumption that the 'composition of capital remains the same'. That is, without taking into account the existence of the 'industrial reserve army'. However, we shall see later that this represents merely a countertendency, which although considerably modifying the tendency of

[25] A metaphor borrowed from the utopian socialist Bray. (See *Wages. Collected Works*, Vol.6, p.422.)
[26] *Capital* I, pp.763, 768-70, 771-72 (613, 617-18, 619).

the formation of wages described in the same section, by no means annuls it.[27] But before this we must look briefly at Marx's very important doctrine of 'relative wages'.

3. Marx's doctrine of relative wages

As early as 1849, Marx wrote in his essay *Wage-Labour and Capital*: 'But neither nominal wages, that is, the sum of money for which the worker sells himself to the capitalist, nor real wages, that is, the sum of commodities which he can buy for this money, exhaust the relations contained in wages. Wages are, above all, also determined by their relation to the gain, to the profit of the capitalist – comparative, relative wages. Real wages express the price of labour in relation to the price of other commodities; relative wages, on the other hand, express the share of direct labour in the new value it has created in relation to the share which falls to accumulated labour, to capital.'

And further: 'A house may be large or small; as long as the surrounding houses are equally small it satisfies all social demands for a dwelling. But let a palace arise beside the little house, and it shrinks from a little house to a hut. The little house shows now that its owner has only very slight or no demands to make; and however high it may shoot up in the course of civilisation, if the neighbouring palace grows to an equal or even greater extent, the occupant of the relatively small house will feel more and more uncomfortable, dissatisfied and cramped within its four walls.'

The same applies to the position of the working class under capitalism: 'Real wages may stay the same, they may even rise, and yet relative wages may fall. Let us suppose, for example, that all means of subsistence have gone down in price by two-thirds while wages per day have only fallen by one-third, that is to say, for example, from three marks to two marks. Although the worker can command a greater amount of commodities with these two marks than he previously could with three marks, yet his wages have gone down in relation to the profit of the capitalist. The profit of the capitalist (for example the manufacturer) has increased by one mark; that is for a smaller sum of exchange-values which he pays to the

---

[27] Even in Volume III, where Marx dropped the assumption of a constant organic composition, he repeatedly pointed to the necessity of wage increases during the prosperity phase of the industrial cycle (e.g. *Capital* III, p.252).

worker, the latter must produce a greater amount of exchange-values than before. The share of capital relative to labour has risen. The division of social wealth between capital and labour has become still more unequal. With the same capital, the capitalist commands a greater quantity of labour. The power of the capitalist class over the worker has grown, the social position of the worker has deteriorated, has been depressed one step further below that of the capitalist.'[28]

This does not represent anything fundamentally new; similar reasoning could already be found in Ricardo,[29] Cherbuliez,[30] and others. What *is* fundamental is the special weight which Marx attaches to the category of 'relative wages', as well as the far-reaching theoretical and practical conclusions he drew from it. Indeed, only in Marx do we find the 'law of the tendential fall of relative wages' (so named by Rosa Luxemburg),[31] by which the 'reciprocal distance' between the working class and the capitalist class – which is of decisive importance here[32] – necessarily grows. Its effects can therefore only be overcome by means of a socialist transformation of the economy.

Rosa Luxemburg has earned the credit for bringing this aspect of Marx's theory of wages into its true light. We read in her *Ein-*

---

[28] *Wage-Labour and Capital. Selected Works*, pp.83-85.
[29] Cf. the passage from Ricardo quoted in *Theories* II, p.424: 'It is not by the absolute quantity of produce obtained by either class, that we can correctly judge the rate of profit, rent, and wages, but by the quantity of labour required to obtain that produce. By improvements in machinery and agriculture, the whole produce may be doubled; but if wages, rent, and profit be also doubled, these three would bear the same proportions to one another as before, and neither could be said to have relatively varied. But if wages partook not of the whole of this increase; if they, instead of being doubled, were only increased one half . . . it would, I apprehend, be correct for me to say that . . . wages had fallen while profits had risen; for if we had an invariable standard by which to measure the value of this produce, we should find that a less value had fallen to the class of labourers . . . and a greater to the class of capitalists, than had been given before.' Marx says in this context: 'It is one of Ricardo's great merits that he examined relative or proportionate wages, and established them as a definite category. Up to this time, wages had always been regarded as something simple and consequently the worker was considered an animal. But here he is considered in his social relationships.' (*ibid.* p.419.)
[30] Cf. *Theories* III, p.396.
[31] See Rosa Luxemburg, *Ausgewählte Reden und Schriften*, II, p.100.
[32] Cf. *Grundrisse*, p.597: 'Further, in the struggle between the two classes – which necessarily arises with the development of the working class – the measurement of the distance between them, which, precisely, is expressed by wages itself as a proportion, becomes decisively important.' For 'the position of the classes to one another depends more on relative wages than on the absolute amount of wages'. (*Theories* III, p.419.)

führung in die Nationalökonomie : 'Capitalist production cannot take one step forward without squeezing the workers' share of the social product. With every new technical discovery, improvement of machinery, every new application of steam and electricity in production and commerce, the worker's share in the product gets smaller, and that of the capitalist, larger.' It is this 'quite invisible power, a simple mechanical effect of commodity production and competition, which deprives the worker of a larger share of his product . . . The personal role of the exploiter is still visible where the question is that of absolute wages, i.e. real living standards. A wage reduction, which leads to a depression of the real standard of living of the workers, is a visible attack by the capitalists against the workers, and will be responded to with an immediate struggle wherever the influence of the unions extends . . .'

The situation is quite different where an invisible reduction in wages takes place as the result of straightforward technical progress, inventions, the introduction of machines, improvements in transportation etc. 'The effects of all these forms of progress on the relative wage of the worker result quite automatically from commodity production and the commodity-character of labour-power . . . Thus the struggle against the fall in relative wages also implies a struggle against the commodity-character of labour-power i.e. against capitalist production as a whole. Thus the struggle against the fall in relative wages is no longer a struggle on the basis of the commodity economy, but a revolutionary, subversive attack on the existence of this economy; it is the socialist movement of the proletariat.'[33]

It now becomes clear why Marx fought so fiercely against Lassalle's 'iron law of wages'. Not only because it was built upon Malthus's doctrine of population, and contradicted the facts; but also because it completely overlooked the category of 'relative wages', and the revolutionary objectives which emerge from it. Marx's own economic theory led to the discovery that the system of wage-labour is fundamentally 'a system of slavery, and indeed of a slavery which becomes more severe in proportion as the social productive forces of labour develop, whether the worker receives better or worse payment',[34] and that consequently the evil of this system can only be overcome with the abolition of wage-labour itself.

'And after this understanding has gained more and more ground in our Party,' he wrote bitterly in the *Critique of the Gotha Programme*, 'one returns to Lassalle's dogmas . . . It is as if, among slaves

[33] Rosa Luxemburg, *Ausgewählte Reden und Schriften* I, pp.717, 719-20.
[34] *Critique of the Gotha Programme. Selected Works*, p.325.

who have at last got behind the secret of slavery and broken out in rebellion, a slave still in thrall to obsolete notions were to inscribe on the programme of the rebellion : Slavery must be abolished because the feeding of slaves in the system of slavery cannot exceed a certain low maximum !'[35]

So much then on the doctrine of 'relative wages'. It was important to look at this doctrine because without it we cannot place Marx's theory of wages in its proper context.[36] It demonstrates that it is not decisive for marxist political and economic theory whether real wages rise or fall – regardless of how important this special question might be in other contexts; and when those who criticise Marx concentrate their attack directly upon this point, all they prove is how little they have grasped the real essence of his theory of wages.

4. The industrial reserve army as regulators of wages

Until this point we have been able to confine ourselves to a simple repetition of Marx's line of reasoning; however, we now come to a point where some critical reservations would seem to be in order.

These are in no way related to the essence of the matter, as the existence of either an industrial reserve army in capitalism, or the significant effect which it exercises on the structure of wages is undeniable. However, sections 3 and 4 of the chapter on accumulation devoted to this theme in *Capital* Volume I seem to exhibit gaps which could lead to incorrect conceptions, and have actually done so. What is Marx's theory in these two sections? In the first place, that the rise in the organic composition of capital, which is necessarily bound up with the progress of capitalist production, would have to lead to a proportionate reduction in the variable part of capital, intended for the purchase of labour-power. Of course, capitalist production continually extends itself, and as a consequence the demand for labour-power grows too, in the long run; but it grows in a 'continually *declining proportion*'. The situation was quite different in capitalism's period of infancy : 'The composition of capital under-

---

[35] *ibid.*

[36] 'In the last analysis it means only grasping half of the law of wages, if one has only recognised the movement of absolute wages. The law of the mechanical fall of relative wages is only fully completed by the capitalist law of wages.' (Rosa Luxemburg, *op. cit.* p.725.) The fact that Henryk Grossmann rebuked Luxemburg for an 'unbelievably barbaric mutilation of Marx's theory of wages', is only of note as a curiosity. (*Das Akkumulations- und Zusammenbruchsgesetz*, p.585.)

went only very gradual changes. By and large therefore, the proportional growth in the demand for labour has corresponded to the accumulation of capital.'[37] However, this was a period in which the variable capital, laid out in the form of wages, heavily outweighed that laid out for machinery, i.e. in which 'manufacture still predominated and large-scale industry was only in its infancy'.[38] At that time one could share Adam Smith's view that the accumulation of capital was identical with a continuously rising demand for labour, and a continual rise in wages, and that the level of wages was simply determined by the relation of the absolute number of workers to the size of the productive capital.

In fact the development of large-scale industry has rendered this optimistic view obsolete. Capitalists were compelled, 'on pain of extinction', to constantly introduce new machinery and perfect the machinery they already had; but 'perfection of machinery means making human labour superfluous'.[39] Owing to the expansion of the machine system, the relation of constant to variable capital must change to the advantage of the former. However, since 'the demand for labour is determined not by the extent of the total capital but by its variable constituent alone, *that demand falls progressively with the growth of the total capital*, instead of rising in proportion to it, as was previously assumed. It falls relatively to the magnitude of the total capital, and at an accelerated rate, as this magnitude increases.'[40] This tendency explains the empirically given fact of a relative surplus population of workers, i.e. a population which exceeds the average valorisation requirements of capital. The surplus population is expressed in enormous armies of unemployed during periods of crisis, which almost trickle away during periods of high prosperity, but always remain in existence.[41] The burden of providing this population with a miserable level of subsistence falls partly on society and partly on the employed work-force. What function does this surplus population have in capitalist production? It is indispensable to capital for two reasons. Firstly, it places at its disposal 'a mass of human material which can be exploited ... for capital's changing valorisation requirements', which it can either employ, or put onto the streets, according to the general level of economic

---

[37] *Capital* I, p.785 (633).
[38] *Theories* III, p.335.
[39] Engels, *Anti-Dühring*, p.324.
[40] *Capital* I, p.781 (629).
[41] Even in the present phase of prosperity there are still millions of unemployed in the USA.

activity. 'Capitalist production can by no means content itself with the quantity of disposable labour-power which the natural increase of population yields. It requires for its unrestricted activity an industrial reserve army which is *independent of these natural limits*.'[42] And secondly, the industrial reserve army acts as a powerful regulator of wages which holds the wage demands of the work-force in check. For, in a developed capitalist society, it is precisely the fact of *'relative surplus population which is the background against which the law of the demand and supply of labour does its work. It confines the field of action of this law to the limits absolutely convenient to capital's drive to exploit and dominate the workers.*'[43] During periods of economic stagnation and at the beginning of upswings it presses down on the 'active army of workers', by not allowing them to push their wage demands too high; and in periods of crisis it often prevents them from making use of their right to strike, to defend themselves against capital's offensive against their living standards. In this sense, 'the general movements of wages are exclusively regulated by the expansion and contraction of the industrial reserve army, and this in turn corresponds to the periodic alternations of the industrial cycle.' They are not regulated 'by the variations of the absolute numbers of the working population, but by the varying proportions in which the working class is divided into an active army and a reserve army, by the increase or diminution in the relative amount of the surplus population, by the extent to which it is alternately absorbed and set free.'[44]

These are the most general elements of the theory of the industrial reserve army. In addition we should note the following.

In the first place it is evident that no conclusions as to the size

---

[42] *Capital* I, p.788 (635).
[43] *ibid.* p.792 (639). The situation was quite different in the last century in the colonies proper, i.e. in countries, such as North America, Australia etc, which were settled by white immigrants. We read in Marx's lecture *Wages, Price and Profit*: 'In colonial countries the law of supply and demand favours the working man. Hence the relatively high standard of wages in the United States. Capital may there try its utmost. It cannot prevent the labour market from being continuously emptied by the continuous conversion of wage-labourers into independent, self-sustaining peasants. The position of wage-labourer is for a very large part of the American people but a probational state, which they are sure to leave within a longer or shorter term.' (*Selected Works*, p.225.) Of course this exceptional situation in North America has long since ceased to prevail; however, the present high wages of the workers there can be traced back to this historical state of affairs.
[44] *Capital* I, p.790 (637).

and specific weight of the industrial reserve army can be drawn from the simple fact of the proportional decrease in the variable part of capital. Everything depends on the concrete conditions: on the one hand, on the extent and speed with which the organic composition rises, as well as the length of the 'intermediate pauses . . . in which accumulation works as a simple extension of production, on a given technical basis';[45] and on the other hand, on the momentum of the process of accumulation itself. It is therefore eminently possible that where capital is strongly expanding and where a large internal (or external) market is at the disposal of the capitalist class, the demand for labour-power could, in the long run grow to such an extent that the disadvantageous consequences of the industrial reserve army could be considerably reduced. (See the development in the USA up to the great depression of 1929.)

Secondly, Marx himself suggests in another passage that the industrial reserve army is more or less absorbed during periods of prosperity i.e. it virtually disappears.[46] When this occurs its effects on the level of wages are consequently cancelled out for a time, or at least reduced.

Thirdly, in the chapter on Accumulation in Volume I, Marx stresses the fact that capital can 'increase its supply of labour more quickly than its demand for workers', by extorting a larger quantity of work from the same number of employed workers, (by) prolonging working-time. 'The overwork of the employed part of the working class swells the ranks of its reserve, while, conversely, the greater pressure that the reserve by its competition exerts on the employed workers forces these to submit to overwork and subjects them to the dictates of capital . . . *The production of a relative surplus population*, or the *setting free of workers*, therefore proceeds still more rapidly than the technical transformation of the process of production that accompanies *the advance of accumulation and is accelerated by it*, and more rapidly than the corresponding diminution of the variable part of capital as compared with the constant.'[47] However, it is clear that this factor, which accelerates the formation of the

---

[45] ibid. p.782 (629).
[46] 'The reverse takes place in periods of prosperity . . . Not only does the consumption of necessities increase. The working class (now actively reinforced by its entire reserve army) also momentarily enjoys articles of luxury ordinarily beyond its reach, and those articles which at other times only constitute, for the greater part, necessary articles of consumption for the capitalist class.' (*Capital* II, p.414.)
[47] *Capital* I, p.789 (635-36).

industrial reserve army, can no longer play the same role as it did in Marx's time, as the introduction of the forty-eight-hour, and then the forty-hour week, and factory legislation, have served to check the exploitative practice of prolonging working-time.

And finally, we already find references in *Capital* to the role of the trade unions, who try 'to organise planned co-operation between the employed and unemployed in order to obviate or weaken the ruinous effects of this natural law of capitalist production [i.e. the law of the surplus working population] on their class'.[48] Clearly this aspect of trade-union activity is of even greater significance today!

It is clear that these are factors which are able to compensate, in part, for the detrimental effect which the industrial reserve army has on wages – factors which surely contributed to the fact that the standard of living of workers not only did not fall in the leading capitalist countries, but actually improved. However, Marx did not deal with these factors in his analysis for methodological reasons, a fact which must have caused his brilliant analysis of the industrial reserve army to be misinterpreted, and drawn numerous marxists to the false supposition that this was not a description of a general historical tendency, but a concrete prognosis for future decades.[49] This must also be the explanation for the fact that bourgeois and reformist caricatures of Marx's conception, such as the so-called 'immiseration theory', could never be adequately refuted from the marxist camp.

5. *The so-called 'theory of immiseration'*

However, didn't Marx himself propose the immiseration theory, and isn't it one of the cornerstones of the marxist system?

Not at all. As evidence against this we have Marx's fierce attack on the conception of the 'physiological minimum of existence', and hence on Lassalle's 'iron law of wages' as well. Without the conception of a physiological minimum of existence the theory of an inevitable and absolute 'immiseration' of the working class is utterly inconceivable. One therefore has a choice: either one admits that Marx rejected the theory of the physiological minimum of existence, in which case one may not lay the theory of immiseration at his door;

---

[48] *ibid.* p.793 (640).
[49] We refer to the sentence which reads in regard to the industrial reserve army: 'This is the absolute general law of capitalist accumulation. Like all other laws it is modified in its working by many circumstances, the analysis of which does not concern us here.' (*ibid.* p.798 (644).)

or, one denies it, in which case one is obliged – against better judgement – to classify Marx as an advocate of the 'iron law of wages' ... which is and always has been precisely the position adopted by those who proclaim the legend of Marx's 'immiseration theory'.

But we should remember that we wish to remain on the terrain of theory. The question is not how Marx and Engels judged the concrete movement of wages at such and such a time in England and on the Continent,[50] but simply this; whether the necessity of a progressive and absolute worsening of the position of the working class (or its 'immiseration') proceeds from Marx's economic system, and the laws of development of capitalist society, as he elaborated them? Whether it is correct that, according to Marx, the concentration and accumulation of capital would not lead to a rise in real wages, but on the contrary to a fall – as Sternberg maintained, for example? Marx's opposition to the idea of a physiological minimum of existence would on its own lead to an emphatic rejection of this view. Nevertheless, even great thinkers can sometimes be inconsistent, and propose contradictory theorems. What is therefore crucial is whether it is possible to find any argumentation in Marx's economic system, which refers to the inevitability of not only a relative, but rather an absolute, worsening of the condition of the working class under capitalism.[51]

The works to be taken into consideration are naturally only the economic works proper, such as the *Grundrisse* (1857-58,) the *Theories of Surplus-Value* (1861-63) and *Capital*, which Marx wrote in the period of his maturity. For we can still read in the *Communist Manifesto*, written in 1847: 'The serf, in the period of serfdom, raised himself to membership in the commune, just as the petty bourgeois, under the yoke of feudal absolutism, managed to develop into a bourgeois. The modern labourer, on the contrary, instead of rising with the progress of industry, sinks deeper and deeper below the conditions of existence of his own class. He becomes a pauper, and pauperism develops more rapidly than population and wealth.'[52]

The *Communist Manifesto* is the only place where we may find the doctrine that wages are at their minimum, a doctrine Marx later

---

[50] We shall see later that they judged the tendencies of the movement, according to the concrete circumstances of the time, in very different ways (and often very pessimistically).

[51] We do not speak of 'immiseration' here, as this terminology seems to us (especially in connection with the term 'relative') contradictory and misleading.

[52] *Communist Manifesto. Selected Works*, p.45.

abandoned.[53] However, regardless of the enormous significance the *Manifesto* has as a document in the history of ideas, no-one would look there for the quintessence of Marx's economic theories. Consequently the passage proves nothing in relation to our present problem, and it is better to treat it with great reserve in this context. Let us therefore return to Marx's economic works proper. Here, the question surely revolves around the well-known passage in *Capital* which reads : '... within the *capitalist system* all methods for raising the social productivity of labour are put into effect at the cost of the individual worker; all means for the development of production undergo a dialectical inversion so that they become means of domination and exploitation of the producers; they distort the worker into a fragment of a man, they degrade him to the level of an appendage of a machine, they destroy the actual content of his labour by turning it into a torment; they alienate from him the intellectual potentialities of the labour process in the same proportion as science is incorporated in it as an independent power.... But all methods for the production of surplus-value are at the same time methods of accumulation, and every extension of accumulation becomes, conversely, a means for the development of those methods. It follows therefore that in proportion as capital accumulates the situation of the worker, *be his payment high or low*, must grow worse.'

And following on from this the sentence which is quoted so often, but usually out of context : 'Finally, the law which always holds the *relative surplus population* or *industrial reserve army in equilibrium with the extent and energy of accumulation* rivets the worker to capital more firmly than the wedges of Hephaestus held Prometheus to the rock. It makes an *accumulation of misery* a necessary condition, corresponding to the *accumulation of wealth*. Accumulation of wealth at one pole is, therefore, at the same time accumulation of misery, the torment of labour,[54] slavery, ignorance, brutalisa-

---

[53] *ibid.* p.47. 'The average price of wage-labour is the minimum wage. i.e. that quantum of the means of subsistence, which is absolutely requisite to keep the labourer in bare existence as a labourer. What therefore, the wage-labourer appropriates by means of his labour merely suffices to prolong and reproduce a bare existence.'

[54] Cf. *Capital* I, p.796 (643) : 'The third category of the relative surplus population, the stagnant, forms a part of the active labour army, but with extremely irregular employment ... It is characterised by a maximum of working-time and a minimum of wages. We have already become familiar with its chief form under the rubric of "domestic industry".' (By the way, it is utterly mistaken to identify the industrial reserve army with 'unemployment', as Sternberg does [*Marx und die Gegenwart*, p.55]. The two concepts in no way coincide.)

tion and moral degradation at the opposite pole, i.e. on the side of the class that produces its *own product as capital*.'[55] It was necessary to quote this passage in full because it is, in fact, the only statement in *Capital* which those critics of Marx who want to attribute the 'immiseration thesis' to him can rely on with any semblance of justification.[56] However, even this semblance disappears on closer examination. What does this passage really mean? Does the last sentence, which speaks of an 'accumulation of misery' in any way negate the preceding sentence which only asserts a relative worsening in the condition of the working class? Not at all. The last sentence merely states that the industrial reserve army grows simultaneously with the growth in accumulation; that consequently, an ever larger part of the work-force becomes superfluous and therefore falls victim to misery, ignorance, brutality and moral degradation. Thus the 'accumulation of misery' relates solely to the 'lazarus-layers of the working class'[57] and not to the working class as a whole. (Or else one would have to suppose that Marx expected this 'ignorant, brutalised and

---

[55] *Capital* I, p.799 (645). The last sentence is repeated in a somewhat changed version on p.929 (763). It reads: 'Along with the constant decrease in the number of capitalist magnates . . . the mass of misery, oppression, slavery, degradation, and exploitation grows; but with this there also grows the revolt of the working class, a class constantly increasing in numbers, and trained, united, and organised by the very mechanism of the capitalist process of production.'

[56] In fact, Fritz Sternberg found another passage, which he cites on p.261 of his book: 'Marx writes, for example in *Wages, Price and Profit*: "These few hints" (on the rising organic composition of capital) "will suffice to show that the very development of modern industry must progressively turn the scale in favour of the capitalist against the working man and that consequently the general tendency of capitalistic production is not to raise, but to sink the average standard of wages, or to push the value of labour more or less to its minimum limit".' However, Sternberg prudently omits the following sentence, which reads: 'Such being the tendency of things in this system, is this saying that the working class ought to renounce their resistance against the encroachments of capital, and abandon their attempts at making the best of the occasional chances for their temporary improvement? If they did, they would be degraded to one level mass of broken wretches past salvation.' (*Selected Works*, p.225.) It has to be admitted that this additional sentence changes the entire complexion of things, and that, according to Marx, the tendency of capitalist production to push the value of labour-power down to its lowest limit, can only go ahead in the absence of a counter-tendency: namely the action of the working class!

[57] Cf. the following passage in *Capital* I, p.798 (644): 'The greater the social wealth, the functioning capital, the extent and energy of its growth . . . the greater is the industrial reserve army . . . But the greater this reserve army in proportion to the active labour-army, the greater is the mass of a con-

morally degraded' working class to establish socialism – something which might perhaps be asserted by Bakunin, but not by Marx!)

In addition, a comparison between Volume I of *Capital*, from which the above quotation is taken, and the *Inaugural Address*, written three years earlier (1864), proves that Marx was far from thinking of an absolute 'immiseration' of the working class as a whole at the time of the publication of *Capital*. We read in the 1864 address: 'Indeed, with local colours changed, and on a scale somewhat contracted, the English facts reproduce themselves in all the industrious and progressive countries of the Continent. In all of them, there has taken place, since 1848, an unheard of development of industry and an undreamed of expansion of imports and exports . . . In all of them, as in England, a minority of the working classes got their *real wages* somewhat advanced; while in most cases the *monetary rise of wages* denoted . . . no real access of comforts. . . . Everywhere the great mass of the working classes were sinking down to a lower depth, at the same rate, at least, that those above them were rising in the social scale.' (Yet another indication, therefore, that even at this time Marx was already reckoning with the possibility of a no more than relative worsening of the situation of the working class.) 'In all countries of Europe it has now become a truth . . . that no improvement of machinery, no appliance of science to production, no contrivances of communication, no new colonies, no emigration, no opening of markets, no free trade, nor all these things put together, will do away with the miseries[58] of the industrious masses; but that, on the present false basis, every fresh development of the productive powers of labour must tend' (in the sense of the doctrine of 'relative wages') 'to deepen social contrasts and sharpen social antagonisms.'[59]

This is Marx's view, which, as research in economic history has demonstrated, corresponds with the prevailing situation at that time (1849-64). But if this represents Marx's assessment of the position of the European working class, how can Sternberg, Strachey et al.[60]

solidated surplus population, whose misery is in inverse ratio to the amount of torture it has to undergo in the form of labour. The more extensive, finally, the pauperised sections of the working class and the industrial reserve army, the greater is official pauperism.'

[58] It is true that Marx speaks of 'misery' here; however the question is whether, in his opinion, 'misery' must be intensified with the development of capitalism; only then could one ascribe a 'theory of immiseration' to him.

[59] Marx-Engels, *Selected Works* in three volumes, Vol.2, Moscow, 1969, pp.14-15.

[60] Strachey's critique in particular seems to us incomprehensible. What is one supposed to say, for example, to his assertion that, according to Marx, 'not only would there be no improvement in the conditions of the wage earners

maintain that three years later he arrived at a theory in *Capital* according to which real wages would have to fall, under all circumstances, and the situation of the working class would necessarily become progressively worse – not merely relatively, but absolutely! This is all the more unlikely as we possess statements from a later period, which, it must be assumed, were unknown to Sternberg and Strachey, and which prove the exact opposite of what they claim. In 1881, during Marx's lifetime, Engels wrote the following, certainly with Marx's agreement and 14 years after the publication of Volume I of *Capital*.[61] 'The great merit of trade unions, in their struggle to keep up the rate of wages and to reduce working hours, is that they tend to keep up and to raise the standard of life. There are many trades in the East End of London whose labour is not more skilled and quite as hard as that of bricklayers and bricklayers' labourers, yet they hardly earn half the wages of these. Why? Simply because a powerful organisation enables the one set to maintain a comparatively high standard of life as the rule by which their wages are measured; while the other set, disorganised and powerless, have to submit not only to unavoidable but also to arbitrary encroachments of their employers ... The law of wages, then, is not one which draws a hard and fast line. It is not inexorable within certain limits. There is at every time (great depression excepted) for every trade a certain latitude within which the rate of wages may be modified by the results of the struggle between the two contending parties. Wages in every case are fixed by a bargain, and in a bargain he who resists longest and best has the greatest chance of getting more than his due. If the isolated workman tries to drive his bargain with the capitalist he is easily beaten and has to surrender at discretion; but if a whole trade of workmen form a powerful organisation, collect among themselves a fund to enable them to defy their employers if need be, and thus become enabled to treat with these employers as a power, then, and only then, have they a chance to get even that pit-

---

as total production increased, but capitalism would, as it were, overstep its own normal laws and actually force down the standard of life of the workers below its true value, which was subsistence level'. (*Contemporary Capitalism*, p.119)? Where did Strachey read all this? Or let us take his explanation of the well-known dispute over the 'iron law of wages'; namely, that Marx only went against Lassalle because he wanted to use the trade unions for the 'revolutionary overthrow of capitalism' – although, from a theoretical point of view he believed in the doctrine of the 'physiological minimum of existence', just like Lassalle etc., etc.
[61] See *MEW* Vol.35, pp.19-20.

tance which according to the economical constitution of present society, may be called a fair day's wages for a fair day's work.'[62]

That was Engels writing in 1881. And he was merely being consistent when he objected ten years later to the sentence in the draft of the Erfurt Programme which read : 'The number and misery of the proletarians becomes ever larger.' He wrote : 'The organisation of the workers, their continually growing resistance possibly serves to set up a certain barrier against the growth of poverty. What certainly does grow is the insecurity of existence.'[63] This is a formulation which we can and must return to today, for, in one part of the capitalist world at least, 'a barrier' has actually been erected against direct, physical poverty.[64] And perhaps an observer who regards the present position through rose-tinted spectacles could conclude from this – in contradiction to the *Communist Manifesto* – that the bourgeoisie in the leading capitalist countries is really capable of 'securing the existence of their slaves, even within their slavery', and that consequently the rule of capital has finally been firmly established. However, the amelioration, or even the elimination of physical poverty is not everything. The major threat to the workers of even the most advanced capitalist countries, and now more than ever before, is the insecurity of their existence : the fact that they have to pass their lives in the shadow of overwhelming crises and wars. Nothing has shown the slightest sign, as yet, of putting a final end to this evil.

Can Engels's remarks be reconciled with some variant of the 'theory of immiseration'? Surely not. Even if these statements are thought of as a 'fighting retreat', as a form of self-criticism, which the founders of marxism made of their earlier views; for in that case it is impossible to see why it should still be necessary to mount an attack on a theory which Engels had quite clearly already rejected in 1881.

Our study of the theory of immiseration has shown that even from a 'semantic' aspect this theory must be consigned to the realm of scientific misunderstanding. The real question is, of course, not how the word 'misery' should be interpreted in Marx's works, but whether the 'theory of immiseration' attributed to Marx can be reconciled with his theory of the determination of the value of labour-power, his polemic against the 'iron law of wages', and his

[62] Engels, articles from the *Labour Standard* in *Engels: Selected Writings*, 1967, pp.102-03.
[63] Engels, *MEW* Vol.22, p.231.
[64] However, one must also consider the North American black population, millions of whom scratch a living which, by present-day standards, has to be characterised as 'misery'.

Marx's theory of wages · 307

theses on the connection between growing intensity and productivity of labour and increases in real wages? In fact we can probably risk the hypothesis that even if Marx had proposed an 'immiseration theory' he would have had to reject it as being in contradiction with the real spirit and content of his theory of wages.

But this should not be taken to mean that the legend of Marx's 'theory of immiseration' is totally without foundation: most scientific misunderstandings have their rationale and are based on actual states of affairs which supply the opportunity for them to be propounded. This also applies in this case. Between the 1840s and the 1860s the situation of the European working class appeared hopeless. This fact was bound to colour the theoretical conceptions of that epoch. Progress was, relatively speaking, so slight and proceeded at such a snail's pace, the actual poverty of the working class was still so immense, that all socialists (and especially revolutionary socialists) were extremely pessimistic about the possibility of any noticeable improvement in the situation of the worker and were consequently inclined towards an 'immiseration theory'. Marx too was naturally in thrall to this empirical fact, and his scientific stature shows itself precisely in the fact that he did not allow himself to be entirely dominated by it in his economic theory ... However, one thing can be conceded to Marx's critics: Marx (and Engels) often overestimated the weight of the factors depressing the condition of the proletariat, and they therefore did not look closely at the possibility of a significant rise in the living standards of the workers, even in the leading capitalist countries. And so in this sense the severe critics (who have the added advantage of writing almost one hundred years after Marx and Engels) are able to accuse the two thinkers of a 'lack of foresight'. But they should also realise that this has nothing at all to do with Marx's theory of wages.

6. The kernel of truth in the 'theory of immiseration'

This is not to claim there are no tendencies towards immiseration in the real capital world; there are more than enough of them – but one has to know where to look. In fact such tendencies emerge clearly in two spheres: firstly (temporary) in all times of crisis, and secondly (permanent) in the so-called underdeveloped areas of the world, which includes not only South and Central America, Asia and Africa, but also the backward capitalist countries of Central and Western Europe (Greece, parts of Italy, Spain and Portugal).

As far as the immiseration of workers during periods of crisis is concerned, we do not have to waste words. Even the world's labour aristocracy – the North American working-class – is not invulnerable, as the experiences of the twelve-year world crisis from 1929 to 1940 show. (Even in the USA there were still 10 million unemployed in 1940!) Naturally, bourgeois economic historians do not like to be reminded of this fact, and prefer to overlook this particularly troublesome contradiction. But not only that; they do not even recognise the existence of the industrial reserve army as it does not appear in the official wages statistics. Rosa Luxemburg wrote on this: 'In representing capitalist wage relations it is quite wrong only to take into account the wages actually paid to the employed industrial workers ... The entire reserve army of the unemployed, from the temporary unemployed skilled worker down to the deepest levels of poverty and official pauperism, enters into the determination of wage relations as an equal factor.' For 'the lowest strata of the rarely employed or totally unemployed destitutes and outcasts are not a kind of excrescence ... but are, on the contrary, connected through all the intermediate links of the reserve army with the topmost and best situated layer of industrial workers by means of internal, living bonds. This inner connection shows itself in numerical terms through the periodic sudden growth in the lower strata of the reserve army in periods when business is poor, and through its contraction during more prosperous periods, and further through the relative reduction in the number of those taking refuge in public charity with the development of the class struggle, and the consequent raising of self-confidence amongst the proletarian masses.' And therefore: 'The living situation of the deepest layers of the proletariat is moved by the same laws of capitalist production, pulled up and down; ... the proletariat constitutes one social class, an organic whole, together with the broad stratum of agricultural workers, with its army of unemployed and with all its layers from the highest to the lowest; a class from whose different levels of poverty and oppression it is possible to grasp the capitalist law of wages on the whole correctly.'[65] However, if this is done, if the position of the working class, both that of the employed and unemployed workers, is taken into account, not only in periods of prosperity but also those of crisis, then the picture painted by the optimistic economists is naturally a much gloomier one and it becomes impossible to deny the presence of tendencies towards immiseration in present-day capitalism, as well.

A study of the so-called 'underdeveloped areas' leads to the same conclusions. It is naturally very pleasant that the industrial

[65] Rosa Luxemburg, *Ausgewählte Reden und Schriften* I, pp.724-25.

workers of the USA possess for the most part their own houses and cars; but how does it come about that the workers from neighbouring Latin America have nothing of the kind, and have to make do, for the most part, with inhumanly low wages? How is it that a North American worker often earns ten times as much as, for example, someone of the same class in Guatemala? And is it really valid to write scholarly treatises on the alleged unbroken improvement in the position of workers in capitalism, if one only takes into account the living standards in the most highly developed capitalist countries? It will be replied: yes, the latter countries are characteristic of capitalism, and it is in fact only in these countries that the position of workers can be regarded as 'normal'; and when areas like Guatemala achieve the same level of labour productivity then workers in these countries will participate in the blessings of capitalism, in the shape of high real wages . . . Our task here is not, however, to look at what might come about, but what actually is the case; not the condition of workers in some imaginary capitalist millenium, but in the real capitalist world, as it exists today. And further: who can say that it is the position of North American, Australian and English workers which is 'normal' whilst that of the rest of the world is 'abnormal'? Doesn't the capitalist world constitute a whole, in which both the highly developed nations (mostly the ruling ones), and the underdeveloped (the ruled and exploited ones) are to be seen as integral parts? And isn't the high standard of living of the workers in the highest developed countries for the most part a product of the fact that the workers of other countries do not possess such a standard of living?

At this point we have to turn back to Marx's theory of the exploitation of the capitalistically underdeveloped nations (primarily agricultural populations) by the highly developed capitalist nations. We do not mean here colonies or semi-colonies in the strict sense, but rather countries which may well be politically 'independent', but which are nonetheless economically exploited by particular capitalist powers. This remains true even when these countries have not been forced to accept damaging trade agreements, and even when they are not, at bottom, merely the fiefs of particular capitalist corporations as, for example, in the case of Guatemala. In other words, we are talking about a form of exploitation which in no way makes use of means of political domination, which is not intentional, but which simply comes about by virtue of the economic laws operating in capitalism.

Which laws are these? First, the law of value. We know that according to the law of value the only labour which counts as socially necessary is that which is required 'to produce any use-value under the conditions of production normal for a given society, and with the average degree of skill and intensity prevalent in that society'.[66] Within one country the differences in intensity and productivity of labour become equalised at one socially average level. But this does not apply on the world market!

'The more intense national labour, as compared with the less intense' not only produces 'in the same time more value, which expresses itself in more money'; here, the law of value 'is yet more modified . . . by the fact that on the world market, national labour which is more *productive* also counts as more intensive, as long as the more productive nation is not compelled by competition to lower the selling price of its commodities to the level of their value.'[67] The result is that an unequal exchange takes place between different nations, so that, for example, 'three days of labour in one country can be exchanged against one in another country. . . . The relationship between working days of different countries may be similar to that existing between skilled, complex labour and unskilled, simple labour within a country. In this case, the richer country exploits the poorer one (even where the latter gains by the exchange)'[68] . . . 'just as a manufacturer who employs a new invention before it becomes generally used . . . valorises the specifically higher productivity of the labour he employs as surplus labour', and therefore achieves a surplus profit.[69] Except in this situation the surplus profit is not temporary, as with the case of the individual manufacturer, but permanent in its nature. In this way the richer country acquires raw materials and products which have been considerably more expensive if they had had to be produced on that country's own territory, and therefore it frees itself from all the disadvantages of its geographical situation, etc. It is not necessary to point out what this unequal exchange means in terms of losses for the poorer country, which thus continually has to give away a portion of its national labour.

In addition to this Henryk Grossmann believed he could put forward another reason why the backward nations are exploited by the advanced capitalist countries in international trade; namely the inequality in the composition of their capitals. Insofar as a tendency to equalisation of the rate of profit exists in international trade, 'the commodities of the capitalistically highly developed

---

[66] *Capital* I, p.129 (39).
[67] *ibid.* p.702 (560).
[68] *Theories* III, pp.105-06.
[69] *Capital* III, p.251.

Marx's theory of wages · 311

country, i.e. a country with a higher than average composition of capital, will be sold at prices of production which are always higher than their values; whereas inversely, in the countries with a lower organic composition of capital, commodities, under free competition, will be sold at prices of production which as a rule must be lower than their value ... In this way *transfers* of the surplus-value produced in the underdeveloped country to the capitalistically higher developed will take place on the world market within the sphere of circulation.'[70] This is the same conclusion as the one reached by Otto Bauer in his *Einführung in die Volkswirtschaftslehre*. He says there: 'It is not true that peoples exchange commodities whose production requires the same amount of labour. Losses and gains from exchange are in fact contained in the prices. Countries with developed industry are the countries which secure a profit in exchange from agricultural countries. That is, the developed countries enrich themselves at the expense of the agricultural countries.'[71]

It is evident that the profits from exchange which the advanced capitalist countries make in their intercourse with the backward countries can be used to some extent to give certain wage concessions to the workers of the former. The room for manoeuvre 'within which the level of wages can be changed as the result of the struggle between the contending parties'[72] will be enlarged by this – apart from the lower prices of the commodities imported from the backward countries, which can also benefit to some extent the workers in the countries receiving the imports. Or, as Otto Bauer succinctly expressed it: 'The workers in the advanced countries are better off. Why? The advanced countries secure profits through exchange; they enrich themselves at the expense of the backward countries.'[73] It

[70] *Das Akkumulations- und Zusammenbruchsgesetz*, pp.431-32. Cf. Marx's *Grundrisse*, p.872: 'From the possibility that profit may be less than surplus-value ... it follows that not only individual capitalists but also nations may continually exchange with one another, may even continually repeat the exchange on an ever-expanding scale, without for that reason necessarily gaining in equal degrees. One of the nations may continually appropriate for itself a part of the surplus labour of the other, giving back nothing for it in the exchange ...'
[71] Otto Bauer, *Einführung in die Volkswirtschaftslehre*, p.165.
[72] Cf. p.305 above.
[73] Bauer, *op. cit.* p.164. However, Bauer's view as quoted here seems to contradict the opinion he advocated at the 1928 Brussels Congress of the Second International. On this we can read in an article by L.Birkenfeld, in ' *Grünbergs Archiv* 1930, p.154: 'The Leninist theory of the labour aristocracy overlooks the fact that as Helene and Otto Bauer proved (in *Der Kampf*, 1928, pp.393ff), the interest which, for example, America draws from Europe, is negligible compared to the amounts of surplus-value of the American capital-

should not of course be concluded from this that somehow the workers in the advanced capitalist countries ought, for better or worse, to build a common front with their own capitalist class;[74] but simply that (1) the increase in living standards cannot accrue to the working classes of all countries, insofar as it derives from this source, but is rather based upon the low living standards of backward countries; and (2) that this increase in living standards in the leading countries can only continue, so long as the agricultural and colonial countries remain backward in their economic development. Today it is more evident than then, 'that no country wishes to remain an agricultural country, because it does not want to be permanently exploited by the industrial states'. Otto Bauer concludes: 'Capitalism will never solve this problem. The agricultural countries will only abandon the idea of industrialisation if they are no longer exploited. But this is unattainable under capitalism. Only socialism can resolve this problem.'[75]

7. Concluding remark

Now that we have seen the other side of the coin, we can conclude our investigation. One final remark is however permissible: it is not difficult to show the superficial and crudely empiricist character of current Marx criticism, as represented by the works of Sternberg and Strachey. However, this is 'pure school-boy's work' (to use an

---

ists, which the latter are able to obtain, owing to the higher productivity of the workers there. A few days after Bauer referred to this in Brussels the Bolshevik leader, Bukharin, asserted at the Congress of the Communist International that he had found a refutation. Bauer, he said, asks where the Swedish colonies are, if a section of the Swedish working class are the highest paid in Europe? Bukharin's reply is that the basis of the labour aristocracy, apart from colonial profits, is also constituted by differential profits for the capitalists, whose firms work with a higher average productivity.'

[74] However, the drive towards this is very strong, as the history of the working-class movement shows! Cf. Engels's letter to Marx of 7 October 1858, in which he expresses the fear that 'the English proletariat is actually becoming more and more bourgeois, so that this most bourgeois of all nations is apparently aiming ultimately at the possession of a bourgeois aristocracy and a bourgeois proletariat alongside the bourgeoisie. For a nation which exploits the whole world this is of course to a certain extent justifiable.' (*Selected Correspondence*, p.103.) And twenty-three years later he complained once more: 'The British working man just does not want to go any further, he has to be shaken up by events, such as the loss of the industrial monopoly. In the meantime, let him keep to himself.' (*MEW* Vol.35, p.20.)

[75] Otto Bauer, *op. cit.* p.166.

Marx's theory of wages · 313

expression of Engels). What is of course much more important and interesting is the study of Marx's theory of wages itself. And here we hope to have shown that we are dealing with a highly elaborate and delicately structured theoretical construction, which – despite the considerable period of time which separates us from its origins – still appears to be in good repair today, and which provides a keen analytical tool. Admittedly this theory carries with it certain dangers (as we saw in the study of the industrial reserve army), which primarily arise from an insufficient regard for the methodological structure of Marx's work. However, these are deficiencies which do not affect the basis of the theory, and do not stand in the way of its fruitful application and further elaboration. It is true of course that anyone who is only interested in superficial appearances in political economy, and is looking for cut-and-dried, complete answers, will not find Marx's strictly scientific and essentially dialectical theory of wages to their liking. The 'thinking readers', however, (to whom Marx appeals in the Foreword to the first edition of Volume 1 of *Capital*[76]) will continue to find great theoretical satisfaction in studying it.

[76] Marx wrote, 'I assume, of course, a reader who is willing to learn something new and therefore to think for himself.' (*Capital* I, p.90 (8).)